# Automobile Industry in India

Driven by Foreign Investment, Fueled for Growth

# Automobile Industry in India

## Driven by Foreign Investment, Fueled for Growth

Dr. Geet

HOW ACADEMICS
an imprint of Highlyy Publishing LLP

ISBN: 978-93-6009-628-1
First Published : 2025


Published by : HOW ACADEMICS

an imprint of Highlyy Publishing LLP

Correspondence Address : 4/30 A II Floor, Double Storey Buildings
Vijay Nagar, Delhi-110009
Editorial: +91 9811026449
Sales : +91 9999953412
Email: info@howacademics.com
Website: www.howacademics.com

# Preface

The journey of this book began as a doctoral thesis, driven by a deep curiosity to understand the evolving nature of Foreign Direct Investment (FDI) and its complex relationship with the industrial performance of a rapidly developing economy like India. With a particular focus on the automobile sector, an industry that has consistently stood as a symbol of modernity, innovation, and international collaboration. This study seeks to uncover the patterns, linkages, and consequences of FDI in shaping domestic industrial capabilities.

India's tryst with FDI has traversed through colonial legacies, post-independence caution, liberalization, and the contemporary push for global competitiveness. Amid this transition, the automobile industry emerged as a critical sector where foreign investment not only brought in capital and technology but also transformed value chains, created employment, and challenged domestic enterprises to rise to new levels of productivity and efficiency.

This book explores these dynamics by analyzing the presence of backward and forward linkages between foreign and domestic firms, offering empirical insights from the period 2011 to 2020. Using panel data and robust econometric models, it captures both the promises and paradoxes of foreign investment in a capital-intensive sector.

While rooted in academic research, this book is written to engage a wider audience including policymakers, industry professionals, scholars, and students interested in the intersections of international finance, industrial development, and economic policy. It aims to contribute meaningfully to the discourse on how emerging economies can strategically leverage FDI not just for growth, but for inclusive and sustainable development.

At its core, however, this work is more than an academic exploration, it is a deeply personal journey. I owe the completion of this book to the enduring strength and silent inspiration of my grandparents, whose values of hard work, humility, and resilience are etched into every word. Their lives taught me that knowledge is not only to be pursued but to be lived with purpose.

To my mother, the quiet force behind all my efforts, your unwavering belief in me, your sacrifices, and your endless encouragement gave me the courage to keep going. This book is, in many ways, a reflection of your strength and love.

What began as a thesis matured into this book through long nights, moments of doubt, and the quiet determination to honour those who stood by me. It is my hope that this book provides not just answers, but also stimulates further questions and inquiries into the evolving role of FDI in India's economic future.

**Dr. Geet**
Assistant Professor
Bhartiya Vidya Bhavan

# Acknowledgement

I take this opportunity to express my sincere regards to my guide and mentor, Dr. Ombir Singh, for keeping faith in my abilities during my research tenure. Your contributions have been a tremendous source of inspiration giving me hope to persist with the rapport built over this period and enrich from it.

It has been kept on track and been seen through to completion with the support and encouragement of numerous people both from the research community and outside of the academic environment. I want to thank all those who have been generous to me and helped me by any means during the past years. This begins with my parents without whom I would not have the courage to continue.

In the last few years, I have worked in an excellent environment with dynamic people. I am also grateful my Ph.D. advisory committee, Prof. Shweta Anand, Dr. Dinesh Kumar Sharma, Dr. Rakesh Srivastava, and Dr. Satish Kumar for their helpful suggestions and comments during my progress report presentations.

Looking back over this period, I feel it was the most productive and intensive stage in my life. This thesis is the finale of my expedition to obtain the Ph.D degree. I consider myself fortunate to have been given the opportunity to work with the most generous fellow research scholars with their uninterrupted benign oversight and marvellous flair for streamlining random ideas have imparted a perfect shape to this manuscript.

The steady and selflessly empathetic demeanour and unflinching professional conviction of institutions such as the Institute of Economic Growth, Institute of Studies in Industrial Development, and Ratan Tata Library also contributed more than expected. I also humbly the entire faculty of the School of Management, Gautam Buddha University, who taught me the basics during the coursework that built upon my theoretical concepts.

**Dr. Geet**

# Abstract

With the advent of the New Economic Policies (1991), the Indian economy has been witnessing the foreign presence with respect to the inflow of the foreign capital classified into various categories such as Foreign Grants and Aid, Loans from International Institutions, External Commercial Borrowings and Intergovernmental Loans etc. at a larger scale. For the most part, it is the foreign presence of the other nations that can be felt with the influx of foreign capital through foreign investments which takes shape in the formation of the fabric of the domestic economy and remodel it according to the international status quo. With the specific purpose of operating in the domestic economy in the form of affiliates, branches and subsidiaries for a long period of time and emphasizing long vested interest, FDI is the preferred source of capital that has also been recognised as an indispensable tool in imparting advantages in terms of the cheaper cost of capital, superior management, high-level technology, marketing strategies, access to raw material and economies of scale etc. However, FDI also tempts international competition that might discourage the efficiency of the domestic companies while contracting their production.

In this context, several studies have been conducted in the foreign academic literature to check the impact of the direct investments in the host countries. In India, major studies have focused mainly on the initial years of the liberalisation period which is not adequate. In order to conduct a comprehensive study of the impact of the foreign presence in the form of FDI in India and the corresponding linkages formed in the automobile industry, the objectives of this study are aimed to observe the trends and patterns of the FDI in the recent decades and analyse the linkages effect with the help of performance and the productivity level, with respect to the main determinants in the automobile industry.

This would help to develop the policy implications in the context of upcoming challenges and opportunities in FDI as well as the automobile industry. This study employs the secondary data. The recent ten years from 2011-2020 has been taken as time period of the study. Due to the presence of the time-invariant panel data, this study has employed fixed effects model in understanding the impact of various determinants. This study has showed negative intra-industry linkages in the automobile industry, indicating at incapability of the domestic firms to harness the positive effects of foreign presence. This study also reflects on the presence of strong backward linkages with somewhat weaker forward linkages in the automobile industry.

# Contents

# Abbreviations

| | | |
|---|---|---|
| ACMA | : | Automotive Component Manufacturers Association |
| ADB | : | Asian Development Bank |
| ADR | : | American Depository Receipt |
| AIAM | : | Association of Automobile Manufacturers |
| API | : | Automobile Products of India |
| BoP | : | Balance of Payment |
| CBU | : | Complete Build Up |
| CIF | : | Cost, Insurance and Freight |
| CKD | : | Complete Knocked Down |
| CMIE | : | Centre for Monitoring Indian Economy |
| DEA | : | Data Envelopment Approach |
| DIPP | : | Department for Promotion of Industry and Internal Trade |
| EPZ | : | Export Processing Zones |
| FCCB | : | Foreign Currency Convertible Bond |
| FDI | : | Foreign Direct Investment |
| FEMA | : | Foreign Exchange Management Act |
| FERA | : | Foreign Exchange Regulation Act |
| FIIs | : | Foreign Institutional Investors |
| FIPA | : | Foreign Investment Implementation Authority |
| FIPB | : | Foreign Investment Promotion Board |
| FIPC | : | Foreign Investment Promotion Council |
| FOB | : | Freight on Board |
| FPI | : | Foreign Portfolio Investment |
| FTZ | : | Free Trade Zone |
| FY | : | Financial Year |
| GCF | : | Gross Capital Formation |
| GDP | : | Gross Domestic Product |
| GDR | : | Global Depository Receipts |

| | | |
|---|---|---|
| GOI | : | Government of India |
| IBEF | : | India Brand Equity Foundation |
| ICT | : | Information, Communication and Technology |
| IMF | : | International Monetary Fund |
| LP | : | Levinson Petrin |
| MNCs | : | Multinational Corporations |
| MNEs | : | Multinational Enterprises |
| NBL | : | Normalised Backward Linkages |
| NEC | : | Not Elsewhere Classified |
| NFL | : | Normalised Forward Linkages |
| NIC | : | National Industrial Classification |
| NRI | : | Non-Resident Indian |
| OECD | : | Organisation for Economic Cooperation and Development |
| OEM | : | Original Equipment Manufacturer |
| OLS | : | Ordinary Least Square |
| OP | : | Olley and Pakes |
| QFI | : | Qualified Foreign Investor |
| R&D | : | Research and Development |
| RBI | : | Reserve Bank of India |
| SDR | : | Special Drawing Rights |
| SEBI | : | Stock Exchange Board of India |
| SEZ | : | Special Economic Zones |
| SFA | : | Stochastic Frontier Approach |
| SIA | : | Secretariat for Industrial Assistance |
| SIAM | : | Society of Indian Automobile Manufacturers |
| SKD | : | Semi Knocked Down |
| TFP | : | Total Factor Productivity |
| UNCTAD | : | United Nations Conference on Trade and Development |
| WIOD | : | World Input-Output Database |
| WIR | : | World Investment Report |
| WPI | : | Wholesale Price Index |

# Chapter 1
Introduction

## Foreign Direct Investment (FDI): A Conceptual Overview

### Definition of FDI

In order to conceptualise the idea of foreign presence in terms of FDI while getting simplified impression of the foreign firms, it becomes essential to describe what internationally and nationally is recognised as FDI. The definition of FDI according to various official organisations is as follows: -

#### *Organisation for Economic Cooperation and Development (OECD)*

According to the *Benchmark Definition* "FDI is a category of cross-border investment made by a resident in one economy with the objective of establishing a lasting interest in an enterprise that is resident in an economy other than that of the direct investor." By *lasting interest*, OECD indicates at an enduring association among the foreign investment concerns and direct investing stakeholders. The Glossary of Terms and Definition document defined "*FDI Enterprise* as an enterprise that resides in one economy and in which an investor from another economy directly or indirectly owns ten percent or more of its voting power for an incorporated or the equivalent, for an unincorporated enterprise."

#### *United Nations Conference on Trade and Development (UNCTAD)*

The World Investment Report as well as the *Methodological Note* of WIR (2017) defined "FDI as an investment involving a long-term relationship." The FDI emphasizes a vested long-term interest and control by the resident in home nation's affiliate firm, situated in any other nation but of foreign direct investor. "Such investment is said to involve both the initial transaction between the two entities and all subsequent transactions between them and among foreign affiliates, i.e., both incorporated and unincorporated."

### *International Monetary Fund (IMF)*

The *Balance of Payments Manual* (BPM, 2009) stated that "the FDI is associated with a resident of one economy having control or a significant degree of influence on the management of an enterprise, that is resident, in another economy." (p. 100.) "Also, a direct investment enterprise is an entity subject to control or a significant degree of influence by a direct investor, when a direct investor directly owns equity that entitles it to 10 percent or more of the voting power in the direct investment enterprise." (BPM6, 2009, p.101.) "Therefore, the definition of direct investment for the BPM6 is consistent with the 4th edition of the OECD *Benchmark Definition* of FDI and with the UNCTAD's World Investment Report" (WIR, 2007, p.245).

### *Master Directions of the Reserve Bank of India (RBI)*

Considering discrepancies in data compilation methods resulting in the underestimation of FDI flows in the 1990s due to outdated definition of FDI, Srivastava (2003) proclaimed "the adoption of 'International Standards' in computing FDI data would automatically raise India's net FDI inflows from the oft-noted $2-3 billion to about $8 billion in 2001." (p. 608) In June 2003, the Report of *Technical Monitoring Group* made proper suggestions to upgrade the reporting system of FDI, including the definitional and methodological issues, in alignment with international reporting practices. With the inclusion of fourteen items to make the data internationally comparable, RBI presented the BoP statement. The Secretariat for Industrial Assistance (SIA) started reporting direct investment inflows in its SIA (now FDI) Newsletter on actual and approval basis stirring headline of The Indian Express issue (Nov 15, 2002) *"India's FDI Inflows Set to Jump Massively".*

The OECD's *Benchmark Definition* and the IMF *Balance of Payments Manual* have acted as a guide to *Master Directions* of RBI. Accordingly, RBI defines FDI as the investment, through capital instruments, by a person resident outside India (a) in an unlisted Indian company, or (b) in ten per cent or more of the post issue paid-up equity capital on a fully diluted basis of a listed Indian company. Following OECD's *Standard Statistical Requirements*, RBI's *Compilation of FDI in India* (2002) report marked that FDI has three components as follows: -

1. "*Equity Capital* which is the foreign direct investor's purchase of shares of an enterprise in a country other than its own.
2. *Reinvested Earnings* comprising the direct investors' share (in proportion to direct equity participation) of earnings not distributed as dividends by affiliates, or earnings not remitted to the direct investor. Such retained profits by affiliates are also reinvested.

3. *Intra-company Loans or Intra-company Debt Transactions* referring to short-term or long-term borrowing and lending of funds between direct investors (parent enterprises) and affiliate enterprises." (p.5)

Therefore, standard guideline of 10% equity ownership of voting stock or ordinary shares decides extant of foreign-invested firms with vested interest and credible voice in the management (to affect the decision-making process).

## Types of FDI

The FDI has been differentiated based on the direction of investment, internal structure, motive, target, different viewpoint or perspectives. The types of FDI based on its *direction,* also acknowledged by OECD Benchmark Definition (2008a), are (i) Inward FDI and (ii) Outward FDI, briefly elaborated as follows: -

### *Inward FDI*

A foreign entity either invests or purchases goods in host economy imbibing an inward investment, as per Chen (2020). The resources from abroad are encouraged by lifting of certain restrictions, low-interest loans, subsidies, and tax breaks etc. Al-Shawaf & Almsafir (2016) observed that through inward FDI, domestic firms in developing countries eventually reach the capability level that enables them to invest abroad.

### *Outward FDI*

As defined by Kenton (2020), an outward direct investment comprises of enlargement of domestic firm's operations in the foreign country in the form of *greenfield* investment or an expansion of the existing facilities, an acquisition, a merger, or encouraged by government-backed insurance and is restricted by tax incentives. Hayakawa & Matsura (2017) concluded that policies that increase outward FDI, contribute in enhancing development.

FDI on the basis of an industry's *internal structure* can be differentiated into (i) Expansionary FDI and (ii) Defensive FDI as following: -

### *Expansionary FDI*

This type of FDI was originally expounded by Hymer (1960) and Caves (1974) in their studies on theory of FDI and Multinational Enterprises (MNEs). "In this case, foreign firms invest in a host country in order to exploit the firm-specific advantage such as scale, R&D intensity and profitability embodied in their intangible asset." (Chen and Ku, 2000, p.154.)

### *Defensive FDI*

Defensive FDI is a survival strategy located in low-wage countries by investing firms to cut uncontrollable increases in production cost in their home countries and also is an effort to protect their export market share that further, determines their international competitiveness."Kojima (1973) called this type of investment labour-seeking FDI." (Chen and Ku, 2000, p.154.)

The types of FDI on the basis of the *viewpoint of the investing firms or the investors* are distinguished as"(i) Horizontal FDI, (ii) Vertical FDI, (iii) Conglomerate FDI and (iv) Platform FDI" (Moosa, 2002, p.4.) stated as follows: -

### *Horizontal FDI*

"In the horizontal FDI, same or similar kinds of goods are produced in a host country as well as in the home country with which monopolistic or oligopolistic gains due product differentiation are harnessed in the process." (Moosa, 2002, p.4.) This type of FDI is market seeking in nature and strengthens the firm's global competitive position. "Horizontal FDI also arises due to high exporting costs from transportation or trade barriers." (Protsenko, 2003, p.3)

### *Vertical FDI*

Phung (2020) states that vertical FDI takes place when multinationals get hold of an operation as either a distributor or a supplier. Hence, companies engaged in such settings aspire to reduce raw material's cost or acquire significant control of the supply chain (hence, becoming resource seeking in nature). It again can be further differentiated into: -

- Backward FDI: Here, foreign affiliates decide to either capture or assemble operations that grants them of the supplier's role. In other words, the investment corporation enters foreign countries to manufacture intermediate products for its home countries' output, in order to provide feed to the investor's existing business, like acquiring raw material sources abroad.
- Forward FDI: In forward FDI, foreign firms assume the role of a distributor to come nearer to the customers by acquiring distribution outlets in the host country i.e., a foreign firm sells its output in the host country by undertaking activities that add value by further processing those products in the home country.

### *Conglomerate FDI*

As stated by FDI India (2020), the conglomerate type of FDI focuses at the overseas firm and industries that manufacture products, not manufactured in the home country. Chen (2020) remarked that this type of investment often takes the form of a venture (joint) between foreign and domestic entities.

### ***Platform FDI***

Ekholm, Forslid and Markusen (2003) observed that platform FDI has the elements of both the horizontal as well as the vertical FDI. "It is an investment from a source country facing a very high cost of production into a destination country, where the cost of production is low, for the purpose of exporting into the third country where again, the cost of production is high." (Markusen, 2003, p.1.)

From the *perspective of host countries* (or investment receiving countries), "FDI can be in the form of (i) Import-Substituting FDI, (ii) Export-Increasing FDI and (iii) Government-Initiated FDI." (Moosa, 2002, p.4.) The three types of FDI are defined as following: -

### ***Import Substituting FDI***

"Import substituting FDI involves the production of goods previously imported by the host country, implying that imports by the host country will decline and so will the exports of the foreign investing country." (Tambunlertchai, 2009, p.11.) It is also emphasized that this type of FDI is brought to the host country in lieu of its structure based on quotas and tariff on the imports.

### ***Export-Increasing FDI***

"The export increasing FDI increases foreign exchange inflow and is motivated by the investing firms' desire to seek new sources of inputs." (Tambunlertchai, 2009, p.12.) The host country, in this case, will tend to improve export of intermediate goods and materials to MNCs' home economy.

### ***Government-Initiated FDI***

"Government-initiated FDI is triggered when the government of the host country offers incentives to allure foreign investors with a view to eliminate the balance of payments deficit." (Tambunlertchai, 2009, p.12.) Kojima (1973, 1975) and Kojima and Ozawa (1985) on the same pattern distinguished FDI as (a) *trade-oriented FDI*, generating excess demand in imports besides excess supply in exports and (b) *anti-trade oriented FDI* that caused obstructions in the activities of trade.

From the *perspective of investment objectives or motivations for establishing,* as first classified by Dunning (1998), FDI is (i) Resource-seeking FDI, (ii) Market-seeking FDI, (iii) Efficiency-seeking FDI and (iv) Strategic Asset-Seeking FDI as follows: -

### *Resource-Seeking FDI*

Resource-seeking FDI, in the host country, operate the aim of exploiting firm-specific advantages in order to make way for privileged access to cheap and natural resources. For example, oil & petroleum resources in Middle East, diamonds in Africa, or low-priced workers of China etc.

### *Market-Seeking FDI*

MNCs subsumes a prime reflex to broaden their investment horizon. In this case, the foreign firms engage in countries with a substantial size of its market and prospects of growth opportunities by protection of existing markets, mitigate competitors and prevention of (potential) rivals from acquiring new markets in the host and home country, mainly by reducing costs, i.e., using cheap resources in the host country.

### *Efficiency-Seeking FDI*

Dunning (2001) observed that firms having comparative advantage, such as scale economies sets to take on efficiency-seeking FDI with the motive to secure cheap factors of production. Here, the investing firms not only aims to access the markets or maintain existing ones but also look forward to gaining international sourcing of inputs, geographical diversification and economies of scope etc.

### *Strategic Asset-Seeking FDI*

The acquisition of some or all of the assets of a foreign firm and the enhancement of the acquiring affiliate's competitiveness, either through improved collaboration or low opposition, is a relatively specialised and occasional incentive for task of strategic asset-seeking FDI. In this situation, the company's mission is not to minimise costs or defend certain markets, but to prevent a competitor from gaining resources owing to resource constraint.

This study attempts to examine the sort of FDI prevalent in India's capital-intensive automobile industry. Nonetheless, resource and market-seeking FDI are the most common types in the majority of host nations.

## Modes of FDI

In modern times, FDI occurs through multinational enterprises, which are primarily composed up of companies and entities operating in various nation that are interconnected in some way to integrate their activities. Accordingly, "an MNE is a parent company that (i) engages in foreign production through its subsidiaries or associates located in several countries, (ii) exercises direct control or influence over the policies of its subsidiaries or associates, and (iii) implements business strategies in production, marketing, finance and staffing that transcend national boundaries." (Root, 1994, p. 17) Some studies have used FDI and MNEs interchangeably. In broader terms, mode of FDI can be interpreted by way of taking FDI and MNEs as separate subject matter and accordingly modes of FDI can be of two types (i) as means/mode of entry routes (ii) as means in MNEs' entry route, i.e., forms in which internationalization of the domestic firms takes place, both of which are discussed as follows: -

## *Mode of Entry Routes of FDI*

In order to attract and promote FDI, the government's attitude is reflected in a flexible policy regime that ensures the process of direct investment to be more investor-friendly. To promote national interest at the global platform, the policy pronouncements on FDI are made through Press Notes by Department for Promotion of Industry and Internal Trade's and on its basis, necessary notifications and policy pronouncements are issued under FEMA, 1999. As notified on Oct 2020, DIPP's Consolidated FDI Policy Circular, a foreign entity is eligible to make an investment in India under the following conditions: -

- Not requiring the governments or RBI's prior approval in the form of automatic route;
- Requiring RBI and the concerned Ministries/Departments' prior approval through DIPP administered FIPB housed in Ministry of Finance (until 2017) that acts as an single point online interface of the Indian government to facilitate investors through government route.

Indian government has permitted 100% FDI under automatic route in the variety of sectors/activities. As per the Ministry of Finance (2020), sectors/ activities with 100% sectoral cap are manufacturing, capital goods sector, auto components, food processing sector (except for trading and e-commerce), single brand retail trading, civil aviation sector, automobiles, urban infrastructure chemicals (with exception of certain hazardous chemicals), electronics system (except defence), railways etc. The sectors/activities that require mandatory government approval are mining (mining and minerals separations of titanium bearing minerals and ores), defence/cases relating to FDI in small arms, satellite (establishment and operations), print media (publications/ printing of scientific and technical magazines/speciality journals/ periodicals and facsimile edition of foreign newspapers), and core investment company having 100% sectoral cap, broadcasting content services and petroleum sector with limit up to 49% multi-brand retail trading up to 51% sectoral cap. Apart from the leading modes of entry of FDI in India, there are Non-Resident Indians' (NRI's) investments that include corporate bodies, societies, trusts, partnership firms and companies with 60% of the equity ownership in the hands of NRIs. This implies that even the entry of non-resident entity is allowed to do involve in direct investments following the permission from the government or RBI's route. Nevertheless, the FDI policy circular (2020) also lists the sectors barred from making any foreign investments, namely: -

1. "Lottery Business including Government/private lottery, online lotteries, etc.
2. Gambling and Betting including casinos etc.
3. Chit Funds.
4. Nidhi Company.
5. Trading in Transferable Development Rights (TDRs).
6. Real Estate Business or Construction of Farm Houses.
7. Manufacturing of cigars, cheroots, cigarillos and cigarettes, of tobacco or of tobacco substitutes.
8. Activities/sectors not open to private sector investment e.g. (I) Atomic Energy and (II) Railway operations. (other than permitted activities)." (p.28)

### *Mode of Entry of MNEs,*

Several qualitative and quantitative studies on multinationals yielded inconclusive results about the determinants of MNEs, based on choices of entry route, because the structure of the company, policies in the host economies and structure of foreign market, varied. In reference to mode through which MNEs enter the host economy, Nocke and Yeaple (2007) claimed that traditionally, FDI is grouped under the head of (i) Mergers & Acquisitions and (ii) non-Mergers & Acquisitions. Furthermore, authors such as Brouthers and Hennart (2007) and Pan and Tse (2000) have distinguished between (i) equity channels and (ii) non-equity channels which constitute not just importing and exporting but also wider range of activities of exchange. The equity channels of acquiring FDI comprise of (a) Greenfield FDI, (b) Brownfield FDI, (c) M&As and (d) Joint Ventures whereas non-equity channels of acquiring mainly covers (a) Licensing, (b) Franchising and (c) *Offshore Outsourcing.*

1. The modes of FDI as the *equity-based entry of MNEs* are described as follows:
   - Greenfield FDI: Similar to greenfield investment, *greenfield FDI*, occurs when a foreign entity establishes the facilities of manufacturing and marketing of goods and services, in the host's markets. Such investment brings about the opening of new establishments and the installation of new factories, plants, buildings and offices. Therefore,

host countries prefer such investments because of their value-adding potentialities. Tripathi et. al. (2019) noticed that since the period of liberalisation in India, greenfield investments have set the pace, bringing not just finance but also understanding of the business ecosystem, job creation, business acumen and technological know-how.

- Brownfield FDI: As highlighted in the World Investment Report (WIR, 2000), the term *Brownfield Investment* is used to denote the investment through cross-border M&As. Similar to brownfield investment, *brownfield FDI*, involves fully replacing the existing firm, by the acquiring firm, while making fresh investments in the original firm to induce a new production activity, then such takeovers result in a *corporate makeover* assimilating improved management and more effective production methods in original corporate entity. However, it does not generate the economic activities that are typically associated with greenfield FDI in host countries.
- Mergers and Acquisitions (M&As): From the investor's perspective, M&A of a running or sick business entity is the easiest way to enter a foreign market as only transfer of assets, to foreign firms from domestic enterprises, occurs because of it. "A *Merger* occurs when two (or more) companies agree to merge into a new single company rather than remain separated for creating business synergies whereas an *Acquisition* is defined as a business transaction between unrelated parties based on terms established by the market where each enterprise acts in its own interest." (OECDa, 2008, p.1) The WIR (2000) also differentiates between *Horizontal M&As* incurred amongst rival firms within the same industry and *Vertical M&As* takes place in firms holding a supplier-buyer relationship in an attempt to minimise transaction costs and lower ambiguity along with *Conglomerate M&As* that may tend to minimize risk and expand scope economies among the firms engaged in independent activities.
- Joint Venture (JV): "A Joint Venture can be described as a mechanism in which most of the assets are *Joint* in a completely new or legally independent *Venture* (entity) of which the JV partners share the equity." (Raff et al., 2008, p.27) In other words, it is a contractual agreement involving two or more partners with the intention to carry out a business venture wherein the stakeholders accept to share the profit and loss realised in the said partnership. It is an efficient strategy to expand in countries with investment restrictions as it enables the

investment firm to benefit from the resident partner's understanding of government rules, value system, and brand building.

2. The modes of FDI as the *non-equity-based entry of MNEs* are stated as follows: -
   - Licensing: These are the agreements under which an innovative company entity provides other entities, the right of patent usage or not as much of regulated technology in its own production processes. In other words, license contract encompasses directions for transferring know-how of various business activities such as production, assembling, testing, and product support assurance and customer care etc. from the licensor to the licensee.
   - Franchising: regards "*Franchising* as an agreement lasting for a definite or indefinite period in which the owner of a protected trademark entitles another economic entity, the right to operate under this trademark, for the purpose of producing and distributing products, or services." (Caves and Murphy, 1976, p.572)
   - Offshore Outsourcing: It is a contract amongst legitimately autonomous companies located in different nations to allow for firm-level inflows of intermediate products and services. For instance, contract manufacturing, contract farming, subcontracting, management contracts, turnkey arrangements, product sharing and concessions etc. also form a part of non-equity modes of entry of FDI.

In surveyed literature, authors such Hennart and Park (1993) Brouthers and Brouthers (2000) Shimizu et al. (2004), Arslan and Larimo (2011), Slangen and Hennart (2007), Demirbag et al. (2008) and Larimo (2003) have emphasized on the advantages of selecting the equity mode of entry of MNEs, especially in the form of the greenfield FDI and even the brownfield FDI as compared to the other modes. This study emphasizes entry mode of FDI based on equity ownership in the overall industry separating domestic and foreign firms.

## Theories of FDI

The idea to go through the economic literature focuses on understanding the concepts underlying the determinants of the FDI and MNEs. The standard classification to the theoretical responses of the exploration of the various schools of literature for FDI has been employed by Agarwal (1980). However, Bajrami & Zeqiri (2019), Denisia (2010) and Moosa (2002) have recently incorporated the frameworks of the major school of thoughts that are divided briefly in theories grounded on the assumption of (i) perfect markets, and those based on the assumption of (ii) imperfect markets.

**(i) The following are the theories based on perfect market: -**

a. The Differential Rates of Return Theory

This theory's central notion and premise is that the "movement of capital takes place from nations with low rates of return to the nations with a high rate of return" (Moosa, 2002, p. 24) The theory of differential rates of return is one of the oldest theories assumes risk neutrality. Hosseini (2005) argued that by introducing risk and uncertainty among nations, this theory loses its predictive ability.

b. The Portfolio Diversification Theory

"The background of this theory can be traced back to the *Theory of Portfolio Selection,* given by Tobin (1958) and Markowitz (1959) with risk as an essential determinant." (Bajrami & Zeqiri, 2019, p.17) According to this theory, Moosa (2002) remarked "capital mobility and FDI will be constrained by the desire to minimize or reduce the risk, which is achieved by diversification". (p.26)

c. The Market Size Theory

Majeed and Ahmad (2008) remarked that "The market size hypothesis argue that inward FDI is a function of the size of the host country market, usually measured by GDP." (p. 87) The main premise of this theory rests on a direct relationship of volume of direct investments from abroad to the size of market. Also, "The market size theory and hypothesis explains the volume and directions of FDI, in light of the market size of the host country." (Bajrami & Zeqiri, 2019, p.17).

**(ii) The following are the theories based on imperfect market: -**

(a)The Industrial Organisation Hypothesis

The firm-specific advantages, such as such as product innovations, advanced knowledge, market segmentation, managerial competence, and access to international markets, according to this supposition, explain why firms penetrate international markets though the direct investments. According to Moosa (2002), a firm seeking to establish a majority stake in some other country may face disadvantages in competing with local businesses due to structural market imperfections, or it may benefit from advantages over competitors.

(b) The Location Hypothesis

Rendering to this hypothesis, "FDI exists because of the international immobility of some factors of production such as labour (in terms of wages paid by foreign investors) and natural resources." (Moosa, 2002, p.33) Therefore, countries with relatively lower wages, fewer allocation costs and large resources are preferred destinations for FDI.

(c) The Internalization Hypothesis

According to Bajrami and Zeqiri (2019), this idea presupposes that FDI results from enterprises' efforts to substitute market transactions with internal activities and the firms strive to internalise various activities. Coase (1937) made the first initial effort to explain the internalisation theory in a national context. They further identified two major determinants of FDI that results in "removal of competition, and advantages that some companies possess in a particular activity." (Denisia, 2010, p.56.)

The OLI Paradigm Hypothesis:

The OLI paradigm emphasizes on the three conditions for a firm to engage in the FDI process. Dunning (2008) postulated these as (a) *ownership (O) advantages* that are defined as the extent to which a firm has sustained ownership-specific gains over all other participants in the industry, (b) the *location (L) advantages* that explains the territorial characteristic of the firms and assets unique to the country and finally, (c) the *internalization (I) advantages* that explain *how* the degree of ownership and control act as the choice between expansion within the firms or to the other firms.

The International Product Life Cycle Theory and Hypothesis.

"Vernon (1966) expounded *four stages of the production cycle: innovation, growth, maturity and decline.*" (Denisia, 2010, p.55). However, as per Moosa (2002), the three stages of the products are central. First, is the initial production with the new product's demand being inelastic, second, when a product reaches maturity, it is relocated to countries with the highest levels of demand and third, is expected harmonization of the product and its manufacturing process.

(e) The Oligopolistic Reactions Hypothesis

Knickerbocker (1973) articulated the notion of imperfections in market and stated two main reasons for selecting a specific nation as a place for establishing an additional enterprise, which are (a) improved market access in the host country, and (b) comparatively substantial resources available in that country. "Knickerbocker (1973) also suggested a third motivation for choosing a location where firms might invest in a country to match a rival's move." (Head, Mayer, & Ries, 2002, p.454).

**(iii) The other theories of FDI are mentioned as follows: -**

The Internal Financing Hypothesis.

This hypothesis is based on the *gambler's earnings hypothesis* of Barlow and Wender (1955) postulating that "MNCs commit a modest amount of their resources to their initial direct investment while the subsequent expansions are financed by the reinvesting profits obtained from the operations in the host country" (Moosa,2002, p.42.). Hartman (1985) on the other hand, explains the theory with the tax-based presuppositions for internalisation of the financial activities.

The Currency Area Hypothesis

FDI was described in terms of relative strength of several currencies by Nayak & Choudhury (2014). This hypothesis was first put forward by Aliber (1970). This theory holds that enterprises from a nation with a strong currency seek to invest overseas and therefore, become the source country of FDI, whereas establishments from a nation with a weak currency become the beneficiary of FDI.

The Hypothesis of Diversification with barriers to International Capital.

According to Agmon and Lessard (1997), for diversification to take place, two conditions must be met. First, there must be impediments or costs to portfolio flows, also investors need to identify foreign corporations providing opportunities which else would be inaccessible. Further, Agmon & Lessard (1977) added that "the flexibility of the MNC in shifting revenue-producing resources among its operating units suggests that even when barriers are nominally the same, direct investment flows will be freer than portfolio flow." (p. 1050.)

The Kojima Hypothesis.

Kojima (1973, 1975) and Kojima and Ozawa (1985) considers comparative advantage between two countries, or between one country and the rest of the world within factor proportions setting. Accordingly, "FDI is classified into (a) trade-oriented FDI that generates excess demand of import and excess supply of export at the original terms of trade leading to welfare improvement of both the countries and, (b) anti-trade oriented FDI that on the other hand has an adverse effect on trade promoting unfavourable restructuring in both countries." (Moosa, 2002, p. 44),

Recently, FDI has been thought of as a necessary driver of long-term growth and development, for the developing countries from linkages with advanced countries.

## Linkages and Spillovers of the FDI

All the major theories discussed in section 1.1.4, try to provide a theoretical base to the explanation of the supply-side elements and motives that would generate a thrust for FDI to probe into the foreign country. Some of such supply-side factors are cost advantages, access to markets, exchange earnings, external economies, locational advantages, risk-averse behaviour of firms, profit augmentation through superior skills and knowledge, and so on. However, FDI is drawn into the host country with accompanying demand-side factors.

The contributions of such demand-side factors can be explained through imitation effects, competition effects, spillovers, linkages, innovation effects, human capital accumulation, internationalisation of R&D, market discipline and strengthening and deepening of the host country's capital markets, and so on. Furthermore, Ray (1998) proposed that FDI inflows improve technology diffusion, resulting in increased productivity and other intangible attributes of the domestic economy.

"The widening gap between the growing importance of MNCs and the static understanding of their effects, created a pressing need by the 1960s to examine, more qualitative attributes of multinationals and the impact of their activities in host countries, such as, their sectoral distribution and technological content along with the nature of the linkages to the local economy." (Jones, 1996, p.6)

According to OECD's International Investment Perspectives (2002), while analysing the general welfare effects of foreign investment, MacDougall (1960) was the first to carefully consider spillovers among the potential implications of FDI. The majority of the studies suggest that spillover effects of the MNEs result in positive direct as well the indirect benefits from the inflows of FDI in the host countries mainly, by way of strength of the horizontal and vertical linkages, existing among the locally-owned firms in the host countries.

Albeit, OECD's International Investment Perspectives (2002) mentioned that although the spillover effects are assumed to be directly associated to the degree of linkages. There are two major types of spillovers based on the vast literature survey, namely, (i) horizontal spillovers and (ii) vertical spillovers, that are discussed briefly as follows: -

(i) Horizontal (intra-industry) Spillovers

The presence of foreign enterprises might result in a rise of the efficiency in internal industry participants, ensuing horizontal spillovers. These are thought to occur via three primary pathways. First, the *demonstration effects,* in which local businesses learn by observing international business functioning at a superior technological level, resulting in product/process improvement. Second, as a result of the competition effect, domestic firms endure intense rivalry from foreign enterprises and are unable to compete with them unless they enhance their own performance. The third pathway is labour mobility, in which personnel trained by or employed by MNCs enters domestic and regional firm or build a new business with firm-specific knowledge.

(ii) Vertical (inter-industry) Spillovers

"The phenomenon of spillovers is not just confined between industries but can also arise as a result of interaction across industries." (Jena & Taggar, 2011, p.130.) The customer-supplier relationship between enterprises is the primary source of inter-industry spillovers. Furthermore, the vertical spillovers process runs downstream (through forward linkages) and upstream (via backward linkages), as outlined as follows: -

(a) Backward Spillovers

Due to host country's significant transportation cost and various restrictions forced by the host nation, and its government, MNCs typically buy their raw material from domestic vendors. According to Lall, (1979), MNCs support domestic enterprises in improving the quality of their manufacturing processes and achieve organisational and technical expertise by offering assistance and training opportunities, as MNCs often abide by high quality requirements for their inputs.

(b) Forward Spillovers

When FDI firms sell their products for input production in local-buyer firms, the high-quality materials enable local buyer firms to extract productivity benefit i.e., forward linkage appears when local buyer firms experiencing improvement in output results from MNE's provide high-quality inputs at a cheaper rate. Javorcik (2004) mentioned the case where the domestic enterprises that are unable to capitalize from such improved quality, would be forced to bear the increased cost of the same.

## Evolution of Foreign Direct Investment Policies and Emerging Trends

The evolution of the FDI policies must be previewed under pretext of historical events that provide the background to the behaviour of the recent trends and patterns of FDI. This study has outlined four discrete stages in the evolution of India's policy towards FDI, as follows: -

### The History of FDI in India

The traditional Indian society in the pre-British era consisted of self-sustaining and isolated villages along with the major cities that acted as the centre of administration, commerce and trade. During the 16$^{th}$ and 17$^{th}$ centuries, India was an industrially advanced economy and held a worldwide reputation for its production of textiles and handicrafts. For these production activities, labour and capital were supplied by the producer, landlord or the moneylender.

The advent of the British, in the form of the East India Company (1757-1858) that coincided with the industrial revolution, led to the disintegration of the traditional Indian society. The British secured the largest possible revenue and engaged in excessive extraction of the financial as well as the natural resources from trade and land respectively, leading to aggressive exploitation of Indian economy. Furthermore, the inflow of foreign capital was disrupted due the industrial transition (revolution).

India became the exporter of the raw material to the British and importer of the manufactured goods leading to the tremendous increase in the productive capacity of the British manufacturers in the face of reduced costs and an unrestricted competition with indigenous producer leading to their systematic destruction. As documented by Tomlinson (1975) "Since the days of the *company firms* of British expatriates had found India a rewarding field for their enterprises." (p. 341) Again, at becoming the British Government of India (1858-1947), the *British Raj* forced India to maintain a favourable balance of trade with Britain. It was only after the World War-I, that the Indian industry was granted some protection. "British capital was invested in the merchant and agency houses of Calcutta and in the railways, other capital schemes and the government debt." (Tomlinson, 1975, p. 341) Out of these, the most sophisticated drainage of profits was seen in the form of system of subsidies offered to the railways known as *the Guarantee.* Hurd (1983) in *Cambridge Economic History of India* mentioned that in return of the *Guarantee*, British investors swiftly made their capital available to the private railway companies in India.

Between 1850 and 1855, the first coal mine, jute mill, and first cotton factory were established, whereby, direct private foreign investment was also made. "The outbreak of World War-I led to the setting up of 70 cotton mills and nearly 30 jute mills along with the foundation of iron and steel industry catering to an urgent demand for the manufactured goods." (Datt and Sundaram, 2013, p. 20) In the 19$^{th}$ and 20$^{th}$ centuries, substantial amount of the overall capital invested in modern establishments such as cotton, tea, coal, jute, tobacco, sugar and rubber etc. was imported from Britain as Indian industries suffered from the lack of adequate capital along with the absence of financial institutions which could finance external trade at such level. Hence, by establishing a trading firm (or an MNE) such as East India Company, the British managed to reap all the benefits as a foreign investor with investment made in the areas of high profits.

The estimates of the foreign capital calculated at the time, suffered the drawback of being patchy. Nonetheless, the conclusion remained unanimous that the influx of the British capital had been rising in the pre-independence era. In Datt and Sundaram (2013), 50% of the foreign investments in companies were registered outside of India as inferred by Findlay Shirras and the *British Chamber of Commerce*. Also, with their operations in India, 20% of the £4000 million British foreign investment were made in the pre-World War-II in India leading to an addition of £500 million in foreign capital to £1000 million in 1933.

**Table 1.1:Estimates of Foreign Capital in India in £ Million.**

| Source | Reference Year | Amount in (£ Million) |
|---|---|---|
| Parish | 1911 | 365 |
| Findlay Shiras | 1929 | 500 |
| British Associated Chamber of Commerce | 1933 | 1000 |

*Source: Adapted from Datt and Sundaram (2013), 69th Edition, S. Chand Publication. p.25.*

Chatterjee (1992) stressed that it was Britain's acute balance of payment crisis, the weak competitive prospects of her exports, and America's desire to align the international environment on the freer lines along with India's political opposition that led India towards freedom. Nonetheless, the journey towards eliminating internal economic incapacities in terms of inadequate capital began with the dawn of independence as the government realised that economic dependence is the key to stimulate investment flows into an economy.

## The Period of Caution and Receptive Attitude towards FDI (1947-1967)

The policy reforms during this phase are characterised by the process of development of domestic industry and revival of agriculture that faced two hundred years of colonial exploitation. On 30th June 1948, the Reserve Bank of India published report on India's foreign liabilities and assets. It got published in 1951 but was changed to December 31, 1953. It was discontinued in 1955, however, in 1961 benchmark surveys instead of census surveys were introduced. "These census surveys made an estimate of foreign investment facilitating the preparation of more accurate estimate of a country's investment position." (Hicks, Mukherjee and Ghosh, 1992, p. 217.) The colonial legacy gave rise to a very low surplus for investment in the Indian economy. "It has been estimated that on the eve of independence the share of foreign enterprises in the total industrial output was only 25% and more than half of this was destined for exports" (Chandra, 1981, p. 15.)

Chandra (1981) documented that the Indian Nationalists vehemently pointed towards the dangers of further economic dependence and domination, but also recognized that some amount of foreign capital would be necessary to fulfil India's massive requirements of capital, imports of machinery, modern technological advancements, and technical personnel in India. After attaining the independence, the Indian government recollected the series of studies on achieving rapid economic growth with the help of specific policies at macroeconomic level.

In 1938, the *National Planning Committee* realised that the ownership or control of all key industries, resources, and services that were likely to become monopolistic in essence and character. "Hence, the key industries were earmarked for further development in the public sector either in view of their strategic nature or anticipated lack of initiative in the private sector because of large capital requirements." (Kumar, 1998, p.1321) The Industrial Policy Resolution (IPR) of 1948 was passed. Ranjan (2018) mentioned that then Prime Minister Pt. Jawahar Lal Nehru made a statement, in *The Wire* (April 1949), to scrutinize every single foreign investment project before giving approval, so that Indians have a fundamental stake in ownership and effective representation but also gave the assurance of the following to the foreign investors: -

- Non-discriminatory treatment of both local and foreign enterprises.
- Permission of plausible facilities of a strong foreign exchange position, remittance of profits and capital repatriation to the foreign investors.
- Fair and equitable compensation to the investor, if foreign undertaking is nationalised.

In 1950, Planning Commission was set up and First Five-Year Plan (1951-1956) was put into implementation. The immediate objective of the same was to attain self-sufficiency in the agriculture in order to rectify the economic imbalance prompted by World War II (1939-1945) and the partition (1947). When the country was going through the industrialization phase during the 1950s, foreign capital came into India through the joint venture route making FDI in India at US$ 8 million. (See Table 1.2).

**Table 1.2:Foreign Investment in India from 1950-51 to 1966-67 in US$ Million and Rs. Crore.**

| Year | RBI | |
|---|---|---|
| | US$ in million | Rupees crore |
| 1950-51 | 8 | 37 |
| 1951-52 | 8 | 28 |
| 1952-53 | 8 | 24 |

| Year | RBI | |
|---|---|---|
| | US$ in million | Rupees crore |
| 1953-54 | 17 | 36 |
| 1954-55 | 17 | 44 |
| 1955-56 | 50 | 30 |
| 1956-57 | 44 | 52 |
| 1957-58 | 6 | 3 |
| 1958-59 | 21 | 10 |
| 1959-60 | 109 | 52 |
| 1960-61 | 59 | 28 |
| 1961-62 | 63 | 30 |
| 1962-63 | - | - |
| 1963-64 | 55 | 26 |
| 1964-65 | 99 | 47 |
| 1965-66 | 38 | 18 |
| 1966-67 | 51 | 31 |

*Source: Handbook of Statistics on the Indian Economy, 2008-09, RBI, p. 248 and p. 250.*

It is to be pointed out that in the Table 1.2, the calendar-wise inflows from 1953 to 1962 and financial year-wise inflows from 1963-64 are mentioned. In consideration of the modification in the period of assessment from calendar year to financial year, it has not been possible to designate the outflows and inflows, throughout 1962-63. In IPR (1956), the role of the state was sharply defined. Nonetheless, due to favourable monsoons in India, agricultural targets set in the First Plan (1951-1956) were achieved, thereby, the focus of attention shifted towards heavy and basic industries in the Second Five Year Plan (1956-1961), with the implementation of Mahalanobis strategy and a focus on the development planning.

The period of 1957 to 1963 saw various sets of fiscal incentives such as concession dividend rates, discounted technical service fees, and preferential tax arrangements for royalties etc. being offered to foreign investors. This led to a tenfold increase to US$ 63 million from US$ 6 million in overall foreign investments, at end of 1962, also depicted in Table 1.2. The government's attitude toward FDI further improved, following the foreign exchange crisis of 1957-58. In the international arena, an unfavourable balance of trade was witnessed and the foreign exchange crisis of 1958 changed the pattern of foreign partnership as follows: -

- Equity participation became the preferable mode of foreign firms to venture
- In lieu of royalties, technical collaborations began to receive the equity participation.

Therefore, in a bid to attract foreign investment, an extension of concessions and incentives was provided, along with comprehensive import controls, such as large quota and high tariffs. Following 1958, Indian enterprises were granted provisional approvals to get a proportion or all of foreign exchange from international investment. Even in conflict with China (1962) and Pakistan (1965), foreign capital in private limited industrial concerns, was allowed up to 49% share in the Third Five Year Plan (1961-66). In special cases, it could go up to 51%, provided Indian resident participation, within a period of 5 years. Foreign investors were, however, forbid to invest in proprietorship as their dividends were prohibited from repatriation.

As per Finance Act (1965), capital gains tax refund ascending from the transfer of NRI's shares in Indian firms was permitted, provided their proceeds were reinvested in India. This was a done for the *Nationalisation* of foreign capital. In 1966, the government decided that to allow NRIs investments in India, yet, the foreign investments declined more than half from 1963-64 to 1965-66 (from US$ 55 million to US$ 38 million), as per Table 1.2. With import-substituting industrialisation called forth a devaluation of the Indian currency. The devaluation of rupee in 1966 was strongly opposed by domestic businesses for expensive imports. This period reflected a deeply contradictory sentiment about foreign investment, as the government had continued with its receptive policy towards foreign capital whereas locally available skills and capabilities could not withstand competitive environment posed by far established nations'.

## The Period of Selective and Restrictive Policy towards FDI (1967-1979)

Despite outward concessions to foreign private capital, the general stance of the Indian government on foreign investment was hostile throughout the 1960s and the 1970s. However, due to the liberal policy towards foreign capital till the mid-1960s, the outflow of capital in the form of remittances, also grew sharply. As described in Datt and Sundaram (2013), in the period of 1966-69, *Plan Holiday* was implemented, whereas, the original draft outline of the Fourth Plan in 1966, was abandoned due to the economic pressures imposed by two consecutive years of drought, rupee depreciation, and recession triggered by inflation. The foreign investments, in the plan holiday period, showed a declining trend from US$ 49 million in 1967-68 to US$ 32 million to 1969-70 as shown in the Table 1.3.

The major disparities in the economy also arose due to the strengthening of the monopoly trends, reinforcing the economic disparities. As reported by the *Monopolies Enquiry Commission* (1965), big business houses had been using the licencing system to the detriment of the small-scale enterprise. "To curb such tendencies and to control the monopolistic and restrictive trade practices of the large business houses, the government of India implemented the Monopolies Restrictive Trade Practices (MRTP) Act in 1969 and the MRTP Commission was set up in 1970." (Mishra & Puri 2013, p. 433). In the year of 1969, the nationalisation of the banks took place, suggesting government's control over the nation's major financial institution network. Also, it was observed by Athreye & Kapur (2001) that with a revised *Patent Act* in 1970, Intellectual Property Rights (IPRs) were severely curtailed. In this context Ahluwalia (1986) added that government in 1972 decided to allow the foreign wholly-owned subsidiaries to establish in India with a condition to export 100% of their output.

With the introduction of the MRTP Act, the industrial framework turned increasingly stringent. Furthermore, to ensure more effective control over concentration of economic power, the definition of large industrial entities based on assets surpassing Rs. 20 crore was introduced, in accordance with the MRTP Act (1969). Also, in 1973, the high priority industries in which significant industrial houses and foreign corporations might invest were determined by the Industrial Policy Statement.

**Table 1.3: Foreign Investment in India as a Component of Balance of Payments in 1967-1980 in US$ Million and Rs. Crore.**

| Year | RBI | |
|---|---|---|
| | **US$ in million** | **Rupees Crore** |
| 1967-68 | 49 | 37 |
| 1968-69 | 37 | 28 |
| 1969-70 | 32 | 24 |
| 1970-71 | 48 | 36 |
| 1971-72 | 58 | 44 |
| 1972-73 | 40 | 30 |
| 1973-74 | 67 | 52 |
| 1974- 75 | 87 | 69 |

| Year | RBI | |
|---|---|---|
| | US$ in million | Rupees Crore |
| 1975-76 | -9 | -8 |
| 1976-77 | -29 | -26 |
| 1977-78 | -12 | -10 |
| 1978-79 | 30 | 24 |
| 1979-80 | 86 | 70 |

*Source: Handbook of Statistics on the Indian Economy, 2008-09, RBI, p. 248 and p. 250.*

This resulted in increase in the foreign investments from US$ 67 million to US$ 87 million from 1973-74 to 1974-1975. Furthermore, the government instituted the FERA (1973), which compelled companies to cut foreign equity holdings to 40%, to be treated as Indian. With foreign equity holding of more than 40%, manufacturing activities of foreign company branches and Indian joint-stock companies in India were also pulled under the ambit of FERA's regime. In addition to foreign investment restrictions, new curbs on technology imports were enforced, with technology acquisition was permitted primarily through licencing instead of financial partnership. However, in industries requiring highly sophisticated technology, such as the core industry, tea plantation industry and drugs and pharmaceuticals sector, non-residents were permitted to continue business and were also spared from obtaining permission from the RBI within the specified licensed capacity, but without any expansion and diversification of their business activities.

The decline in foreign investments from 1975-76 to 1977-1978 resulted from the negative effects of external factors like *oil shocks* in 1973 and 1974, generating inflation. The policy that permitted NRIs (with authorised equity ownership of up to 74%) to build industrial facilities in India by taking in imported machinery was enforced by 1976. Nonetheless, the year of 1976-1977 marked the severe decline of US$ (-) 29 million. "Because of FERA and some other radical measures that strongly controlled domestic industry, India under Indira Gandhi's leadership was, indeed, the most comprehensively regulated market economy in the world" (Tendulkar and Bhavani, 2007, p. 23)

With this, in few cases, the Indian government permitted foreign participants to have majority control in the company. Also, such foreign participation was subjected to modifications at the hands of bureaucratic arrangements. To avoid delays in clearances of foreign collaborations, the authorities also granted a broad array of tax breaks to foreign firms and simplified the industrial licencing system. As documented in GOI (1969), it was clarified that foreign collaboration efforts were persuaded merely to fill a crucial gap and did not exclude the effective utilisation of indigenous know-how.

The *Industrial Policy Statement* (1977) emphasized on the small-scale sector along with cottage and tiny industries to hamper some reduction in the concentration of the economic power of the large business houses. The earlier approvals taken by the multinationals as the foreign collaboration were not renewed in the territory where foreign know-how were not required but exceptions were made in highly export-oriented and/or sophisticated technology area only. The government maintained a strategy of unplanned import liberalisation throughout 1977-78 and the two years that followed, at a time when the export surge had practically peaked.

Lall and Mohammad (1983) stated that, the entire expanse of foreign capital permitted by government throughout the eleven-year period (1966-1979), amounted to only US$ 70 million, with a negative net capital inflow. "India's reputation for hostility towards foreign economic participation though was mostly due to the restrictions on equity participation and export obligations imposed during the 1970s." (Mahambare & Balasubramanian, 2005, p.6.) This adoption of a receptive attitude towards FDI by the government forced to make fervent attempts to adopt the market-oriented reforms suggested by developed economies.

## The Period of Partial Liberalization Policy with the Progressive Reduction of Regulations towards FDI (1980-1990)

The importance of the 1980's is reflected in the fact that most of the studies on the Indian economy are done on basis of comparison of the pre (1980-90) and post (1991 onwards) reform period. From 1980-1990, period of *partial liberalisation* came under the sixth and seventh Five Year Plan, whereby, the respective actual average annual GDP growth rates of 5.7% and 6.0% were achieved. It is emphasized by Virmani (2003), that for most of the people, the story of increased rate of growth follows New Economic Reforms (1991), succeeding the BoP crisis, but even so, it actually took place from partial liberalisation process in the 1980s.

Nevertheless, the period of 1980s also witnessed the unprecedented strains on the external payments situation. This period began and ended with the crisis. In 1973, the oil crises, tailgated inflationary pressures, endangering economic growth. Strikingly, after the second oil crisis in 1979-1980, as a result of inflation, rising import bills depleted the forex reserves. This situation was further impelled by hikes in crude and stagnant economic state of affairs in 1982-83. To get over the problems posed by BoP, the government in November 1981 secured a US$ 5 billion SDR loan under IMF's extended fund facility (EFF) and headlined in *India Today* (1981) also. The *Technology Policy Statement* (1983) covered a whole range of policy measures relating to liberalising of the licensing provisions related to imported technology. In light of the course of events, foreign investment was distinguished in the 1980s as a conduit of technology transfer not available, locally.

This resulted in a substantial spurt in the foreign collaborations that joined hands with domestic big business houses to diversify and expand its production activities of the latter. This would be clear from Table 1.4 that of the total 12,285 foreign collaboration agreements approved in the 40 years between 1948 and 1988, as many as 4,201 (i.e., 34.20%) contracts were approved during the eight years between 1981 and 1988. The formal data from Stoever (1989) on the number of foreign collaboration agreements approved from 1948 to 1988 (Jan-Jun) is reported in Table 1.4. It signifies that despite the tenfold increase in the number of the foreign collaborations approved between 1980 and 1988, the absolute number of agreements to be observed were rather small for India considering its size and scale.

**Table 1.4:Number of Foreign Collaboration Agreements Approved in India (Jan, 1948-Jun, 1988).**

| Year | Total Number of Cases Approved | Cases Involving Foreign Technical Participation |
|---|---|---|
| 1948-55 | 284 | - |
| 1956 | 82 | - |
| 1957 | 81 | - |
| 1958 | 103 | - |
| 1959 | 150 | - |
| 1960 | 380 | - |
| 1961 | 403 | 268 |
| 1962 | 298 | 174 |
| 1963 | 298 | 183 |
| 1964 | 403 | 280 |
| 1965 | 242 | 171 |
| 1966 | 202 | 153 |
| 1967 | 182 | 120 |
| 1968 | 131 | 101 |

| Year | Total Number of Cases Approved | Cases Involving Foreign Technical Participation |
|---|---|---|
| 1969 | 135 | 106 |
| 1970 | 183 | 151 |
| 1971 | 245 | 199 |
| 1972 | 257 | 220 |
| 1973 | 265 | 231 |
| 1974 | 359 | 304 |
| 1975 | 271 | 231 |
| 1976 | 277 | 238 |
| 1977 | 267 | 240 |
| 1978 | 307 | 263 |
| 1979 | 267 | 235 |
| 1980 | 526 | 453 |
| 1981 | 389 | 332 |
| 1982 | 590 | 477 |
| 1983 | 673 | 544 |
| 1984 | 752 | 601 |
| 1985 | 1,024 | 786 |
| 1986 | 957 | 717 |
| 1987 | 852 | 610 |
| 1988 (Jan- June) | 450 | 134 |
| Total | 12,285 | 8,522 |

*Source: Adapted from Stoever, Foreign Collaborations Policy in India: A Review. (1989), p.489, further mimeographed from various issues of Indian Investment Centre, New Delhi.*

As per *the Annual Report* of RBI (1990-91), the gross fiscal deficit rose from 4.1% of GDP in 1975-76 to 6.2% in 1980-81. "It continued rising during the 1980s to reach a peak of 8.4% of GDP in 1990-91, making the macro-economic situation vulnerable to external shocks." (Virmani, 1997, p. 2064). The government undertook a broad series of economic reforms in response to the BoP crisis. However, Kumar (2003) observed an increasing dependency on the private business sector spawned by the reforms, initiated in the mid-1980s, allowing for hefty relaxations of imports control and de-licensing process to augment industrial expertise. "The change in India in the early 1980s is accordingly best described as pro-business rather than pro-market." (Rodrik & Subramanian, 2004, p.4) This is reflected in the adoption of the industrial policy of 1980.

However, it was the latter part of the 1980s that exacerbate the signs of a partially liberalised regime. In 1985, the first Long-Term Fiscal Policy (LTFP) was unveiled. Other tax arrangements included the conversion of multipoint excise taxes into a MODVAT tax, which allowed manufacturers to deduct excise duties and countervailing duties paid on locally produced inputs and its imports, respectively, against their liabilities. Furthermore, several export incentives were introduced (for e.g., EXIM Bank in 1982) to provide exporters/importers with a comprehensive range of financial and allied facilities.

In the direction of disseminating stability and proclaim continuity of trade, the Export-Import (EXIM) policy was announced in 1985 over a three-year span in its first phase. Furthermore, export-oriented FDI became the centre of attraction for which Export-Processing Zones began to be installed in 1985. "Imports of designs and drawings and capital goods were permitted under a liberalised *Technical Development Fund Scheme*." (Sahoo et al., 2013, p. 43) The Stock Exchange Board of India was put in place in 1988-89 to allow stock market to complement the new industrial reforms. Morris (1994) emphasised that the 1980s saw a resurgence of FDI into India after a period of very low or negative investments in the 1970s.

In Table 1.5, Foreign Direct Investment under the component of BoP's current account during the 1980s in the RBI's *Handbook of Statistics* (2008-09). Earlier presented as RBI's *Monograph on India's Balance of Payments (July 1993)*, (EPWRF, 2005), these series follow its own set of flaws. Firstly, data are not available for the period of 1980-1981 to 1985-1986. No official data collection was carried out during this time. Also, the time period of 1987-1988 to 1989-1990 follow the same fate. Although, an increasing trend can be seen in the FDI from Rs. 249 crores in 1986-1987 to Rs. 683 crores in 1989-1990.

In dollar terms, FDI rose from US$ 195 million in 1986-1987 to US$ 434 million in 1987-1988 and further, rising to US$ 410 million again in 1989-1990. However, for an updated coverage ensuring data consistency for FDI inflows in India from 1980-1990, Table 1.5 has also depicted the statistics according to the UNCTADSTAT database on the inward flow of the FDI in US$ at the current prices, revealing a substantial annual rise in the value of inward FDI flows (in US$ million) from 1980 to 1990. Accordingly, the severity of balance of payments situation, also discussed earlier, is reflected in the period of 1983-1984, whereby, inward FDI flows stood at US$ 6 million.

**Table 1.5: Foreign Direct Investment in India from 1980-1990 in US$ Million and Rs. Crore from RBI and in US$ at current prices in millions and as a percentage of GDP from UNCTADSTAT.**

| Years | RBI | | UNCTAD | |
|---|---|---|---|---|
| | US$ in million | Rupees Crore | Inward FDI flows at current prices (US$ million) | FDI inflows as a % age of GDP |
| 1980-81 | - | - | 79 | 0.04 |
| 1981-82 | - | - | 92 | 0.05 |
| 1982-83 | - | - | 72 | 0.04 |
| 1983-84 | - | - | 6 | 0.00 |
| 1984-85 | - | - | 19 | 0.01 |
| 1985-86 | - | - | 106 | 0.05 |
| 1986-87 | 195 | 249 | 118 | 0.05 |
| 1987-88 | 434 | 563 | 212 | 0.08 |
| 1988-89 | 357 | 517 | 91 | 0.03 |
| 1989-90 | 410 | 683 | 252 | 0.08 |

*Source: Compiled from Handbook of Statistics in the Indian Economy (2008-09), RBI, p. 249 and p. 251, UNCTADSTAT, 1980-1990.*

Furthermore, in Table 1.5, it can be seen that the annual inflows, as a percentage of GDP throughout the decade have been revolving around the average of 0.04% of GDP. The decade ended with FDI in India with highest FDI inflows at US$ 252 million standing at 0.08% of GDP due to realisation of the effects of the various policies undertaken to fix the balance of payments problem. The rising trend in the FDI throughout the decade gave India the confidence it required, towards encouragement of foreign private capital in the coming decade in the face of New Economic Policies.

## The Period of Post Liberalisation with the advent of New Economic Reforms (1991-2000).

By the end of 1990s, due to the external upheavals such as the Gulf War, India's low ranking on Moody's bond ratings, and unfitted fiscal budget, India sought short-term loans and intensified the existing economic crisis. In October 1990, as an outcome of relatively high inflation rate, a rise in rupee's real exchange rate and the *twin deficit problem* in the BoP culminated at the end of the pre-reform period. This led to justification for the implementation of economic reforms. On July 24, 1991, also detailed in Kumar (1998), the *New Industrial Policy* (NIP), funded by the IMF and the World Bank, was unveiled as part of programme encompassing macroeconomic stabilisation and structural adjustment. This instigated the process of full-scale liberalisation and deepened India's integration with the world economy. The *Macroeconomic Stability Programme* part of the New Economic Policy (NEP) reforms included fiscal adjustment, exchange rate correction, monetary objectives, and inflation control programmes. The NEP reforms (1991) also included the *Structural Modification Programme*, which was backed up by modifications such as FDI, banking and financial sector reforms, trade liberalisation and industrial deregulations.

In order to re-establish global credibility and provide a foundation for further liberalisation of FDI regulations in the future, the New Industrial Policy 1991 called forth (a) up to 51% of foreign equity approval in 34 high-priority industries demanding huge investments and sophisticated technologies (i.e., if the foreign equity insured the forex requirement involved in capital goods imports), (b) payment of dividends of the foreign firms to be monitored through the RBI, (c) *Foreign Technology Agreements* were granted automatic permission, and enterprises were allowed to negotiate technology transfer arrangements based on their own financial judgement while recruiting foreign technicians, and lastly, (d) foreign ownership of equity up to 51 percent was permissible for trading enterprises, chiefly embroiled in export activities, in order to gain access to global markets for foreign products. "The newly created Foreign Investment Promotion Board (FIPB) in 1992 ensured the speedy approval of FDI proposals outside the ambit of the automatic route." (RBI, Vol IV, p.508)

The consequence of this move was that both FDI and FPI increased throughout the decade from 1991-1992 to 1999-2000 from US$ 129 million to US$ 2,155 million and US$ 4 million to US$ 3,026 million respectively, as shown in Table 1.6. FDI, valued at US$ 316 million in 1992-1993, rose in following five years, with an average inflow of US$ 3,557 million. In the Table 1.6, numbers on the acquisition of shares of Indian enterprises by non-residents have been included as part of FDI, since 1995-1996, under the purview FEMA (1999), which was formed for the control and monitoring of foreign exchange. FDI, on the other hand, was a positive development in the years 1995-1996 and 1996-1997, also it virtually matched net FPI inflows for the first time since 1992-1993, and turned up as a vital component of the capital account. This also recognised India as one of the initial beneficiaries of the FPIs' equities market.

**Table 1.6: FDI and FPI in India (1991-2000) in Rs. Crore and in US$ in Million.**

| Year | Direct Investment | | Portfolio Investment | | Total (A+B) | |
|---|---|---|---|---|---|---|
| | In Rs Crore | In US$ Million | In Rs. Crore | In US$ Million | In Rs Crore | In US$ Million |
| 1990-1991 | 174 | 97 | 11 | 6 | 185 | 103 |
| 1991-1992 | 316 | 129 | 10 | 4 | 326 | 133 |
| 1992-1993 | 965 | 315 | 748 | 244 | 1713 | 559 |
| 1993-1994 | 1,838 | 586 | 1,188 | 3,567 | 13026 | 4,153 |
| 1994-1995 | 4,126 | 1,314 | 12,007 | 3,824 | 16133 | 5,138 |
| 1995-1996 | 7,172 | 2,144 | 9,192 | 2,748 | 16,364 | 4,892 |
| 1996-1997 | 10,015 | 2,821 | 11,758 | 3,312 | 21,773 | 6,133 |
| 1997-1998 | 13,220 | 3,557 | 6,794 | 1,828 | 20,014 | 5,385 |
| 1998-1999 | 10,358 | 2,462 | -257 | -61 | 10,101 | 2,401 |
| 1999-2000 | 9,338 | 2,155 | 13,112 | 3,026 | 22,450 | 5,181 |

*Source: Compiled from data of RBI Bulletin 2001, Handbook of Statistics on Indian Economy, 2001-2002, 2008-09 and 2011-12 and India's Balance of Payments Concepts, Compilation and Recent Scenario (1950-51 to 2003-04) EPW Research Foundation, Feb, 2005.*

The influx of foreign based equity was supposed to help develop the domestic capital market by drawing in finest practises from around the world and encouraging competition. "Over the decade, India not only permitted foreign investment in almost all sectors of the economy (barring agriculture, and, until recently, real estate), but also allowed foreign portfolio investment, thus practically divorcing foreign investment from the erstwhile technology acquisition effort." (Nagraj, 2003, p. 1701) The foreign equity investors were also able to appraise and spread the potential prospects which brought good news with respect to the disposal of FDI in India. However, the Asian financial crisis (1997) inflicted certain setbacks to the global financial order of newly industrialised countries. But India was relatively safe from the shocks that were felt across the world, especially in Asia.

**Table 1.7: FDI inflows in India, Asia, Developing Economies and Developed Economies from 1990-2000 in US $ million.**

| Year | India | Asia | Developing Economies | Developed Economies |
|---|---|---|---|---|
| 1990-1991 | 236.69 (0.07) | 24,916.36 (0.45) | 34,648.57 (0.87) | 170,176.6 (0.94) |
| 1991-1992 | 75 (0.03) | 25,688.8 (0,42) | 39,309.87 (0.93) | 114,464.3 (0.60) |
| 1992-1993 | 252 (0.09) | 36,538.66 (0.54) | 53,456.64 (1.16) | 107,860.7 (0.53) |
| 1993-1994 | 532 (0.19) | 58,351.31 (0.77) | 75,689.48 (1.50) | 141,378.6 (0.69) |
| 1994-1995 | 974 (0.30) | 70,732.16 (0.87) | 102,386 (1.90) | 150,590 (0.68) |
| 1995-1996 | 2,151 (0.58) | 84,781.62 (0.92) | 117,763.2 (1.94) | 219,760.9 (0.90) |
| 1996-1997 | 2,525 (0.64) | 101,184.3 (1.13) | 147,139 (2.22) | 236,348.9 (0.96) |
| 1997-1998 | 3,619 (0.85) | 116,545.4 (1.34) | 185,391.8 (2.66) | 285,576.6 (1.19) |
| 1998-1999 | 2,633 (0.61) | 101,736.7 (1.29) | 174,995.2 (2.67) | 508,699 (2.08) |
| 1999-2000 | 2,168 (0.47) | 134,776.1 (1.54) | 216,251.4 (3.25) | 852,848 (3.33) |
| 2000-2001 | 3,587.99 (0.75) | 159,186.3 (1.68) | 231,588.8 (3.19) | 1,119,102 (4.32) |

*Source: Compiled from UNCTADSTAT database*

*Figure 1.1: FDI Inflows at Current Prices in US$ Million for the years 1990-2000 in India, Asia, Developing Economies and Developed Economies.*

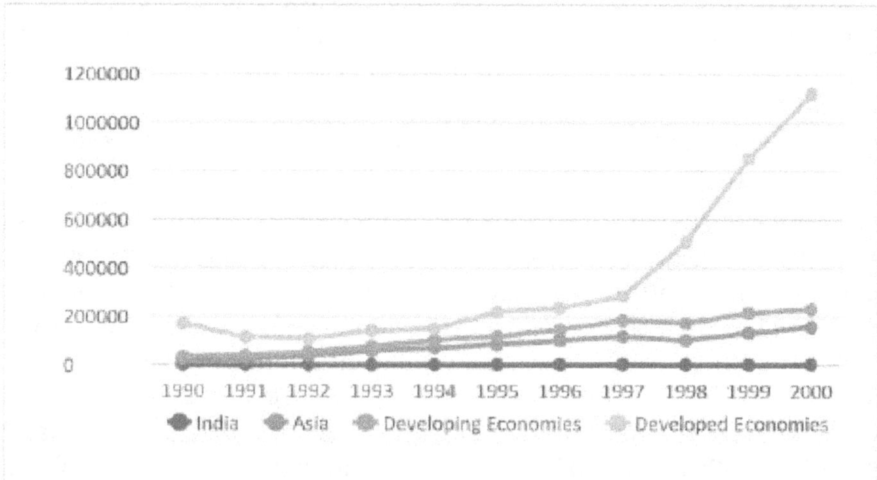


*Source: Table 1.7.*

The Table 1.7 on FDI inflows to India is given from 1990-2000 on the basis on UNCTADSTAT database. Along with it, the data on FDI inflows in Asia, developing nations and developed nations for the year 1990-2000 is also presented. Looking into the FDI inflows to India after implementing liberalisation policies, in the Table 1.7, it is seen that the FDI inflow has increased almost to a tenfold level from US$ 236.69 million in 1991-1992 to US$ 2,168 million in 1999-2000. FDI flows increased as a result of improved infrastructure, a more vibrant banking sector, and strong economic fundamentals. However, Asia's inward FDI during this period ended at 1.54% of its GDP.

Moreover, developing nation's inward FDI increased continuously from US$ 39,309.87 in 1991-1992 to US$ 2,16,251.4 in 1999-2000 welcoming the FDI inflows at 3.19% to their GDP. The share has dropped since then, but at a variable rate. The rising trend in India, Asia, developing nations and developed nations FDI inflows, in the post-liberalisation period in Table 1.7 is visually represented in Figure 1.1. The massive rise in the FDIs is witnessed only in the developed economies, since 1997-1998 onwards. Earlier than that Asian Financial Crises made through the western world and the developed nations especially in 1994-1995. "Monetary tightening and rising interest rates in the US, beginning in February 1994, the Mexican crisis in December 1994 and bullish stock OECD countries, particularly the US, had the effect of lowering the flows to emerging markets." (RBI, Vol IV, p. 508)

It is also to be noticed that Asia forms an essential proportion of the overall FDI inflows in the developing nations. Regardless, the developing nations were able to grab more of FDI inflows than Asia, proving other nations in South America, Africa and former Soviet bloc., were able to dust off the effects of the Asian financial crises. According to Nagraj (2003), the role of European countries as key sources inflows of FDI to India had also steadily continued to fall over the liberalisation period, while the western superpower, the United States, has emerged as perhaps the most significant cause of FDI influx in India.

Furthermore, Nagraj (2003) reflected on the fact that many of the operations of branches of foreign firms were not documented in RBI's survey of financial performance, despite the fact that various estimates regarded approved FDI were a valuable data source. However, external sector policies, according to Virmani (2003), were among the most significant reforms implemented in India throughout the 1990s that hampered opening up the economy, strengthened the external account, therefore, making it less vulnerable to shocks. Therefore, the decade of 1990s, resulted in simplified FDI procedures and greater flexibility in case of the external environment.

## The Recent Period of Confluence of the Global Environment in India (2000-2020).

The spirit of market-driven competition was matched by the dynamic confluence of the global environment, from the outset of 2000s. Nonetheless, the major structural changes of the 1990s, became the reason that average growth rate in Indian economy paced from 2000 to 2010 at 8.8%. Whereas, the global slowdown owing to the financial crisis (2009) placed India's economic growth averaging at 7.1% between 2010 and 2019. In order to understand how the changes in the FDI took place in the last two decades in India (2000-2001 to 2010-2019), it is to be taken into account that up to 1999-2000 the official RBI data on inward and outward FDI included equity capital of unincorporated firms (mainly international banks in India and Indian banks operating abroad) as well as equity capital of incorporated organisations. The data from the year 2000-01 onwards is not comparable to the earlier data. "In India, FDI inflow was recorded under five heads of (i) RBI's *automatic approval* route for equity holding up to 51 percent, (ii) FIPB's or SIA's *discretionary approval* route for larger projects with the equity holding greater than 51 percent, (iii) *acquisition of shares* route since 1996 (relating to the acquisition of shares of Indian companies by non-residents under Section 29 of FERA), (iv) RBI's *NRI schemes*, and (v) external commercial borrowings (ADRs/ GDRs and euro equities)." (Mishra and Puri, 2014, p. 531) Since 2000-01, the coverage of FDI data, in order to match with the international best practices has been expanded to include, 'other direct capital' (inter-corporate debt transactions) and 'reinvested earnings' (including retained earnings) besides equity capital (i.e., SIA/ FIPB route, automatic route, NRI route). Also, the definition of FDI was brought in line with IMF's definition that included external subordinated debt, reinvested earnings and commercial borrowings. Mishra and Puri (2014) argued that as a result of this revision, FDI in 2000-01, according to the earlier definition at US$ 2,339 million but was later estimated to be US$ 4,029 million.

The year of 2000 also signalled at the government's commitment to install confidence in the investors with announcement for setting up *Special Economic Zones* for upsurging investment of the foreign sources. Along with it, Sahoo (2006) emphasized the importance of the Foreign Investment Implementation Authority (FIIA) in 2000 that provided after-service care to international investors by easing the process of acquiring the necessary compliance. The Competition Act (2002) replaced MRTP Act (1969) and was deemed applicable equally to both the domestic and foreign companies governing M&A and cartels.

**Table 1. 8: FDI Inflows at Current Prices in US$ Million for the years 2000-2019 in India, Asia, Developing Economies and Developed Economies.**

| Year | India | Asia | Developing economies | Developed economies |
|---|---|---|---|---|
| 2000 | 3,588<br>(0.26) | 159,186<br>(11.73) | 231,589<br>(17.07) | 1,119,102<br>(82.5) |
| 2001 | 5,478<br>(0.70) | 134,518<br>(17.40) | 215,994<br>(27.95) | 548,464<br>(70.98) |
| 2002 | 5,630<br>(0.95) | 110,412<br>(18.72) | 166,239<br>(28.18) | 413,630<br>(70.12) |
| 2003 | 4,321<br>(0.78) | 146,577<br>(26.62) | 194,852<br>(35.39) | 337,931<br>(61.37) |
| 2004 | 5,778<br>(0.83) | 195,925<br>(28.29) | 261,897<br>(37.82) | 401,644<br>(58.00) |
| 2005 | 7,622<br>(0.80) | 237,232<br>(25.03) | 331,298<br>(34.96) | 585,747<br>(61.80) |
| 2006 | 20,328<br>(1.45) | 310,022<br>(22.08) | 403,666<br>(28.76) | 941,067<br>(67.04) |
| 2007 | 25,350<br>(1.34) | 395,479<br>(20.91) | 522,392<br>(27.61) | 1,282,083<br>(67.77) |

| Year | India | Asia | Developing economies | Developed economies |
|---|---|---|---|---|
| 2008 | 47,102<br>(3.16) | 433,210<br>(29.07) | 578,020<br>(38.79) | 794,313<br>(53.30) |
| 2009 | 35,635<br>(2.88) | 352,841<br>(28.54) | 460,252<br>(37.23) | 714,028<br>(57.76) |
| 2010 | 27,417<br>(1.96) | 437,900<br>(31.36) | 622,011<br>(44.55) | 710,394<br>(50.88) |
| 2011 | 36,190<br>(2.24) | 446,899<br>(27.67) | 664,817<br>(41.16) | 870,823<br>(53.92) |
| 2012 | 24,196<br>(1.61) | 438,263<br>(29.34) | 666,167<br>(44.59) | 762,695<br>(51.06) |
| 2013 | 28,199<br>(1.94) | 448,632<br>(30.81) | 655,954<br>(45.04) | 716,491<br>(49.20) |
| 2014 | 34,582<br>(2.46) | 498,863<br>(35.53) | 677,340<br>(48.25) | 703,520<br>(47.69) |
| 2015 | 44,064<br>(2.16) | 544,435<br>(26.66) | 729,889<br>(35.75) | 1,274,405<br>(62.42) |
| 2016 | 44,481<br>(2.24) | 519,575<br>(26.20) | 651,979<br>(32.87) | 1,265,245<br>(63.79) |
| 2017 | 39,904<br>(2.35) | 545,310<br>(32.06) | 700,636<br>(41.20) | 950,150<br>(55.88) |
| 2018 | 42,156<br>(2.82) | 536,960<br>(36.04) | 702,196<br>(46.77) | 734,535<br>(50.92) |
| 2019 | 50,558<br>(3.28) | 560,152<br>(36.60) | 734,389<br>(47.99) | 795,837<br>(52.00) |
| 2020 | 64,062<br>(6.41) | 578,126<br>(57.87) | 670,352<br>(67.10) | 328,540<br>(32.89) |

*Source: Compiled from UNCTADSTAT database from 2000-2019.*

*Figure 1.2: FDI Inflows at Current Prices in US$ Million for the years 2000-2019 in India, Asia, Developing Economies and Developed Economies.*

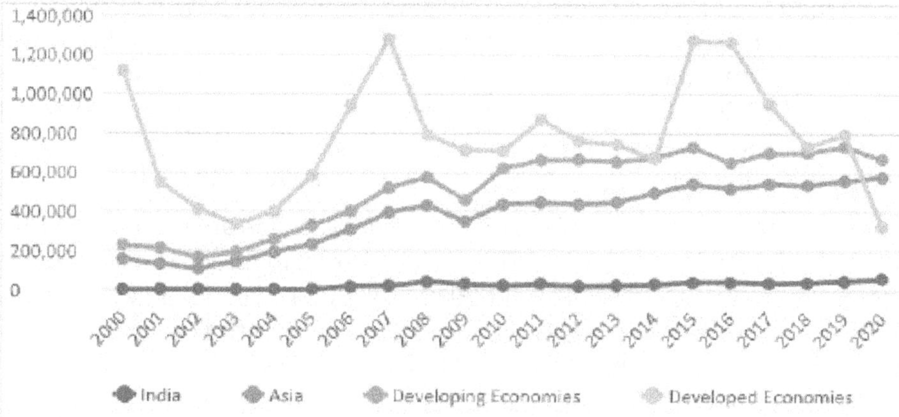


*Source: Based on Table 1.9*

With all the above-mentioned changes in the domestic trajectory and at the global front, FDI inflows at US$ million (at current prices) in India in comparison to that of Asia, developing economies and developed economies are presented in Table 1.8. It also puts forward FDI as percentage share of the world (the brackets) in Asia, developing economies and developed economies for the period of 2000-2020. After implementing the policies relating to foreign investments throughout the entire decade of 1991 to 2000, FDI inflows in India turned out to be US$ 3,588 million only which was equivalent of 0.26% share of the world. With each passing year in the decade 2000s, the first five years (2000-2005) in India saw a rather slower trend in the FDI flows on the account of dot-com collapse and global recession of 2001.

In Table 1.8, a decline in FDI inflows in 2003 at US$ 4,321 million from a slow moving US$ 5,630 million in 2004 was seen. From US$ 5,630 million in 2004, FDI flows increased to US$ 7,622 million in 2005. A slight rise in FDI percentage share in the world from 0.80% in 2004 to 0.83% in 2005 was also registered. In the developed nations, the impact of market speculations and recession of 2001 was pronounced in 2004. Although the situation in the developing nations, especially in Asia showed resistance to downfalls of the developed economies, from 2000 to 2005. Overall, the FDI flows as percentage share, rose for Asian countries from 11.73% in 2000 to 28.29% in 2005 and for developing economies, it moved from 17.07% in 2000 to 37.82% in 2005. Afterwards, global boom incurred and contributed to the exponential rise of the FDI inflows.

The magnitude of rise in FDI inflows was, though greater in the developed nation, hovering about 60% share of the world till 2008. In 2008, this trend in

FDI growth was severely hit by the American debt crises which affected Indian markets in 2009. Nonetheless, India was relatively secured on the account of the managed floating exchange rate and average annual growth rate of GDP at 8.9% from 2008-2010. An early insinuation of worries was reflected in the fact that though, the absolute FDI inflows in US$ million were increasing in the years 2006-2009, the FDI inflows as a percentage share of world was moving back and forth with a noticeable decline. Such, global uncertainty caused a reduction in the FDI inflows for India from 2.88% in 2008 to 1.96% in 2009.

Even, in the first half of 2010-2015, the *Great Recession* affected the FDI flows with a sigh of relief in second half. This is clearly seen in foreign inflows to India, declining from US$ 27,417 million in 2010 to US$ 24,196 million in 2012, even though increasing to US$ 44,064 million in 2015 again. With Make in India (2014) initiative, an increase to US$ 44,481 million in 2016 from US$ 44,064 million in 2015 was seen in India. The developing economies, especially Asia witnessed a great deal of fluctuations from 2015 to 2020, mainly due to the adoption of the protectionist policies by the developed nations.

Nonetheless, the developing nations also witnessed increase in FDI flows in 2020. The overall FDI inflows in the developed nations actually declined from US$ 12,82,083 million to US$ million 328,540 in 2020 but FDI as a percentage share to world turned out to be mimicking adverse effects of the protectionist attitude. The Figure 1.2, based on Table 1.8, shows the data for the FDI inflows in US$ million at current prices. A pronounced fall in the FDI inflows in the developed nations in 2020 can be seen. In 2020, 67.10% of world share of FDI stood with the developing nations. Of the developing economies, Asian countries were able to grab a 57.87% share of world's FDI inflows.

The WIR (2021) has stated that a decrease in Global FDI flows by up to 35% in 2020 brought FDI below US$ 1 trillion for the first time since 2005, as a result of COVID-19. Nonetheless, Asia was the only region that witnessed an increase of 5% of the FDI flows. Amidst the global disorder, India also faced some struggles within the domestic economy such as implementation of GST and demonetization. The share of world FDI inflows in India grew from 3.28% in 2019 to 6.21% in 2020. After three decades of liberalisation, FDI has become an important source of foreign presence in the Indian economy.

## Importance of FDI in India

FDI inflows offer significant benefits to the economic activities in India. That is why at the beginning of the current millennium, Athreye and Kapur (2001) emphasized that the concept of growth-led FDI is more likely to be persistent rather than FDI-led growth. The access to new consumption and production markets were established by MNCs and business operations of the local firms were also expanded. The new market of the host economy offers opportunities to the foreign investors ranging from the availability of fresh resources to economies of scale. According to OECD (2002), the home countries acknowledged that multinational corporations can supplement the development efforts with help of the following: -

a. Expansion of development-related financial resources,
b. Aiding jobs market and broadening the skill base,
c. Fostering competitiveness in the global market,
d. Augmenting technological capacities (generation, transfer and diffusion), and
e. Promoting social and environmental responsibility.

To comprehend the importance of FDI in the Indian context, Mishra and Puri (2013, p.525.) have made some specific mentions. Therefore, in the broader area of evaluation of the foreign presence and foreign investment, in terms of FDI, is considered critical for overall economic development not only because of the limited resources present in the home countries but also due to the benefits accruing to the labour, management, technology transfers, reduced cost of production, cheaper source of raw materials and tax advantages that to the host countries undertaking FDI. Hence, FDI is considered important in India due to the reasons mentioned as follows: -

1. **Accommodating for a Low Level of Saving.** With low savings rate in India, resource gap emerges in the savings and investment. Whereas, investment require mobilisation of savings in the productive resources. Savings in India mostly takes the form of hoarding which contributes not only to the loss of opportunities in creation of the productive capital but also to the inequality of wealth. In addition, there is a limit on saving due to general poverty of the masses in India. As a result, there is an operational discrepancy between savings and investment. The foreign capital in FDI form takes care of such discrepancies.
2. **The Gap in Technological Catch-up.** Developed nations possess a high level of technological effects as compared to developing countries, in both relative and absolute terms. This calls for technology imports in both embodied and disembodies form. However, it possesses a strong urge for modernisation of its economy with the efforts made in the digitalisation and automation. Such technology that can compete with foreign countries is frequently accompanied by a foreign presence in the form of foreign direct investment or foreign partnership.

3. **Acquisition and Extraction of Natural Resources.** India has always been wealthy being the possessor of the natural resources that awaits correct usage but exploitation. While most of the time multinationals have been found guilty of overutilization of resources, awareness towards environmental concerns and global warming have urged the MNCs to comply with the new norms. It has to be kept in mind that India does not have the necessary skills and technical expertise to perform such operations. Hence, India has to understand the interdependence on the international economies to take up the challenge of optimum usage of its natural resources.
4. **Shortage of Foreign Exchange.** In today's globalised world, a large amount of foreign exchange is necessary to pay for the import bills, especially, in the case of crude oil and raw materials to meet demands of the consumers for variety of goods and service that would further lead to economic development. Since India's balance of payments has been chronically unfavourable, the revenue generated by the exports is not sufficient to meet foreign exchange requirements. India needs foreign investments for this purpose. With foreign investments, foreign exchange would allow smooth payments to the imports of much-needed goods.
5. **Requirements of Economic Infrastructure.** Due to poor infrastructure many foreign companies refrain to invest in new projects in India. With its inadequate capital, building up the economic infrastructure on its own is a difficult job. Thus, India requires the assistance of foreign direct investment that leads to certain benefits such as construction of roads, transportation facilities, generation and distribution of electricity, development of irrigation facilities and creation of market places etc., in the area it operates. The foreign companies operating in the backward areas are also granted special tax benefits and concessions.
6. **Generation of Employment Opportunities.** India comprises of the youngest workforce waiting to be employed. It is also expected to experience the demographic dividend. In the light of the above, without the generation of specific skillsets and persistence of cut throat competition, India would not be able to generate the employment opportunities to subsume the entire population. With the direct foreign investment, the avenues for the working population would increase and the growing insecurity towards limited employment opportunities will be reduced.

Nagraj (2003) advocated channelling of foreign investment inflow in the desired directions that results in maximising long-term returns to the economy. By facilitating the entry of foreign organisations into the domestic marketplace,

FDI in India has helped to create a global manufacturing centre and an R&D hub by providing a competitive environment that is pronounced in various industries. The automobile industry is the prime example of the same. "The automotive industry has been regarded as a classic example of a producer-driven commodity chain". Gereffi (1994, p. 176). The automobile industry consists of job-creating skilled and semi-skilled labour in vehicle manufacturing and the components manufacturing (ancillary industry).

The FDI in the automobile industry has also pushed domestic firms in India to continuously enhance their processes, product offerings while fostering innovation (For instance, Ashok Leyland, Tata Motors and Mahindra & Mahindra etc.). The importance of FDI in the automobile sector is prominent due to the large scale of operations, capital-intensive nature, and technology-driven product cycles. Such joint ventures, mergers and acquisitions of the major automobile companies have also contributed to the capital formation of the manufacturing industry. Therefore, FDI in the automobile industry provides for an eminent research topic for current landscape of academic literature.

## Work Outline of the Study

### Type of Research

This study consists of exploratory and empirical objectives to reflect on effects of FDI using panel data. The research topic has focused on the FDI in India and the contribution of the variables pertaining to the important determinants in the selected firms in presence of foreign establishments, reflecting on linkages in the overall Indian automobile industry, in the recent time period of 2011-2020.

### Statement of the Research Problem

Broadly, problem statement is "To study the trends and patterns of FDI, ascertaining the strength of sector-wise linkages, and investigating for the performance and productivity levels with respect to various sources at the firm-level as a result of foreign presence in the Indian automobile industry.'

### Objectives of the Study

The problem statement has contributed in forming the following objectives: -

*Objective 1. To study the trends and patterns of FDI in India during the selected period from 2000 to 2020.*

*Objective 2. To study the industry-wise backward linkages and forward linkages in the automobile industry in India from 2010 to 2020.*

*Objective 3. To examine the performance linkages of the selected firms in the presence of foreign-invested firms in the automobile industry from 2011 to 2020.*

*Objective 4. To examine the productivity linkages of the selected firms in the presence of foreign-invested firms in the automobile industry from 2011 to 2020.*

## Time Period of the Study

This study probes the research question for the recent time period of 2011-2020. The research period is pivotal in a variety of ways. The year 2011 marked a year of revising the statistical standards with the upgraded industrial classification standards namely, National Industrial classification (2008). Along with this, the data National Accounts Statistics, Office of Economic Advisory and the Annual Survey of Industries has also been updated with respect to the base year 2011-12.

## Data Type of the Study

This study has tried to fulfil the objectives by employing the secondary data in automobile industry at the industrial-level and firm-level.

## Data Source of the Study

The source of the secondary data has been extracted from various issues of the DIPP's Quarterly Factsheet on FDI, SIAM's Annual Reports, UNCTADSTAT, EPWRF, RBI's KLEMS Database, Office of Economic Advisor, National Accounts Statistics, Annual Survey of Industries and CMIE's Prowess IQ.

## Research Technique

In order to meet the study's first objective, the technique of cumulative percentage change and the compound annual growth rate have been employed. The second objective is based on the theme of the linkages (forward & backward) calculated from the input-output analysis. The review of literature has contributed towards the selection of the determinants based on the recent studies in the Indian context.

In order to identify the intra-industry repercussions of FDI in terms of foreign presence, the Horizontal FDI variable has also been constructed in the study. It is based on the output share of foreign firms to the ratio of total output in overall automobile industry. With third objective, the findings were made on the automobile industry's firm-level output estimates, calculated with the following equation: -

Due to the presence of the time-invariant variables, the fixed effect regression-based method has been finalised by the Hausman test. The fourth objective is based two-part approach. In the first part the total factor productivity estimates have been obtained using the Levinsohn and Petrin (2003) model that assumes proxy variable of energy (E), free input variables of labour (L) and raw material (M) and an endogenous input variable of capital (K) in production function with Cobb-Douglas specifications where output is explained through the mentioned variables expressed in the following function: -

that makes use of the following equation: -

In the equation (ii) , , , , mark the logarithm value for the output variable and input variable of capital, labour, material (raw) and energy. The error term of the estimation is . This is the result of , where connotes at time *t,* the mean level of productivity across firms, represents the productivity difference with firm-specific notions of the predictors (independent variables) and depicts the measurement error uncorrelated to the input variables. In second step, this study formulates and estimates the panel data regression with a variety of explanatory variables on the productivity of firms as the dependent variable presented as following equation: -

In the subsequent analysis, the Hausman test designates the technique of fixed effects or the random effects to estimate results of panel data for 139 domestic firms in the automobile industry.

## Organisation of the Thesis

The thesis is presented as a study of six chapters as follows: -

Chapter 1. *INTRODUCTION* familiarises with the subject matter of the study by presenting a conceptual overview of the FDI consisting of the definition, types, modes, theories and linkages and spillover effect of FDI. It also contributes to analysing the policy matters adopted from time to time, from independence to the recent period and also reflected on the importance of FDI in India.

Chapter 2. *EVOLUTION OF THE AUTOMOBILE INDUSTRY stresses* its structure, followed by its evolution from the independence to the current decade inciting various policies and events inducing segment-wise aspects of growth in the numbers of the automobile units covered in the scenario of the Indian automobile sector.

Chapter 3. *REVIEW OF THE LITERATURE explores* research gaps by thoroughly surveying updated literature in the foreign as well as the Indian context of FDI linkages and spillover effects. This chapter ends with the preferred approach based on a literature survey.

Chapter 4. *RESEARCH METHODOLOGY explains* the construction of the extracted drivers and variables from the surveyed literature and presents the needed tools and techniques including measures formulas and models in the research framework while describing their purpose with respect to the objectives of the study.

Chapter 5. *DATA ANALYSIS AND INTERPRETATION utilises* formulas and models while finding the numerical measures and estimates of the relationships among variables with relevant data and while presenting point-to-point analysis, examines the proposed explanation for the relationship in line with the objectives of the study.

Chapter 6. *FINDINGS DISCUSSION AND CONCLUSION summarizes* the results and the conclusion of the study while discussing the contribution of this study to the academic and the industry in India. Lastly, it presents the limitations and further scope of this study.

# Chapter 2
Evolution of The Automobile Industry

## Overview of Structure of the Indian Automobile Sector

In the simplest words, an automobile is a vehicle with an internal combustion engine that is used to carry people and goods over land. An automobile can also be defined as a self-moving vehicle, such as a car, jeep, bus, truck, scooter, and so on. The essential locomotive (vehicle and component) manufacturing stood as a key benefactor to range of economic sectors. The operations of the automobile sector have a strong manifold impact on the developmental prospects in any economy, according to the National Auto Policy (Draft Version 2. 2018). In addition, the automobile industry's scale, skill, experience, and innovation have the potential to aid other industries.

*Figure 2.1: Structure of Indian Automobile Industry.*

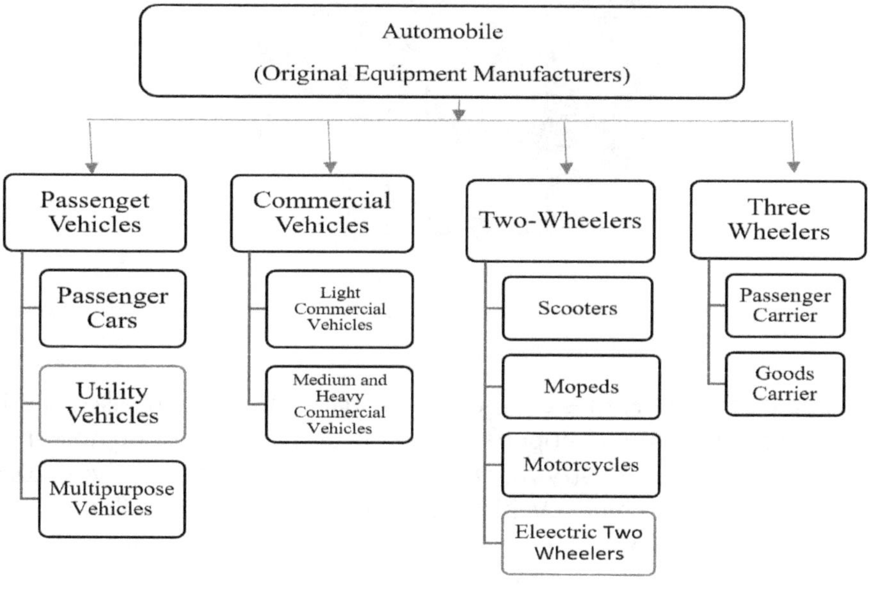


*Source : SIAM*

G. & Vashisht (2013) identified two separate group of actors, in the Indian automobile industry. The first are the producers, who produce components, parts, bodies, and chassis, among other things, and the second are builders of automobile, identified as Original Equipment Manufacturers (OEMs), who assemble all of these components. The automobile sector concerning OEMs is compartmentalized into four different segments which as shown in Figure 2.1 comprising of (i) passenger vehicles including utility vehicles, cars, and multipurpose vehicles, (ii) commercial vehicles that include (a) light commercial vehicles and (b) medium and heavy commercial vehicles, (iii) two-wheeler comprising of scooters, mopeds and motorcycles and electric two-wheelers, and (iv) three-wheeler including passenger carriers & goods carrier. SIAM's *Industry Composition* (2020) data on the domestic market share of each of the individual segments of the automobile sector. Accordingly, the passenger vehicle held 13% of the total market share for 2019-20 and commercial vehicles and the three-wheelers were at tie at an equal domestic market share of 3% each.

*Figure 2.2: Domestic Market Share as per the Composition of Indian Automobile Industry for the year 2019-20. (In Percentage)*

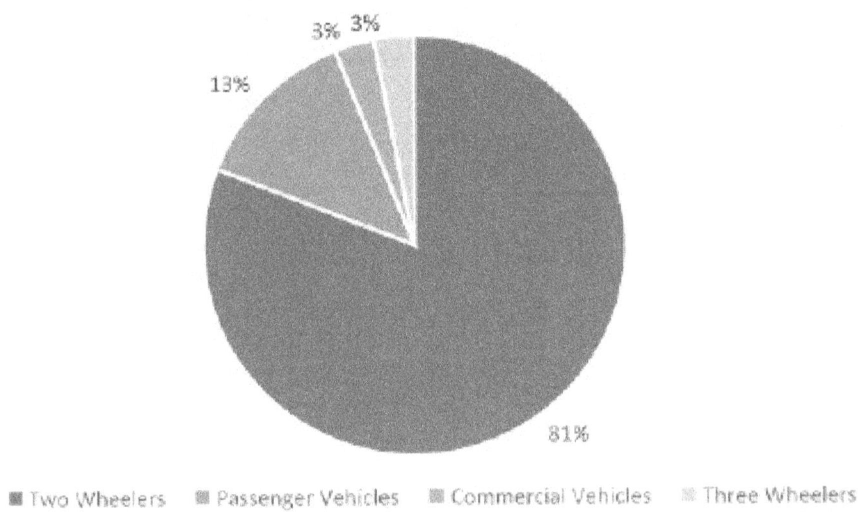


*Source: SIAM*

As depicted in the Figure 2.2, the market share data by SIAM also stated that the two-wheeler segment happened to be the dominant position holder of the domestic automobile industry with 81% of the market share in the year 2020. As per ETAuto (2020), commercial vehicles and passenger vehicles building has been doubled, also the two-wheelers making has virtually tripled in India, reflecting the new achievements of the existing manufacturers. The composition of the automobile also establishes a deeper insight on the fundamental structure of the automobile industry.

The data on the market share of OEMs in the passenger segment, for the month of June 2020, is shown in the Figure 2.1. Figure 2.3, 2.4, 2.5 and 2.6 are based on automobile dealers' body FADA that reports monthly data based on the units of vehicles' registration from Ministry of Road Transport and Highways of India's *Vahan* database. Its counterpart, SIAM maintains the database of the number of vehicles dispatched from factories to dealers. In Banerji (2019), SIAM claimed that *Vahan* data is unauthentic due to its wide fluctuations resulting from daily upgradation. Albeit, this doubt occurred only in sales data for the month of Oct 2019. Nonetheless, data from SIAM and FADA have the tendencies to even out during a period of time. For this reason, the FADA database for understanding only the market holding of various firms has been considered.

## Passenger Vehicles (PVs)

The Multipurpose Vehicles (MUVs), Utility Vehicles (UVs), along with cars comprise the *passenger vehicle segment*. Therefore, this segment primarily caters to the domestic, as well as, foreign demand of the end consumer. According to Figure 2.3, the market share of top five passenger vehicle makers in India that are the leading players in the production of Cars and MUVs segment and UVs have been compared for Jan 2019 to that of Jan 2020, capturing their year on the year growth rate. It can be observed that only two out of top five carmakers increased their market share in Jan 2020.

*Figure 2.3: Market Share of Top Five Passenger Vehicles in Jan,19 to Jan,20. (In Percentage)*

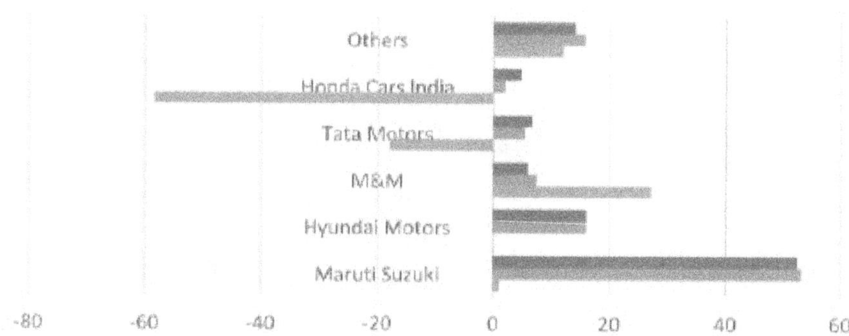


*Source: FADA Journal (January,2020), Vol 19, Issue no.10, p.54.Retrieved from http.www.fada.in.*

Among the top five, two companies posted lower growth sequentially. First, the Tata Motors was at -17.91% from Jan 2019 to Jan 2020. Second, Honda Cars

India in particular, declined to little less than half from 4.8% in Jan 2019 to 2% in Jan 2020 at growth rate of -58.33%. Hyundai Motors, which began as a leading exporter of small cars from the country, experienced zero-digit growth with the same level of market share at 16% in both Jan 2019 and Jan 2020. However, the double-digit growth rate was noted in Mahindra and Mahindra Ltd. (M&M) from Jan 2019 to Jan 2020 at 27.12%. It is also the leading player in the MUVs segment. Besides the top five, the other OEMs for instance, Toyota, Honda Motors and Ford, etc. that operate in the premium cars segment, grew at the rate of 12.06% in Jan 2020.

## Commercial Vehicles (CVs)

According to the Invest India (2020) report, the overall commercial vehicle segment, which includes Medium and Heavy Commercial Vehicles (M&HCVs) and Light Commercial Vehicles (LCVs), grew 17.55% in Apr-Mar 2019. Whereas, as per the same Invest India (2020) report, India became 5th largest auto-producing country after China, the USA, Japan and Germany. Currently, the Indian automobile industry is named as the world's seventh-largest manufacturer of commercial vehicles. Aside from light commercial vehicles, in the international heavy vehicle market a robust spot is held by India with the heavy truck manufacturing, production of busses and tractor building.

*Figure 2.4: Market Share of Top Five Commercial Vehicles in Jan,19 to Jan,20. (In Percentage)*

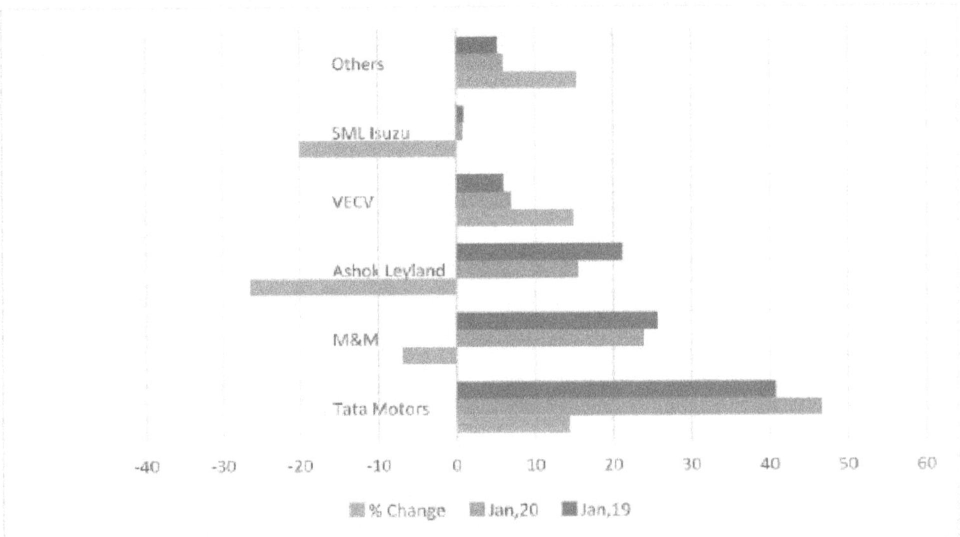


*Source: FADA Journal (Jan 2020), Vol 19, Issue no.10, p.54. Retrieved from http.www.fada.in.*

As per SIAM's Annual Report (2018), the commercial vehicle segment, crossed one million domestic sales marks in FY18-19. According to Mishra (2020), with a growth of 17.6%, the commercial vehicle manufacturers dispatched 10,07,319 units from their factories across India in the FY19 compared to 8,56,916 units in FY18, as per SIAM's database. Furthermore, the top three players namely Tata Motors, M&M and Ashok Leyland, which commanded more than 86% of the market, grew at a dissimilar pace of 14.46%, -6.98% and -26.42% respectively. This led to varied changes in their market share from Jan 2019 to Jan 2020, also shown in Figure 2.4.

There has been a positive increase in the market share of the VEVC Ltd. and other market players from 6% (Jan 2019) to 6.9% (Jan 2020) and 5.2% (Jan 2019) to 6% (Jan 2020) respectively. According to CRISIL Impact Note (2020), the CV makers were already hit by macroeconomic challenges on the producer's side in 2019 from the disrupted supply chain, weakened financial profile of fleet operators and significant price hikes on the account of transition to Bharat Stage-VI emission norms.

## Two-Wheelers

The market share of the top five two-wheelers from Jan 2019 to Jan 2020 is given in Figure 2.5 while incorporating level of change in percentage. Accordingly, Hero MotoCorp and Honda Motorcycles and Scooters India Limited (HMSIL), continued their rule in top two positions with 36.4% and 27.90% of the total market share respectively in Jan 2020. Another holder of a large market share (14.3%) in Jan 2019 was TVS Motor. It declined by -0.15% Jan 2019 to 12.2% in Jan 2020.

Although, Bajaj Auto, third in the rankings has seen a decline in market share from 12.7% in Jan 2019 to 11.8% in Jan 2020. The listed reasons were lower consumer sentiments, rising fuel prices, liquidity crunch, higher interest rates and GST. As seen in Fig 2.5, among the top five OEMs, India Yamaha dipped by 22.86% from 3.5% to 2.7% from Jan 2019 to Jan 2020. The other OEMs of two-wheelers, such as Suzuki Motorcycle India and India Kawasaki Motor and Piaggio Vehicles etc. have reported a growth in their market share from 8.7% to 9.1% in Jan 2020.

*Figure 2.5: Market Share of Top Five Two Wheelers in Jan,19 to Jan,20. (In Percentage)*

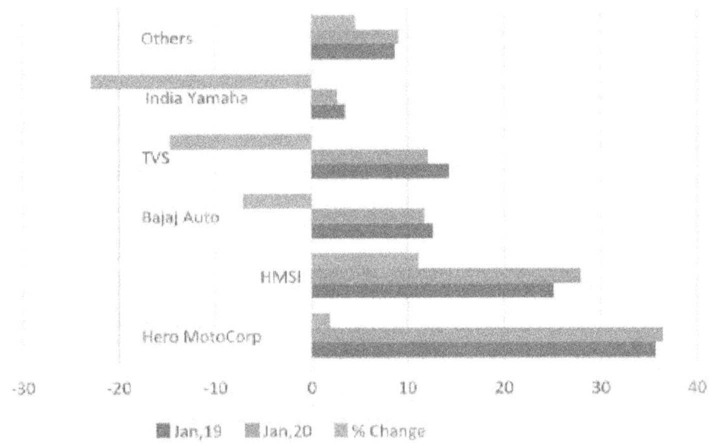


*Source: FADA Journal (Jan 2020), Vol 19, Issue no.10, p.53. Retrieved from http.www.fada.in.*

## Three-Wheelers

In terms of both sales and production, India holds world's principal market meant for three-wheeler vehicles. The top-three players in the market, the leader, Bajaj Auto, Piaggio the second-largest and M&M, the third largest accounted for 87.3% of the total market share in the FY 2019. Bajaj Auto, the market leader in the three-wheeler segment, increased its market share by 10.58%, from 52% in Jan 2019 to 57.5% in Jan 2020. Piaggio, the next leading OEM, saw its market share falling by -23.91% between Jan 2019 and Jan 2020. It should be noted that Bajaj Auto is also the market leader in the passenger vehicle segment, while Piaggio is the market leader in the goods segment. M&M, the third in line, faced a double-digit positive growth rate of 24.07% (in Figure 2.6) in the total market share of top five three-wheelers from Jan 2019 to Jan 2020.

The other big names such as Atul Autos and TVS both faced a decline in the share of the three-wheeler segment -8.20% and -20% from 2019 to 2020 respectively. Atul Auto held a market share of 6.1% in Jan 2019 that declined to 5.6% in Jan 2020 and TVS was the market shareholder with a 1.9% share in Jan 2020. Other OEMs in the three-wheeler segment, such as Scooters Auto, Lohia Auto, JS Auto, and others, saw a -20% decline in market share from Jan 2019 to Jan 2020. The domestic market's growth in India has stalled after a meteoric rise in 2018 and 2019, owing to liquidity constraints, a shifting regulatory environment, a high base and the advent of electric models and in the export market.

*Figure 2.6: Market Share of Top Five Three Wheelers in Jan,19 to Jan,20. (In Percentage)*

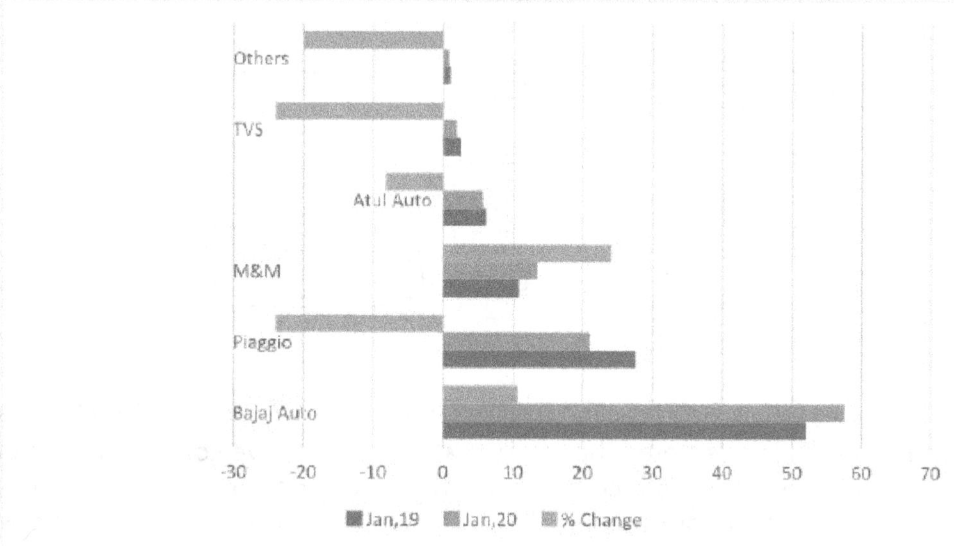


*Source: FADA Journal (Jan,2020), Vol 19, Issue no.10, p.55. Retrieved from http.www.fada.in.*

## Automobile Component Industry

A diverse range of engineering, designing, manufacturing, marketing, and selling of vehicles and auto components etc. constitutes trades and businesses of the automotive establishments. As discussed briefly, the automobile industry is also composed automobile component industry in the production of high-quality precision instruments. India has the preferred designing and manufacturing base for most of the global automobile OEMs. Through Make in India (2014) and its supplementary programmes, export, manufacturing and engineering of vehicles and their components would push India to move to the top three in the world.

According to the Automobile Components Manufacturers Association (ACMA, 2019), auto components are divided into sub-sectors such as drive transmission and steering parts, engine parts, suspension and braking parts, body and chassis, electrical parts, equipment, along with others including such as die castings, fan belts, and metal sheet parts etc. (but exclude tires, batteries, and fuel) shown in Figure 2.7

*Figure 2.7: Decomposition of Automobile Component Industry in India.*

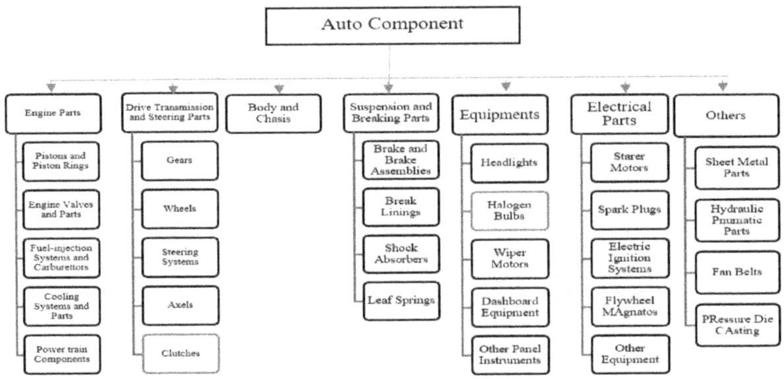


*Source: ACMA (Automotive Component Manufacturers Association of India)*

It should also be noted, however, that the automotive component sector excludes industries dedicated to the maintenance of automobiles, once they are delivered to motor gasoline filling stations and automobile repair shops, these being the consumers of the final product. As per ACMA database, in 2019-2020, on the supply-side of the auto-component, the engine components comprise the major share of 25.90%, suspension system serves 16%, bodies and chassis form 14% and drive transmission and steering consists of 13.30% share of the total auto-component companies. As elaborated in Figure 2.8, electricals and electronics form 12.40% of the total companies. Within the auto-component industry, interior works excluding electronics make 10.50% of the total companies. Finally, rest of the miscellaneous works form 6.30%, of the total companies in the auto-component industry.

On the demand side of the auto-component industry, lies the OEMs of the automobile industry, with the passenger vehicles segment forming a 43% share in the consumption in 2019-20 for the locally produced auto-components companies as well as its imports in India. In Figure 2.9, share of the total consumables of the auto component sector is depicted. It is followed by two-wheelers with 20.50%, LCVs with 14.80% and HCVs with 10.40%, respectively, as share in consumption in 2019-2020.

*Figure 2.8: Top Auto components Manufactured in the India in 2019-20. (In Percentage)*

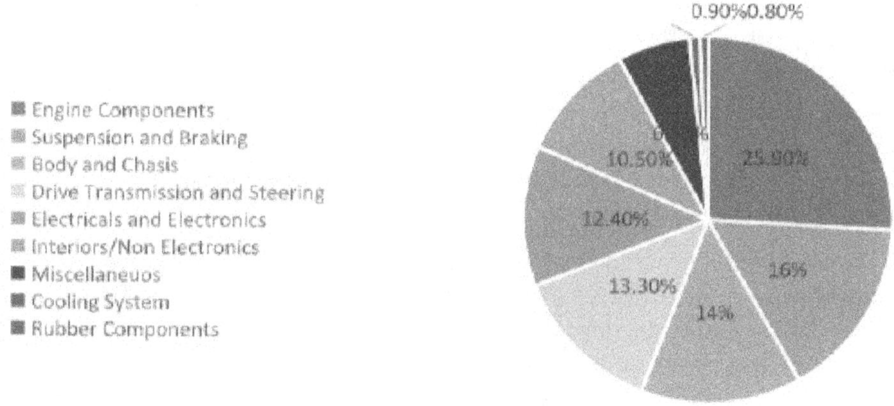


*Source: ACMA*

*Figure 2.9: Top Auto Components Consumables in the India in 2019-20. (In Percentage)*

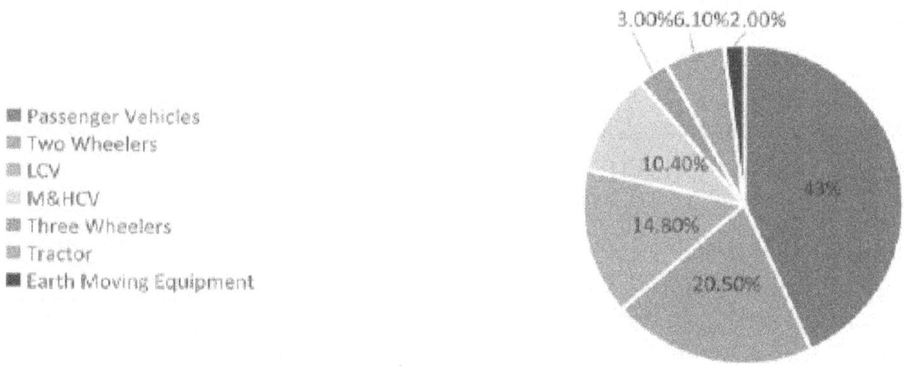


*Source: ACMA*

Additionally, segments of three-wheelers at 6.10%, tractors at 3% and earth moving equipment at 2% share respectively, in 2019-20, also formed a share in the consumption of the auto component industry.

## Evolution of Policy Reforms in the Indian Automobile Industry

The evolution of India's automobile sector has been consistent with the country's industrial policy framework. Porter (1990) emphasised the importance of industrial strategy, arguing that the economic climate, which ultimately changes an industry's comparative advantage, is dependent on its industrial policy. According to Lall (1987), Narayana (1989), and Kathuria (1996), in India, state engagement in the form of policy choices was critical in initiating and continuing the industrialization process. There was a lack of manufacturing facilities and channels in India, primarily being an agrarian society. "During the British regime, India had no auto industry to begin with and all the automobiles were imported from global auto manufacturers such as General Motors and Ford Motors." (G. and Vashisht, 2008, p.76) According to Narayana (1989), the quantity of such imported automobiles by the winding up of World War I, was around 4000 units per annum.

The eminent statesmen as well as businessmen at the time suggested the establishment of automobile industry native to India. "In the 1940s, Hindustan Motors and Premier Motors were established by Indian entrepreneurs, by importing know-how from General Motors and Fiat respectively." (G. and Vashisht, 2008, p.76) The prime focus of these companies was the manufacturing of passenger vehicle. According to Ranawat and Tiwari (2009), both companies were initiated with foreign technical assistance and practise of progressive building of Complete Knocked Down (CKD) vehicles, but owing to sluggish development, the actual making of vehicles in these companies began afterwards the freedom from the British. Therefore, a brief account of the study of evolution of the industry in question is as follows: -

## Phase of Protection, Indigenisation and Regulation of the Domestic Market: (1947 to 1965)

During 1947 to 1965, the Indian auto industry was severely restricted to foreign competition due to licencing requirements and protective tariff rates. The alliances with the foreign establishments were permitted afterwards a due deliberation only, in addition they were put through operational restriction by corporations in India. In the wake of independence, Indian government took a very strategic framework for boosting the automobile industry, making changes in the policy framework for enriching the substantial gap in the capital requirement, which had an extensive weight on domestic and foreign direct investment to shape them. The Industrial Policy Resolution (1PR, 1948) divided industries of the nation into different categories (see sub-section 1.2.1) in accordance with their critical role in enhancing the national income. The manufacturing units under automobile industry were also prone to government regulatory system because it was categorised as the basic industry by the IPR (1948). In this way, the state acted as a controller, whereby, the projects exclusive to the industry were bequeathed to the private arrangements.

The first automotive policy was formulated in 1949, in accordance with the objectives of IPR (1948). Singh (2014) witnessed a ban on the import of completely build vehicles in 1949. However, as Narayan and Vasishta (2008) noted while, while foreign assemblers were permitted to assemble CKD vehicles, the majority of them imported components until the middle of 1950s, just before when *Import Substitution Programme* was unveiled. The two-wheeler segment was also given its due importance. "The early 1950s saw the entry of API in the two-wheeler segment." (Piplai, 2001, p.2892.) As per Narayan and Vasishta (2008), a limited number of manufacturers, namely Bajaj Auto, Ashok Motors (in partnership with Leyland Motors) and finally, Mahindra and Mahindra (1945) seeped in the two-wheelers and commercial vehicles market in 1950s. "However, IPR (1948) along with the Industries Development and Regulation Act (1951) created an elaborate licensing system surrounding the Indian industries, including the automotive industry." (Ranawat and Tiwari, 2009, p.22)

In 1953, the government organised the *Tariff Commission*, which recommended that only enterprises with a *Progressive Manufacturing* approach to CKD vehicles and components be legally recognised to run. Furthermore, this strategy opposed price control. "Since 1953, when the government of India launched its import substitution programme, vehicle manufacturing and component producing activity became separate and distinct." (Piplai, 2001, p.2892.) Kathuria (1987) while describing the Tariff Commission (1953) report, argued that there were 12 firms producing or assembling cars and commercial vehicles by that time with a manufacturing programme. "The ministry also stated that although, the import duties on automobiles and components were not shown as 'protective' in the Indian Customs Tariff Schedule, the automobile industry was to be treated as 'protected'." (Kathuria,1987, p. 1810)

The foreign exchange crunch of 1957, forced the government to modify the approved manufacturing programmes of the recognised manufacturers as progressive indigenisation became a necessity. "However, the performance of the automotive industry (especially passenger cars) throughout the 1950s had been unsatisfactory." (Ranawat and Tiwari, 2009, p. 24) The institutional support for the automobile industry was in sight with the establishment of the *Automotive Component Manufacturers Association* in 1959. The Association of Indian Automobile Manufacturers (AIAM, now SIAM) was set up in 1960 as a voluntary organisation of vehicle and vehicle engine manufacturers providing information and services for its members to manage the technology changes and shifting competitive markets. According to Ranawat and Tiwari (2009), the L. K. Jha Committee published its findings in January 1960, stating that the high costs of vehicles were due to abandonment and shortfalls in manufacturing, caused by a dearth of domestic competitiveness. Though the consequence was that the small-scale industry ensued encouragement in 1965.

## Phase of Disparate Segmental Growth Due to Increased Regulation: (1966 to 1979)

Kathuria (1987) observed that the 1960s and 1970s marked the entry of new manufacturers like Bajaj Tempo, TELCO, Mahindra & Mahindra in the commercial vehicle segment. These companies started their production activities by entering into a licensing agreement with other major foreign companies for importing the Complete Knocked Down (CKD) or Semi Knocked Down (SKD) units, thereafter, localising the same in India. Staelin (1974) observed that the Tariff Commission's third and final inquiry in 1966 addressed the subject of automobile industry protection which was set to expire in 1967 and directed to enquire into the composition of costs and affordable price of sales of various categories of vehicles also. It also recommended that the automobile industry should *continue to be protected.*

The Automotive Research Association of India was founded in 1966 to provide applied research services to the vehicle industry. The MRTP Act was enacted in 1969 to prevent the abuse of power by the dominant firm and forbid deterring practises prompted by the intensification of control by few in critical trade and industrial activities, and many automobile manufacturers were subject to its provisions due to their soaring investment levels. The Industrial Policy Statement in 1973, as observed by Kathuria (1987), amended the earlier Industrial Licensing Policy of 1970 and enlarged the list of core industries to let open for participation of MRTP companies, and also to foreign concerns and subsidiaries, while excluding private vehicles. In September 1973, the government established FERA, which fostered the development of the non-luxury part of the automobile industry. The government pursued the policy of pushing forward the growth of the two-wheeler segment, to deliver movement to the expanding population, while keeping utilisation of fuel at a moderate level under the fifth Five Year Plan (1974-1979). To that reason, the FERA (1973) restricted the operation of international alliances and the imports of supplies, as well as levied additional restrictions on the import of components, raw materials, and expertise for the manufacturing segment and the automobile sector, in particular.

With passing of such policies, the regulations encompassing the automobile sector were empowered. Nonetheless, "the unanticipated oil shocks of 1973 and 1979 created problems of demand, exacerbating the situation created by high costs, heavy taxation and general recessionary conditions in the economy". (Kathuria, 1987, p.1811) Non-MRTP and Non-FERA enterprises manufacturing scooters, tractors and commercial vehicles etc. were authorised to expand with no restriction, and adjustments to licencing laws were made, beginning in 1975.

The government relaxed some of its tougher norms on foreign exchange equity ventures in 1978, which had a positive effect in the 1980s.

## Phase of Controlled Liberalisation and Foreign Partnerships: (1980 to 1990)

Between 1970s and 1980s, the automotive industry started growing and demand surged but to a smaller extent for tractors, commercial vehicles and scooters. The Industrial Policy Statement (1980) articulated this transition in government policy from previous regulatory policy frameworks and implemented efforts to make companies more competitive. For instance, the licensing system was eased, FDI in export and technology-oriented sectors were allowed, import restrictions were relaxed and joint ventures were encouraged. The 6$^{th}$ Five Year Plan (1980-1985), which was implemented immediately in 1981, revealed such alterations in policy. According to Miglani (2019), the government issued a *Letter of Intent* to Indian producers for the making LCVs, namely Allwyn Nissan, Swaraj Mazda, Eicher Mitsubishi and DCM Toyota in 1981. All four of these firms were in financial-cum-technical partnership with Japanese corporations. Apart from these four, other popular collaborations were HML producing a heavy-duty truck with Isuzu, LCVs produced by BTL (Daimler-Benz collaboration), Mahindra & Mahindra (Peugeot collaboration), and TELCO (indigenous). "In February 1981, an Indian company called the Maruti Udyog Limited (MUL) was incorporated as a government company with Suzuki Motor Corporation as a minor partner to make an efficient people's car for the middle-income class in the country." (Miglani, 2019, p. 443)

In 1982, with the efforts of the Indian government MUL went into a joint venture with a Japanese firm Suzuki to start mass production of different new models of small cars and in two-wheeler segment companies. Telco took advantage of the opportunity and united utility vehicles, commercial vehicles and cars in a single merchandise group called "On-Road Four-Wheelers," by venturing into the commercial (light) vehicle segment with a locally designed prototype. Correspondingly, broad-banding put entire two-wheelers into one category, which was eventually extended to embrace three-wheelers in 1986. The government announced the *Minimum Economic Scale* initiative in 1986, promising to aggressively promote enterprises to reach the economic scale of operations. Despite this, the relatively low liberalisation that occurred all through this period, a profound effect on the performance of automobile industry took place. "Additionally, the *Motor Vehicles Act* (1988) mandated the components used in the Indian vehicles to be certified under the standards laid by the Bureau of Indian Standards." (Ranawat and Tiwari, 2009, p. 32)

Of the two-wheeler manufacturing companies, Bajaj Auto, TVS Motors and Escorts entered into a technology collaboration with Kawasaki, Suzuki and Yamaha, respectively, under the changing scenario to upgrade their model. The most significant development, according to Kathuria (1987), was the liberalisation of government policy as well as the arrival of domestic undertakings, two decades afterwards, in the commercial vehicle, two-wheeler, and passenger automobile sectors. "Around this time, the government also put in place a Phased Manufacturing Programme (PMP) for localization of components, under which domestic OEMs had to increase the proportion of domestic inputs used in their output over a specific period." (Miglani, 2019, p. 443)

## Liberalisation and Globalisation: Post 1991

Encompassing the essence of the liberalisation, privatization and globalisation, a wide range of macroeconomic stability and structural reforms were introduced in the Indian economy with the advent of the new economic reforms 1991. "In line with the 1980s' policy changes, a comprehensive reform package was announced in the early 1990s allowing entry of foreign firms along with the removal of restrictions on the import of raw material and technology." (Singh, 2014, p. 249) The major role of the public and private sectors was evaluated in the context of the New Industrial Policy of 1991, and industrial licencing was eliminated, throughout, in automotive, i.e., vehicle segments (excluding passenger vehicles) and auto component segments. In May 1993, the passenger automobile category was delicensed. In a simultaneous bid to encourage the automobile industry, the mass emission standards in 1991 were first proposed for petrol vehicles, and in the following year for diesel vehicles; however, the government restrained the use of petroleum by levying 25% supplementary charges on its products in order to avoid any supply shortages. As a result, *motor vehicle licencing* was discontinued in April 1993.

Before the implications of the trade reforms of 1991, heavy excise duty imposed by the government on the selling price of all automobiles, acted as a deterrent for the growth of the automobile sector. Kathuria (1996) added that the peak tariff rate for auto-related imports got reduced from 150% in 1991 to 110% in 1992, 85% in 1993, 65% in 1994 and to 50% in 1995. The MRTP (1969) clearance was also terminated. As a result of multiple global companies joining the Indian automobile industry were now free to participate, grow, specialise, team up and get hold of the domestic market. As a result, in terms of foreign investments, FDI up to 51% was automatically permitted in a broad range of sectors.

"Thus, the lowering of trade barriers, the possibility of making direct investments and the promising growth potential of the domestic market, brought India onto the radar of international automotive players." (Ranawat and Tiwari, 2009, p.34) As a result, various foreign entities entered the car market in India, primarily through joint ventures with domestic firms. For example, beginning from 1994, Premier *Automobiles* Ltd. (PAL) collaborated with Peugeot, Hindustan Motors Limited (HML) went into partnership with General Motors, Tata Engineering and Locomotive Company (TELCO) made an alliance with Mercedes-Benz. In the successive year, SIEL Ltd. went into forming an alliance with Honda Motors at the same time as DCM-Toyota was acquired by Daewoo. Similarly, such arrangement was followed in 1966 when Hyundai became a fully owned subsidiary whilst Mahindra and Mahindra partnered with Ford Motors. In 1997, Tata Motor was chosen by FIAT motors for collaboration whereas Kirloskar Group teamed up with Toyota.

Covering the same time period of 1997, Ministry of Environment and Forests officially published fuel requirements that were first unveiled in 1996. In the same year, the policy aimed for national highways was confirmed, imbibing a significant influence over the automotive industry. By the middle of 1990s, Tatra had entered into a partnership with Vectra Motors (1997) in the commercial vehicle segment, while Volvo had entered the Indian market through its wholly owned subsidiary (1997). Following the 1991 reforms, global manufactures and first-class dealers entered India, paving pathway in the upturn of assortment, technology, and component makers. Since then, vehicle manufacturers such as Mahindra & Mahindra, Maruti Suzuki India Ltd., and Tata Motors Ltd. among others have risen to the position of prominent automobile manufacturers in the country. Since the year 2000, key regulatory policies such as *GST, Bharat Stage* norms, safety regulations, efficiency rules focusing on alternative fuels, upgradation to hybrid and electric vehicles and end-of-life strategy for old vehicle, and harmonisation of vehicle protocols, among others, were subsumed in major policies.

## Recent Policy Environment and Government Initiatives since 2000

In the 1990s, FDI was mostly market-seeking, and the inflow of FDI was aided by government policies and local content requirements, which led to further FDI influx and helped various industries compete with foreign competitors. The OEMs, across a certain period, were required to intensify the percentage of domestic inputs exploited in their output in order for Indian firms to reap after technology transfers bringing foreign equity inflows. The landmark events of the 1990s opened the groundwork for continued expansion. This began with the *industrial delicencing,* shelving of *phased manufacturing programme,* elimination of necessary MRTP requirement in 1991, which facilitated the entry of global assemblers, a reduction of tariffs from 87% to 20.3% in 1997, as well as automatic approval of FDI in joint ventures with 51% bulk portion of foreign equity. Since the beginning of the year 2000, the government has adopted the following initiatives: -

### *Auto Policy (2002)*

In 2002, the Ministry of Heavy Industries presented an official document titled 'Auto Policy 2002' made specifically for the automobile industry imbibing the goal of building a worldwide competitive industry together with its expansion not later than 2010. The primary goal is to achieve integrated, phased, long-term, and self-sustaining growth in the automobile sector. It succeeded the earlier auto policy, launched in 1997, in order to pursue best worldwide practises that would result in India becoming a crucial locale for building two-wheelers and tractors, a universal centre for auto-components and a global centre intended for small cars. In 2002, 100% of FDI equity flows into the automobile industry were permitted under the automatic approval route.

### *National Automotive Testing and R&D Infrastructure Project (NATRIP 2005)*

The Cabinet Committee on Economic Affairs (CCEA) authorised the NATRIP in 2005 towards constructing a R&D infrastructure, validation, and testing by means of an initial capital spending of Rs 1,718 crore meant for the establishment of vehicle testing facilities in 7 sites, throughout India, by 2011. In partnership with SIAM, NATRIP programme aims at testing and homologation of automobiles, through building infrastructure, with the goal of assisting the industry in adopting as well as implementing top-notch performance, emissions, and safety standards for the local firms. The Ministry of Heavy Industries has been delegated the authority to carry out the NATRIP project under its guidance and administrative direction.

### *Regulations Relating to Emission, Safety & Noise (2005)*

Under these policies, *Bharat Stage II* norms were introduced across the country for all four-wheelers, two-wheelers and three-wheelers. In the 11 major cities, *Bharat Stage III* norms were also introduced. The safety regulations included lamps, bulbs, interior fittings headlamps levelling devices etc. Along with it, the tight *noise norms* were made. In 2007, SIAM also made a presentation to the Executive Committee on the 'Future Emission Roadmap' at Chennai regarding *Bharat Stage V and Bharat Stage VI.*

### *Automotive Mission Plan (AMP 2006)*

In 2006, the Ministry of Heavy Industries and Public Enterprises formulated the Draft Automotive Mission Plan. This plan, consistent with SIAM (2017), was carrying the vision "To emerge as the destination of choice in the world for design and manufacture of automobiles and auto components with output reaching a level of US$ 145 billion accounting for more than 10% of the GDP and providing additional employment to 25 million people by 2016". A number of initiatives were examined as part of this plan, such as increasing budget by 150% for R&D pursuits, removal of weighted R&D expenses, and creating an outstanding R&D testing set-up, maintaining the duty on raw materials around 5 %t to 7% and reducing the duty of cars to 16% in the automobile sector.

### *National Electric Mobility Mission Plan (NEMMP 2013)*

The NEMMP (2013) was established with the goal of promoting Electric Vehicles (EVs) and Hybrid HEVs Electric Vehicles (HEVs) while boosting indigenous production proficiencies to safeguard environmental and fuel. As part of the implementation of the NEMMP, the authority has been promoting the development of indigenous battery technologies and charging facilities. The implementation of NEMMP is predicted to lower vehicular emissions and greenhouse gas emissions such as carbon dioxide during the same time period. It envisioned ways of achieving the goal of efficient, ecologically friendly, and economical EVs by 2020, with annual production of an entire spectrum of EVs of Rs. 6-7 million units and fuel savings of Rs. 2.2 to 2.5 million tonnes.

### *Faster Adoption and Manufacturing of Hybrid and Electric Vehicles (FAME 2015)*

This proposal aims to encourage electric mobility in the country and support the development of Electric Vehicles (EVs) as well as Hybrid and Electric Vehicles (HEVs) throughout the transport categories such as commercial means of transport, motorcycles, and buses. The advancement towards HEVs along with EVs, envisions to provide the essential power and fuel security along with reduced pollution, while also stimulating the development of indigenous technologies and R&D capabilities. AMP (2006-16) emphasizes this concept as well. The current Phase-II budget is Rs.10,000 crores for the three-year period 2019-2022. According to SIAM (2017), with the determination of carrying out EVs initiative followed by steering it to realize 100% of overall production of EVs by 2030 comprehensively, the FAME India initiative has recently been passed to NITI Aayog.

### *Smart Cities Mission (2015)*

In 2015, Smart Cities Mission was set out to endorse one hundred inclusive and sustainable metropolises which were equipped with unpolluted surroundings, low priced and eco-friendly modes of conveyance, basic infrastructure, and an acceptable life quality for the residents. In order for cities to be balanced and smart, NITI Aayog developed a 3-year strategy that combines a number of major programs for the encouragement of low-carbon transportation. With an overall outlay of 2,05,018 crore, 3789 projects worth of 60,602 crore have been completed so far.

### *Automotive Mission Plan (AMP 2016)*

In AMP (2016-26), the vehicles, auto-ancillary and tractor industry are to increase with respect to size and job creation, and contribute to India progress, worldwide footprint, technological advances, minimizing carbon footprints competitiveness, institutional structure and capabilities in time-oriented policies generating 65 million employments by the end of 2026 and expanding exports of vehicles by fivefold. This plan seeks to enhance universal mobility and imagined the end-of-life approach of vehicles.

## Scenario of the Indian Automobile Sector

This section depicts the state of the automobile industry's major segments, namely two-wheelers, three-wheelers, commercial vehicles, and passenger vehicles based on production, domestic sales, and export data compiled from various Annual Reports of SIAM. SIAM became the successor organisation of AIAM (founded in 1960) in May 1999, with eight members, international and national importance served as a key network of disseminating information for the automobile industry through numerous publications, reports, seminars, and conferences. The most recent data for observing trends in the major segments of the vehicle sector, ranging from 2001-02 to 2019-20, has been collected but was available until March 2020. This is because the vehicle sector's data came under the limits of the consequences of the nation-wide lockdown caused by COVID-19 since March, 2020.

### *Production*

The Table 2.1 shows the segment-wise trends in production of the automobile sector in India from 2001-02 to 2019-20 in numbers. The segment-wise diagram on the trends in production of the automobile sector in India from 2001-02 to 2019-20 in numbers, based on the Table 2.1, is shown in Figure 2.10 for the passenger vehicles, Figure 2.11 for the commercial vehicle,

**Table 2.1: Segment-wise Trends in Production of the Automobile Sector in India from 2001-02 to 2019-20. (in Numbers)**

| Year | Passenger Cars | Utility Vehicles | Vans | Total Passenger Vehicles | MCVs & HCV's | LCV'S | Total Commercial Vehicles | Three-Wheelers | Scooters | Motorcycles | Mopeds | Total Two-Wheelers | Grand Total |
|---|---|---|---|---|---|---|---|---|---|---|---|---|---|
| 2001-02 | 500,301 | 105,667 | 63,751 | 669,719 | 96,752 | 65,765 | 162,508 | 212,748 | 937,506 | 2,906,323 | 427,498 | 4,271,327 | 5,316,302 |
| 2002-03 | 557,410 | 114,479 | 51,441 | 723,330 | 120,502 | 83,195 | 203,697 | 276,719 | 848,434 | 3,876,175 | 351,612 | 5,076,221 | 6,279,967 |
| 2003-04 | 782,562 | 146,325 | 60,673 | 989,560 | 166,123 | 108,917 | 275,040 | 356,223 | 935,279 | 4,355,168 | 332,294 | 5,622,741 | 7,243,564 |
| 2004-05 | 960,487 | 182,018 | 67,371 | 1,209,876 | 214,807 | 138,896 | 353,703 | 374,445 | 987,498 | 5,193,894 | 348,437 | 6,529,829 | 8,467,853 |
| 2005-06 | 1,046,133 | 196,506 | 66,661 | 1,309,300 | 219,295 | 171,788 | 391,083 | 434,423 | 1,021,013 | 6,207,690 | 379,994 | 7,608,697 | 9,743,503 |
| 2006-07 | 1,238,021 | 222,495 | 84,707 | 1,545,223 | 294,258 | 225,724 | 519,982 | 556,126 | 943,944 | 7,112,281 | 379,987 | 8,466,666 | 11,087,997 |
| 2007-08 | 1,426,212 | 246,038 | 105,333 | 1,777,583 | 294,957 | 254,049 | 549,006 | 500,660 | 1,074,933 | 6,503,532 | 430,827 | 8,026,681 | 10,853,930 |
| 2008-09 | 1,516,967 | 219,498 | 102,128 | 1,838,593 | 192,283 | 224,587 | 416,870 | 497,020 | 1,161,276 | 6,798,118 | 436, 219 | 8,419,792 | 11,172,275 |
| 2009-10 | 1,932,620 | 272,883 | 151,908 | 2,357,411 | 250,133 | 317,423 | 567,556 | 619,194 | 1,494,409 | 8,444,857 | 571,070 | 10,512,903 | 14,057,064 |
| 2010-11 | 2,453,097 | 313,142 | 216,533 | 2,982,772 | 345,818 | 414,917 | 760,375 | 799,553 | 2,134,585 | 10,510,189 | 704,575 | 13,349,349 | 17,916,035 |
| 2011-12 | 2,537,170 | 370,945 | 237,954 | 3,146,069 | 384,801 | 544,335 | 929,136 | 879,289 | 2,659,340 | 11,982,669 | 785,523 | 15,427,532 | 20,382,026 |
| 2012-13 | 2,423,086 | 568,538 | 239,434 | 3,231,058 | 280,677 | 551,972 | 832,649 | 839,748 | 3,026,512 | 11,925,690 | 791,954 | 15,744,156 | 20,647,611 |
| 2013-14 | 2,322,578 | 568,692 | 196,703 | 3,087,973 | 221,556 | 477,479 | 699,035 | 830,108 | 3,676,213 | 12,474,626 | 732,210 | 16,883,049 | 21,500,165 |
| 2014-15 | 2,422,158 | 626,296 | 172,965 | 3,221,419 | 268,558 | 429,740 | 698,298 | 949,019 | 4,722,747 | 13,011,219 | 755,345 | 18,489,311 | 23,358,047 |
| 2015-16 | 2,565,970 | 717,809 | 181,266 | 3,465,045 | 341,287 | 445,405 | 786,692 | 934,104 | 5,276,138 | 12,816,203 | 737,886 | 18,830,227 | 24,016,599 |
| 2016-17 | 2,711,911 | 909,555 | 180,204 | 3,801,670 | 342,761 | 467,492 | 810,253 | 783,721 | 5,926,499 | 13,088,208 | 919,032 | 19,933,739 | 25,330,967 |
| 2017-18 | 2,746,658 | 1,093,346 | 180,263 | 4,020,267 | 344,592 | 550,856 | 895,448 | 1,022,181 | 7,117,795 | 15,167,481 | 869,562 | 23,154,838 | 29,094,447 |
| 2018-19 | 2,710,057 | 1,098,578 | 217,412 | 4,026,047 | 444,202 | 667,974 | 1,112,176 | 1,268,723 | 7,095,163 | 16,502,734 | 905,189 | 24,503,086 | 30,915,420 |
| 2019-20 | 2,175,242 | 1,124,973 | 133,798 | 3,434,013 | 233,979 | 518,043 | 752,022 | 1,133,858 | 6,027,198 | 14,359,418 | 649,678 | 21,036,294 | 26,362,282 |

*Source: Compiled from the Annual Report of SIAM (2001-02 to 2019-20)*

Figure 2.12 for the three-wheelers and Figure 2.13 for the two-wheelers segment, respectively. According to the 4th Annual Report of SIAM (2002), the production of the automobile industry recorded a growth of 13% in 2001-02 over the previous fiscal year and the dominant segment of two-wheeler recorded a growth of 16%. In the year 2002-03, the production of passenger vehicles increased from 669,719 units to 723,330 of which passenger cars contributed 557,410 units to the total production.

**Figure 2.10: Trends in Production of the Passenger Vehicles in India from 2001-02 to 2019-20.**

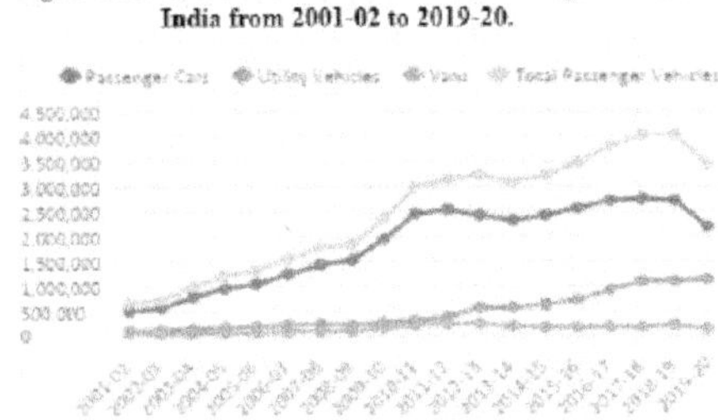

**Figure 2.11: Trends in Production of the Commercial Vehicles in India from 2001-02 to 2019-20.**

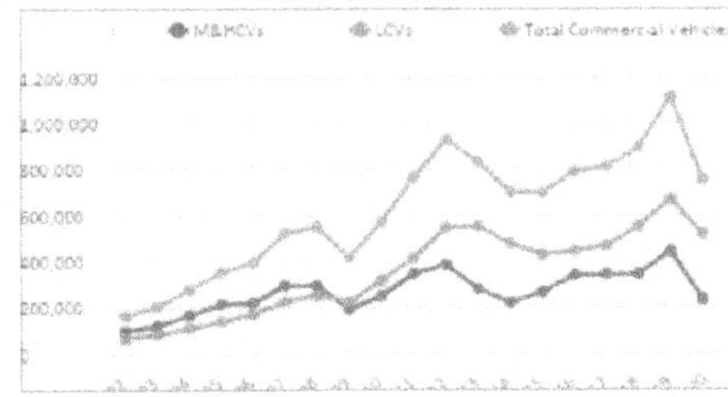


**Figure 2.12: Trends in Production of the Three-Wheelers in India from 2001-02 to 2019-20.**

**3: Trends in Production of the Two-Wheelers in India from 2001-02 to 2019-20.**

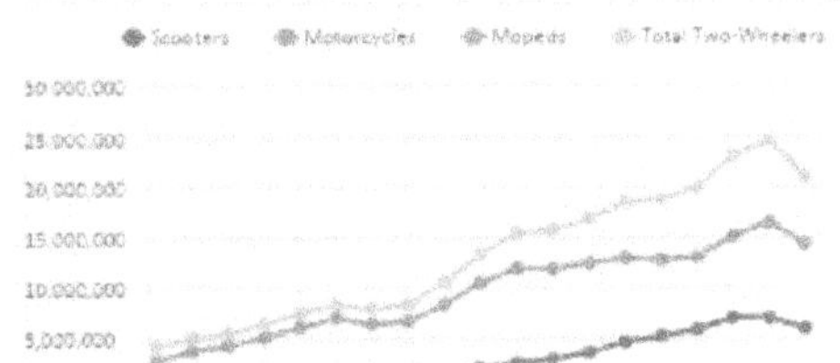


In October 2003, the *National Auto Fuel* policy was approved and aimed to provide a roadmap for stringent vehicular emission norms, bringing about an increase in the making of overall passenger vehicle segment from 7,243,564 units in 2003-04 to 8,467,853 units in 2004-05. The year 2005-06 saw an increased level of overall production by 15%. In September 2006, the Draft Automotive Mission Plan (DAMP) was unveiled.

In addition to this for passenger cars, two wheelers and three-wheelers, custom duty was retained at the current level tariff for CBU units were proposed to be delinked from other tariffs pegged at a 40% bound rate. Therefore, the passenger cars grew at the rate of around 15% over the year of 2007-08 as compared to that of 2006-07, total commercial vehicles rose by 29,024 units in the same period. In the 13th Annual Report (2011) of SIAM, two-wheelers occupied one-third of the total of 17,916,035 units in 2010. (In Figure 2.13 based on trends of two-wheelers) In the Figure 2.13, the production of two wheelers crossed the 10 million marks in 2010. The auto industry successfully emerged from a downturn in 2008 but the year 2012-13 resulted in spiralling inflation, rising interest rates and rapid rise in the petrol prices that took its toll on the overall sentiments in the market.

As compared to 2010-11 the overall production grew at 20.26% in 2011-12. In addition, the excise duty on cars in the commercial vehicles segment was also increased in 2012-13. As a result, the cumulative production data for the year 2012 shows production growth of somewhat greater than 1.3% over the same period last year with 20,647,611 units of automobiles produced as per 13th Annual Report (2011) of SIAM. In the 14th Annual Report (2012) of SIAM, overall production showed signs of improvement in 2013-14 with 21,500,165 as compared to 20,647,611 units in 2012-13.

In 2014-15, except for the production of vans at 172,965 units that passenger vehicles segment had performed well at 12.07% over the previous year of 2013-14. The positive aspects in the automobile sector were further facing positive expectations with the government's announcement on *Make in India* (2014) focusing on the manufacturing industry of which the automobile sector forms a huge part. Although the air pollution activism and various regulations such for safety and emission efficiency and launch of *National Electric Mobility Mission Plan (2013)* are described as one of the key highlights of year 2015, also in reality 2015-16 witnessed overall progress of the commerce, across exports, domestic sales and production, whereby, overall production, grew by 2.58% in 2015-16.

In Apr-Mar 2016, the sector built 25,330,967 vehicles, comprising of two-wheelers, three-wheelers, commercial vehicles and passenger vehicles compared to 24,016,599 units in Apr-Mar 2015, showing a 2.58% increase compared to the same period last year. After almost a year, overall growth of 4.16% in 2017 was registered.

The first six months of 2018-19 saw an impressive overall growth of 11%, the latter half of the year saw a continuous slide of fortunes of the industry resulting in a degrowth of about 1% also, as explained in the 19th Annual Report of SIAM. The industry persevered to move from manufacturing emission standards BS-IV to BS-VI with effect from the implementation date of April 1st, 2020. However, according to SIAM's 22nd Annual Report (2020), de-growth of (-) 14.73% was marked in all the segments with an overall of 26,362,282 units in Apr-Mar, 2020, in contrast to 30,914,874 units in Apr-Mar, 2019.

### *Domestic Sales*

The Figure 2.14 presents the sub-components of the passenger vehicle segment along with the overall units. The Figure 2.15 gives the visual information on the segments of the commercial vehicle, as well as the total commercial vehicle segment. The three-wheelers are presented in the Figure 2.16, whereas the sub-segments are depicted in the Figure 2.17. The data for the respective figures is based on various reports of SIAM's database compiled from the period pf 2001-02 to 2019-2020. According to the 4th Annual Report (2002) of SIAM, the domestic sales for the passenger cars, commercial vehicles and three-wheelers segments showed a negative growth rate in 2001-02 over the previous fiscal year.(see Table 2.2)

In 2002-03, as shown in the Figure 2.14 based on the Table 2.2, the domestic sales of passenger vehicles registered a decline. Domestically, the commercial vehicle segment performed strongly, growing by 30% over the previous year. (See Figure 2.15 for the commercial vehicle segment) In the two-wheeler segment, only the motorcycles segment showed a positive growth. (See Figure 2.17 for the two-wheeler segment) The reduction in the excise duty on the passenger cars and utility vehicles, announced in the Union Budget 2003-04, positively impacted their domestic sales growth by 6.5% and 9.65% respectively in 2003-04.

In 2004-05 the passenger vehicles segment grew by 18%, the commercial vehicle segment grew at 22%, and two-wheelers as a whole grew by over 15% on the account of the upward trend of purchasing power in the hands of rural people. In 2005, SIAM also became a member of the International Manufacturers Association. In the same year, the two-wheeler segment grew by over 13% and crossed 7 million mark in domestic sales. The commercial vehicle segment also saw a positive growth rate at 10% in 2005-06 which could have been higher but issues relating to certification and the non-availability of diesel required to meet the new emission norms. The emphasis on the two-wheeler sector was, further noticed in the form of a negative growth of 8.89% during 2007-08 over the year 2006-07 on the account of a decline in the motorcycles segment of 14.5%. The marginal growth in the domestic sales for the passenger vehicles segment was also witnessed during 2008-09 at 0.13% over the year 2007-08.

According to the 10th Annual Report (2008) of SIAM, the domestic sales in the case of commercial vehicles also declined by (-) 21.69% in 2008-09 due to a whopping fall in the domestic sales of the M& HCVs at (-) 33.16%. As observed in Figure 2.16, three-wheelers declined by (-) 4.13% in 2008-09 on the account of a major decline in the goods carrier at (-) 37.52%. In the 12th Annual Report (2010) of SIAM, the overall commercial vehicles segment took charge with 38.31% of growth at 15,513,156 units, whereas the passenger vehicles segment was at 25.57% growth in 2010-11. The challenge in 2011 was indeed the rise in inflation which prompted RBI to tighten the monetary policy with the rate of interest putting a direct impact on sales.

**Table 2.2: Segment-Wise Trends in Domestic Sales of the Automobile Sector in India from 2001-02 to 2019-20. (In Numbers)**

| Category | Passenger Cars | Utility Vehicles | MCV's | Total Passenger Vehicles | M & HCV's | LCV'S | Total Commercial Vehicles | Three Wheelers | Scooters | Motorcycles | Mopeds | Total Two-Wheelers | Grand Total |
|---|---|---|---|---|---|---|---|---|---|---|---|---|---|
| 2001-02 | 509,088 | 541,491 | 61,775 | 675,116 | 89,999 | 56,672 | 146,671 | 200,276 | 908,268 | 2,877,184 | 408,263 | 4,203,725 | 5,225,788 |
| 2002-03 | 541,491 | 113,620 | 52,087 | 707,198 | 115,711 | 74,971 | 190,682 | 231,529 | 825,648 | 3,647,493 | 338,985 | 4,812,126 | 5,941,535 |
| 2003-04 | 696,153 | 146,388 | 59,555 | 902,096 | 161,395 | 98,719 | 260,114 | 284,078 | 886,295 | 4,170,445 | 307,509 | 5,364,249 | 6,810,537 |
| 2004-05 | 820,179 | 176,360 | 65,033 | 1,061,572 | 198,506 | 119,924 | 318,430 | 307,862 | 922,428 | 4,964,753 | 322,584 | 6,209,765 | 7,897,629 |
| 2005-06 | 882,208 | 194,502 | 66,366 | 1,143,076 | 207,472 | 143,569 | 351,041 | 359,920 | 909,051 | 5,810,599 | 332,741 | 7,052,391 | 8,906,428 |
| 2006-07 | 1,076,582 | 220,306 | 83,091 | 1,379,979 | 275,556 | 192,209 | 467,765 | 403,910 | 940,617 | 6,547,195 | 354,760 | 7,872,334 | 10,123,988 |
| 2007-08 | 1,203,733 | 245,284 | 100,865 | 1,549,882 | 274,582 | 215,912 | 490,494 | 364,781 | 1,050,109 | 5,768,342 | 413,759 | 7,249,278 | 9,654,435 |
| 2008-09 | 1,220,475 | 225,621 | 106,607 | 1,552,703 | 183,495 | 200,699 | 384,194 | 349,727 | 1,148,007 | 5,831,953 | 431,214 | 7,437,619 | 9,724,243 |
| 2009-10 | 1,528,337 | 272,740 | 150,256 | 1,951,333 | 244,944 | 287,777 | 532,721 | 440,392 | 1,462,535 | 7,341,122 | 564,584 | 9,370,951 | 12,295,397 |
| 2010-11 | 2,016,115 | 367,012 | 234,945 | 2,618,072 | 348,701 | 460,831 | 809,532 | 513,251 | 2,562,841 | 10,096,062 | 697,418 | 13,435,769 | 15,513,156 |
| 2011-12 | 2,031,306 | 363,772 | 234,761 | 675,116 | 349,216 | 460,283 | 809,499 | 513,281 | 2,558,981 | 10,073,303 | 776,866 | 13,409,150 | 17,361,769 |
| 2012-13 | 1,874,055 | 553,662 | 237,298 | 707,198 | 268,689 | 524,522 | 793,211 | 538,290 | 2,923,424 | 10,085,000 | 788,761 | 13,797,185 | 17,793,701 |
| 2013-14 | 1,786,826 | 525,839 | 190,844 | 902,096 | 200,618 | 432,233 | 632,851 | 480,085 | 3,602,743 | 10,481,115 | 722,920 | 14,806,778 | 18,423,223 |
| 2014-15 | 1,877,706 | 552,135 | 171,395 | 2,601,236 | 232,755 | 382,193 | 614,948 | 532,626 | 4,500,920 | 10,726,013 | 748,628 | 15,975,561 | 19,724,371 |
| 2015-16 | 2,025,097 | 586,576 | 177,535 | 2,789,208 | 302,397 | 383,307 | 685,704 | 538,208 | 5,031,678 | 10,700,406 | 723,767 | 16,455,851 | 20,468,971 |
| 2016-17 | 2,103,847 | 761,998 | 181,737 | 3,047,582 | 302,567 | 411,515 | 714,082 | 511,879 | 5,604,673 | 11,094,547 | 890,518 | 17,589,738 | 21,863,281 |
| 2017-18 | 2,174,024 | 922,322 | 192,235 | 3,288,581 | 340,781 | 516,135 | 856,916 | 635,698 | 6,719,909 | 12,620,690 | 859,518 | 20,200,117 | 24,981,312 |
| 2018-19 | 2,218,549 | 941,461 | 217,426 | 3,377,436 | 390,740 | 616,579 | 1,007,319 | 701,011 | 6,701,469 | 13,599,678 | 880,243 | 21,181,390 | 26,267,783 |
| 2019-20 | 1,695,441 | 946,010 | 132,124 | 2,773,575 | 224,806 | 492,882 | 717,688 | 636,569 | 5,566,036 | 11,214,640 | 636,940 | 17,417,616 | 21,546,390 |

*Source: Compiled from the Annual Report of SIAM (2001-02 to 2019-20)*

The year 2012-13 from the prospects of the passenger segment showed a decline, majorly in the passenger car segment's domestic sales at 1,874,055 units from 2,031,306 units the previous year as depicted in Figure 2.14. According to the 16th Annual Report (2014) document, the overall sales on the domestic front in 2013-14 increased to 19,724,371 units in 2014-15, hampering an increase of 7.06% in 2014-15. As per the 17th Annual Report (2015), the sales (domestic) saw progress altogether in 2015-16. The sales passenger vehicle increased by 7.24% between Apr-Mar 2016 as compared to the same time previous year. Among the passenger segment, cars, utility motors, besides vans increased from Apr-Mar, 2016 by 7.87%, 6.25%, and 3.58%, correspondingly.

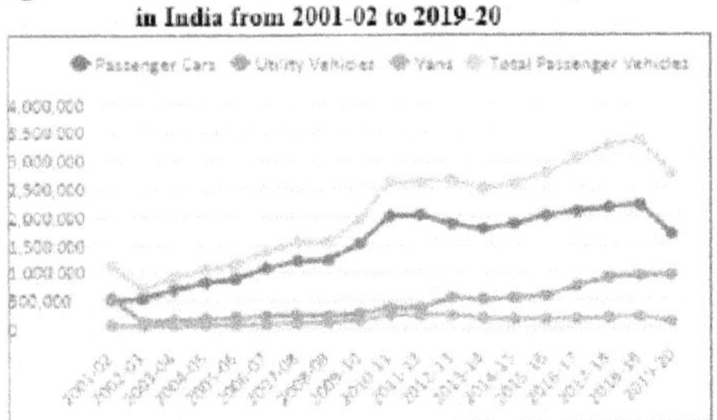


**Figure 2.14: Trends in Domestic Sales of the Passenger Vehicles in India from 2001-02 to 2019-20**

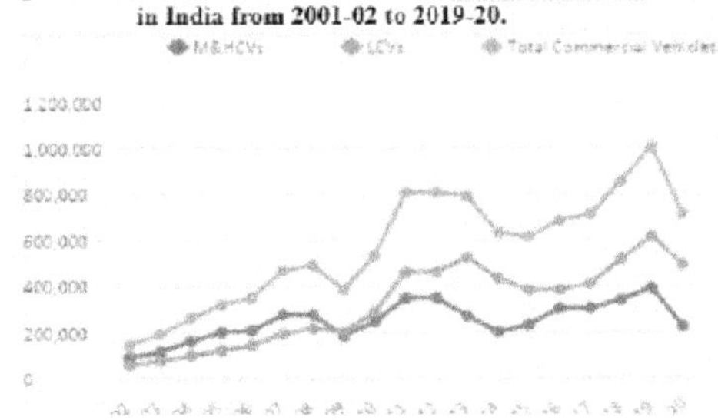


**Figure 2.15: Trends in Domestic Sales of the Commercial Vehicle in India from 2001-02 to 2019-20.**

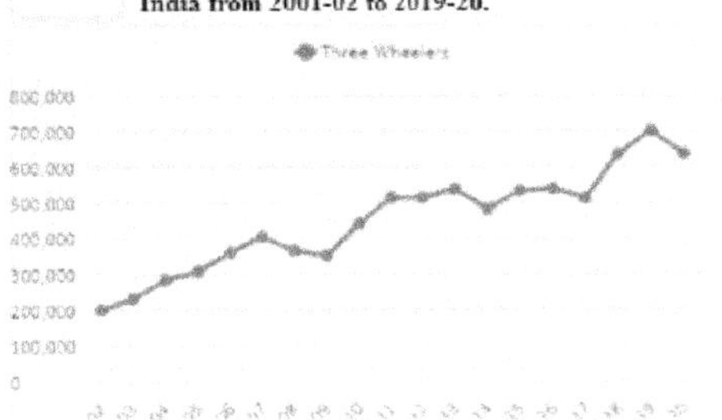


**F [illegible]: Trends in Domestic Sales of Three-Wheelers in India from 2001-02 to 2019-20.**

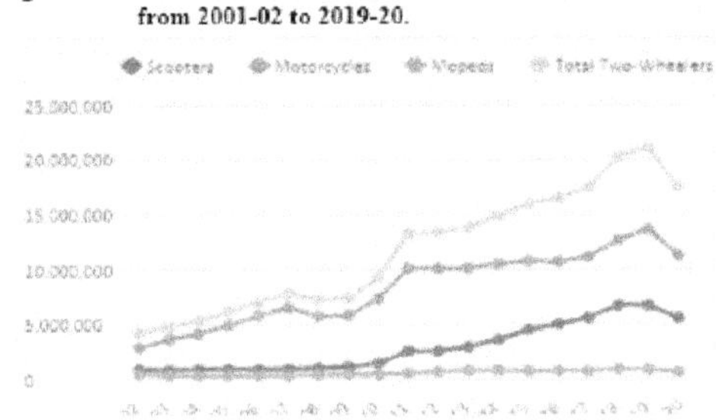


**Figure 2.17: Trends in Domestic Sales of Two-Wheelers in India from 2001-02 to 2019-20.**

*Source: Compiled from the Annual Report of SIAM (2001-02 to 2019-20)*

The industry's overall performance in 2017, in 20th Annual Report (2018), was the electric assortment that made plan for the future in EVs. With respect to the latest estimates of the domestic sales in the 22nd Annual Report (2020) for 2019-20, the overall passenger segment witnessed a decline from 3,377,436 to 2,773,575 units. A stark reduction in the domestic sales was also observed for the commercial vehicle segment. Also, the two-wheeler segment led by the motorcycles, showed a decline from 13,599,678 units to 11,214,640 units in 2019-20.

### *Exports*

With exports for various segments and sub-segments being described in SIAM's various Annual Reports, the Table 2.3 presents the data from 2001-02 to 2019-20 compiled on the basis of the categories of two wheelers, three wheelers, commercial vehicles and passenger vehicles. The Figure 2.18 used Table 2.3 to depict the data on the passenger vehicle segment from 2001-02 to 2019-2020. Figure 2.19 shows the sub-segments in the commercial vehicles segment with respect to the exports in the 2001-02 to 2019-20. The three-wheelers can be seen in Figure 2.20 and finally, two-wheelers and its sub-components are shown Figure 2.21, from the year 2001-02 to 2019-20. According to the 4th Annual Report (2002), the overall exports for the year 2002-03 grew by 60% over the year of 2003-04. The passenger vehicles in 2004-2005, crossed the hundred thousand units. Also, the two-wheelers and three-wheelers crossed three hundred thousand units for the first time in 2004-05. The export performance was also encouraging with respect to the commercial vehicles segment, which went beyond 40,000 units growing at a rate over 35% in 2005-06. In 2006-07, the exports in overall automobile industry reached 1,011,529 units. The automobile exports also witnessed growth, at 16.9% in 2007-08, with three-wheelers bagging the maximum increase of 31.5%. The year of 2008-09 registered an increase in the exports with a growth of 23.61% in all the segments except commercial vehicles (-27.67%) segment. (See Figure 2.19)

The overall exports in 2011-12, stood at 29.64% over the past year of 2010-11, whereas marginal growth at 1.64% was recorded for passenger vehicles. There was a continued volatility, witnessed in the prices of the crude oil since 2011, along with the depreciation of rupee in the international market whereas, interest rate had risen substantially leading to a relentless rise in the price of the price of the diesel and petrol cars cumulating to depressed market conditions and loss in the consumer confidence at the domestic front. But the exports were at 3,110,584 units in 2013-14. The commercial vehicle segment recorded an increase of 12.83% in 2014-15 in the units exported as shown in Figure 2.19. The bounce back of heavy vehicles in CV category and car in PV category sectors together with the enduring upsurge of the scooters in two-wheelers category was of great importance in the year 2015-16. (See Figure 2.20) In 2016-17, overall automobile exports grew by 1.91%. According to SIAM's 21st Annual Report, total exports increased by 14.50% during the financial year 2019, while exports of passenger vehicle decreased by 9.64%.

**Table 2. 1 Segment-Wise Trends in Exports of the Automobile Sector in India from 2001-02 to 2019-20. (in Numbers)**

| Category | Passenger Cars | Utility Vehicles | Vans | Total Passenger Vehicles | M&H-CV's | LCV's | Total Commercial Vehicles | Three Wheelers | Scooters | Motorcycles | Mopeds | Total Two-Wheelers | Grand Total |
|---|---|---|---|---|---|---|---|---|---|---|---|---|---|
| 2001-02 | 49,273 | 3,077 | 815 | 53,165 | 4,824 | 7,046 | 11,870 | 15,462 | 28,332 | 56,880 | 18,971 | 104,183 | 184,680 |
| 2002-03 | 70,263 | 1,177 | 565 | 72,005 | 5,638 | 6,617 | 12,255 | 43,366 | 32,566 | 123,725 | 23,391 | 179,682 | 307,308 |
| 2003-04 | 125,320 | 3,049 | 922 | 129,291 | 8,188 | 9,244 | 17,432 | 68,144 | 53,687 | 187,287 | 24,078 | 265,052 | 479,919 |
| 2004-05 | 160,670 | 4,505 | 1,227 | 166,402 | 13,474 | 16,466 | 29,940 | 66,795 | 60,699 | 277,123 | 28,585 | 366,407 | 629,544 |
| 2005-06 | 169,990 | 4,489 | 1,093 | 175,572 | 14,078 | 26,522 | 40,600 | 76,881 | 83,934 | 386,054 | 43,181 | 513,169 | 806,222 |
| 2006-07 | 192,723 | 4,399 | 1,330 | 198,452 | 18,610 | 30,927 | 49,537 | 143,896 | 35,397 | 545,592 | 38,655 | 619,644 | 1,011,529 |
| 2007-08 | 211,112 | 6,283 | 1,006 | 218,401 | 22,093 | 36,901 | 58,994 | 141,225 | 25,482 | 776,007 | 18,224 | 819,713 | 1,238,333 |
| 2008-09 | 331,535 | 3,034 | 1,160 | 335,729 | 16,819 | 25,806 | 42,625 | 148,066 | 25,816 | 971,018 | 7,300 | 1,004,174 | 1,530,594 |
| 2009-10 | 441,709 | 2,823 | 1,613 | 446,145 | 20,425 | 24,584 | 45,009 | 173,214 | 30,125 | 1,102,978 | 6,905 | 1,140,058 | 1,804,426 |
| 2010-11 | 438,214 | 3,746 | 2,366 | 444,326 | 28,349 | 45,694 | 74,043 | 269,968 | 50,646 | 1,474,678 | 6,295 | 1,531,619 | 2,339,333 |
| 2011-12 | 501,546 | 5,221 | 2,016 | 508,783 | 28,495 | 63,763 | 92,258 | 361,753 | 94,440 | 1,871,595 | 9,076 | 1,975,111 | 2,937,905 |
| 2012-13 | 547,222 | 10,423 | 1,769 | 559,414 | 19,524 | 60,503 | 80,027 | 303,088 | 91,062 | 1,862,008 | 3,308 | 1,956,378 | 2,898,907 |
| 2013-14 | 551,218 | 43,433 | 1,491 | 596,142 | 23,813 | 53,237 | 77,050 | 353,392 | 93,931 | 1,982,817 | 7,252 | 2,084,000 | 3,110,584 |
| 2014-15 | 542,112 | 77,025 | 2,204 | 621,341 | 30,652 | 56,287 | 86,939 | 407,600 | 195,407 | 2,252,066 | 9,993 | 2,457,466 | 3,573,346 |
| 2015-16 | 532,630 | 118,741 | 1,682 | 653,053 | 35,197 | 67,927 | 103,124 | 404,441 | 257,481 | 2,210,615 | 14,780 | 2,482,876 | 3,643,828 |
| 2016-17 | 602,134 | 154,257 | 2,336 | 758,727 | 43,719 | 64,552 | 108,271 | 271,894 | 292,828 | 2,027,297 | 20,152 | 2,340,277 | 3,480,725 |
| 2017-18 | 580,153 | 166,317 | 1,896 | 748,366 | 44,093 | 52,772 | 96,865 | 381,002 | 314,284 | 2,483,307 | 17,412 | 2,815,003 | 4,042,841 |
| 2018-19 | 513,912 | 158,252 | 4,029 | 676,193 | 48,674 | 51,257 | 99,931 | 567,689 | 398,316 | 2,865,851 | 16,674 | 3,280,841 | 4,629,054 |
| 2019-20 | 490,748 | 183,671 | 2,892 | 677,311 | 24,162 | 36,551 | 60,713 | 502,169 | 369,998 | 3,136,519 | 13,859 | 3,520,376 | 4,765,754 |

*Source: Compiled from the Annual Report of SIAM (2001-02 to 2019-20)*

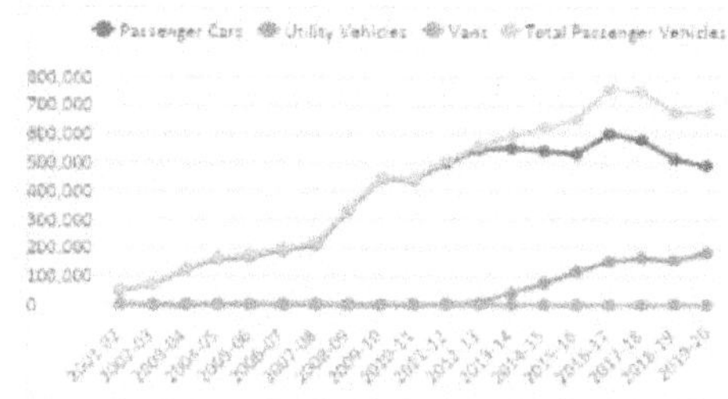


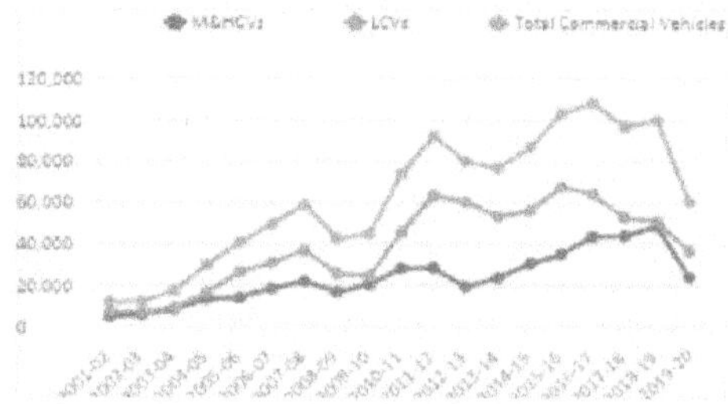


**Figure 2.20: Trends in Exports of the Three-Wheeler Vehicles in India from 2001-02 to 2019-20.**

**Figure 2.21: Trends in Exports of the Two-Wheeler Vehicles in India from 2001-02 to 2019-20.**

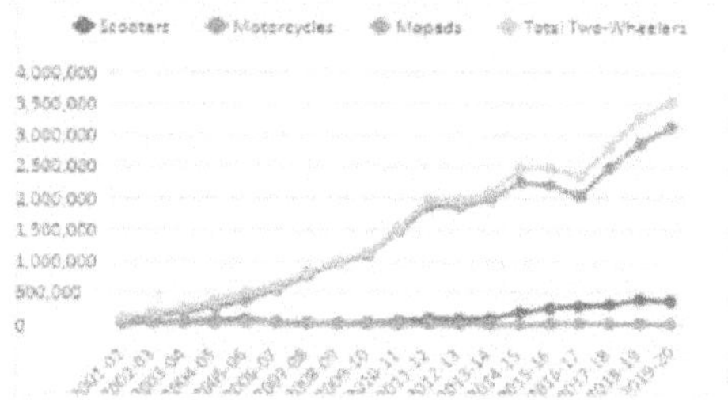


*Source: Compiled from the Annual Report of SIAM (1998-99 to 2019-20)*

In April-March 2019, commercial vehicles increased by 3.17%, three-wheelers increased by 49%, and two-wheelers increased by 16.55%, respectively. According to the 22nd Annual Report of SIAM, the latest numbers for the Apr-Mar 2019-20 exports show that passenger vehicles fell from 513,912 units in 2018-19 to 490,748 in 2019-20. The dominant sector of two-wheelers also saw an increase in exports to 3,136,519 units in the financial year, 2020. It is to be noted that Table 2.1, Table 2.2 and Table 2.3 does not include the new additions of the quadricycles and electric sub-segments to avoid the confusion with the base data. This study has taken into consideration the entire automobile industry that also resonates with the automobile and ancillaries' data in the Prowess IQ database. The details of the automobile industry provide a base to understanding the fundamentals of the automobile industry in this study.

# Chapter 3
Review of the Literature

## Foreign Direct Investment and Economic Growth

This section begins elaborating the major studies on the FDI and economic growth emphasizing on positive, negative as well as mixed growth effects of the FDI in line with aggregation, data's nature, absorptive capacity, trade openness, etc. in various countries. The studies on the FDI and economic growth are as follows: -

Borenzstein, et al. (1988) within the cross-sectional regression framework during 1970-89, found the positive effect of FDI from 67 developing countries on their respective economic growth. While highlighting process of technology diffusion, the study also reflected on the fact that the magnitude of the relationship amongst foreign investments and growth or *crowding in* foreign investment is dependent on the host country attaining a specific level of human capital.

De Mello (1999) estimated both panel and time-series data of OECD and non-OECD nations from 1970 to 1990. In the study it was found that the long-term positive relationship does exist in the economic growth and direct investments from abroad. However, magnitude of the relationship had been subjected to the degree of complementarity and substitutability between domestic and foreign based investment.

Balasubramanyam, et al. (1999) analyzed role of FDI in promoting economic growth by employing cross-sectional annual data in 46 developing nations from 1970 to 1985. With size of the domestic market, level of competition prevailing besides interactions between FDI and human capital, the stress was laid on such factors exerting an important influence upon economic growth.

Nair-Reichert & Weinhold (2001) emphasized on the techniques of Mixed, Fixed and Random coefficient approach in panel database to deal with the heterogeneous variables. The relationship between FDI and growth over 25-year period, also, revealed that firms with foreign equity participation has more effect on the productivity level but only in small enterprise. Also, the efficacy of FDI was found to be higher in the economies that facilitated more liberalized trade regimes of 24 developing countries.

Aggarwal (2002) found the existence of a positive affiliation amongst FDI and growth in Nepal, Sri Lanka, Bangladesh and India for the period 1965-1996. Along with the presence of a complementary relationship between foreign and national investor was also documented after the process of liberalization with cross-section and time-series data analysis.

Carkovic and Levine (2002) with the help of pooled cross-section and time-series data analysis put data averaging from 1960-95 to use and determined that the exogenous FDI component wielded unreliable and negative impact on the economic growth. Such a relationship depended on host country's level of openness, financial development and educational attainment,

Chakraborty and Basu (2002) revealed FDI was not the reason for improvement in GDP, but GDP caused FDI to cultivate, in the period of 1974-1996.This was primarily observed in the case of the time-series cross-sectional data. Also, the trade liberalization policy of the Indian government had some positive short-run impact on the FDI which was labour displacing in nature. The structural cointegration model method was employed for the findings.

Bengoa and Sanchez-Robles (2003) revealed employed panel-based analysis and revealed that FDI inflows are directly determined by the liberty prevailing in the host economy throughout 1970-1999. While exploring the interplay between economic freedom, FDI and economic growth in 18 Latin American countries, it was seen that these were, subject to the existence of liberal markets, stable economy and suitable human capital.

Alfaro et al. (2004) probed various relations among economic growth financial markets, and FDI and concluded that the level of development of local financial markets was crucial for the positive effects of the FDI on the economy since 1975 to 1995. Thus, nations through better monetary systems were exploiting FDI and were contributing to economic growth more efficiently, and not otherwise.

Li and Liu (2005) examined whether international investments influence GDP in the presence of factors such as human capital, exchange rate fluctuation and infrastructure, using both single equation and simultaneous equation system with panel data for 84 economies in 1970. It was showed that that reciprocity between human capital and foreign investments cast an upshot in developing countries' growth prospects, though a significant inverse impact of FDI in the countries with a technological gap was also seen.

Vu et al. (2008) estimated a direct and significant consequence of FDI on growth in both countries was observed, especially within secondary sector. The impression of FDI on growth in China for 12 economic sectors and Vietnam for 11 economic sectors from the time period of 1990 to 2004 was evaluated. In order to assess the impact, firm-level micro-econometric analysis using a regression equation,

Chakraborty and Nunnenkamp (2008) employed a panel cointegration framework, and allowed for heterogeneity in data across 15 industries in the primary, secondary and tertiary sectors in India. The dynamic inter-relations of economic growth and FDI was explored throughout 1987-2000. In conclusion, the arrival of foreign investments contributed to flourishing growth in India during the same time period.

Herzer (2012) explored the role of global investments in improving the growth prospects in 44 developing nations during the time period of 1970-2005 using heterogeneous panel cointegration techniques. This technique generates robust estimates to account for endogeneity. As the result shows, a negative effect on growth in developing countries, on average, was found, yet with large differences across countries, in effect. In addition, a general-to-specific model-selection approach explained such cross-country differences in the growth effects of FDI.

Belloumi (2014) applied Auto-Regressive Distributed Lag (ARDL) technique from 1970 to 2008 to find the relationship between the openness, growth and overseas investment in the Tunisian economy. The results of bounds tests suggested relationship between long-run growth and the foreign investments. In the short run, the growth also led to improvement in the trade sector. Nevertheless, the situation also indicated an insignificant cause and effect stream took place from foreign investments and trade to economic evolution.

Mahembe and Odhiambo (2014) reviewed the theoretical literature on the cause of liaison amongst growth and FDI. It was established that direct investments from abroad acted as a key contributor to the pecuniary expansion in the host country as the FDI had the capacity to foster the embracing of innovative expertise in the manufacturing progression by means of technology spillovers. It was suggested that FDI might also stimulated transfer of knowhow in terms of organizational practices, management, training the workforce and gaining specialization.

Iqbal et al. (2014) employed the *Cobb-Douglas* production function to test the cause of association between the national income and foreign investments over the duration of 30-years from 1983 to 2012 in Pakistan. While examining the descriptive statistics of the same, an affirmative relationship between the former and latter was disclosed. Along with this, a much larger effect of FDI was realized in the regimes supporting openness that were consistent with culture and the situation of the country.

Pegkas (2015) found an affirmative co-integrating relation between economic growth and foreign investments prevailing in the Euro-zone nations. The study investigated the liaison of the economic growth and the foreign direct investment by means of the panel data over the interval of 2002 to 2012. Moreover estimation technique of Dynamic OLS (DOLS) and Fully Modified OLS (FMOLS) was also implemented.

Elboishi (2015) suggested that the host countries' characteristics such as liberalized external sector, skills and expertise of the labor, capital infrastructure and financial market etc. form pre-condition to growth effects of FDI. The study is supported with the selected panel data from the developing countries through the period of 1970-2005, using Generalized Method of Moments (GMM) panel data technique. Although, the notion of positive influence of the FDI on the development was preserved throughout the study.

Iamsiraroj & Ulubaşoğlu (2015) discovered the relationship amongst 140 countries with respect to the foreign investments (direct) and growth in 1970 through an econometric analysis exploiting a comprehensive model. It was concluded that FDI positively affected the economic growth in the developing world and the similar relationship was also found globally. Furthermore, it was the regional distinction and contemporary FDI, in addition to capability to absorb the expertise which signified for economic advancement.

Gunby et al. (2017) applied meta-analysis and quadratic specifications to the corresponding empirical literature from 2001 to 2015 to find whether the spillover effect from the FDI has been of satisfactory magnitude to impact progress at a cumulative level in precondition of productivity in China. It was recognized that the economic growth in China impact of FDI stood much less significant than anticipated due to overabundance of valuations centered on less preferred studies and publication bias.

Sunde (2017) found an encouraging relationship between long run economic growth, exports and the FDI. The study applied the Autoregressive Distributed Lag Model (ARDL) from 1990 to 2014. In addition, the Vector Error Correction Model (VECM) obtained cause and effect relationship streaming from foreign investments to economic growth and foreign investments to exports, respectively. However, causality in both ways was detected amongst exports and growth.

Sirag et al. (2018) tried to find the effects of FDI and financial development on economic growth in Sudan by means of yearly time-series data through Fully Modified OLS (FMOLS) and the Dynamic OLS (DOLS) techniques. The data throughout the time period 1970 to 2014 is evaluated in the presence and absence of structural break estimated in long-run model. It was found that the overseas investment and financial expansion are critical in expounding positive growth in Sudan.

Carbonell and Werner (2018) found no evidence for growth invigorating FDI during the period of 1984-2010 in the Spanish economy. In spite of this, the macro-variables-based analysis projected an idyllic condition for international investments with the help of Autoregressive Distributed Lag (ARDL) model. In addition, it is stressed in the study that direct effect of overseas investment on economic growth lies on the financial maturity of the host country.

Sengupta and Puri (2018) outlined the summary of major trends of the direct investments from abroad in the subcontinent comprising of nations such as Sri Lanka, Bangladesh, Pakistan, Nepal and India to discover the cause and effect between Gross Domestic Product (GDP) and foreign investment. The technique of Granger causality, stationarity, panel data analysis, unit root test were employed and it was estimated that FDI inflows had triggered an acceleration of economic growth in India and its neighborhood countries, in the last two decades since 2000.

Bhattarai and Negi (2020) while finding an optimistic relationship between economic growth and direct investment from abroad with Prowess' panel database 2004 to 2018, determined that positive sentiments of FDI are to be experienced in 2019. Furthermore, sectors that encompass the ability to avert diminishing returns on investment are anticipated to contribute more towards sustainable development future. Also, positive contributions of foreign investment have been realized to profit, employment wages besides sales of firms in India emanating from Make in India (2014).

## Major Studies on Linkages and Spillover Effects in Foreign Firms and Industries

There exists a body of literature on the linkages explained by spillover effects in the foreign firms and industries in the foreign context, the majority of which have been explored as follows: -

Caves (1974) established that in case of Canadian manufacturing suggested that productivity level was mildly affected by the foreign subsidiary, whereas in Australian manufacturing industries, productivity levels did show a strong tendency to the presence of foreign subsidiaries. For this purpose, data of 81 manufacturing sectors was employed for 1962 and 1966. In the regression equation, value added per worker was studied with explanatory variables of average profit before taxes, assets, number of firms etc.

Koizumi and Kopecky (1977) explicitly modelled a partial equilibrium framework to study technological transfers from the direct investments. The major findings of this technical paper made aware of the conditions ensuing the steady state equilibrium. The most important variable in the study was the capital stock of the host country. It was also shown that following different paths, two countries with different saving rates will reach different levels of equilibrium owing to varying capital intensity. A high saving rate would grant a reduced necessity of the foreign capital.

Blomström and Persson (1983) established the direct relationship between the partial productivity and the presence of the foreign entities. This study described advances in the efficiency of the firms in the domestic economy of Mexico with the help of assets, concentration of the market power, wages and categorization of the workers, as the predictors in the regression model. The analysis was performed with the help of cross-section data retrieved for 1970 for 215 four-digit industries.

Blomström (1986) verified that the entrance of overseas firms had a substantial effect on average productivity in 230 four-digit Mexican industrial entities. For this intention, a comprehensive efficiency index was constructed with the help of average value-added per employee ratio. The study employed panel data for the year 1970 and 1975. Nevertheless, transmission of technology was not influenced by foreign firms as domestic establishments with low level of productivity were also maintaining no stimulus on technical progress. The direct investments helped in intensifying competition to stimulate efficiency.

Wang and Blomström (1992) established a dynamic optimization solution to the strategy and proved that transfer of foreign technology via multinational can be developed endogenously with the help of interaction among the former and the latter. The less costly the technological spillovers from the parent to subsidiary firms, the faster the technology transfer is incurred. The interdependent investment decisions in such scenario are sought to play a critical role to enable capitalization of profit.

Haddad and Harrison (1993) conjectured those indirect effects of the foreign investments were transpired through narrow difference between the productivity level of foreign and domestic firms. The study was conducted with the firm level panel data on barriers to exports in the form of tariffs and quotas. The sample was taken of 4,236 Moroccan firms during 1985 to 1989. With the help of stochastic frontier approach, it was seen that low technology-based firms in various sectors induced competition, further enhancing productivity concentration among them, but in the latter half of the 1980s.

Kokko (1994) verified that indirect effects of the foreign investments are positively related the size of the technological gap between domestic firms and foreign firms in 1970. The study performed linear assessments test for 230 four-digit manufacturing industries in Mexico. The regression encompassed predictors such as quality of labor, capital-labour ratio, foreign presence and the industrial concentration along with explained variable of value-added per worker.

Olley & Pakes (1996) using homogenous *Cobb-Douglas* production function between 1974-87, on the balanced panel data, estimated the parameters to scrutinize the progress of firm-level productivity for the equipment industry taking into condition the endogeneity of the inputs in the U.S. telecommunications equipment industry. The study was also suggesting a large bias in the negative direction, as a result of the application of simple OLS estimates forming the problem of endogeneity.

Aitken and Harrison (1999) grasped that equity involvement of foreign establishments is negatively associated with productivity of the domestic entities. This conclusion was assessed by utilizing a *log-linear* function for a group of domestic firms in Venezuela. By exploiting the panel data, for the period of 1976 with 3,955 firms to 6,044 firms in 1989, a negative relationship was observed to be robust for small companies. However, they also found that the indirect advancements in the productivity were primarily harnessed by the joint ventures.

Chuang and Lin (1999) revealed direct investments from abroad held a direct relationship with the level of productivity along with the variable of research and development activity in Taiwan. This study was accompanied by the evaluation of the Probit model with Heckman's two-stage estimation for data comprising of 13,330 manufacturing units. By applying this method firm's size, market's structure and labor's quality were deemed to suggest a positive effect on the productivity level whereas R&D activities turned to be substitutes for the foreign presence.

Okamoto (1999) made three major findings, first, the US firms were productive than domestic enterprises in Japan, however, in 1992. Secondly, the suppliers on inputs of the US origin upgraded their operations progressively during 1982 to 1992 and lastly, transfer of technology from Japanese to US resulted in performance advancement as a result of competition in the 1980s and in the initial years of 1990s. The study assessed the hypothesis for the indirect effects using firm-level data for Japanese investment in the US components industry from 1982 to 1992.

Sjöholm (1999) provided evidence in favor of spillovers to domestic firms, through the competition effect in 8,086 establishments from 1980 and 16,382 establishments from 1991. The study employed regression analysis with specialization effects, variety effects, investment effects and competition effect as predictors. Moreover, this study conducted in Indonesia was ambiguous on the impact of technological gap on the level and growth of productivity of the domestic firms.

Djankov and Hoekman (2000) found an adverse indirect FDI effects in the local manufacturing sectors in Czech Republic through the period of 1992-1996. This study has applied OLS estimation and Random Effects Model. The results from the examination revealed that joint-venture participate extensively further in novel expertise and technological know-how relative to domestic establishments by reason of the insufficient capacity to captivate the expertise brought together by foreign organizations.

Flores et al. (2000) investigated the domestic firms in 9 manufacturing sectors in Portugal in the period from 1992 to 1995. In the study, the effect on the productivity performance with respect to overseas investments was inspected. In the findings, it was ascertained that diffusion of the indirect as well as the direct benefits from such investments is linked with contemporary manufacturing entities in which the foreign concerns have an advantage on the domestic ones, in addition to other specific factors.

Liu et al. (2000) examined productivity spillovers for the period 1991 to 1995. With panel data evaluation this study focused on three-digits based 48 manufacturing industries in U.K. In the findings of the study, presence of foreign firms was noticed to be optimistic and substantial for the productivity progress by means of spillover effects. In addition, coefficients of intangible assets per worker and human capital were found to be affirmative of such effects with convincible stock of native expertise and knowledge capabilities.

Konings (2001) found discouraging impact of foreign entities in domestic concerns insinuating that crowding out effects encompassing competition, overshadows the positive effects of technological transfer in Romania and Bulgaria. This study was conducted by means of regression analysis using the panel data. The study was for the time period 1993-1997. To control for firm-level fixed effects and log-linear production function at the firm-level GMM estimators were used. However, no sign of advances to domestic firms in Poland was seen.

Liu et al. (2001) inspected spillovers through productivity from overseas investment in manufacturing industries in the form of rivalry amongst foreign and local firms. The data covering 191 industries in China, confirmed a substantial as well as positive impact of capital intensity, labour quality on the domestic firms whereas spillovers from productivity were adversely associated with technology gap. These findings also put forth the notion that market-oriented FDI generated spillovers by ever-increasing competition effects. Although, FDI preoccupied with international trade did not induce competition effects in 1955.

Barrios and Strobl (2002) showed an increase in firms' productivity level through a greater degree of market concentration as well as access to foreign markets through FDI in the Spanish economy. Also, with the help of the regression-based equation, it was suggested that only companies imbuing essential absorptive capacity might gain via positive externalities from FDI as firms indulging in R&D expenditure were seen to be having greater capacity to absorb spillover for the period of 1990-1998.

Glass and Saggi (2002) presented the literature surveyed in the review papers throughout the 1980s and 1990s. An encouraging consequence of trade on domestic firms' productivity level were witnessed. Furthermore, the study pointed at the ambiguous outcome of knowledge absorption incurred due to transfer of international technology, generating an overall view that foreign investments provide an optimistic results on the economic progress in the investment accommodating nation.

Hu and Jefferson (2002) observed that the productivity of domestic firms is negatively affected by the direct foreign investments. This study has correspondingly examined the market-stealing effects of Foreign Direct Investment in the short-run. The cross-sectional data employed a long-difference estimator in long-run and short-run regression function-based relations, in China's electronic and textile industries' firms, from 1995 to 1999.

McVicar (2002) found that negative competition or market stealing effect might dominate positive horizontal FDI spillovers. Employing the annual panel data covering seven UK manufacturing sectors of food, paper, chemicals, metal manufacturing, mechanical engineering, electrical engineering and transport equipment for the period 1973-1992, an increase in its own R&D stock over the same period of time was also seen.

Liu et al. (2002) investigated the relationship amongst foreign presence and productivity advances. By making use of industrial data substantial and optimistic effects of spill-overs within complete and sub-sample of local companies was witnessed. The integration and cointegration properties of quarterly panel data are analyzed from 1981-97 using the Vector Autoregression (VAR) model. The conclusion was that FDI, exports, and economic development give the impression to be strengthened reciprocally under China's open-door policy.

Chuang and Hsu (2004) confirmed technology-gap learning theory and observed substantial indirect benefits from the foreign presence in China's industries based on low technology-gap group, however, not otherwise. In the study, the data on the domestic plants from 1995 is retrieved from Chinese Industrial Census. Moreover, trading with more advanced countries and in particular, Asian Tigers and the OECD, contributed optimistically to the productivity at the firm level.

Javorcik (2004) established that spillovers incurred in the case of inter-industry, as MNCs prevented the outflow of know-how to domestic players, while having no motivation to avoid the technology dissemination to its customers and suppliers in the manufacturing industry of Lithuania. The study took unbalanced panel covering the period 1996-2000. By employing a semiparametric model based on the firm-level data, the study specified that spillovers are realized by means of ventures.

Photopoulos and Louri (2004) extended the literature survey to include new groups of variables i.e., extent of foreign ownership besides technological spillover to the study of foreign direct investment in Greece, from the time period of 1992-1997.This was achieved using quantile regression technique for 2640 manufacturing firms, which explained more integrated picture of the underlying relations.

Sinani and Meyer (2004) argued that spillovers fluctuate with the extent of external presence in Estonia. In the study, to evaluate the effect of technology transfer from foreign entities on the output growth of domestic companies during 1994 to 1999 a Heckman two-stage procedure is followed. It was also assured to be influenced by the recipient firm's size, its ownership structure, and its trade orientation when evaluated through panel data technique.

Alvarez and Lopez (2005) tried to find if selling abroad generated positive efficiency spillovers in firms operating within the similar industry and/or dissimilar industries, or not. The study was conducted using plant-level data econometric analysis in Chilean manufacturing industries. It was documented that exporters did not improve the competence of firms buying intermediate inputs, but helped sellers of the same, along with the indication of positive horizontal spillovers for the year 1990 to 1999.

Görg and Strobl (2005) established that foreign presence has unalike consequences on productivity and wages in non-exporting and exporting enterprises in the Irish economy by taking labor productivity and TFP as the predicted variable in dynamic wage equation settled for the endogeneity of inputs in the manufacturing firms. The agonized impression of exporters from crowding out in labour-market by multinationals was observed whereas non-exporters in domestic region did not make an advance in productivity level in Ireland.

Dimelis (2005) examined the FDI spillover effects in the Greek manufacturing industries for the period of 1992 and 1997. The study consisted of 2,589 firms. As per the estimates of this regression-based study, higher growth was seen in segments with greater foreign shares and the output increased to the proportion of external ownership. Moreover, the results of this study were in line with the *absorptive capacity hypothesis* that established positive relationship between spillover benefits and the technological capability.

Görg and Strobl (2005) used value-added and total factor productivity as a dependent variable in data of manufacturing firms comprising the years from 1991 to 1997. The *Cobb Douglas* production function was used to postulate a schematic illustration of the labor mobility for (horizontal) spillovers. The study suggested that of the conglomerates' selected knowledge was industry-specific and untransferable to firms of different industries in Ghana. Furthermore, specific training followed in foreign corporations had not altered their performance.

Narula and Marin (2005) formulated a question that despite the growing role of FDI in most economies, no evidence of positive and significant indirect technological spillovers were observed yet positive direct spillover effects were seen from FDI in Argentina between 1992 and 2001.This paradox was examined, using the firm-level panel data analysis, conducted with the help of introducing the variables ,that reflected changes in competition on the sectoral basis, in terms of the employment, research and development as well as the import penetration.

Ruane and Uğur (2005) examined the productivity spillovers in the Irish manufacturing industry, with the help of the panel data at two-digits, three-digits and four-digit industries covering an average of 4,600 companies for the period 1991 to 1998, and it was seen in the manufacturing sector that no substantial productivity spillovers from FDI existed in Ireland. Furthermore, the regression technique confirmed that foreign presence was negative but statistically insignificant in three-digit industries.

Takii (2005) examined the Indonesian manufacturing industry for productivity improvements resulting from the presence of transnational firms for the period, 1975 to 2001. The industries with the small technological gap showed a larger magnitude of direct and indirect benefit, especially the domestic enterprises engaged in innovation especially in 1995. The result also reveal that at 1% level of significance, the impact of the foreign share variable stood critical in positive direction.

Marin and Bell (2006) analyzed the technology spillover impact of FDI in Argentina manufacturing industries, for the period 1992 to 1996 on the firm-level data collected from the Argentine Innovation Survey, with 283 foreign affiliates. It was observed that domestic firms that were positioned in industries along with foreign holdings, had comparatively a huge outlay on training and skill intensity of employment and therefore, also experienced positive and significant spillover effects.

Pawlik (2006) investigated cross-section industry-level data for the period 1993 to 2002 and using the econometric model. It was found that FDI spillover effect in the Polish manufacturing industry were at significant levels, whereas, the overall mean productivity of private domestic corporations was high for private firms and low for public firms. However, the negative association of foreign firms with local productivity showed that there was no transfer of tacit knowledge from foreign corporates.

Buckley et al. (2007) found evidence of coexistence of linear as well as curvilinear natured relationships among the FDI influx and the productivity of domestic corporates. The study was using multivariate analysis to capture firm's size effects the Chinese manufacturing industry. The findings of the study suggested the curvilinear shape as suitable form for the spillovers from direct investments.

Crespo and Fontoura (2007) put forward the mixed evidence about FDI spillovers to domestic firms supplemented the investigation of surveyed features that determined the sign and proportions following the existence of FDI spillovers. This also suggested numerous aspects contributed to the indirect as well as direct advantages generated via foreign presence in particular, with an indeterminate effect. Furthermore, the absorptive capacity of domestic region and firms was deemed as preconditions for incorporating the benefits of FDI spillovers.

Crespi et al. (2007) explored the role of knowledge flows and TFP growth in the United Kingdom by means of direct survey in 52 firms, then discovered a statistically significant association between Total Factor Productivity (TFP) growth and FDI inflows with respect to average information flows from competitors, also regarded as the spillovers, whilst the positive relationship between information flows and the industry R&D and MNEs was also noticed in the study.

Driffield and Love (2007) developed a theoretical relation among FDI spillovers and determination of the stakeholders to invest. The study was conducted by estimating the FDI impact on productivity in the United Kingdom. It was cognized that diverse categories of FDI had demonstrated diverse productivity spillovers. Also, FDI influx driven by contemplations of sourcing technology indicated at absence of direct and indirect gains. The study exploited a panel comprising of 30 countries for 11 years (1987-1997) provided by ONS, OECD's ANBERD and STAN databases.

Jabbour and Mucchielli (2007) observed that technology spillovers were inadequate to form vertical linkages in Spain. In addition, such effects were majorly influenced by the gap between foreign associates and domestic corporations of technology bundle. The study undertook data during 1990 to 2000. The regression-based estimation also observed for the technology spillovers by the features of overseas associates.

Reganati and Sica (2007) examined the Italian manufacturing industries for horizontal and vertical spillovers, with an unbalanced panel, employed for 1997 to 2002. The main results showed absence of productivity gains accompanying the foreign presence. Also, no spillovers to domestic companies from foreign enterprises at intra-firm level were visible as coefficient of foreign ownership was positive, which implied insignificant productivity gains from foreign equity for the horizontal and vertical spillover effect.

Tian (2007) found that optimistic spillovers from foreign-invested enterprises to local concerns occurred mainly by means of tangible assets, domestic consumption of 'traditional' products and using the services of unskillful labor in China. The study employed panel of 11,324 firms as of 1996-1999, with an estimate of basic log-linear production functions. In the findings the affiliates also generated adverse spill-overs by employing skilled labor and export of new products.

Chudnovsky et al. (2008) analyzed the Argentine manufacturing sector on the basis of the role of FDI in addition to the grasping capabilities of local establishments for the period 1992 to 1996 and 1998 to 2001. The regression equation-based estimation generated the coefficient of foreign equity share that was statistically substantial and positive, implying that concerns with external control had higher level of productivity than local concerns.

Girma et al. (2008) analyzed panel-based data of local firms from 1992 to 1999 to examine the exporting activities, effects of their presence, linkages and productivity spillovers from FDI in UK's manufacturing industries. With the help of regression-based econometric technique, substantial intra-industry spillovers in addition to backward linkages were observed from export-oriented transnationals to local exporters in the study.

Jordaan (2008) found that FDI created negative externalities within industries via horizontal links dominated by the competition effect, whereas positive externalities between industries were exacerbated through backward links caused by the vast technological differences between FDI and Mexican companies, as well as the concentration of industries in several Mexican regions in the 1990s.

López (2008) found a positive spillover effect from technology licensing in upstream sectors in Chile in the 1990s, justifying subsidizing the importation of technology in sectors that provide inputs to the domestic market, whereas the downstream effects of licenses suggested that suppliers were producing high-quality inputs at low prices in the manufacturing sector at the time. To finish, no indication of intra-industry spillovers was noticed.

Marcin (2008) took an unbalanced panel to examine the presence of indirect benefits generated by foreign investments in the host nation. The study was employing panel in the Polish corporate sector for the period 1996-2003. In its main findings, local firms with the industry were benefitting from external incidence. Correspondingly, the absorptive capacity of local establishments was extremely sensitive to the magnitude of external benefits, while the inter-industry spillovers were greater in knowledge intensive establishments, and intra-industry concerns devoted to spend on the foreign intangibles gained substantially from the same.

Salim (2008) empirically estimated the Productive Capacity Realization indices by means of the stochastic frontier approach and analyzed a number of estimates describing the indices across panel data following Battese and Coelli (1995) in Bangladesh food manufacturing. The results of the study suggested that firms were yielding far behind the full capacity. Furthermore, the policy-related variables included in the regression-based estimation were statistically insignificant for the period 1992 to 1999.

Barbosa and Eiriz (2009) examined the Portuguese manufacturing industry for productivity spillovers by using an unbalanced panel data over a period of 1994 to 1999. Despite the study's findings, there was no strong evidence to support claims of knowledge spillovers or horizontal or vertical linkages at the industry level that could potentially raise firms' productivity. The study used econometric estimation to analyse 21 different manufacturing companies at two-digit level. In addition, firm-specific choices of inputs in estimation accounted for most of the productivity differences.

Blake et al. (2009) estimated the productivity spillovers on 998 firms in China from five manufacturing sectors for the year 2000. The study based on the regression analysis presented an estimation of horizontal spillover effects having a noteworthy and adverse impact on the productivity of local firms, but conversely, also had a substantial and optimistic impact on the productivity of state-owned enterprises.

Yang et al. (2009) investigated 35 industries, from 1999-2003 and looked for the productivity spillovers from overseas investments in China. In its findings, the study showed that (i) coefficient of labour and capital were direct and statistically considerable; (ii) resulting in sizeable backward linkages, nonetheless, (iii) irrelevant horizontal spillovers through movement of labour, competition, imitation among labour intensive and capital-intensive production units also existed.

Hoang and Thanh (2010) observed that FDI spillovers from foreign establishments to domestic concerns are substantial and optimistic in numerous characteristics, such as variations in intensity of capital, expertise, intensity of skills, technical know-how etc. The study was grounded on observed statistics at firm-level throughout 2003 to 2007 in Vietnam, while finding the productive efficiency inducing effects of foreign investment spillovers.

Waldkirch and Ofosu (2010) analyzed the period of 1991 to 1997 and found the consequence of external presence on the productive efficiency of manufacturing establishments in Ghana. By using the panel data and reflecting upon evidence, the study concluded that local corporations are unfavorably altered by external incidence as any optimistic outcomes owing to spillovers and learning were in effect counterweighed by increased competition effects. Also, it was noticed that the existence of external establishments had a constructive effect on concerns, if handled competition.

Agarwal and Milner (2011) discovered that the regional economic advancement was not progressively influencing the FDI spillovers in China during period of the study. In the study, a panel of 20,460 was utilized for manufacturing concerns throughout 2001 to 2005. The methodology applied non-parametric besides parametric techniques of estimation to explore the fundamental link amongst the economic expansion in China and direct investment spillovers with the help of simple *Cobb-Douglas* production function. It was

Du et al. (2011) investigated the implications of various features of foreign institutions on the nature of spillovers on the sample size of 1,545,626 Chinese firms during the time period of 1998-2007.These institutions as different sources of FDI were comprising of three institutional features of China's special characteristics including heterogeneous ownership structure and industrial promotion to FDI. In its results, the study found positive and significant linkages to domestic firms in the same industries via horizontal foreign investment and industrial promotion policies.

Ghali and Rezgui (2011) derived the data on balanced panel for 674 manufacturing firms over the period of 1997 to 2001 from Tunisian industrial database. The study, with the help of regression-based analysis showed that over the period of time, overseas corporations, were more competent than local firms, on an average, nevertheless, presence of influence from more efficient foreign firms depended on the absorptive capacity, trade size and market share of domestic firms.

Havránek and Iršová (2011) concluded that the average spillover to upstream industries and downstream industries was statistically substantial, however, magnitude was smaller for the latter. Also, larger spillovers were acknowledged by nations with undeveloped financial arrangements and larger openness in international trade. Such gains were yielded by stakeholders who came from far-off nations and had an minor technical edge over domestic concern. The period of the study was taken for the data set including 3626 estimates of semi-elasticities from 47 countries during 2002-2008 and regression-based technique was applied.

Javorcik and Spatareanu (2011) worked out the Olley-Pakes approach and Levinsohn-Petrin approach to inspect the foreign presence effects on the productivity level of national concerns within European countries, including Romania, for the period 1998-2003. The study found an optimistic relation amongst the productivity level of the Romanian establishments in the upstream segments and the American corporations in downstream segments. Nonetheless, no noteworthy association in in the European conglomerates was observed. In findings, patterns from downstream presence were dependent on shipping costs in Romanian firms but same was not the case in European affiliates.

Jordaan (2011) analyzed the cross-sectional estimates from unpublished data for the year of 1994 with the help of Mexican manufacturing census. The study had been employing OLS method of calculating the impact of FDI on Mexican firms. The study concluded that the results of foreign contribution was drastically divergent from the anticipated results achieved with the econometric technique, validating that the fundamental OLS estimate yielded a biased evaluation.

Le and Pomfret (2011) found positive and significant results for backward spillover effects while examining the technology spillovers in Vietnam. The study took place for the period 2000 to 2006. This study was conducted with the econometric based regression technique. In findings, the effect of overseas firms' being on the productivity of domestic concerns was found significant also negative but was significant only for small and medium firms.

Du et al. (2012) took an unbalanced panel dataset for the duration of ten years for the period of 1998 to 2007. This dataset was including all state-owned enterprises that were 162,033 in 1999 to 336,768 in 2007. The study worked at finding foreign presence originating outside of Macao, Hong Kong and Taiwan was only linked with advanced production efficiency. The findings, however, showed no positive horizontal spillovers from the foreign investment but indicated at the presence of positive backward and forward spillovers having a noteworthy influence on the productivity of the local enterprises.

Ito et al. (2012) took panel for 31 provinces in China for the period 2000 to 2007, while addressing the spillovers effects from foreign-invested enterprises into two categories of innovation, first, on the basis of (i) process innovation by the means of TFP and (ii) the product innovation by the means of patent applications. Nonetheless, the study found no knowledge spillovers emerging from foreign enterprises to the R&D source contained in the same industry. However, prominent forward effects as well as a backward effects in comparison to the horizontal effects were, indeed seen.

Masron *et al.* (2012) showed that the crowding-out phenomenon occurred in the industries producing goods such as the paper and printing products, petroleum and coal products, metal products and other transport equipment within the manufacturing sector in Malaysia for the period of 1999 to 2004 by employing simple correlation analysis. This study took on time-series data from the ASEAN database.

Negara and Adam (2012) analyzed panel from 1995 to 2005 then covered 20,000 manufacturing firms in Indonesia. The study while employing regression-based econometric technique, concluded that an increased foreign share variable (FDI) led to an increase in the firms' level of productivity further showing the positive and significant effects of horizontal spillovers and insignificant for the backward spillovers on the firms' productivity levels.

Iršová and Havránek, (2013) collected panel data on 1,205 estimates of spillovers studies in the region of Europe and examined the factors that influenced the spillover magnitude by means of Levinsohn-Petrin method. The findings of the study suggested that the direction in addition to scale of the horizontal spillovers depended comprehensively on the features of the host economy and overseas stakeholders. Furthermore, it depended on the investments from countries having subtle technology lead that created the principal gains for the internal market in 45 countries in the study.

Suyanto and Salim (2013) observed the cases of foreign investment, by exploiting an unbalanced panel of 210 firms at five digits ISIC level, from 1990 to 1995. The study observed, as per the estimates from the production frontier, the coefficient of FDI horizontal was insignificant and, therefore, no considerable spillover effects to domestic concerns in the related market of the Indonesian pharmaceutical sector were seen.

Baltagi et al. (2014) assessed the causes of productivity spillovers in electric and electronic industry which had been distinguished by its dependence on expertise. Especially, by means of panel data of 25,360 concerns, the study was carried out for the period 2004-2007. The conclusion of the study was that there existed robust spillovers in establishments engaged in exporting firms than those not engaged in the same, being either overseas or domestic in ownership. However, spillover effects differed across sub-sectors, when calculated in coefficients employing the Törnqvist index.

Medda and Piga (2014) suggested that participation of local firms in innovative activities accounted for substantial production efficiency advances in Italy. This study took bedded sample of 5,000 companies during period of 1998-2000. The study presented this, with findings that TFP dynamics of local establishments were being directly induced by its own R&D expenses while the technical spillovers brought forth by the intra and inter-sectoral level were also corrected for selection bias and endogeneity, concurrently.

Suyanto et al. (2014) empirically examined the indirect effects pf foreign presence on the technological effectiveness. The stochastic frontier approach has employed 3318 manufacturing firms, in the study, examined throughout 1988 to 2000. The findings revealed the substantiation of direct FDI spillover effects on technological effectiveness of the firms. Fascinating deviations, nevertheless, also emerged once the samples were separated into different levels of effectiveness. The study concluded that wider the efficiency gap amongst foreign as well as domestic concerns easier it was to extract spillover benefits from the foreign firms in Indonesia.

Zhou (2014) took unbalanced panel data for the study. The time period from 1991 to 2003 was taken in the study to investigate the influence of FDI on company's technical efficiency. In the study, mixed effects of FDI in the manufacturing industry were found in China. The coefficients of the efficiency were measured using stochastic frontier analysis. This suggested that the foreign ownership increases the efficiency more than any other type of private ownership and so does the size, age and openness of the firm.

Albulescu & Tămăşilă (2015) explored the impact of FDI on the entrepreneurial activity using GEM database. This data allowed for understanding the distinction between opportunity determined and necessity determined flows of international investment as independent variables and the entrepreneurial activity as the dependent variable. The study took the panel data from 2005-2012 and used fixed effects panel technique. It concluded that FDI have an adverse effect on the entrepreneurs holding opportunity-determined investments whereas it optimistically impacts entrepreneurs' investments determined by necessity in Europe.

Anwar and Sun (2015) found the effects of backward linkages based on the likelihood analysis of entry from FDI in electric machinery and equipment and transport equipment industries. The study applied panel data as of 2005-2007 and was carried out with Probit model revealing that international influx of investment in innovation in addition to associated spillovers had a critical effect on the prospects of entry and exit of local companies in Chinese economy.

Kim (2015) investigated productivity spillovers of FDI then tried to assess role of the absorptive capacity in indigenous enterprises of South Korea. The study indicated at the effects of exports and innovation soaking up the heterogeneous spillovers, dependent on the conditional distribution of productivity. The study was evaluating the results from simultaneous quantile regression for the manufacturing industries as of 2006 to 2009. Such additional spillovers were generated through encouraging strategies such as regulatory exclusions and tax stimuli for drawing in extra overseas investment.

Yi et al. (2015) examined the part of area-specific organizations in describing spillovers from FDI. The dataset being considered in the study constituted native corporations and multinational enterprises operational. The time of the study was taken for the period 2005-2007 and the results were calculated with the help of the regression-based econometric technique. The findings of the study reflected to the important role if the region-specific institutions in transfer for technology and resources from foreign direct investment in the Chinese manufacturing industry.

Ali et al. (2016) emphasized that literature on endogeneity suggested that foreign R&D besides own R&D, is diffused via ways of knowledge spillovers with domestic productivity growth as the explained variable covering 1995 to 2010. This was although a necessary condition but was not a sufficient condition for the foreign firms to transmit spillovers. The data sample in the study covered and included 20 nations in Europe, mainly testing for cointegration technique.

Demena and Bergeijk (2016) analyzed the spillover values for exploratory research papers printed throughout 1986 to 2013 and looked for the intra-sector heterogeneity of productivity spillovers from FDI. The study reported that spillovers evaluations were altered by model misspecification along with, publication predisposition especially in the case of the key studies. It was also mentioned that such bias overstated the genuine coefficients while remaining economically and statistically significant.

Hassine et al. (2016) emphasized that the influence of foreign R&D spillovers was more pronounced in addition of being significant than those of reverse R&D spillovers in France. The study investigated spillover effects from the FDI inflows in the form of the foreign firms for the period 1990 to 2009.The study also took

13 manufacturing industries and by using *Crepon, Duguet and Mairesse (CDM)* model to unbalanced panel data, studied the bearing of R&D spillovers on firm performances in the host economy.

Ubeda & Pérez-Hernández (2016) investigated the influence of FDI on productivity growth in case of 2722 Spanish manufacturing firms. The study concluded that the domestic firms with high absorptive capacities incorporate the more multifaceted know-how specified by multinationals, and moreover, generated positive spillovers. The Threshold revealed a non-linear association linking production efficiency and influx of foreign investment in local corporations the as of 1993 to 2006, constrained by the geographical distance and absorptive capacity.

Wang and Xie (2016) investigated the heterogeneous productivity level and the corresponding spillover effects from overseas subsidiaries to domestic enterprises in China with the help of firm-level data between 2000 and 2007. This data varied with the distance distribution between them. For this reason, a partial equilibrium model estimated the results that the foreign subsidiaries may generate productivity spillovers to local firms by providing intermediate inputs that embodied advanced technology. The results of the study were robust after controlling for workers' mobility, capital good market externality, and endogeneity.

Mukunoki (2017) concluded that when the trade costs and fixed costs of the direct investment are neutral the speediest technology embracing takes place along with maximum prosperity of the consumer. Furthermore, the study added on the various literature surveyed suggesting that the preferential liberalization in foreign investments promoted the adoption of technology but then the customers were discouraged. The technology choice was studied by employing dynamic model of technology adoption with dataset comprising of 663 entrants per year from 1998 to 2012.

Berrill et al. (2018) extended the specimen of R&D spillovers by furthermore investigating FDI as a vital link aimed at knowledge based spillover effect besides the influence of trade on domestic productivity. They explored the purpose of education and FDI in clarifying the contribution of entrepreneurship using a database across 75 countries between 2001 and 2015, country-level data on entrepreneurship with GEM data. It was concluded in the study that inward FDI led to job creation in the labour sector in countries that consisted of highly educated labour forces.

Kaulihowa and Adjasi (2019) tested the non-linear effects of foreign presence on the levels of human capital development in nine carefully chosen nations. The study was constructed on panel data comprising of African nations as of the period of 2000 to 2017. To ensure robustness, the estimation technique with instrumental variable was employed in the study. The calculation in the study indicated that various levels of human capital conveyed mixed results on spillover effects.

Teplova and Sokolova (2019) anticipated an index of efficiency imbuing foreign presence and its transition into growth and innovation. The study ranked numerous advanced and evolving economies from OECD website. The outcome of multivariate causality test, nonparametric DEA based Malmquist Index showed that FDI activates intellectual capital flows and economic progress in identified countries by the quality of FDI management. The study concluded that a change in efficiency over time was highly influenced by government effectiveness.

Velde (2019) identified six major factors to analyse the effects of foreign presence in emerging nations that include firm-specific aspects, investment, technical advancement, movement of labor, linkages, financial proficiencies and training of employees from reviewing literature of various first-hand studies in the developing nations to understand role of the public policies with respect to the FDI in those countries.

Haider et al. (2020) calculated how the growth of total factor productivity level was affected by R&D, trade, information and communication technology. The study took into consideration of the catching up time period in a sample of 12 European countries, from 1990 to 2006.This study estimated the results using Malmquist Index on the Capital, Labour, Energy, Materials and Services (KLEMS) sub-category and concluded that catching-up effects are statistically important and large differences between the frontiers existed and persisted between sectors and countries in the period of study.

## Drivers and Variables of Linkages from Spillover Effect: An Exploration in the Indian Context

The drivers and variables of linkages by way of analysing the spillover effects have made majorly in the case of various industries concerning the output level, value added and the total factor productivity (TFP). The studies that have hugely contributed to the literature on the impact of FDI with respect to various determinants are as follows: -

Lall (1978) employed a narration like rundown for Indian external economy that took place from the time period of colonialization to the creation of UNCTAD and argued that reasons that led India to adopt its competence as an open economy in the New International Economic Order were placed by the western countries. This happened for improving the terms of trade, increasing development assistance, and tariff reductions etc. of the latter.

Page (1984) investigated the interrelationship concerning firm size and technical efficiency in four major manufacturing sectors in India using a panel estimation following a trans-log function to evaluate the level of efficiency. It was concluded that the firm size was positively related to productive efficiency (relative) in one out of four major sectors from 1979 to 1981.

Lall (1986) sought to explore the influences of the technological determinants such as on the firm-level export performance in India's chemical industry and engineering industry respectively over the period of 1978-1980 on the 145 firms using the econometric analysis. The study found that product-targeted R&D had an adverse impact on exports related performance whereas process-targeted R&D in chemical industries had positive effect on the exports related performance in the engineering industries.

Das (1987) employed a dynamic framework quadratic cost functions assuming (a) domestic labour as non-inferior input and (b) higher employment of domestic labour by the foreign subsidiary. In analyzing the optimal behaviour of a subsidiary, it was seen that after subsidiary imported better technology from home country such transfer had not benefitted the host country's firms in spite of the know-how, nonetheless such transfer boosted the host country.

Katrak (1990) used multiple regression analysis on the primary data from the period of 1980 to 1984. In the study, it was found that upsurges in the volume of partnership contracts and size of the firm induced just an equi-proportionate growth in the technical efforts resulting in favorably affecting enterprises' technological efforts. This, furthermore, favored the argument that the private advantages of technological imports were apparently more than the social gains in India.

Siddharthan (1992) dealt with the determinants of the in-house R&D of the national concerns to find impact of transfer of technology on R&D expenses during 1985-1998. With 69 firms from the private corporate sector in the analysis, the transaction cost framework employed in the study. The results of the study indicated that the affiliates of MNCs in India put greater in-house R&D endeavors, but then again same was not observed in the third world, other things remaining constant.

Dua and Rashid (1998) examined the interdependence between India's economic activity and FDI. The study undertook the post-liberalization period for the period 1992-1998 collected monthly data from the Monthly Review of the CMIE on foreign investment that were approved and foreign investment inflows in actual. Furthermore, innovation accounting causality tests and suggested that actual FDI movements responded to industrial manufacturing but, however, did not cause the industrial output to rise.

Kathuria (2001) concluded that propensity of R&D of the domestic firms was negatively affected by the rise in FDI inflows in seven major Indian industries. It was further added that this negative effect of FDI inflows gradually diminished in the latter years of the post-liberalization period in sub-periods from 1994-1996 and 1999-2001. This study took place with a sample of 10,000 firms and making use of the *Tobit and the Probit model* that analyze explanatory variables affecting the probability of investment in R&D in the medium as well as the high technology firms of the Indian manufacturing sector.

Hasan (2002) found direct and statistically significant contributions of technology imports on the productivity levels of local companies comprising of prominent technological opportunities together with investments. Also, a negligible impact of firms' R&D was found. The study took place using panel data for 286 Indian manufacturing firms during 1976-1977 to 1986-1987. The fixed effects analysis with translog production function (Cobb Douglas) were applied.

Narayanan (2004) used estimation of the growth function, for the period 1980-81 to 1995-96, with two-way fixed effects in order to analyze the growth determinants in India's automobile industry by taking firm-level data for eleven firms. The results showed that variables encapsulating technology paradigm, for instance vertical integration, determined the inter-firm differences of growth patterns in the automobile industry.

Nikaido (2004) in order to arrive at policy implications for small scale industries analyzed the effects of the firm size and agglomeration of the firms on technical efficiency measured with stochastic frontier approach for the year 1987. With the help of the Annual Survey of Industries database, the study indicated at a negative effect of the size of the firm on the technical efficiency, whereas positive effect of agglomeration of the firms on the efficiency was also noticed.

Banga (2005) evaluated the inducement of foreign presence on wages and employment a in organized manufacturing industries. The study was conducted from 1991-92 to 1997-98. Then with dynamic panel data model for 78 industries at three-digit level was calculated in India. In the results, differential impact of FDI (technological and trade) progress on the dependent variable was found.

Siggel and Agrawal (2009) reported the findings of a survey from 1987-88 to 1997-98 in the case of various manufacturing enterprises in the Delhi region.

The study tried to prove a point regarding the advantageous effect of economic reforms in India in making foreign technology accessible and reducing the cost of production by importing intermediate goods and capital goods.

Zheng (2009) realized that aspects of borrowing cost, market size and exports were critical to China's FDI whereas factors such as cultural distance and geographical location were significant in India's FDI in a comprehensive analysis conducted by employing panel data sets from both the nations as of 1990 to 2004. The observed outcome showed that in case of both the countries policy liberalization, political risk, low cost of labor, cheaper imports and market growth were also important as determinants.

Ranjan and Agrawal (2011) concluded that labour force and gross capital formation were not the critical determinants of FDI inflows in BRICS economy whereas growth prospects, macroeconomic stability, size of the market, openness, infrastructure and cost of labor were significant determinants of the same from 1975 to 2009. The study used random effects model on panel data.

Dash and Parida (2012) studied the association between FDI inflows, production, trade, and services with quarterly data from 1996 to 2011 at sectoral levels using co-integration approach. The presence of a bidirectional causal relationship between FDI and economic production was found in the data. Similarly, direct relation between service exports and economic output was established. The complementarity of the relationship between services export and FDI was proven by a feedback interaction between them.

Rath and Bal (2014) examined the dynamic relationship with Zivot and Andrews test between direct investment (private and public) for the period 1978-79 to 2009 in India. The structural breakpoints in the data were to be understood. The Vector auto-regression (VAR) was employed to evaluate results from the structural model indicating that FDI crowded in the shocks along with this, the evidence suggested that cyclic shocks positively improved the FDI inflows.

## Studies on Linkages and Spillover Effects with respect to Determinants of Productivity in India

Sinha (1993) made an attempt to establish the between a variety of arrangements of the technical efficiency and foreign presence at 164 large manufacturing groups in India. It was observed that technical efficiency had a significant and positive relationship with one industry group, together with, an insignificant and negative linkage with exports in three groups, respectively. Furthermore, a direct and sizeable influence of foreign hold of equity on the dependent variable in 1987-1988 was found. By using stochastic frontier approach the concurrence of the output level in the direction of specified array of input measures was determined.

Tybout (2000) presented the literature review of the studies employing the stochastic frontiers from 1987 to 1985 and found that the manufacturing sectors India and that of other less developed countries (LDCs) had been relatively protected traditionally, while being subjected to a hefty regulation, and therefore, performed poorly. As a result of this, cross-firm productivity dispersion remained high, oligopolists exploited monopoly power, and scale economies went unexploited.

Kathuria (2000) made use of the stochastic frontier approach for 368 large firms and medium firms in the manufacturing industry during 1975 to 1976 and 1988 to 1989 in India. In the study it was found that establishments have its place at the scientific sub-groups signified the presence of strong R&D capabilities, whereas, firms belonging to the non-scientific group faced a greater degree of competition effect due to the foreign presence.

Aggarwal (2002) tested large data set of *Tobit* estimates in the manufacturing sector in India for fag end period of 1990s. The study provided results that in high-tech industries, MNE affiliates performed no better than their local counterparts making efficient labor (or manpower) and R&D as critical determinants of competitiveness in high and medium-high technology-based sectors, at the foreign front, with large firms being export-oriented due to imports of raw materials.

Kathuria (2002) observed the results of 487 firms belonging to 24 manufacturing industries in India over 1989-90 to 1996-97, employing the SFA regression-based method with fixed effect model and found that only the non-FDI scientific firms experienced a positive impact of the liberalization but spending more on in-house R&D activities was prime condition for inducing greater spillover effects in the domestic firms whereas in non-scientific subgroup the productive efficiency growth of the local firms was positively affected by the foreign presence itself.

Driffied and Kambhampati (2003) analyzed the effects of the new economic reforms of 1991 in India on the efficiency of firms in the manufacturing sector. With panel data covering 1800 medium and large native concerns for the period 1987-1994, this study applied Stochastic Frontier Approach (SFA) regression-based method. With this study, it was concluded that enterprises imbibing an eminent market share as well as advanced R& D activity were tending to be efficient, more than others. In addition, overall surge in effectiveness in five sectors of the manufacturing industry was also seen.

Unel (2003) found that in the manufacturing sector during the 1980s, the TFP and labour productivity levels were marked better than that of the preceding decades in the liberalization trend analysis. Their growth rate further picked up after 1991 reforms. The study has been using the data from the CSO's Annual Survey of Industries for the period of 1979-1980 to 1997-1998.

Banga (2004) studied the U.S. and Japanese economies in search of their spillover effects in India on the basis of TFP growth. This study showed contribution towards the literature using a balanced panel estimates and a *Cobb-Douglas* function-based regression for 153 firms. The study was conducted for the years of 1993-94 to 1999-2000 across 25 industries at both industry and firm level. The results showed a net positive spillover effect with Japanese FDI spillovers outweighing the insignificant spillovers from the U.S. FDI.

Banga and Goldar (2004) emphasized the role of services as an input in the process of production, as well as the productivity in Indian manufacturing industry. This study was based on panel data estimated on 148 industries for 18 years' time period from 1980-81 to 1997-98. This study was conducted by constructing a Multilateral Total Factor Productivity Index and multiple regression analysis. The analysis brought out a significant favorable effect of the service input on the output growth in the post-liberalization period of the 1990s, by the way of trade reforms in the growth of the services to the Indian manufacturing industry.

Goldar (2004) concluded the study indicating at the positive influence of economic reforms on the productivity level in local undertakings of Indian manufacturing industry. Also, such success, in the post-reform period, was accompanied by a decline in growth rates of total factor productivity. By employing panel data in 17 industries for the period 1981-82 to 1997-1998, this study employed translog production (value-added) function, estimated with the fixed effect model. This study contradicted the earlier conclusions made by Unel (2003) and Tata Services Limited (TSL) (2003) noting an acceleration in TFP post the economic reforms.

Goldar et al. (2004) employed stochastic frontier approach in addition to multiple regression with estimation techniques in line with companies-based panel data in the engineering industries. This study in the post-reform period from 1990-91 to 1999-2000 indicated that, in terms of the efficiency, the domestic firms converged with the foreign enterprises in the Indian engineering sector but foreign firms were experiencing technical efficiency a higher level.

Ray (2004) employed panel data at firm-level of the Capitaline Ole' database during period of 1991-2001 in the Indian manufacturing sector. While working with the Data Envelopment Approach, in the study, it was found that ownership of domestic firms by multinationals enhanced the efficiency of 27 industry groups and the firms belonging to them. The findings indicated that the average efficiency decreased during 1991 to 1996 and never reached 1991 levels.

Siddharthan and Lal (2004) checked the influence the productivity of firms of FDI spillovers in a cross-section data in the post-liberalization years of 1993-2000 in India. This analysis was tested using an unbalanced panel regression estimated through fixed and random effect models. The study found a strong and increasing trend in the presence of the entry and exit of firms, through coefficient of the spillover variable with unclear realization of liberalization process.

Patibandla and Sanyal (2005) estimated results for panel data at firm level from 1989 to 1999 across eleven industries having 1,132 firms of India. In the post-reform period, the direct and indirect productivity effects generated by foreign investment using regression with OLS technique were studies. Albeit, the study showed mixed results, i.e., external presence held an insignificant influence on productivity as well as R&D spending levels of the local firms. Nevertheless, the local firms benefited from foreign investment in their industries.

Pattnayak & Thangavelu (2005) studied the economic reforms (1991) and its effects of on the manufacturing industries in India with the help of *translog cost function* from 1981 to 1998. The data on 121 industries comprised of panel data. It was observed that improvements in TFP took place, after the post-1991 reforms, for most of the industries. During this time period, the study shows the enhancements in economic efficiency as a result of various government initiatives.

Bergman (2006) made a conclusion of non-existing productivity spillover effects in organized sector of the Indian pharmaceutical industry for 43 pharmaceutical firms, at the plant level. By applying the regression method with the OLS technique with White's test for heteroskedasticity, this study produced the negative results in the context of productivity spillover effects. These effects were explained by a technology or productivity difference between domestic and multinational firms in pharmaceutical industry.

Patibandla (2006) employed *Cobb Douglas* production function as well as *Data Envelopment Approach* for the panel data from the period of 1983 to 1984 in Indian manufacturing industries, to investigate the discrepancies in specific characteristics of structural performance all the way through small and large entities. It was found that technical efficiency in manufacturing industry was maximum in medium-sized companies subject to the structural conditions in the manufacturing sector.

Ray (2006) investigated the factors explaining industrial efficiency in India using panel data for 23 industrial groups. This study was made on the data for three years 1991, 1995 and 2001. This study also tried to answer whether there had been a change in these factors since the liberalization of 1991, with the help of production function. The results exhibited a non-negative and substantial relationship between efficiency as well as net exports of raw materials and royalty payments, in 2001 that were insignificant in 1991.

Sasidharan and Ramanathan (2007) with firm-level data for the period of 1994-2002, employed a log-linear augmented Cobb-Douglas specification with independent variables of inputs such as materials, labor and capital, to be regressed on output level among the manufacturing industries to examine both horizontal and vertical spillovers. There was, however, no proof of horizontal spillovers but vertical spill-over effects were found to be negative.

Kathuria (2010) found that domestic firms imbibed more productivity than foreign firms in a large number of industries. This finding was based from 1995 to 2005 and by employing regression with *Cobb-Douglas* production function and White test on a panel data for 1,840 firms. The foreign firms with a substantial size of the technology gap did not indicate at any spillover effects being generated.

Marin and Sasidharan (2010) found a positive effect of competence creating subsidiaries on the host economy. The negative impact of competence exploiting subsidiaries was indicated, independently of the absorptive capability of local firms. This study was done by regression estimation of a log-linear transformation in a *Cobb-Douglas* setting following ta semi-parametric approach on panel dataset between 1994 and 2002 for 2,696 firms.

Pant and Mondal (2010) looked into the factors and policies that determined the transfer of indirect benefits via spillover effects in domestic firms with respect to productivity in five Indian manufacturing industries assuming a *Cobb-Douglas* function. This study took place with the help of regression on a sample consisting of 1,168 firms covering three years of 2000-01 to 2006-07. The conclusion of the study indicated that by abandoning the policies of the 1980s that fostered purchasing of foreign technology, pushing for foreign presence as well as institutional factors in the 1990s, was a better choice for the transfer of technology.

Mishra (2011) put forward the research question of the direct impact of firm as well as indirect effects of FDI in India, concerning the 22 sectors of the manufacturing industries in India from 2006-2010. Applying Levinsohn-Petrin (2003) approach to estimate productivity on a panel-based data robust model, an insignificant, marginal and inverse impact of foreign investment inflow on productivity level from forward linkages as well as backward linkages was found.

S.N. (2011) examined the efficiency levels in order to design supporting in the informal manufacturing sector on the basis of the whole sector and five broad industry-wise groups in Kerala, using the translog production function for period of 2000-2001 with a sample of 6797 firms. The firm-level study found that seasonality of operation, region (location), ownership, and size had a significant influence on the level of technical efficiency.

Saxena (2011) concluded that Indian manufacturing firms had been heavily influenced by knowledge and technology spillovers in post-liberalization period from 1994 to 2006 following India's economic reforms (1990s). Furthermore, while using the fixed effects estimator, results indicated that the labor-intensive industries gained from this spillover when compared to capital intensive industries. The study employed the generalized moment's method estimates for unbalanced panel data with 42,794 observations.

Behera (2012a) analyzed the spillover effects of FDI across balanced panel data of 16 manufacturing industries in Indian manufacturing industries with 2,379 firms. The multiple regression equations with random effects model had been employed. The results showed that in industries such as non-metallic mineral products, chemicals, drugs and pharmaceuticals, food products and textiles, a positive relationship between technical efficiency and trade orientation existed.

Mandal & Madheswaran (2012) applied stochastic frontier approach for the period of 1989-1990 to 2006-2007 and showed that cement industry had experienced productivity growth in India, not on the basis of technical efficiency but time-invariant progress and its scale component. In this context, it was observed that the economic policy reform in the early 1980s did result in the phenomenal growth of the sector in study.

Sharma (2012) evaluated performance of Indian pharmaceutical firms as a consequence of R&D activities by means of employing data throughout 1994 to 2006. In the post reform period, with the help of two empirical frameworks, namely growth accounting and production function whereby the results from former suggested a direct and substantial impact of R&D intensity on the dependent variable, whereas, output elasticity to R&D capital fluctuating from 10% to 13% is suggested by the study.

Ghosh and Roy (2013) employed Generalized Method of Moments estimates and Hausman-Taylor estimation techniques on a dynamic panel data with 3,469 firm-level observations, across industries for the period 1991-2010 and revealed that the raw materials imports and capital goods imports, explained growth in exports at firm-level in domestic firms post the period of 2000, whereas the presence of foreign ownership did not affect the export performance any significantly different than domestic firms across industries in Indian manufacturing sector.

Jadhav and Reddy (2013) investigated spillover effects in India's capital goods industry sector in India to evaluate the contribution of FDI to 286 Indian manufacturing firms from 1976 to 1977 and 1986 to 1987 with multiple fixed effects regression while assuming the Translog production function. The results witnessed no major gap between the *average turnover ratio* of domestic and foreign firms whereas *rate of capital employed* of foreign businesses was considerably greater than domestic enterprises.

Petkova (2013) employed a consistent TFP index with LP (2003) methodology and studied growth in productivity and performance of firms in Indian manufacturing sector, by compartmentalizing effects of foreign investment into FDI and FII. This conditioned taking a panel data set over 1988-2008 of 23,000 firms and by. It was concluded that relaxation of credit constraints was caused by foreign firms and technology transfer never resulted from the same, under favorable corporate governance.

Behera (2014) examined productivity spillovers of the local firms with the foreign presence. The study was conducted in a cross-industry data for manufacturing industry in India with a panel dataset for 2,379 firms. The time of the study was for a period of 2001 to 2010 and the analysis was done using Cobb-Douglas production technology function-based regression analysis along with GMM estimates. It was seen the R&D intensity and the technological imports intensity were the key drivers responsible for the positive horizontal spillovers. This study, therefore, emphasized the trade liberalizing policies to harness the benefits of the FDI through spillovers.

Mitra et al. (2014) examined manufacturing firms' productivity and efficiency in the purview of liberalization of 1990s over the period 1994-2008 in India. The research was done in terms of level improvement due to imports (capital goods, intermediate goods, and total goods) and exports as a result of technology transfer, infrastructure endowment R&D and trade liberalization. In findings of the study infrastructure was portrayed as a significant determinant of performance in manufacturing sector.

Mondal and Pant (2014) investigated the effects of the presence of the foreign firms instead of purchasing foreign technology in electrical goods, power and fuel, industrial machinery, transport equipment and chemical industries of the Indian manufacturing industries. The balanced panel dataset comprised of 1,168 firms covering the years from 2000-01 to 2006-07. The results from regression estimation using OLS production function with Olley and Pakes (1996) estimator and fixed-effect models saw demonstration effects of foreign presence and absorptive capacity at the firm were more likely to lead to higher competitiveness of the domestic firms.

Sahu and Solarin (2014) estimated the efficiency and productivity levels of foreign and domestic firms with the help of stochastic frontier approach and a direct relation of an increase in foreign equity at firm and sectoral level and improved productivity level was observed for 616 firms from the period 1999-00 to 2009-10. This finding was followed by fixed effects model following the Cobb-Douglas production function-based regression and indicating towards presence of positive horizontal spillover due to superiority of the foreign firms.

## Studies on Linkages and Spillover Effects with respect to Determinants of Export Performance in India

Basant and Fikkert (1993) undertook the microlevel panel data for the period of 1974-75 to 1982-83 in the Indian manufacturing firms and revealed the substitutability, flanked by the local and overseas enterprises, with respect to R&D spending and technology purchases, which, after controlling international and domestic R&D spillovers resulted in increased productivity level, as well as the social benefits surpassing the private benefits for domestic firms.

Kumar and Siddharthan (1993) addressed the export behavior based on the inter-firm variation in 13 Indian manufacturing industries. The study estimated the results using the Tobit model. Also, the study utilized the panel data from 1987-88 to 1989-2000. The findings suggested that a) higher level of technology was a main component in clarifying the export behavior of establishments and b) a U-shaped relationship between export behavior and firms' size existed.

Bhavani and Tendulkar (2001) found variables affecting (a) the export decision function, and (b) the function for export performance Garment and Apparels making entities in Delhi by exploiting Tobit *and Probit* model, that were implemented as the research techniques to find the estimated increase in the minimal influence of variables, such as scale sales share in expenses on the likelihood of selling abroad for the period of 1987-1988.

Joseph and Reddy (2009) examined the export performance of companies in the Indian manufacturing industry in relation to horizontal and backward spillovers, covering the years 1993-2008 with 1,466, firm-level panel database. It was concluded from the study that domestic Indian firms through their export performance did not benefit from buyer-supplier relations forming the backward linkages with MNEs as well as the horizontal spillovers due to increased competition and crowding-out effects by putting regression with OLS estimation into use.

Franco and Sasidharan (2010) in the period 1994-2006 tested the effectiveness of different channels as well as the role played by the technological efforts of local firms on more than 7000 firms using the econometric based regression model. The study suggested that in-house R&D was critical than the supply of technical know-how from the outside to internalize the positive spillover effect from multinationals. It was found the export spillovers were mainly caused by competition effect in India, as opposed to China, where a demonstration effect was prevalent.

Sharma and Mishra (2011) revealed that moving into the external trade market did not enhance the efficiency level but exiting, export market, adversely affected the same in India. Such conclusion was reached by questioning the hypothesis of self-selection and learning-by-exporting and uncovering an interdependence amongst productivity performance and exporting of manufacturing firms during 1994 to 2006, with the help of causality analysis.

Kuntluru et al. (2012) revealed an adverse effect of international presence on the performance of exports of domestic enterprises. In the case of India's pharmaceutical industry, the regression equation with the fixed effects (within) model was calculated to study the effect of direct foreign investments on the performance of exports employing panel data from 103 pharmaceutical firms in India from 1997-98 to 2004-05.

Keshari (2013) analysed the determinants of export performance for 55 large industries by employing two linear regression equations estimated by Ordinary Least Squares (OLS) method on exports as a proportion of its sales during 3 years period from 1981-1982 to 1983-1984. The Indian machinery industry and its skilled workforce (employed in production engineering, export marketing, and product innovation/adaptation), greatly contributed to increased exports growth.

Siddharthan and Nollen (2014) claimed that MNE affiliate exports were higher due to larger foreign equity participation from 1974-1975 to 1982-1983, which allowed for more tacit knowledge transfers while complementing FDI benefits. Although for licensees and domestic enterprises, intensity of capital and size of the firm intensity had the most bearing. The study took balanced panel data for 7,000 concerns in the information technology sector. The pooled Tobit regression and fixed effects model of estimation was used for analysis part of the study.

## Studies on Linkages and Spillover Effects with respect to Determinants of Innovation in India

Kathuria (2000) demonstrated that, in 1994-1996 and 1999-2001, domestic firms did not gain, in terms of output, through the presence of multinationals. Nonetheless, such firms made capital stock advances. The study was evaluated on panel data from 26 industries in India using a stochastic production frontier. The spillover effects in the presence of foreign firms was also observed in scientific industries that invested in R&D activities, implying complementarity between the two.

Parameswaran (2009) calculated a micro-level unbalanced panel of 2,100 Indian firms from 1988-1989 to 2000-2001 to study the impact of trade facilitating R&D spillovers and its inter-sectoral variation to evaluate the domestic investment's crucial role in plant and machinery, technology imports and R&D in augmenting manufacturing industry's productivity. The semi-parametric Levinsohn-Petrin (2003) with GMM estimators was employed for estimation. The findings suggested the existence of trade-related R&D spillovers along with the positive effects of R&D spillovers on productivity.

Madsen et al. (2010) examined whether endogenous growth theories (second-generation second-generation) are in line with India's economic performance. The study employed the cointegration approach for firm-level data from 1993 to 2005. The post-reform growth boom was observed to be influenced by economic reforms, that began in the 1980s and gained traction after 1990, as well as indications of large R&D spillovers in India.

Sasidharan and Kathuria (2011) investigated the relationship between R&D and FDI in the post-liberalization era using regression based technique on unbalanced panel data for 1,843 domestic firms in India's manufacturing sector from 1994 to 2005 to determine whether the entry of foreign firms allowed domestic firms to compete with them. The findings revealed that FDI and R&D were complementary in nature. Also, FDI inflows encouraged to invest in R&D in high-tech industries.

Behera (2012b) investigated the presence of the technology spillover effect of FDI in manufacturing industries using an Innovation production function and Generalized Methods of Moments (GMM) estimates with panel data across rural and city area clusters located firms in India. The results were mixed, with some clusters benefiting from cluster-specific FDI as a whole as well and also the region-specific technology stock varying over a period from 2000 to 2007.

Ambrammal and Sharma (2014) investigated the innovative activity of Indian enterprises investing in R&D (via patents) from 1995 to 2010 using Heckman's two-step technique. The study used data from high-tech and medium-high-tech enterprises with Hurdle count model to investigate the determining factors of R&D equation. It was discovered that changes in patent policy had a considerable impact on R&D and patenting intensity in the domestic sectors.

Goldar and Sharma (2014) tried to assess the performance indicators by analyzing the impact of FDI in Indian manufacturing firms using *Probit Model* with a difference in difference estimators for unbalanced panel data containing 63 firms during the period of 2000-01 to 2011-12 for the sample of 775 manufacturing industries. It was discovered that there were large positive productivity spillover effects from exports, growth, and profitability from transnational corporations to domestic firms in the initial years of 1990s.

Mrinalini et al. (2014) conducted a quantitative study of sectoral and cluster preferences of multinational businesses investing in India. As pointed out, a significant proportion of investments in R&D was limited to businesses such as IT, pharma/biotechnology, and automobiles; additionally, such FDI inflows did not bring growth, but rather targeted growth-oriented sectors. The quantitative assessment, using regression, of R&D-intensive inflows was done from 2003 to 2009, as R&D began to pick up from 2003 onwards.

## Research Updates on the Study

In this section, the studies after the year 2015 have been emphasized on the account of greater leniency towards the most recent studies that are fundamental in understanding the factors and determinants explaining technological paradigm shifts in the Indian industrial sector. Some of such studies are mentioned as follows: -

Goldar and Ghosh (2015) examined the trends in employment growth and the determining factors of employment generation such as labour market reforms, non-native technology and raw materials brought in from abroad in India's manufacturing sector. It was found that the labour market reforms significantly boosted job creation for the period of study from 1999-20 to 2011-12 Furthermore, it was concluded that relative changes in factor prices and growth in output had a significant impact on the generation of employment in the Indian manufacturing sector.

Malik (2015) scrutinized the case of the manufacturing industry at the firm level in India and employed a semi-parametric model to look into the FDI technology spillover in the form of vertical linkages from 2000-2001 to 2007-2008. The study showed that the productivity improvements were experienced in domestic firms through backward linkages confirming that enterprises incurring high-tech benefit the most from FDI.

Rijesh (2015) used firm-level data from 1995 to 2010 to evaluate the importance of technology imports on productivity, as estimated by Levinsohn and Petrin (2003) approach in India's organised manufacturing sector. As per the findings, both embodied and disembodied kinds of technology import had a positive and statistically significant effect on productivity levels in medium technology-intensive enterprises.

Thakur and Burange (2015) studied the manufacturing sector and obtained productivity spillovers, from FDI, in India from 2000 to 2010. The study consisted of 3,029 firm-level panel data to be estimated with Cobb-Douglas production function-based regression along with fixed effects estimation. As a result, through forward and backward linkages positive spillover effects (especially in industries like cosmetics, chemicals and fertilizers, drugs & pharmaceuticals solely through backward vertical spillovers), but negative effects of human capital affecting TFP in the manufacturing industry were found.

Mohapatra and Gopalaswamy (2016) used 17 years of panel data from 1996 to 2012 to investigate the long-term relation involving domestic investment as well as FDI flows in 32 Emerging Market Economies (EMEs). The unit root approach was designed to monitor the presence of unit root while utilising Fully Modified OLS and Dynamic OLS. The result was that, in addition to FDI inflow, FDI outflow was equally significant for EMEs in augmenting domestic investment.

Khachoo and Sharma (2016) examined input-output tables from 2000 to 2013 for the presence of spillovers and found positive horizontal and backward spillovers. It was also emphasised that the upstream industry benefited more than the downstream sector. The repercussions of direct foreign investment on the domestic enterprises of India's manufacturing sector were assessed positive, with statistically significant impacts of 1% and 5%, respectively, in supplying sectors.

Singh (2016) used the Cobb-Douglas technique to analyse the links between R&D and productivity spillovers for a sample of 42 domestic computer firms and 56 domestic machine tool firms in the Indian manufacturing sector from 2001 to 2012. The findings revealed that firms that invest in technological know-how and engage in ICT are more productive.

Klein (2017) examined the productivity spillovers from inward FDI for respective high technology and low technology firms in the manufacturing industry with the help of unbalanced panel from 2001 to 2016. This study employed the Levinsohn and Petrin (2003) approach for a sample of 9,561 enterprises. Insignificant positive horizontal spillovers were observed for low technology firms, whereas substantial horizontal spillovers were found for high technology firms in India's manufacturing industry.

Pradeep et al. (2017) with *Generalized Method of Moments* (GMM) estimator *applied on Cobb Douglas* production function and the subsequent the random effect mode took balanced panel data from over 1,000 Indian manufacturing firms from 1994 and 2008. The study established positive productivity spillover effects (especially with R&D) due to better FDI environment and low costs of manufacturing. The findings showed that foreign presence had a positive and significant impact on manufacturing sector of exports and varying R&D efforts.

Rawat (2017) estimated TFP of the manufacturing firms and the formulated relationship with other determinants using pooled OLS and fixed-effects model and found that materials were one of the largest contributors to productivity and output growth, and productivity formed an inverse-U shaped relation to firm size and it was also increasing in export intensity. It was concluded that capital intensive firms have seen more TFP growth, but labor-intensive firms that also export incur fast TFP growth in the period 2000-2017

Aggarwal (2018) evaluated the notion of whether the modes of technology acquisition and technology intensities are linked to firm ownership in India with the help of the Prowess database from 2003 to 2014. In conclusion, the results indicated a little justification for the relocation of R&D activities to India due to the global financial crisis in the 2,000 firms based data set.

Mondal and Pant (2018) applied the semi-parametric *Levinsohn and Petrin (2003) approach and subsequent* fixed-effect model on an unbalanced panel dataset on 5,923 domestic firms in the manufacturing sector during 1994 to 2010. This was done to investigate horizontal and vertical linkages induced productivity spillovers as a consequence of direct investments. The focus on a firm's absorptive capacity was also made. It was observed that the Indian firms' productivity growth level was negative with respect to horizontal spillover channels while being insignificant with respect to the vertical linkages.

Sur and Nandy (2018) utilized stochastic frontier approach for the period 2001-2014 and compared the technical efficiency of foreign firms in regard to domestic firms in the automobile industry. In the conclusion, the study on the domestic automobile firms in India, revealed demonstration effects as the main channel for transmission of horizontal spillovers. In the process, the firm-specific variables were emphasized.

Malik (2019) examined balanced panel data of 54 three-digit industries from the ASI database to look into the employment effects of direct foreign investment in manufacturing industries in India, from the year 2008-2016. When type of employees' variable was controlled with the use of a dynamic labour demand model via the GMM estimator, the inadequacy of FDI as a significant avenue for job creation in India's manufacturing sector was revealed.

Therefore, an insignificant impact of FDI on domestic demand for labour in India's manufacturing industries was observed.

Murthy et al. (2019) questioned on distinguishing features between foreign and local firms on the basis of their determinants such as R&D intensity, import intensity and export intensity etc. and their respective spillover effects in the domestic economy. Logistic regression has been used to study panel data on 1,846 firms from 2001-2010. The conclusion, in terms of spillover effects, indicated that unless the explanatory variables were added to the model one by one, the results would demonstrate that foreign enterprises acted differently than local firms.

Padmavathi (2019) adopted the *stochastic frontier analysis* to examine the efficiency with the help of *National Sample Surveys* data in India's unorganized food processing industry. This sector demonstrated a disproportionate increase in the capital accumulation not enhancing the firm level efficiency in terms of higher output levels. Being labour-intensive in nature, yet a lack in the skills of the labour, inaccessibility to credit and presence of only half-time workers contributed to the inefficiency of enterprises in this sector.

Goldar and Banga (2020) checked panel estimates for around 7,338 Indian firms for 15 years from 2000-01 to 2014-2015 in manufacturing industries and applied Levinsohn-Petrin (2003) approach for analysing total factor productivity with regression assuming production function with Cobb-Douglas specifications with fixed effects model. They discovered that while there were positive and significant horizontal spillover effects, there was only a limited backward spillover effect due to FDI in the Indian manufacturing sector.

Pant and Mondal (2020) investigated the impact of FDI induced efficiency spillovers in the organized manufacturing sector in India taking an unbalanced panel of 5,956 domestic firms for 23 manufacturing industries, for 1994-2010 and employing the *SFA* regression-based method, following *Battese and Coelli (1995)* found that there were negative absorption effect of R&D expenses, disembodied technology imports and export activities on efficiency in 1994-2001 while the absorption effect became positive in 2002-10 effects of disembodied technology imports and export activities were insignificant in 2002-10.

Paul and Kumar (2020) created an *import intensity index* using the input-output tables for the Indian organized manufacturing and unorganized manufacturing for the years 2005-2006, extrapolated for 2010-2011 and 2015-2016. As a result of free-trade agreements, both regionally and bilaterally, the gains to the domestic market from global competition were realised in the early 2000s. According to the study, an increase in imported inputs in the export industry had a negative influence on exports, to enhance firms' productivity level.

Rijesh (2020) used a panel analysis based on OLS and random effect regression to inquire into the impact of embodied and disembodied technology imports on manufacturing exports from 1995 to 2016 in India. He discovered that embodied technology-facilitated intermediate and capital goods exports while disembodied technology-aided consumer and capital goods exports. While R&D had a statistically significant impact on Indian export, technology imports showed an insignificant impact.

Kale (2021) employed a macro framework to investigate the innovation effort on the part of the Indian economy with R&D expenditure with ARDL regression analysis. The possibility of innovation was considered with the help of three variables namely, patent, industrial design and trademark from 1981 to 2017. The findings of the study suggested a significant impact of remittances and human capital on innovation. Along with it, an insignificant impact of openness, with a small impact on FDI was also witnessed.

## Research Gap in the Literature Survey

The following points summarise the research gap in the existing literature: -

- The existing literature on FDI with respect to linkages and its spillover effects vary, showing mixed results.
- Most of the available studies conducted are found in the context of foreign countries.
- Of those studies available in the foreign countries, mostly are conducted pertaining to particular FDI projects and the results cannot be easily generalized.
- Most studies reckoned the cross-sectional characteristics, which, due to the presence of endogeneity, posed the challenge in establishing the direction of causality among the variables.
- There are also foreign studies navigated for spillovers at the firm-level with panel data but failed to explain 'how' in the question.
- There are very few studies conducted in India in the automobile industry as most of the studies pertain to much broader manufacturing sector and the tertiary sector.

The studies in the Indian context were surveyed for FDI effects, in the instance of influencing performance and productivity in the Indian firms and industries. The number of studies in analysing the effect of FDI taking place in domestic economy, though, are relatively sparse in India as compared to other developing nations. However, the studies in the Indian context, in the literature surveyed suggest the methodology of narrowing down FDI effects on the basis of factors and determinants, resulting in estimates that are available in the quantifiable values to allow for the empirical analysis.

## Major Estimation Approach in the Literature Survey

On the basis of the literature surveyed, every firm in the studies happens to have private knowledge of its level of productivity, which indeed affects its decision to leave or stay in the industry, its choice of inputs, and reinvestments etc. Olley and Pakes (1996) provided an algorithm for estimating the production function parameters which takes into account the self-selection bias induced by liquidation (known as exit time of the firm) and the simultaneity bias introduced by the endogeneity of the input demands (or decisions) by developing a semiparametric estimator for the production function parameters for the U.S. telecommunications equipment industry. This estimator seemed to be consistent with a quite general version of the theoretical framework as per Olley and Pakes (1996) and rely on the assumption that "there is only one unobserved state variable that causes the difference in the firm's productivity level." (p.1265.). Olley and Pakes (1996) also demonstrated how a proxy for investment can regulate the association among the unobserved productivity shock and the level of inputs used.

By modifying Olley and Pakes (1996) method, Levinsohn and Petrin (2003) showed that intermediate inputs are essentially the inputs that are subtracted from the gross output to reach a value-added production function. This process also has an ability to solve the simultaneity problem along with advantages of expanding the choice set to include the proxy's inputs. The L-P approach has an advantage that, these are no more difficult to implement than OLS. The semi-parametric model of Olley and Pakes (1996) has been contemporarily employed for estimation of the technical efficiency in Javorcik (2004), Aggarwal and Milner (2010), Javorcik (2011), Irsova and Havaranak (2013), Petkova (2013).

On the other hand, latest studies such as Parameswaran (2009), Mishra (2011) Mondal and Pant (2014), Malik (2015), Rijesh (2015), Klein (2017), Mondal and Pant (2018), and Goldar and Banga (2020) have made use of the same in the Indian context. However, with respect to the simple yet efficient estimates, the Levinsohn and Petrin (2003) technique allows for incorporation of the primary as well as intermediate inputs in finding the productivity level of an industry. This technique of finding the productivity level has been considered in this study to account for the simultaneity bias also.

# Chapter 4
# Research Methodology

## Statement of the Research Problem

This research study is descriptive as well as empirical in nature. In its empirical part, this study focuses on the performance linkages and productivity linkages of FDI inflows with the help of the output and the TFP, respectively, in the Indian automobile industry. The research topic was chosen to furnish the possibility of obtaining results that could provide an understanding of the automobile industry as a key sector. Hence, the problem statement of this study is stated as follows: -

'To study the trends and patterns of FDI, ascertaining the strength of sector-wise linkages, and investigating for the performance and productivity levels with respect to various sources at the firm-level as a result of foreign presence in the Indian automobile industry.'

## Objectives of the Study

This study aims to investigate the foreign presence, in the form of Foreign Direct Investment (FDI) and its impact on domestic firms in the Indian automobile sector. This study employs the panel data techniques by incorporating the effect of explanatory variables in an empirical model. In line with the statement of the problem, this study has identified various objectives that are stated as follows: -

*Objective 1. To study the trends and patterns of FDI in India during the selected period from 2000 to 2020.*

*Objective 2. To study the industry-wise backward linkages and forward linkages in the automobile industry in India from 2011 to 2020.*

*Objective 3. To examine the performance linkages of the selected firms in the presence of foreign-invested firms in the automobile industry from 2011 to 2020.*

*Objective 4. To examine the productivity linkages of the selected firms in the presence of foreign-invested firms in the automobile industry from 2011 to 2020.*

## Summary of the Variables

In the review of the literature, the entire manufacturing sector in India has been investigated in search of the linkages and its spillovers by Goldar and Banga (2020), Sur and Nandy (2018), Murthy et al.(2019), Mondal and Pant (2014, 2018), Klein (2017), Thakur and Burange (2015), Sahu and Solarin (2014), Sahu and Solarin (2014), Behera et al. (2012a, 2012b), Petkova (2013), Malik (2011), Mishra (2011), Marin and Sasidharan (2010), Pant and Mondal (2010), Bhattacharya et al. (2008), Sasidharan and Ramanathan (2007), Bergman (2006), Patibandla and Sanyal (2005), Banga (2004), Goldar et al. (2004), Pradeep et al.(2004), Ray (2004,2006), Siddharthan and Lal (2004), and Kathuria (2001, 2002 and 2010).

Nonetheless, limited research has been carried out in the automobile industry in India. This may be due to the limitation in variables and the number of sample firms available for the purpose. For instance, due to the limitation in the availability of sufficient data, export performance and innovation variables cannot be cosidered as the dependent variable, for the purpose of investigation of the effects incurred due to foreign presence. However, most studies, in the recent literature, have favoured these as the independent variables in presence of foreign firms. The variables used in this study are described in detail below as follows: -

### *Capital (K)*

Capital is one of the main inputs in the calculation of the productivity level and forms a huge part of the in-house research and development activities. The foreign-invested firms might boost the domestic firm in the host countries that are capital abundant nations to indulge in the capital-intensive industries due to a cheaper (relative) price of capital, namely rent. Not only that, the capital-intensive goods are used, further, as the intermediate product to create the final product. For instance, automobile engine is used in the process of assembly. On the other hand, host countries that are labour abundant might be capital deficient. Owing to the relatively expensive capital stock, industries in such countries are unable to realise the benefits of the latest cutting-edge technology. Petkova (2013), Mondal and Pant (2014), Malik (2015), Pradeep et al. (2017), Joseph and Reddy (2009), Parameswaran (2009), Behera et al. (2012b), Rijesh (2015) and recently, Goldar and Banga (2020), and Pant and Mondal (2020) harnessed perpetual inventory method for calculating the capital stock

### *Labour (L)*

India is a labour abundant country that produces mainly labour-intensive goods. An increase in labour in a firm or an industry leads to a decline in its capital-labour ratio. The labour variable also acts as the major input in the productivity analysis. In general, Hasan (2002), Banga (2004), Goldar et al. (2004), Parameswaran (2009), Joseph and Reddy (2009), Jadhav and Reddy (2013), Keshari (2013), Mondal and Pant (2014), Malik (2015), and Rijesh (2015), along with the average wage rate, have used wages and salaries paid by a firm as a proxy for labour in scouting for factors such as competitiveness, productivity, and efficiency etc.

### *Raw Materials (M)*

Raw materials act as the intermediate variable, as well as, the control variable in finding the productivity level. This has mainly been the case in the studies such as Hasan (2002), Driffield and Kambhampati (2003), Banga (2004), Banga and Goldar (2004), Ray (2006), Marin and Sasidharan (2007), Parameswaran (2007), Keshari (2013), Petkova (2013), Kuntluru et al. (2012) and Klein (2017) etc. In the process of manufacturing, raw materials are used for transformation into final product. The recent studies that included raw material expenses as the explanatory variable comprise mainly Ghosh and Roy (2013), Pant and Mondal (2020) and Goldar and Banga (2020).

### *Energy (E)*

Energy was used as an intermediate input in Banga (2004), who defined energy input simply as an expenditure on power and fuel. Energy expenditure contributes to an increase in a firm's or industry's production activity. Ray (2004, 2006) calculated fuel intensity as a cost-to-sales-turnover ratio. Rijesh (2015), then again, included the value of raw materials, power, and fuel use in raw material expenses. Goldar (2004) defined it as the value of intermediate inputs constructed by adding materials, power and fuel, and other intermediate inputs while calculating productivity, whereas, Goldar and Banga (2020) computed the nominal energy input for a firm as the sum of its expenses on power and fuel.

### *Export Intensity (XI)*

In general, export activity promotes engagement with foreign buyers and international markets, along with learning from them, which enhances the firm's scale and productivity in the domestic country. There are studies such as Kathuria (2000,2001,2002), Banga 2004, Banga and Goldar (2004), Goldar et al. (2004), Ray (2004), Patibandla and Sanyal (2005), Sharma and Mishra (2011), Ghosh and Roy (2013), Pradeep et al. (2017), Seenaiah and Rath (2018), and Goldar and Banga (2020) that support the existence of performance linkages and productivity linkages by taking export intensity as one of the explanatory variables in their respective study. As per Pant and Mondal (2020), increases in the export intensity of a firm exposes it to advanced technology available abroad, in turn, boosting the productivity of domestic firms.

### *Import Intensity (MI)*

According to Driffield and Kambhampati (2003), import intensity influences efficiency because firms can import capital goods and the latest technology. The studies in the Indian context, especially, Banga (2004), Ray (2004), Banga and Goldar (2004), Sasidharan and Kathuria (2011), Ghosh and Roy (2013), Seenaiah and Rath (2018), Murthy et al. (2019), Goldar and Banga (2020) and Pant and Mondal (2020) analysed the effect of import intensity as the explanatory variables on the TFP.

### *Research and Development Intensity (RDI)*

In studies pertaining to the Indian context, it has been well established that R&D intensity is a key determinant of firm performance, as well as, productivity improvement. Behera (2014) saw R&D investment as a crucial variable that evaluates the systematic efforts of firms to build their knowledge base and use that stock of knowledge to develop new applications. R&D efforts also augment as well as enhance the firm's absorptive capacity to new technologies, improve product quality, and reduce costs. According to Sasidharan and Kathuria (2011), foreign equity participation in high-tech businesses encourages them to engage in R&D.

### *Age of the firm (Age)*

Age is among the major firm-specific variables that try to project the learning effect of the firm, based on the year of its establishment. Petkova (2013) put into use, the age of the firm while constructing the TFP index. The majority of the studies regarded the firm's age to act as a proxy for accumulated knowledge and skill in production and marketing. The very recent study by Sur and Nandy (2018) has focused on the firm's age to find the technical efficiency in the Indian automobile industry. Nonetheless, a negative relationship between age and technical efficiencies of domestic firms was found. Kathuria (2000, 2001, and 2002) also recommended introducing control variables such as age to limit the likelihood of bias caused by omitted variables.

### *Size of the firm (Size)*

According to Ghosh and Roy (2018), larger enterprises are seen to possess a superior risk perception of foreign markets and a larger resource base. In addition, Kathuria (2009), Joseph and Reddy (2009), Jadhav and Reddy (2013), Keshari (2013), Goldar and Sharma (2015), Klein (2017), and Seenaiah and Rath (2018) have studied this firm-specific variable. These studies make us understand that the size of the film depicts the scale of operation of firms. Because the Indian automobile industry operates on such a large scale in the manufacturing sector, the size of the firm in the automobile industry must play a significant role in influencing the foreign and domestic share of output, implying a critical effect on firms' performance and productivity level. For example, Bergman (2006) discovered that the size variable had a positive as well as a substantial impact on the productivity levels of local enterprises in the pharmaceutical sector in India.

### *Capital Intensity (KI)*

The capital intensity variable is checked in the studies of Banga (2004), Goldar (2004), and Behera et al. (2012a, 2012b) to measure its effects on performance and productivity. High capital intensity indicates that the amount of physical capital available per worker in the production process is also high. With higher levels of physical capital, the labour-intensive technique becomes more efficient in utilizing the benefits of new technology introduced in the host economies as a result of the foreign presence. The automobile industry by design must be incorporating a higher capital intensity.

### *Herfindahl-Hirschman Index (HHI)*

HHI is a measure of market concentration. HHI was utilised by Kathuria (2000), Sasidharan and Kathuria (2011), Behera (2012b), and Ambrammal and Sharma (2014) to capture market structure. Klein (2017), like Javorcik (2004), adopted the HHI index to measure industrial concentration. Furthermore, Banga (2004) investigated the effect of foreign market share on the TFP growth of domestic concerns. Nonetheless, with HHI, a more concentrated industry may imply a reduced competition effect, lowering the productivity of firms in the industry.

### *Horizontal FDI*

Most recent studies, such as Seenaiah and Rath (2018), Murthy et al. (2019), Goldar and Banga (2020), and Pant and Mondal (2020), have included Horizontal FDI in the study to measure the foreign share of overall output in the industry. It is, therefore, a constructed variable, describing the foreign presence at the firm in the same industry. This variable signifies intra-industry linkages or the with-in firm analysis in a given industry, thus, assisting in examining competition and demonstration effects of FDI.

## Construction of the Variables in the Study

Some of the key variables collected in this study are sales, salaries and wages, gross fixed capital, power and fuel expenses, raw material expenses, export of goods, total spending, total assets etc. for the overall automobile and ancillaries' industry. These are retrieved from CMIE's Prowess database at NIC (2008) classification. The construction of several important variables in this study are as follows: -

### *Output: Sales*

The dependent variable of output is taken as the logarithm of the deflated sales plus the change in stocks variable. The data field of Sales corresponds to the main income of non-financial companies in the CMIE's Prowess IQ data directory. The gross output of a firm is actually the sales with a change in the stock of finished and semi-finished goods. The sales variable was deflated using three-digit industry-level price deflators, constructed from the Wholesale Price Index (WPI) (2011-12=100) series obtained from the Office of the Economic Advisor, Ministry of Commerce and Industry.

### *Total Factor Productivity (TFP)*

With the respect of TFP, estimates from Levinsohn and Petrin (2003) approach are used. This method employs the following production function: -

$$y_{it} = \beta_0 + \beta_l l_{it} + \beta_k k_{it} + \beta_m m_{it} + e_{it} \text{ or,}$$

$$y_{it} = \beta_0 + \beta_l l_{it} + \beta_k k_{it} + \beta_m m_{it} + u_t + v_{it}$$

where, $y_{it}$ is the logarithm of the firm's output, which is commonly expressed as gross revenue, $l_{it}$ and $m_{it}$ are the logarithm values of the freely variable labour and intermediate inputs, and $k_{it}$ is the logarithm of the state variable capital. For specificity, two freely variable inputs, labour and materials (raw), are employed. The proxy variable of energy is also used. The error term $e_{it}$ has two components, one of which is the transmitted productivity component given as $u_t$ and an error term that is independent to input choices $v_{it}$. The key difference between $u_t$ and $v_{it}$ is that the former is a state variable and influences the firm's decision rules, while the latter is not observed by the econometrician and can influence input choices, predisposing to the well-known simultaneity problem in the calculation of TFP. Inconsistent results will be produced by OLS estimators that ignore the correlation between inputs and these unobservable components. The following are the inputs utilised in the computation of TFP: -

### *Capital: Gross Fixed Assets*

The Perpetual Inventory Method has been utilized to estimate capital stock in studies such as Basant and Fikkert (1993), Parameswaran (2009), Petkova (2017), Malik (2015) Rijesh 2015, Mondal and Pant (2018) Goldar and Banga (2020). In this method, capital stock in the subsequent year is calculated by adding the total number of investments () in year *t* to the capital stock at replacement cost ($K_t$)

$$K_{t+1} = K_t + I_{t+1}$$

$$K_t = K_{t-1} + I_{t-1}$$

$$K_{t-2} = K_t - I_t - I_{t-1}$$

and so on.

Gross Fixed Assets (from the Prowess IQ database) are catalogued at the historical cost of all fixed assets in a company's possession and control on the last day of an accounting period and are converted into gross fixed assets valued at replacement cost at the most recent base year 2011-12 (with the largest number of observations) on the basis of a revaluation factor from the values of price of the capital (p) and growth rate of investment (g). In other words, the revaluation factor is applied to convert capital in the base year to capital at replacement cost (at current prices).

$$\text{Revaluation Factor} = \frac{(1+g)(1+p)-1}{g(1+p)}$$

In Parameswaran (2009), the price (p) of the capital is assumed to be changing at a constant rate $(p = \frac{P_t}{P_{t-1}} - 1)$,, where, $P_t$ measures the price of the capital stock, prepared with the help of data on the Gross Fixed Capital Formation from source of National Accounts Statistics and the growth rate of investment (g) at 1992-93 prices is assumed to be the same for all the firms $(g = \frac{I_t}{I_{t-1}} - 1)$. With $I_t$ as the real investment at time t, and is calculated as the difference between the gross fixed assets (GFA) in two consecutive years, i.e.,

$$I_t = GFA_t - GFA_{t-1}.$$

Gross Fixed Asset $_t$ at historic cost equals to the formula as follows: -

$$P_t I_t = \left(\frac{(1+g)(1+p)}{(1+g)(1+p)-1}\right)$$

, and at replacement cost equals to the formula as follows: -

$$P_t I_t = \left(\frac{(1+g)}{(g)}\right)$$

Following the literature surveyed, the lifespan of the plant and machinery is assumed at 20 years. This ensures that no enterprise has capital stock in 2011-12 that is older than 1992-93. As a result, in firms formed after 1992, the earliest vintage capital underlying their capital mix is dated back to the year of establishment. This study uses WPI for Machinery and Equipment to deflate the capital stock variable at replacement cost at the constant price (2011-12=100).

### *Labour: Salaries and Wages*

The Prowess IQ makes available data on salary and wage for a company, but the number of employees. The number of employees is calculated by dividing salaries and wages by the average wage rate of the industry to which the firm belongs for the given year. The same can be presented as follows: -

Number of Employees in a $\text{firm}_t$ = (Salaries and $\text{wages})_t$)/(Average wage $\text{rate})_t$

where, Average Wage $\text{Rate}_t$ = Total $\text{Emoluments}_t$/Total Persons $\text{Engaged}_t$

The average wage rate is calculated by dividing Total Emoluments by Total Persons Engaged in each firm using data from the Annual Survey of Industries (ASI) on total emoluments and total persons engaged from 2011-2020.

### *Raw Materials Expenses*

The raw material variable is created by deflating the firm's raw material expenditures in CMIE's Prowess IQ database with the RBI's raw material input deflator (2011-12=100). As per CMIE's Prowess IQ data directory, stores and spares consumed are a part of *other expenses* and are not added to raw materials to construct raw materials stores and spares etc. that is deflated using raw material price deflators (2011-12=100).

### *Energy: Power and Fuel Expenses*

According to CMIE's Prowess IQ data directory, power and fuel expenses are the costs of using energy, which include the costs of consuming electricity, petroleum products, coal, and other sources of energy for carrying out a company's activity. The energy variable is calculated by discounting the firm's power and fuel expenditures with the RBI's energy input deflator (2011-12=100).

### *Export of Goods Intensity: Export of Goods (F.O.B.)*

In the Prowess IQ data directory, export of goods refers to any items that are to be transported from India to a location outside of India on a Free on Board (F.O.B.) basis i.e., when an exporter pays all charges involved in getting them actually aboard the ship up to a certain delivery point. In this study, export intensity is defined as the ratio of a firm's goods exports to sales value.

### *Import Intensity: Total Spending*

The import intensity variable is computed as the ratio of final goods imports to sales variables. The import of finished goods is determined at the Cost, Insurance, and Freight (C.I.F.) value of finished goods, which means that the cost of goods imported includes such charges. The Prowess IQ database reports this data field as the value of finished goods imported by the company.

### *R&D intensity: R&D Expenses*

R&D expenses are included in the prowess database as current expenses incurred and reported by the company on research and development (salaries, rent, repairs depreciation etc.). It excludes capital expenditures for research & development. In this study, the variable of R&D intensity is produced by dividing R&D expenses by firm-level sales.

### *Age: Year of Incorporation*

The Prowess database contains the age group of companies at historical periods to which they belong and are assigned the age categories, based on their incorporation year. Ambrammal and Sharma (2015) used company age as a control variable in determining industry productivity. However, in this study, the age of the firm is computed using the logarithm of the difference between the year of incorporation and the year under consideration (i.e., 2020), as suggested by Franco and Sasidharan (2010).

### *Size: Total Assets*

According to the Prowess IQ database directory, the sales variable is the most commonly quoted indicator for size in most references to a company as it reflects an outcome of a company's business and is the least contaminated by valuation complications. Nonetheless, sales are vulnerable to industry-specific business cycles and company-specific events. However, Jadhav and Reddy (2013) pointed out that the valuation of different companies entails different rates of depreciation. Hence, total assets in the firm at the start of the year must be preferred to calculate the size of the firm. Therefore, the logarithm of the total assets is used in this study.

### *Capital Intensity: Gross Fixed Assets*

Following Goldar and Banga (2020) and Rijesh (2020), capital intensity has been calculated by dividing gross fixed assets to sales ratio from Prowess IQ database. The gross fixed assets (in Prowess IQ database) variable is reported at the historical cost.

### *Herfindahl-Hirschman Index (HHI): Sales*

The Herfindahl-Hirschman Index (HHI), explained as the sum of an industry's squared market shares, has been estimated as follows: -

$$\text{HHI}=\sum_{ij}\left(\frac{Sales_i}{\sum Sales_{ij}}\right)$$

where, is the total sale of $i^{th}$ firm in the $j^{th}$ industry ($j$ is the automobile industry).

### *Horizontal FDI: Foreign Presence*

According to Malik (2015) and Klein (2017), the foreign presence within the industry can be studied in the form of the Horizontal FDI variable. Following this, the notation used in the standard literature to construct the variable is as follows: -

$$Horizontal\ FDI_{jt} = \frac{\sum_{i\in j} Y_{it}.\,Foreign\ Share_{it}}{\sum_{i\in j} Y_{it}}$$

where, $i$, $j$, and $t$ denote firm, industry, and year. It measures the foreign firm's share of output in the total output of the industry. In other words, the same can be defined as follows:-

$$Horizontal\ FDI_{jt}=\frac{\sum_{i=1}^{m} Y_{it}^{f}}{\sum_{i=1}^{n} Y_{it}}$$

where $y_t$ is the total output of firm $i$ in year $t$, $y_{it}^{f}$ is the output of the foreign firm $i$ in the same year, $n$ is the number of firms in an industry, consisting of both domestic and foreign firms, and $m$ denotes the number of foreign firms in an industry. In this study, the standard threshold of 10% foreign equity ownership has been taken to denote foreign direct investment in a firm.

## Research Design

This section presents a detailed plan for the execution of the objectives in a systematic way. It also tries to provide the steps and procedures harnessed, in the collection of related data and information for purpose of analysis in this study.

## Type of Research

This study is exploratory as well as empirical in nature. The research is twofold with four objectives. The first objective and the second objective are associated with the exploratory nature of this study. The first objective of this study is elaborated as follows: -

### *Objective 1. To study the trends and patterns of FDI in India during the selected period from 2000 to 2020.*

The Compound Annual Growth Rate (CAGR) is an important tool that is used to measure the cumulative growth rate of an investment over a specified period of time, usually more than one year. The analysis of FDI inflows in India with respect to its trends and patterns for 2000-2020 is calculated by employing CAGR. It would measure the performance of the FDI inflows from one value to another, over a period of time in percentage with the help of the following formula: -

**Compound Annual Growth Rate=(Final Value/Initial Value)$^{1/N}$-1**

To fulfil the first objective of this research study, the value of N will remain at five years. The reason for selecting five years as a period to observe the trends is that, in order to calculate the investment, CAGR must consider the time period from three to seven years for greater accuracy. For reliable results, this study took the average of the same, i.e., five years. Also, if the time period selected for studying the CAGR is more than that of ten years, then, there remains a high possibility of the hidden sub-trends, discouraging the accuracy of the findings. The measure of CAGR is employed to further assess the performance of FDI inflows as per the availability of data (i) by the sectoral distribution, with the financial year-wise data taken from April-March 2005-06 to April-March 2019-20, (ii) by the source country, for which financial year-wise data has been taken from April-March 2005-06 to April-March 2019-20 and finally (iii) by destination in India, for which financial year-wise data has been taken from April-March 2010-11 to April-March 2019-20. All values are expressed in US dollars (million) or as percentage shares of the same, as per the availability of data from various issues of DIPP's Quarterly Factsheet on FDI.

### *Objective 2. To study the industry-wise backward linkages and forward linkages in the automobile industry in India from 2010 to 2020.*

In order to evaluate the second objective of this study, the classical input-output model has been employed in line with the interdependencies of various sectors in India. The total backward linkage and total forward linkage along with their respective normalized values are calculated to show inter-sectoral linkages in the domestic economy. The time period selected for the second objective comprises the latest ten years from 2011 to 2020 in the study. This time frame has aided in working with the recent database for the analyses. To achieve the second objective, the Asian Development Bank Input-Output Database, which is based on the updated Multi-Regional Input-Output Tables (MRIOTs) and World Input-Output Database (WIOD) database, was employed. The Central Statistic Organisation has not issued input-output tables after 2007-08. However, in order to obtain a more detailed picture of the interrelationships between various sectors, particularly the automobile industry, a 35-sector based classification constructed on the United Nation's International Standard Industrial Classification (ISIC) Rev. 3.1, has been used.

All values of the (ISIC) Rev. 3.1 database are expressed in US dollars (in millions). Therefore, sectoral classification comprising thirty-five distinguished industries was important to induce a comprehensive analysis. The ISIC 3.1 classification corresponds to National Industrial Classification (NIC, 1998) and NIC (2004) at a two-digit level. It is to note that NIC (2008) is a revised version of NIC (2004) which is analogous to the ISIC 4 classification. Albeit, the revised NIC (2008) appears to provide a more contemporary industrial classification system, yet, the delegations, mergers, the nomenclature of industries, as well as industrial classifications due to the same, caused complex changes causing unavailability of data, inadvertently. Hence, with the emphasis on the relevance of the objective the ISIC Rev 3.1 in line with NIC (1998) and NIC (2004) (up to two digits) recent time period of 2011-2020 has been selected for the calculations. The list of various industries as per the thirty-five based classification in the Asian Development Bank Input-Output Database is presented in the following Table 4.1: -

**Table 4.1: Indian Industries classification of 35-sectors based on ISIC Rev. 3.1.**

| | |
|---|---|
| D1. | Agriculture, hunting, forestry, and fishing |
| D2. | Mining and quarrying |
| D3. | Food, beverages, and tobacco |
| D4. | Textiles and textile products |
| D5. | Leather, leather products, and footwear |
| D6. | Wood and products of wood and cork |
| D7. | Pulp, paper, paper products, printing, and publishing |
| D8. | Coke, refined petroleum, and nuclear fuel |
| D9. | Chemicals and chemical products |

| | |
|---|---|
| D10. | Rubber and plastics |
| D11. | Other non-metallic minerals |
| D12. | Basic metals and fabricated metal |
| D13. | Machinery |
| D14. | Electrical and optical equipment |
| D15. | Transport equipment |
| D16. | Manufacturing, recycling |
| D17. | Electricity, gas, and water supply |
| D18. | Construction |
| D19. | Sale, maintenance, and repair of motor vehicles and motorcycles, retail sale of fuel |
| D20. | Wholesale trade and commission trade, except of motor vehicles and motorcycles |
| D21. | Retail trade, except of motor vehicles and motorcycles, repair of household goods |
| D22. | Hotels and restaurants |
| D23. | Inland transport |
| D24. | Water transport |
| D25. | Air transport |
| D26. | Other supporting and auxiliary transport activities, activities of travel agencies |
| D27. | Post and telecommunications |
| D28. | Financial intermediation |
| D29. | Real estate activities |
| D30. | Renting of M & Eq and other business activities |
| D31. | Public administration and defence, compulsory social security |
| D32. | Education |
| D33. | Health and social work |
| D34. | Other community, social, and personal services |
| D35. | Private households with employed persons |

*Source: ADB Database.*

In order to find the inter-industry linkages among the industries in the Indian economy, Table 4.2 throws light on the simple input-output table format used to determine the same. The sectors in the left-most column in Table 4.2 are the sectors engaged in the supplying and distribution of the goods and services in the production process, while the sectors shown across the top row (from D1. to D35.) are the buyers of such the goods and services in the production process in India. Thus, sum of each row generates the gross output equal to its corresponding total input, indicating the absorption of the output of each industry bringing about the purpose of studying the forward integration, while each column shows the input sources of each sector to execute the analysis of the backward integration. The intermediate uses depict the consumption of goods and services resulting in value-added (*Zi*) is equal to total inputs *(Xi)*.

**Table 4.2: Input output table for the Indian economy.**

| | | Intermediate Uses | | | | | | Final Uses | | | | | | |
|---|---|---|---|---|---|---|---|---|---|---|---|---|---|---|
| Industry | | D1. | D2. | D3. | ... | ... | D35. | Final Consumption Expenditure by House-holds | Final Consumption Expenditure by NPISHs | Final Consumption Expenditure by govt. | Gross Fixed Capital Formation | Changes in Inventories and valuables | Exports | Gross Total Output |
| Intermediate Inputs | D1. | $X_{11}$ | $X_{12}$ | $X_{13}$ | ... | ... | $X_{1,35}$ | $Y_{11}$ | $Y_{12}$ | ... | ... | ... | $Y_{16}$ | $X_1$ |
| | D2. | $X_{21}$ | ... | ... | ... | ... | ... | ... | ... | ... | ... | ... | ... | .. |
| | ... | ... | ... | ... | ... | ... | ... | ... | ... | ... | ... | ... | ... | ... |
| | ... | ... | ... | ... | ... | .. | $X_{34'35}$ | ... | ... | ... | ... | ... | ... | ... |
| | D35. | $X_{35'11}$ | ... | ... | ... | ... | $X_{35'35}$ | $Y_{35'1}$ | ... | ... | ... | ... | $Y_{35'35}$ | $X_{35}$ |
| | Gross Value Added | $Z_1$ | $Z_2$ | $Z_3$ | ... | ... | $Z_{35}$ | | | | | | | |
| | Output | $X_1$ | $X_2$ | $X_3$ | ... | ... | $X_{35}$ | | | | | | | |

*Source: Asian Development Bank Input-Output Tables Database.*

The *final uses* comprise household consumption, non-profit organisations and institutions serving households (NPISHs), government, gross capital formation (fixed), inventory changes, and exports. The output matrix of any sector is the sum of intermediate transactions and final demand vector. The linkage effect becomes operationalized in the input-output table with intermediate flow $z_{ij}$, from sector $i$ to sector $j$. The level of production, remains consistent with the assumption of constant returns to scale due to the fact that the ratio between input and output remains fixed in the Leontief system. Thus, the technical coefficients, $a_{ij} = \frac{x_{ij}}{x_j}$ describe the production structure of given economic activities. These coefficients are also assumed to be stable. The initial work on the backward and forward inter-industry linkages method has been documented by Rasmussen (1957). The input-output system's basic equation is stated as follows: -

$AX+Y=X$ rewritten as,

$X\text{-}AX=Y$ and can be further simplified as,

$X(I\text{-}A)=Y$, where A = technology coefficient matrix = total production, and Y = final demand. The first condition to solve the system of input-output matrix is to calculate the inverse matrix of (I-A).

i.e., $X=(I\text{-}A)^{-1}\,Y$

The value of backward linkage captures the demand side impact of any change in a sector's output on the sectors producing and supplying its input requirements. In this regard, simple output multipliers are emphasized in the study. Morrissey and O' Donoghue (2013) observed backward linkage to orient itself towards assigning multiple inputs to each single output and therefore, in the input-output model $X=(I\text{-}A)^{-1}\,Y$ can be written as $GY$ where $G=(I\text{-}A)^{-1}$ The total backward linkage of the sector $j^{th}$ can then be derived as the sum of the elements of the $j^{th}$ column of the *Leontief Inverse* G. Forward linkage value, on the other hand, captures the supply-side implications of any change in a sector's output on the sectors that buy and consume its output as an input in their own production. In this case, Morrissey and O'Donoghue (2013) established that multiple output values are to be assigned to a single input and hence, total forward linkage, is derived for the sector as the sum of the elements of the row of the Ghoshian matrix H where $X'=m'(1\text{-}B)^{-1}$ that can be written as $m'$H.

According to Guerra and Sancho (2010), both the Leontief model (1956) and the Ghosh model (1958) are simultaneously equivalent in their partial effects, provided that the output ratios remain constant. It means that there are no changes in quantities, neither endogenous nor exogenous. However, in order to evaluate the relative strength of interindustry linkages, the normalised values of backward and forward linkages must be obtained by dividing the sectoral value by the mean value of all sectors and offering interpretations for either stronger or weaker linkage effects. These values are used to identify key sectors with high growth-inducing effects, which aids in assessing the potential implications of internal and exogenous shocks. The Normalized Backward Linkage (NBL) for sector *j* is computed with the formula as follows: -

Normalised Backward Linkage = $\frac{Backward\ Linkage_j}{\frac{1}{n}\sum_{j=1}^{n} Backward\ Linkage_j}$ , in addition

Normalized Forward Linkage (NFL) in sector $i$ can be calculated with the formula mentioned as follows:- -

Normalised Forward Linkage = $\frac{Forward\ Linkage_i}{\frac{1}{n}\sum_{i=1}^{n} Forward\ Linkage_i}$

The focus of this study would remain on the automobile industry. In this regard, Miller and Blair (2009), with the help of Table 4.3, defined the method of identifying the key sectors, and accordingly, sectors in the first quadrant with NFL>1 and NBL>1 have substantial values of forward and backward linkages, showing a significant dependency on both suppliers and consumers of output in other industries. The second quadrant shows that sectors that are more dependent on others utilise their output (NBL>1) and are less dependent on others producing their inputs (NFL<1). In the third quadrant are those sectors that have lower dependence in the relative terms on other sectors (NFL<1, NBL<1) are stated. Finally, the fourth quadrant has sectors with high dependence on their buyers (NFL>1) and less dependence (NBL<1) on other sectors, supplying their output to be used as inputs.

**Table 4.3: Identifying the Key Sectors based on NBL and NFL.**

| **NFL>1** | | **Normalised Forward Linkage Coefficients** | |
|---|---|---|---|
| | | **NFL<1** | **NFL<1** |
| Normalised Backward Linkage Coefficients | NBL>1 | | |
| | NBL<1 | | |

*Source: Miller and Blair (2009)*

The third objective and the fourth objective respectively, in this study are associated with the empirical estimation based on the summary of variables and their construction.

***Objective 3. To examine the performance linkages of the selected firms in the presence of foreign-invested firms in the automobile industry from 2011 to 2020.***

In order to measure the performance of the domestic firms in the presence of the foreign-invested firms, the output variable is constructed as the logarithm of sales plus the change in stocks as the dependent variable. First, the pooled OLS estimates are applied. Following the OLS results, the Hausman test was used, which preferred the fixed effects model. The following equation is estimated to investigate the relationship between output and various sources in the overall automobile industry: -

$$lnOutput_{it} = \beta_0 + \beta_1 XI_{it} + \beta_2 MI_{it} + \beta_3 RDI_{it} + \beta_4 Age_{it} + \beta_5 Size_{it} + \beta_6 KI_{it} + \beta_7 HHI_{it} + \beta_8 Horizontal\ FDI_{it} + e_{it}$$

where,

$i$ is the number of domestic firms (i.e., $i$=139), and

$t$ is the time period ($t$=10 years, i.e., 2011-2020).

$Output_{it}$ stands for the logarithm of the sales plus change in stocks of firm $i$ at time $t$. $XI_{it}$, is the export intensity and $MI_{it}$ is defined as the import intensity, both variables form the trade source or the source related to the export activities. The innovation and/or the absorptive capacity as a source of the output is explained by the independent variable of research and development intensity ($RDI_{it}$). $Age_{it}$ is the age of the firm, $Size_{it}$ is the size of the firm and $KI_{it}$ is the capital intensity of the firm $i$ at time $t$. These three variables are the firm-specific variables whereas the industry-specific variable $HHI_{it}$ or the Herfindahl-Hirschman Index is calculated using each firm's market share. $e_{it}$ is the residual term. Turning to proxies for foreign effect on the domestic firms, $Horizontal\ FDI_{it}$ captures the extent of foreign presence in sector $j$ at time $t$. It is defined on the basis of foreign equity participation evened over total firms in the sector, weighted by each firm's share in total industrial output where $Foreign\ Share_{it}$ measures the share of firm's total equity, of ten percent or more, owned by foreign investors.

$$Horizontal\ FDI_{it} = \frac{\sum_{(i\ for\ all\ i \in j)} Foreign\ Share_{it} * Y_{it}}{\sum_{(i\ for\ all\ i \in j)} Y_{it}}$$

### *Objective 4. To examine the productivity linkages of the selected firms in the presence of foreign-invested firms in the automobile industry from 2011 to 2020.*

From the review of the literature, it is well understood that with TFP once estimated, the question turns to its sources at the firm-level data. With the total factor productivity as the dependent variable, first, the pooled OLS estimates are applied. In order to examine the relationship between productivity and various sources in the overall automobile industry, the following equation, is estimated: -

$$lnTFP_{it} = \beta_0 + \beta_1 XI_{it} + \beta_2 MI_{it} + \beta_3 RDI_{it} + \beta_4 Age_{it} + \beta_5 Size_{it} + \beta_6 KI_{it} + \beta_7 HHI_{it} + \beta_8 Horizontal\ FDI_{it} + e_{it}$$

where,

$i$ is the number of domestic firms (i.e., $i$=139), and

$t$ is the time period ($t$=10 years, i.e., 2011-2020).

The variable $TFP_{it}$ stands for the Total Factor Productivity of firm $i$ at time $t$. Similar to the third objective, the independent variable in the equation comprises the trade source of $XI_{it}$, as the export intensity and $MI_{it}$ as the import intensity. The innovation source of productivity has been explored by the independent variable of research and development intensity $RDI_{it}$. The firms' characteristics are reflected in the variable such as $Age_{it}$ describing the firm's age, $Size_{it}$ as the firm's size and $KI_{it}$ as the capital intensity of the firm $i$ at time $t$. The Herfindahl-Hirschman Index, $HHI_{it}$ reflects the market share of each firm in the industry. The residual term is $e_{it}$. The presence of the foreign-invested firms is reflected with the $Horizontal\ FDI_{it}$ variable in sector $j$ (automobile industry) at time $t$. The formula for the Horizontal FDI is as follows: -

$$Horizontal\ FDI_{it} = \frac{\sum_{(i\ for\ all\ i \in j)} Foreign\ Share_{it} * Y_{it}}{\sum_{(i\ for\ all\ i \in j)} Y_{it}}$$

It is based on the foreign equity participation in the automobile industry averaged over all firms, weighted by every firm's share in total industrial output (based on sales).Here the foreign share is taken as the total equity owned at ten percent or more from 2011-2020.

## Type of Data and Source of Data Collection

This study is mainly grounded in secondary data foundations. In *Objective 1*, the source that has been employed is from the DIPP's *Quarterly Factsheet* on FDI. Objective 2 constitutes data from the Asian Development Bank's database. This study deals with the multiple variables over multiple time periods with respect to *Objective 3* and *Objective 4*. The type of data that has been employed for the empirical study, therefore, resorts to the space as well as time dimensions. In the econometric literature, this type of data is identified as panel data, pooled, micro panel or longitudinal data. It consists of the elements of both the time-series and cross-sectional data. Within the panel data, as per Gujrati (2011), the cross-sectional unit (here, a firm) is surveyed over time or movement over time of cross-sectional units is studied. There are, however, certain characteristics of the panel data as listed in Gujarati (2011) that are as follows: -

1. Over time, heterogeneity is conditioned to exist in panel data units relating to persons, firms, states, countries, and so on. The panel data estimate techniques can explicitly account for heterogeneity while accounting for individual specific variables.
2. It gives "more informative data, more variability, less collinearity among variables, more degrees of freedom and more efficiency" (pp.637-638), as it consists of combined elements of time-series of cross-section units.
3. It is suitable for investigating the dynamic forces of change by studying the repeated cross-sectional observations.
4. It allows for the detection and measurement of impacts that would otherwise go undetected in pure time-series as well as a pure cross-section.
5. It assists in analysing complex behavioural patterns. It might handle events of technological advancement and scale better than pure cross-section or time-series data.
6. It helps to minimize the bias occurring while aggregating persons or organisations into broad measures while dealing with thousands of units, i.e., it can enhance empirical research in ways that cross-section or time-series data cannot.

In this study, the main data source for the panel data is the Centre for Monitoring the Indian Economy's Prowess IQ database, which publishes data from audited financial statements of listed and unlisted companies. The data in the study pertains to the automobile and ancillary industry. As per the requirement of the study, firm-level data on the foreign promoters (companies' percentage share), firms' incorporation year, sales, change in stock gross fixed assets, total assets, salaries and wages, power and fuel, raw material expenses, export of goods (F.O.B.), total forex spending, R&D expenditures are extracted in US$ million. The construction of the variables such as export intensity, import intensity expenditure, firm size, firm age, and HHI has already been covered in section 4.2.

In order to deflate the primary and intermediate variables such as sales, capital, labour, energy and materials, this study has worked with various deflators. For instance, the Wholesale Price Index (WPI) from the Office of Economic Adviser, with the base year 2011-12, in particular, has been employed to get the deflated values of the output variable and capital variable using WPI for all commodities and WPI for machinery and tools respectively. For the energy and material variable, i.e., the intermediate inputs, RBI's KLEMS database is taken. Also, Annual Survey of Industries (ASI), National Accounts Statistics (NAS), following NIC (2008) concordance with the base year 2011-20 have been used, in order to provide the most efficient estimates for the study.. In order to get the labour input, data on the total emoluments and total persons engaged is retrieved from the Ministry of Statistics and Programme Implementation's Annual Survey of Industries (ASI).

The data pertaining to the Indian automobile industry in the ASI at NIC (2008) is reported at the two-digit (division) level of Division 29 i.e. the manufacture of motor vehicles, trailers and semi-trailers have been taken includes group 291 of the manufacture of motor vehicles, group 292 on the manufacture for motor vehicles of bodies (coachwork), manufacture of trailers and semi-trailers and finally group 293 on the manufacture of parts and accessories for motor vehicles also follows NIC (2008). The data for Gross Fixed Capital Formation in the Perpetual Inventory Method has been collected from NAS (2011) and NAS (2021) from the Ministry of Statistics and Programme Implementation.

## Time Frame and Size of the Variables in the Study

In this study, the first objective constitutes the time period from 2000-2020. With respect to the second objective, the time period in the study is from 2011-2020. Similarly, this study covers the ten-year time period from 2011 to 2020 to address the third and fourth objectives. The primary reason for selecting this time period for this study was the availability of the relevant database up to the latest financial year of 2020. Since the CMIE's Prowess IQ database provides wide panel data according to the annual financial statements at the companies' level, it becomes much easier to understand the implication of the objectives with respect to the latest developments that have taken place in the automobile sector. Secondly, it is also to be noted that in this study, the industrial as well as the firm-level data from 2011 onwards, follow the NIC (2008) classification along with 2011-12 as the new base year and therefore, adds to the relevance of the data. With respect to the year 2020, however, it must be remembered that it is not the financial year 2020 but the financial year 2021 that was stricken by the arrival of a global pandemic in India. Since the pandemic has not ended but is ongoing in nature, any study that takes up the objective of studying its aftermath on the economy would have to wait for more than three years, for its economic realisation. It is to be emphasized that this study has not included the time period of 2021, as the data pertaining to this period got influenced by the event of the global pandemic and as a result, forms part of the scope of further research. Therefore, this study has taken the data from the annual financial statements of 1053 companies in the overall automobile and ancillaries' sector in India from CMIE's Prowess IQ database from 2011 to 2020.

Because the original data comprised a large number of unreported or missing values. The process of filtering and cleaning the data by removing the missing values in the data is important, especially, in the case of the panel data or else it fails to provide its true form as the balanced panel or the unbalanced panel. This process left 170 companies in the overall automobile industry. Although after taking on the selected firms, this study was left with 139 domestic companies generating 1390 observations from 2011-20.

## Tools and Techniques

This section discusses the main tools and techniques used for econometric estimation. In Objective 1, the technique of compound annual growth rate is applied. The technique of input-output analysis for the Objective 2 has been used to find the backward and forward linkages. This study attempts to investigate the effects of foreign presence mainly in the form of FDI with respect to various performance linkages (Objective 3) and the productivity linkages (Objective 4) in the overall Indian automobile industry. Since only the automobile industry is selected, this study calls for intra-firm level analysis.

The impact of foreign-invested firms' presence on the performance as well as productivity levels in the domestic establishments are examined, with respect to the export activities as foreign-invested firms ensure the build-up of an extensive international distribution network. The innovation activities reflect the possession of knowledge and international technology either in the entire industry or at the firm level. The firm-specific characteristics based variables and the industry-specific characteristic-based variable shows the inert capacity of the firms to adopt the technology transfer and know-how leading to performance improvements and gains in productivity in domestic firms, respectively.

In this study, the econometric analysis with respect to the Objective 4, consists of two steps. In the first part, the level of Total Factor Productivity from the firm-level primary and intermediate inputs has been empirically estimated in the overall automobile sector, with the help of the Levinsohn-Petrin approach. In the second step, this study formulates and estimates the panel data regression model with the productivity of the firms as the explained variable on a number of independent variables formulating the performance linkages, including an intra-firm measure of FDI (i.e., horizontal FDI). The estimates of the pooled OLS are primarily shown in this study. The Hausman test is used in this study to choose between the random effects/fixed effects techniques amongst the presence of the individual-specific effects. This setup then estimates the results of panel data for 139 domestic automobile firms.

### *Total Factor Productivity*

The purpose of the empirical objectives of this study is to examine whether the foreign presence affects the performance or the productivity level of the local firms, irrespective of the sources. The study of productivity as the response variable becomes imperative in this study. However, the emphasis has been put on the TFP in the review of the literature to evaluate the variations in the industry over a period of time. This is because the assessment of partial factor productivity overemphasizes one input factor, and therefore, cannot represent the overall economic health of the automobile industry. The Total Factor Productivity fits as the broadest measure of productivity and efficiency in the usage of resources. However, the difference between efficiency, performance and productivity must now be understood in the context of what these terms imply. On one hand, productivity can be regarded as the rate at which goods and services are produced as output with respect to a unit of input, however, efficiency implies the ability to produce goods and services without wasting materials, time and energy. The term performance describes the gap between the expected and the actual work done depending on the output level.

There are several procedures in the review of the literature to measure productivity by its source. One such measure is the Malmquist index number, calculated as the ratio of an index of output change to that of change in its input. However, this measure presents itself with the limitation of requiring knowledge of prices and quantities of input utilized and output manufactured. An alternate method is the econometric estimation of the production function, which does not necessitate any assumptions about the firm's behaviour or technological level. As a result, employing the production function methodology to estimate TFP allows us to acquire more accurate estimates that account for biases. In this study, the semi-parametric Levinsohn-Petrin (LP) technique is applied.

The technique involves reckoning output as a function of the inputs and then deducting the estimated output from actual output to encapsulate productivity as the residual. To estimate TFP at the firm level, the various studies highlight the Levinsohn-Petrin (LP) approach which produces consistent estimates of productivity used as the dependent variable. These productivity estimates are found by using the major inputs of capital, labour, intermediate input of raw material, and the energy consumption at the firm level. A Cobb-Douglas production function is assumed, with output determined by capital as the endogenous input variable, power and fuel (energy) as proxy variables, and labour and raw materials as free input variables. The following is an equation for the production function: -

$$Y_{it} = A_{it}K_{it}^{\beta_k}L_{it}^{\beta_l}M_{it}^{\beta_m}E_{it}^{\beta_e} \qquad .....(i)$$

In (i), $Y_{it}$ represents the output of the firm $i$ at period $t$. $A_{it}$ is the productivity coefficient. The state variable capital $K_{it}$, free variable labour $L_{it}$ and raw materials , $M_{it}$ and the proxy variable for intermediate input i.e., energy $E_{it}$. Using natural log in equation (i) the production function is as follows: -

$$y_{it} = \beta_0 + \beta_k k_{it} + \beta_l l_{it} + \beta_m m_{it} + \beta_e e_{it} + \omega_t + \varepsilon_{it} \qquad .....(ii)$$

In the equation (ii), $y_{it}$, $k_{it}$, $l_{it}$, $m_{it}$, $e_{it}$ denote the log value of output, capital stock, labour, raw material and energy variable, respectively. The error term is $\omega_t+\varepsilon_{it}$. This is the result of $\ln(A_{it})=\beta_0+\omega_t+\varepsilon_{it}$ where $\beta_0$ measures productivity level across the firms at time $t$, $\omega_t$ denotes the firm-specific productivity level difference within each firm that is not captured by predictors in the equation and $\varepsilon_{it}$ stands for the error component uncorrelated to the input choices. Using the estimated coefficients of the production function the productivity is shown in the functional form as follows: -

$$lnTFP_{it} = y_{it} + \hat{\beta}_k k_{it} + \hat{\beta}_l l_{it} + \hat{\beta}_m m_{it} + \hat{\beta}_e e_{it}$$

Olley and Pakes (OP, 1996) used a similar estimating technique utilising investment as a proxy. The OP technique needs investment to strictly increase with productivity and only non-negative investment values can be used in calculations. This study follows the Levinsohn-Petrin (LP, 2003) approach since it overcomes the major drawback of OP approach (1996) which would otherwise lead to a significant loss of efficiency, as warned by Goldar and Banga (2020). The LP (2003) procedure also addresses the problems of simultaneity and selection bias at the firm level in the Indian automobile industry throughout 2011 to 2020.

There are also several other issues and criticism associated with the use of the value-added as a variable for estimating the performance. This study considers the sales variable more appropriate as a measure of output, as it has been used to calculate the performance in the recent review of the literature. In the second part of the study after the estimation of the Output and TFP, econometric regression estimation has been done with the panel regression model which constitutes two major models namely, the fixed effects model and the random-effects model. These models are explained as follows: -

### ***Panel Data Models***

The panel data is a cross-sectional time-series data set that includes various entities with repeated observations at varying time intervals. The group effect in the panel data is estimated with the help of the (i) fixed effects model and (ii) random effect models. These two panel data regression models are briefly discussed as follows: -

**Fixed Effects Regression Model**

The fixed effects is applied to investigate the effect of variable quantities that change over time. This model estimates group differences in constant terms, assuming that all firms have the same slopes and variance. Because the effect of a group or an individual is time invariant. It is allowed to be correlated to other regressors because it is regarded as a part of the intercept and the error term in the regression equation. The effects of those time-invariant characteristics are removed in fixed effects regression to determine the net effect on the dependent variable of the independent variables.

**Random Effects Regression Model**

In the panel data regression model, the random effects assume a 'composite error term' that consists of both the cross section and time-series error components. It also comprised of components of error term that are random and uncorrelated with the independent variables. This is also why the random effect regression model is also known as the error component model. Individual error components are also unrelated to each other. This requirement allows time invariant variables to act as explanatory variables in the panel data regression model. This model also represents the case of extrapolating the inference derived from the sample.

### *Estimation Tools*

In this work, the STATA software programme is employed for data analysis so as to accommodate panel data. The Prowess IQ database is accessible in a wide panel form. As a result, the data is cleaned and filtered in MS Excel. This command computes the Cobb-Douglas revenue production function, using capital and labour as the primary inputs, energy as the intermediate input, and materials as the proxy variable. This study employs firm-level panel data that is secondary and quantitative in nature. The following tools are used to conduct the analysis: -

**Pearson's Coefficient of Correlation**

The correlation coefficient has been used to construct a correlation matrix to inspect the degree of strength and nature of the association amongst the independent and dependent variables.

**Hausman Test**

Since this study has employed the panel data, therefore, it called for regression-based on the fixed effects (FE) or random effects (RE) to be performed using the software packages. In order to choose between these two techniques, the Hausman specification test is employed following $\chi^2$ distribution at a 0.05% level of significance. The statement of purpose in this test is that 'there is no systematic difference between the two estimators $(\widehat{\theta_1})$ and $(\widehat{\theta_2})$', where $(\widehat{\theta_2})$ is estimator of the random effects and $(\widehat{\theta_1})$ is the estimator for the fixed effects. If the statement of no difference is rejected, we can conclude that the random effect model is inapplicable also that it would be better off utilising the fixed effects model for the panel data.

The issues of multicollinearity and heteroscedasticity, which most estimators suffer from in the panel data, are verified with the Variance Inflating Factor and the Breusch-Pagan test, which are briefly mentioned below: -

**Variance Inflating Factor (VIF): Multicollinearity**

The variances and covariances of the OLS estimators are large in the presence of severe multicollinearity, resulting in larger confidence intervals and acceptance of the null hypothesis. As a result, even though the t-ratio of one or more coefficients might be statistically insignificant, they possess a large value of $R^2$. Also, the OLS estimators in addition to its standard errors are perceptive to the slightest data alterations. A VIF (average) score of less than 5 suggests that no explanatory variable should be eliminated from the model.

**Breusch-Pagan (BP) Test: Heteroscedasticity**

Another one of the OLS assumptions is that the conditional variance of $Y_i$ given $X_i$, remains equal to $\sigma^2$ regardless of the values taken by the independent variable. In mathematical terms:-

$$E(u_i^2) = \sigma^2$$

The error terms are considered to be heteroscedastic if their variance is not constant. Heteroscedasticity produces biased and misleading parameter estimates. The BP test detects any linear form of heteroscedasticity. If the computed value of the $\chi^2$ square statistic surpasses the critical $\chi^2$ value at the 0.05%, the statement of 'no difference' in homoscedasticity can be rejected; else, it is not rejected.

## *Estimation Issues*

The estimation issues in this study are stated as follows: -

### The Issue of Endogeneity

A common concern in the empirical literature of various studies was the emergence of endogeneity from OLS estimates. Several studies in the review of literature reflected upon the treatment of error term in the case of panel data with the following equation: -

$$y_{it} = \alpha+\beta X_{it}+\varepsilon_{it}$$

*where i* (cross-section identifier) = 1, 2, 3, 4, …, N, *t* (the time identifier) = 1, 2, 3, 4,.., *T*, and X includes all explanatory variables. The error term in the case of panel data can be decomposed into two independent terms as follows: -

$$\varepsilon_{it} = u_t+v_{it}$$

where $u_t$ is the permanent, unobserved heterogeneity across firms in their technologies, and $v_{it}$ type etc., and is a period-specific shock, independent over time and across firms. It is difficult to get an unbiased and consistent estimation of the equation because it violates the assumptions of OLS estimators. The error term $\varepsilon_{it}$ becomes heteroscedastic. However, both the fixed effects and random effects models can handle heteroscedasticity.

### Missing Values or Non-reporting of Certain Variables

In this study, the non-reporting of certain variables in the CMIE's Prowess IQ database has allowed us to use data from various sources. For instance, ASI data for the labour variable, NAS (2021) data for calculating the capital construction and RBI's KLEMS database for deflating energy and material etc.

- The Effects of Pandemic

This study has taken the time period of 2011-2020. It does not take into consideration the database of the same variables pertaining to the financial year 2021 (i.e., 2020-2021), because most of the companies had not released their data for the same in the CMIE's Prowess IQ database. It is also to be understood that the effects of an ongoing pandemic will be fully realised by the Indian economy as a whole after at least 3-5 years.

# Chapter 5
Data Analysis and Interpretation

## The Trends and Patterns of FDI in India from 2000 to 2020

### *Objective 1. To study the trends and patterns of FDI in India during the selected period from 2000 to 2020.*

In line with Objective 1 of the study, this section throws light on the trends and the pattern of FDI inflows in India. This is done with the help of source, sectoral classification destination of FDI inflows on the basis of the recent Quarterly Factsheets on FDI inflows maintained by DIPP. The developments from the new economic reforms in 1991 resulted in the liberalisation, privatization and the globalisation of the Indian economy and also in the confluence of a global environment (see section 1.2). In the area of foreign investments, this phenomenon was witnessed following international best practices. From 2000 onwards, many new additions to the definition of FDI were made to rectify any discrepancies in available data on FDI inflows. In addition to this, the recent time period from 2000 onwards is crucial because of a cent per cent automatic approval of the FDI inflows in the automobile sector in 2002. After this, a general increase has been observed in the production, domestic sales and the exports of the various segments. (Section 2.4).

In this section, Table 5.1 shows the FDI inflows in US$ million. It is to be noted that data from 2018-19 to 2020-21 given in Table 5.1 are provisional. Up to 1999-2000, equity capital formed the main part of FDI inflows in India. However, the FDI coverage from 2000 to 2001 was broadened to encompass, besides equity capital, inter-corporate debt transactions among entities in the form of other capital and reinvested earnings. In Table 5.1, apart from the equity of incorporated bodies, data on FDI also shows equity of (foreign) bank branches in India and Indian branches operational out of the country as unincorporated entities. It is observed that the FDI inflows through FIPB/RBI's automatic route have been increasing since 2003. This trend is followed by an increase in reinvested earnings component of FDI on the account of persistent easing of FDI norms across sectors. Although, the reinvested capital component of the FDI shows improvement in trend but with fluctuations.

Table 5.1 shows that around the beginning, total FDI inflows of US$ 4,029 million (in April 2000), the FDI inflows worth US$ 2,339 million came through the FIPB route or automatic route (taken as total FDI flows by definition) (See section 1.1.1). In addition, US$ 61 million came from the equity capital of unincorporated entities and US$ 1,350 million were reinvested earnings and a further US$ 279 million formed the component of the other capital. The FII fund, however, in 2000-01, stood at US$ 1,847 million. In the duration of the entire decade of 2000-10, the highest year on year growth rate was seen at 155% for the year 2006-07. This was the result of government efforts, on raising the FDI limit, in various sectors. For instance, in the year 2004, the limits of FDI flows were raised in major sectors, such as, in the petroleum product marketing, printing scientific and technical magazines, periodicals and journals;and the banking sector etc. Besides, the existing restrictions of the foreign investors setting up business in India were reviewed and fresh guidelines were issued in 2005 that required the foreign investors to give detailed circumstances under which they found it necessary to set up a joint venture with the Indian industries. Also, a distinct change that occurred in 2006-07, was that the share of FDI surpassed the share of the portfolio investment. This situation took place as SEZ Act (2005) generated additional economic activities and the year 2006-07 saw a substantial increase in FDI and portfolio investment.

This resulted in FDI inflows that grew even more than double in that year. The visual representation of Table 5.1 is depicted in Figure 5.1, where total FDI inflows in India as per financial year 2000-2020 in US$ (million), are compartmentalised on the basis of its components. It must be noted that it was the year 2006-07, where an actual increase in the total foreign investment was observed. The subsequent year of 2007-08 also marked a positive increase in the FDI inflows with a 53% increase. The FII sector witnessed an abrupt rise in inflows from US$ 3,225 to US$ 20,328 in 2007-08. It was, however, the year 2008 that registered the increase in FDI inflows at US$ 41,873 million while the FII fund registered degrowth at a negative US$ 15,017 million. This situation took place because of the recession in the economies of developed nations (mainly the U.S.A.). As a result of this global FIIs withdrew a large number of resources from the Indian economy in 2008-09. This time period also reflected the investors' confidence in the FDI as compared to FIIs.

As shown in Table 5.1, the FII fund rose to US$ 29,048 million in 2009-10 and similar to it, the automatic route-based component of FDI equalled US$ 25,606 million as portfolio investment whereas total FDI inflows stood at US$

37,745 million. The share of FII in the total foreign investment inflows in this year was as high as 63.9 per cent. In 2009-10 and 2010-11, the total FDI inflows saw degrowth (-) 10% and (-) 8%, respectively. In 2009-10, the effects of the global financial crises (2008) were felt in India causing a situation of panic, among the investors. Albeit, the government had relaxed the foreign ownership norms in aviation, mining, oil refining, real estate, commodity exchange and credit industries in the same year. The average economic growth of 7.8% sustained the momentum of economic activities, especially during the global economic crisis of 2009-10. In totality, the solid economic fundamentals of India motivated and assisted the sharp surge in FDI flows during 2000-2010.

**Table 5.1: Foreign Direct Investment Inflows in India from 2000-01 to 2020-21 (P). (In US$ million)**

| S. No. | *Financial Year (April-March)* | Foreign Direct Investment Inflows in India | | | | | | Investment by Foreign Institutional Investors Fund (net) |
|---|---|---|---|---|---|---|---|---|
| | | Equity | | *Reinvested Earnings* | *Other capital* | FDI flows into India | | |
| | | *FIPB Route/ RBI's Automatic Route/ Acquisition on Route* | *Equity capital of unincorporated bodies* | | | Total FDI Flows | *%age growth* | |
| 1. | 2000-01 | 2,339 | 61 | 1,350 | 279 | 4,029 | - | 1,847 |
| 2. | 2001-02 | 3,904 | 191 | 1,645 | 390 | 6,130 | (+) 52% | 1,505 |
| 3. | 2002-03 | 2,574 | 190 | 1,833 | 438 | 5,035 | (-) 18 % | 377 |
| 4. | 2003-04 | 2,197 | 32 | 1,460 | 633 | 4,322 | (-) 14 % | 10,918 |
| 5. | 2004-05 | 3,250 | 528 | 1,904 | 369 | 6,051 | (+) 40% | 8,686 |
| 6. | 2005-06 | 5,540 | 435 | 2,760 | 226 | 8,961 | (+) 48% | 9,926 |
| 7. | 2006-07 | 15,585 | 896 | 5,828 | 517 | 22,826 | (+)155% | 3,225 |
| 8. | 2007-08 | 24,573 | 2,291 | 7,679 | 300 | 34,843 | (+) 53% | 20,328 |
| 9. | 2008-09 | 31,364 | 702 | 9,030 | 777 | 41,873 | (+) 20% | (-) 15,017 |
| 10. | 2009-10 | 25,606 | 1,540 | 8,668 | 1,931 | 37,745 | (-) 10 % | 29,048 |
| 11. | 2010-11 | 21,376 | 874 | 11,939 | 658 | 34,847 | (-) 08 % | 29,422 |
| 12. | 2011-12 | 34,833 | 1,022 | 8,206 | 2,495 | 46,556 | (+) 34% | 16,812 |
| 13. | 2012-13 | 21,825 | 1,059 | 9,880 | 1,534 | 34,298 | (-) 26% | 27,582 |
| 14. | 2013-14 | 24,299 | 975 | 8,978 | 1,794 | 36,046 | (+) 5% | 5,009 |
| 15. | 2014-15 | 30,933 | 978 | 9,988 | 3,249 | 45,148 | (+) 25% | 40,923 |
| 16. | 2015-16 | 40,001 | 1,111 | 10,413 | 4,034 | 55,559 | (+) 23% | (-) 4,016 |
| 17. | 2016-17 | 43,478 | 1,223 | 12,343 | 3,176 | 60,220 | (+) 8% | 7,735 |
| 18. | 2017-18 | 44,857 | 664 | 12,542 | 2,911 | 60,974 | (+) 1% | 22,165 |

| S. No. | *Financial Year (April-March)* | **Foreign Direct Investment Inflows in India** | | | | | | **Investment by Foreign Institutional Investors Fund (net)** |
|---|---|---|---|---|---|---|---|---|
| | | **Equity** | | ***Reinvested Earnings*** | ***Other capital*** | **FDI flows into India** | | |
| | | ***FIPB Route/ RBI's Automatic Route/ Acquisition on Route*** | ***Equity capital of unincorporated bodies*** | | | **Total FDI Flows** | ***%age growth*** | |
| 19. | 2018-19 (P) | 44,366 | 689 | 13,672 | 3,274 | 62,001 | (+) 2% | (-) 2,225 |
| 20. | 2019-20 (P) | 49,977 | 1,757 | 14,175 | 8,482 | 74,390 | (+) 20% | 552 |
| 21. | 2020-21 (P) | 59,636 | 1,787 | 16,216 | 4,082 | 81,722 | (+) 10% | 38,097 |
| Cumulative Total (From Apr, 2000 to Mar, 2021) | | 532,513 | 19,005 | 170,509 | 41,549 | 763,576 | - | 252,899 |

*Notes: (P) stands for Provisional Data*

*Source: RBI's Bulletin for March, 2021 dt.17.05.2021 (Table 34 - FOREIGN INVESTMENT INFLOWS). DIPP, Ministry of Commerce and Industries, https://dipp.gov.in/*

*Figure 5.1: Foreign Direct Investment Inflows in India since 2000-01 to 2020-21 (P). (In US$ million)*

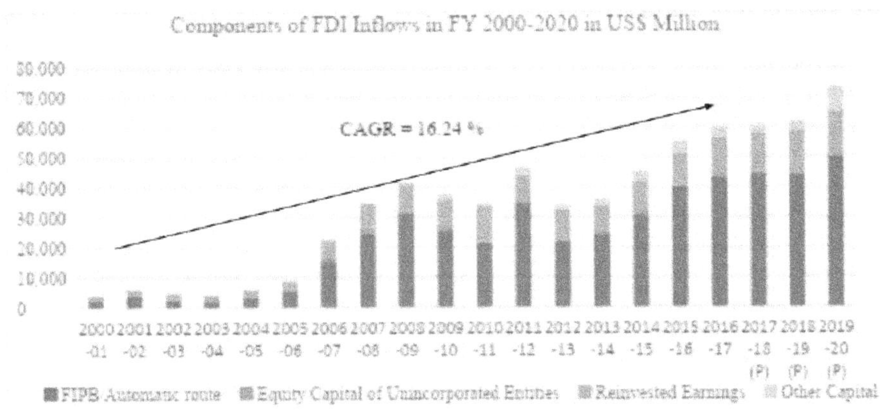


*Note: (P) stands for Provisional Data*

*Source: Table 5.1*

The negative growth rate was again visible with a massive decline of (-) 26% for the year 2012-13. It was attributed, almost, entirely to a weakened industrial growth and the depreciation of the Indian currency. In Figure 5.1, this decline can be observed in 2012-13. The FII inflows registered an impressive growth in 2014 at US$ 40,923 million but declined in 2015 to US$ (-) 4,016 million.

Thereafter, a slight increase was seen in the FII inflows at US$ 7,735 in 2016-17. Such fluctuations were not witnessed in total FDI inflows in 2014 which stood at a solid US$ 45,148 and registered a growth rate of 25%, over the preceding year 2013. In 2015, total FDI inflows rose to US$ 55,559 million. Also, the FDI inflows increased at a rate of 8% in 2016-17 over 2015-16. Since the year 2015, FDI has shown a revival on the account of the Make in India (2014) initiative, specially designed for the betterment of the manufacturing sector. Mint (2017) mentioned that in spite of the mess in the banking sector, weak exports, drying up of investment demand and back-to-back droughts India's economy managed to thrive in 2014-15 and 2015-16. In 2017-18 and 2018-19, total FDI inflows were at US$ 60,974 million and US$ 62,001 million, respectively.

These figures showed a year on year growth rate of 1% and 2% respectively. With FII fund, the year 2018-19 witnessed a decline to a figure of US$ (-) 2,225 million over 2017-18. For this, demonetisation, GST and the rising value of Non-Performing Assets (NPA) were reasoned. With the fear of the global pandemic (COVID-19) and due to its subsequent lockdown, the FII fund in India declined in the financial year 2019-2020 at US$ (-) 552 million but increased to US$ 38,098 million in the financial year 2020-21. Nonetheless, the total FDI inflows in the year 2019-20 and 2020-21 stood at US$ 74,390 million and US$ 81,722 million respectively. This way the FDI inflows showed quiet resilience as compared to FIIs from 2018-19 to 2020-21. The Cumulative total FDI inflows from Apr 2000 to Mar 2021 stood at US$ 763,576 million, due to improvement in the government's attitude towards easing policy procedures and sectoral limits of the automatic route as a mode of FDI. With Compound Annual Growth Rate, over the course of 21 years from Apr 2000 to Mar 2021 stands at 16.24%.

**Table 5.2: The Compound Annual Growth Rate of total FDI inflows and FII fund in percentage from 2000-2021. (In Percentage)**

| Year | CAGR of Total FDI Inflows | CAGR of Total FII Inflows |
|---|---|---|
| 2000-2001 to 2004-2005 | 8.47% | 36.29% |
| 2005-2006 to 2009-2010 | 33.04% | 23.96% |
| 2010-2011 to 2014-2015 | 5.32% | 6.82% |
| 2015-2016 to 2019-2020 | 6.01% | -32.76% |
| 2016-2017 to 2020 -2021 | 6.3% | 37.56% |

*Source: Table 5.1*

The CAGR of total FDI inflows and FII inflows in percentage is shown in Figure 5.2 on a five-year basis from 2000 onwards. It is seen that from 2000-01 to

2004-05, the CAGR in the case of total FDI was 8.47%. The FII for the same period of time was at a whopping 36.29%. From 2005-06 to 2009-10, the compounded inflows on the annual basis irrespective of the yearly inflows were the highest in total FDI inflows at 33.04%, whereas, FII inflows were occurring at 23.96%. The highly difficult period of 2010-11 to 2014-15 seemed grim with CAGR at 5.32%, in the case of FDI inflows and 6.82%, in the case of FII inflows. The five-year time period from 2015-16 to 2019-20, witnessed a huge decline in the FII inflows at -32.76%. During the time period of 2015-16 to 2019-20, CAGR in case of total FDI inflows, was at 6.01%.

Abiding the five-year time period of calculating the CAGR, the time period from 2016-17 to 2020-21 is also to be read. In this time period, the CAGR stood at 6.3% with total FDI inflows, whereas, the FII inflows showed better performance at 37.56%. Figure 5.2 based on Table 5.2 shows the recent CAGR values from 2016-17 to 2020-21, in the case of both FDI and FII.

*Figure 5.2: The Compound Annual Growth Rate of Total FDI inflows and FII fund from 2000-2021. (In Percentage)*

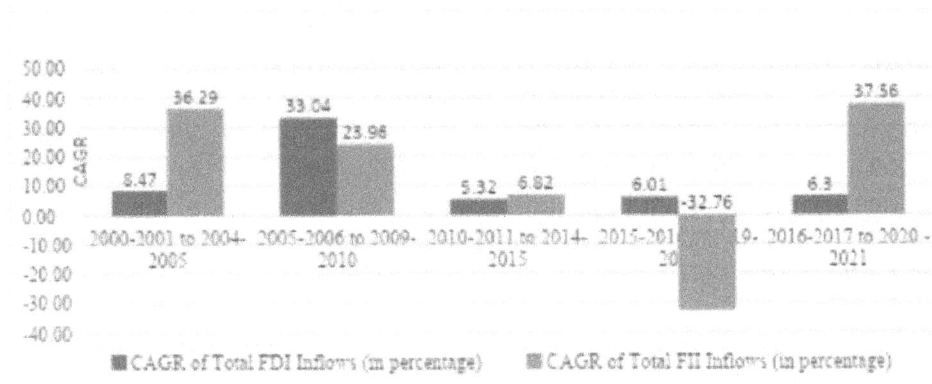


*Source: Table 5.2*

Significant changes were also found in the sectoral composition of the FDI. Table 5.3 depicts the sectoral data of the top ten industries that attracted the most FDI inflows over the years 2005-06 to 2019-20 in US$ million. The sectors shifted with respect to the rankings in the five-year period of 2005-2006 to 2009-2010, 2010-2011 to 2014-2015 and from 2015-16 to 2019-2020. From 2005-2006 to 2009-2010, the top sector that attracted the FDI inflows has been the service sector. The computer software and hardware sector was the second-largest sector, attracting FDI inflows.

**Table 5.3: Top Ten Sectors attracting largest FDI inflows in India in the year 2005-2006 to 2019-2020. (In US$ Million)**

| Rank | Sector | 2005-2006 April-March | 2006-2007 April-March | 2007-2008 April-March | 2008-2009 April March | 2009-2010 April March | Sector | 2010-2011 April-March | 2011-2012 April-March | 2012-2013 April-March | 2013- 2014 April-March | 2014-2015 April- March | Sector | 2015-2016 April-March | 2016-2017 April-March | 2017-2018 April-March | 2018-2019 April-March | 2019-2020 April-March | Cumulative Inflows in Apr, 2000-Mar,2020 | % age to total inflows |
|---|---|---|---|---|---|---|---|---|---|---|---|---|---|---|---|---|---|---|---|---|
| 1 | Services Sector | 543 | 4,664 | 6,615 | 6,116 | 4,353 | Services Sector | 3,296 | 5,216 | 4,833 | 2,225 | 3,253 | Services Sector | 6,889 | 8,684 | 6,709 | 9,158 | 7,854 | 82,003 | 17% |
| 2 | Computer Software & Hardware | 1,375 | 2,614 | 1,410 | 1,677 | 919 | Construction Development: | 1,663 | 3,141 | 1,332 | 1,226 | 758 | Computer Software & Hardware | 5,904 | 3,652 | 6,153 | 6,415 | 7,673 | 44,911 | 10% |
| 3 | Telecom Sector | 624 | 478 | 1,261 | 2,558 | 2,554 | Telecom Sector | 1,665 | 1,997 | 304 | 1,307 | 2,895 | Telecom Sector | 1,324 | 5,564 | 6,212 | 2,668 | 4,445 | 37,271 | 8% |
| 4 | Housing & Real Estate | 38 | 467 | 2,179 | 2,801 | 2,844 | Computer Software & Hardware | 780 | 796 | 486 | 1,126 | 2,200 | Trading | 3,845 | 2,338 | 4,348 | 4,462 | 4,574 | 27,595 | 6% |

| Rank | Sector | 2005-2006 April-March | 2006-2007 April-March | 2007-2008 April-March | 2008-2009 April March | 2009-2010 April March | Sector | 2010-2011 April-March | 2011-2012 April-March | 2012-2013 April-March | 2013- 2014 April-March | 2014-2015 April- March | Sector | 2015-2016 April-March | 2016-2017 April-March | 2017-2018 April-March | 2018-2019 April-March | 2019-2020 April-March | Cumulative Inflows in Apr, 2000-Mar,2020 | % age to total inflows |
|---|---|---|---|---|---|---|---|---|---|---|---|---|---|---|---|---|---|---|---|---|
| 5 | Construction Activities Including Roads & Highways | 151 | 985 | 1,743 | 2,028 | 2,862 | Drugs & Pharmaceuticals | 209 | 3,232 | 1,123 | 1,279 | 1,523 | Construction Infrastructure | 113 | 105 | 540 | 213 | 617 | 25,662 | 5% |
| 6 | Automobile Industry | 143 | 276 | 675 | 1,152 | 1,208 | Automobile Industry | 2,354 | 4,041 | 1,537 | 1,517 | 2,570 | Automobile Industry | 2,527 | 1,609 | 2,090 | 2,623 | 2,824 | 24,211 | 5% |
| 7 | Power | 87 | 157 | 967 | 985 | 1,437 | Chemicals Other Than Fertilizers | 1,299 | 923 | 292 | 878 | 669 | Construction Infrastructure Activities | 1,917 | 1,861 | 1,308 | 2,258 | 2,042 | 19,768 | 5% |
| 8 | Metallurgical Industries | 147 | 173 | 1,177 | 961 | 407 | Power | 1,272 | 1,652 | 536 | 1,066 | 657 | Chemicals (other than fertilizers) | 1,470 | 1,393 | 2,730 | 1,981 | 1,058 | 17,639 | 4% |

| Rank | Sector | 2005-2006 April-March | 2006-2007 April-March | 2007-2008 April-March | 2008-2009 April March | 2009-2010 April March | Sector | 2010-2011 April-March | 2011-2012 April-March | 2012-2013 April-March | 2013- 2014 April-March | 2014-2015 April- March | Sector | 2015-2016 April-March | 2016-2017 April-March | 2017-2018 April-March | 2018-2019 April-March | 2019-2020 April-March | Cumulative Inflows in Apr, 2000-Mar,2020 | % age to total inflows |
|---|---|---|---|---|---|---|---|---|---|---|---|---|---|---|---|---|---|---|---|---|
| 9 | Petroleum & Natural Gas | 14 | 89 | 1,427 | 412 | 272 | Metallurgical Industries | 1,098 | 1,786 | 1,466 | 568 | 472 | Drugs & Pharmaceuticals | 754 | 857 | 1,010 | 266 | 518 | 16,847 | 4% |
| 10 | Chemicals other than Fertilizers | 390 | 205 | 229 | 749 | 362 | Trading | 308 | 993 | 3,259 | 1,343 | 2,761 | Hotel & Tourism | 1,031 | 997 | 1,132 | 1,076 | 2,938 | 16,501 | 4% |

*Source: Compiled from various issues of the Quarterly factsheet on FDI inflows in India. DIPP. Ministry of Commerce and Industry.*

In 2009-2010, the sector attracting the largest FDI inflows was the telecom sector that received US$ 2,558 million. The housing sector was at US$ 2,844 million in 2009-10. In the same time period, the FDI inflows were further secured by the construction sector at US$ 2,862 million. Considering the year 2005-2006 to 2009-2010, the automobile sector incurred US$ 1,208 million worth of inflows. The metallurgical industries also saw the largest inflows of US$ 1,177 million in 2007-08. On similar lines, the petroleum sector also received US$ 1,477 million in 2007-08.

Nonetheless, the final spot was taken by the chemicals industry with the largest FDI inflows at US$ 749 million. In the time period 2010-2011 to 2014-2015, the service sector again gained the top spot and the largest inflows were experienced in 2011-2012. The second-ranking was taken by the construction sector. The telecommunication sector took the third ranking and received the largest inflows in 2014-2015. With this, the fourth largest sector, namely, the computer software and hardware sector witnessed FDI inflows at US$ 2,200 million in 2014-2015. The fifth-largest sector that attracted FDI inflows was drugs and pharmaceuticals. The automobile sector stood stable in the sixth place from 2010-2011 to 2014-2015. The power sector witnessed the largest inflows in 2014-2015 at US$ 2,570 million. The chemicals industry climbed the seventh spot in 2009-2010 from the tenth spot in 2005-2006. The metallurgical industry lost its spot, over the period from 2005-2006 to 2009-2010. Out of the other industries, the tenth spot got captured by the trading sector. The shares (in percentage) of the top ten sectors receiving the FDI inflows during the time 2015-2020 are shown in Figure 5.3 based on Table 5.3 is depicted as follows: -

*Figure 5.3: Share of the Top Ten Sectors Receiving FDI in India from 2000-2020. (In Percentage)*

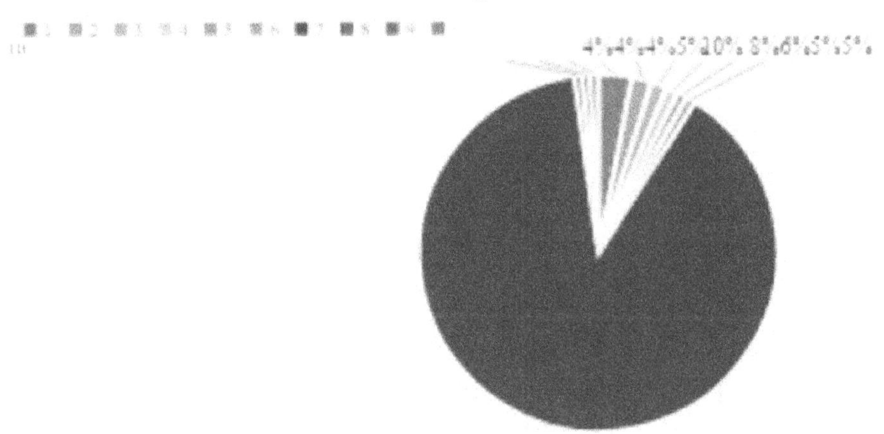

*Source: Table 5.3.*

The FDI's sectoral composition data in India from 2015-2016 to 2019-2020, majorly comprised the service sector at 17% share of the total. The second place was kept by computer software and hardware at 10%, over the same course period of time. The telecommunication industry was also shining at the third spot by FDI inflows. The trading sector from the tenth spot in 2010-2011 to 2014-2015. The automobile industry retained its spot at sixth rank. Furthermore, construction infrastructure, drugs and pharmaceuticals and hotels and tourism, all have a 5% share in the total direct flows. The attention must also turn to the fact that the highest amount of FDI inflows was experienced by 2019-2020. These last six sectors together accounted for a cumulative FDI of US$ 94,966 million from Apr 2000 to Mar 2020, whereas the cumulative FDI arrivals to the service sector alone accounted for US$ 82,003 million. With respect to the compounded average performance for the various sector for the respective five-year time period i.e., 2005-06 to 2009-2010, and 2010-11 to 2014-15, Table 5.4 and Table 5.5 shows the CAGR for the top ten sectors as follows: -

**Table 5.4: The Compound Annual Growth Rate of Top Ten Sector Receiving FDI Inflows in 2005-2006 to 2009-2010. (In Percentage)**

| Sector | Year |
|---|---|
| | **2005-2006 to 2009-2010** |
| Services Sector (financial & non-financial) | 51.63% |
| Computer Software & Hardware | -7.74% |
| Telecommunications, Radio, Paging, Cellular Mobile, Basic Telephone Services | 32.55 % |
| Housing & Real Estate | 134.04 % |
| Construction Activities Including Roads & Highways | 80.11% |
| Automobile Industry | 53.23 % |
| Power | 75.22% |
| Metallurgical Industries | 22.59 % |
| Petroleum & Natural Gas | 81 % |
| Chemicals (other than Fertilizers) | -1.47% |

*Source: Table 5.3*

**Table 5.5: The Compound Annual Growth Rate of Top Ten Sector Receiving FDI Inflows in 2010-2011 to 2014-2015. (In Percentage)**

| Sector | Year |
|---|---|
| | 2010-11 to 2014-2015 |
| Services Sector | 0.26 % |
| Construction Development: Townships, Housing, Built-Up Infrastructure | -14.54 % |
| Telecommunications (Radio Paging, Cellular Mobile, Basic Telephone Services) | 11.69 % |
| Computer Software & Hardware | 23.04% |
| Drugs & Pharmaceuticals | 48.76 % |
| Automobile Industry | 1.77 % |
| Chemicals (other than Fertilizers) | -11.65 % |
| Power | -12.37 % |
| Metallurgical Industries | -15.53 % |
| Trading | 55.06% |

*Source: Table 5.3*

The largest CAGR has been witnessed in the case of the housing and the real estate sector and the lowest CAGR was seen in the computer software and hardware sector from 2005- 06 to 2009-10. The second-largest CAGR based on the FDI inflows took place in the power sector. The time period from 2005-2006 to 2009-2010 was relatively stable due to low inflation and a high average annual growth rate. The effects of the US financial crises reached India in 2009-2010 as a result of global turmoil from the down gradation of the U.S. bonds. This also meant the direction of the FDI inflows for various sectors, in India, was readjusted from the year 2010 onwards. In the troubled time period from 2010-11 to 2014-15, the services sector, of both financial and non-financial nature did not stand the test of time and saw a CAGR of 0.26%. On the other hand, the trading sector was the one that recorded the highest CAGR of 55.06%. Among the industries in the negative range, the metallurgical industries were seen with (-) 15.53% CAGR from 2010-11 to 2014-15.

**Table 5.6: The Compound Annual Growth Rate of Top Ten Sector Receiving FDI Inflows in 2015-2016 to 2019-2020. (In Percentage)**

| Sector | Year |
|---|---|
| | **2015-16 to 2019-2020** |
| Services Sector | -5.98 % |
| Computer Software & Hardware | 34.66 % |
| Telecommunications | -21.60 |
| Trading | -7.47 % |
| Construction Development: Townships, Housing, Built-Up Infrastructure and Construction Development Projects | 30.15 % |
| Automobile Industry | -8.31 % |
| Construction and Infrastructure Activities | 32.65 % |
| Chemicals (other than fertilizers) | -10.44 % |
| Drugs & Pharmaceuticals | 14.59% |
| Hotel & Tourism | 18.57% |

*Source: Table 5.3*

From 2015-16 to 2019-20, the services sector actually was taking the blow of the economic disturbances and recorded a negative (-) 5.98%. The compound annual growth rate was 34.66%, the highest in the computer software and hardware sector. This was attributed to a greater inclination towards the information, communication and technology industries providing multifaced services to the various economic sector, especially the education sector. The smallest CAGR of (-) 10.44% was seen in the chemicals industry. These FDI inflows were coming from the specific countries that with their aim and motivation shifted places in the top ten spots in the financial year 2005-2006 to the financial year 2019-2020. In this regard, Table 5.7 is presented as follows: -

**Table 5.7: Top Ten Source Countries of FDI in India from 2005-2006 to 2014-2015. (in US$ million)**

| *Rank* | *Country* | 2005-2006 April-March | 2006-2007 April-March | 2007-2008 April-March | 2008-2009 April March | 2009-2010 April March | *Country* | 2010-2011 April-March | 2011-2012 April-March | 2012-2013 April-March | 2013- 2014 April- March | 2014-2015 April- March | *Country* | 2015-2016 April-March | 2016-2017 April- March | 2017-2018 April- March | 2018-2019 April- March | 2019-2020 April- March | Cumulative Inflows in Apr, 2000-Mar,2020 | % age to total inflows |
|---|---|---|---|---|---|---|---|---|---|---|---|---|---|---|---|---|---|---|---|---|
| 1 | Mauritius | 2,570 | 6,363 | 11,096 | 11,208 | 10,376 | Mauritius | 6,987 | 9,942 | 9,497 | 4,859 | 9,030 | Mauritius | 8,355 | 15,728 | 15,941 | 8,084 | 8,241 | 142,710 | 30% |
| 2 | Singapore | 275 | 578 | 3,073 | 3,454 | 2,379 | Singapore | 1,705 | 5,257 | 2,308 | 5,985 | 6,742 | Singapore | 13,692 | 8,711 | 12,180 | 16,228 | 14,671 | 97,670 | 21% |
| 3 | U.S.A. | 502 | 856 | 1,089 | 1,802 | 1,943 | U.K. | 2,711 | 7,874 | 1,080 | 3,215 | 1,447 | U.S.A. | 4,192 | 4,709 | 2,095 | 3,139 | 4,223 | 33,852 | 7% |
| 4 | U.K. | 266 | 1,878 | 1,176 | 864 | 657 | Japan | 1,562 | 2,972 | 2,237 | 1,718 | 2,084 | Netherlands | 2,643 | 3,367 | 2,800 | 3,870 | 6,500 | 33,499 | 7% |
| 5 | Netherlands | 76 | 644 | 695 | 883 | 899 | Netherlands | 1,170 | 1,115 | 1,856 | 2,270 | 3,436 | Japan | 2,084 | 1,483 | 1,633 | 2,965 | 3,226 | 29,779 | 6% |

| *Rank* | *Country* | 2005-2006 April-March | 2006-2007 April-March | 2007-2008 April-March | 2008-2009 April March | 2009-2010 April March | *Country* | 2010-2011 April-March | 2011-2012 April-March | 2012-2013 April-March | 2013- 2014 April- March | 2014-2015 April- March | *Country* | 2015-2016 April-March | 2016-2017 April- March | 2017-2018 April- March | 2018-2019 April- March | 2019-2020 April- March | Cumulative Inflows in Apr, 2000-Mar,2020 | % age to total inflows |
|---|---|---|---|---|---|---|---|---|---|---|---|---|---|---|---|---|---|---|---|---|
| 6 | Japan | 208 | 85 | 815 | 405 | 1,183 | U.S.A. | 1,213 | 1,409 | 557 | 806 | 1,824 | U.K. | 898 | 2,379 | 847 | 1,351 | 1,422 | 28,211 | 6% |
| 7 | Cyprus | 70 | 58 | 834 | 1,287 | 1,627 | Cyprus | 913 | 1,587 | 490 | 557 | 598 | Germany | 986 | 1,069 | 1,124 | 886 | 488 | 12,196 | 3% |
| 8 | Germany | 303 | 120 | 514 | 629 | 626 | Germany | 200 | 1,622 | 860 | 1,038 | 1,125 | U.A.E. | 985 | 604 | 417 | 898 | 339 | 10,748 | 2% |
| 9 | France | 18 | 117 | 145 | 467 | 303 | France | 734 | 663 | 646 | 305 | 635 | Cyprus | 508 | 675 | 511 | 296 | 879 | 8,539 | 2% |
| 10 | Switzerland | 96 | 56 | 211 | 219 | 258 | Switzerland | 341 | 353 | 83 | 64 | 41 | Cayman Islands | 985 | 979 | 1,237 | 1,008 | 3,702 | 7,536 | 2% |

*Source: Compiled from various issues of the Quarterly Factsheets on FDI inflows by DIPP.*

The majority of FDI inflows in the 1990s were routed from U.K. and U.S.A. as a direct implication of the colonial ties. This dominance of western dependence has been declining since the mid-2000s. From 2005-06 to 2009-10, Mauritius provided FDI flows worth US$ 1,096 million (in 2008-2009) which were the highest compared to other countries. In the same year of 2008-2009, the U.S.A. contributed FDI flows amounting to US$ 1,802 million whereas the contribution from the U.K. was only US$ 854 million. From 2010-11 to 2014-15, Japan rose as the fourth major FDI inflows source country for India which were even greater than the U.S.A. In the five-year time period ending in 2014-15, US$ 2,084 million came from Japan in India, as compared to US$ 1,824 million from the U.S.A. In 2015-16 to 2019-20, Singapore was the highest FDI providing the country with US$ 14,671 million.

The islandic winds in case of foreign direct inflows came majorly during 2005-06 to 2019-20 where countries such as Mauritius (the largest source country of FDI), Singapore, and Japan together amounted to 57% of the total FDI inflows. However, it must be taken into consideration that India has a double tax avoidance agreement (DTAA) with Mauritius, making it a preferred route for the US investments and investments of other developed nations. The *Double Tax Avoidance Agreement* qualifies a foreign investor for paying the taxes either in India or in Mauritius. Also, there was an addition of the Cayman Islands jumping at number ten in rankings in 2015-16 to 2019-20 that also holds the notoriety of being the tax haven. Therefore, the rising FDI inflows from such nations being the source countries must be taken with a greater level of accountability.

*Figure 5.4: Share of the Top Ten Countries Receiving FDI in India from 2000-2020. (In Percentage)*

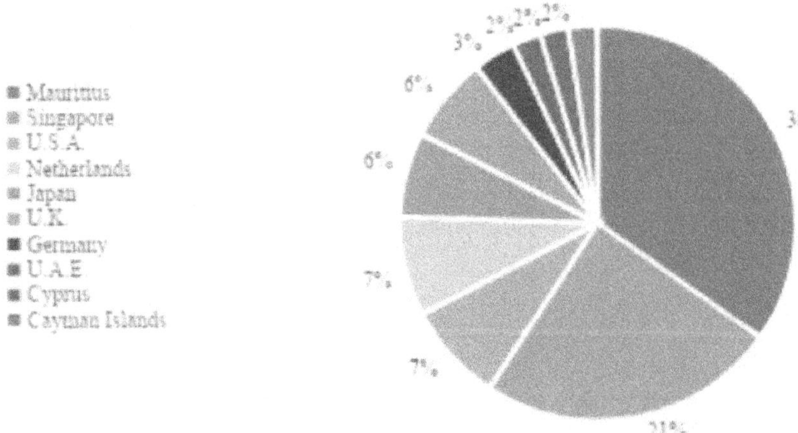


*Source: Table 5.7.*

In India, the portion of the top ten sectors in accordance with the influx of total FDI (percentage) from the year 2000-01 to 2019-20 is also visually represented in the pie diagram in Figure 5.4. With respect to the source country of inflows, from the year 2000-01 to 2019-20, the highest inflows over the entire period of the financial year 2000 to 2020 were received from Mauritius (of about 30% of the total). Singapore scored second ranking with a share of 21% in the total FDI inflows. Also, the Netherlands is the third with a 7% share in the total. Whereas, Japan and U.S.A. & U.K. have a 6% share each, as observed in Figure 5.4. Finally, countries such as U.A.E., Cyprus and Cayman Islands share a small percentage of 2% in the total FDI inflows. With respect to CAGR, in the period of 2005-2006 to 2009-2010, Cyprus with 87.61% made largest growth.

**Table 5.8: The Compound Annual Growth Rate of Top Ten Sector Receiving FDI Inflows in 2005-2006 to 2009-2010. (In Percentage)**

| **Country** | **Year** |
|---|---|
| | **2005-2006 to 2009-2010** |
| Mauritius | 32.19 % |
| Singapore | 56.06 % |
| U.S.A. | 31.08 % |
| U.K. | 19.82 % |
| Netherlands | 62.27 % |
| Japan | 41.57 % |
| Cyprus | 87.61 % |
| Germany | 15.61 % |
| France | 75.88 % |
| Switzerland | 21.86% |

*Source: Table 5.7.*

**Table 5.9: The Compound Annual Growth Rate of Top Ten Sector Receiving FDI Inflows in 2010-2011 to 2014-2015. (In Percentage)**

| Country | Year |
|---|---|
| | 2010-2011 to 2014-2015 |
| Mauritius | 5.26 % |
| Singapore | 31.64 % |
| U.K. | -11.13 % |
| Japan | 5.93 % |
| Netherlands | 24.04 % |
| U.S.A. | 8.50 % |
| Cyprus | -8.11 % |
| Germany | 41.26% |
| France | -2.85 % |
| Switzerland | -35.54% |

*Source: Table 5.7.*

At 19.82%, the U.K. was holding on to the lowest growth compounded for the five-year period from 2005-06 to 2009-10. This is shown in table 5.8, although in Table 5.9, the CAGR for the U.K. was in negative value (-11.13%). In Table 5.9, the highest CAGR was observed for Germany at 41.26%. The lowest CAGR, however, was seen in the case of Switzerland. The worst performance in terms of the CAGR was shown by Mauritius in the year 2015-2016 to 2019-2020. Alternatively, the realisation in terms of CAGR was with the U.K. This scenario is presented in the Table 5.10 as follows: -

**Table 5.10: The Compound Annual Growth Rate of Top Ten Sector Receiving FDI Inflows in 2015-2016 to 2019-2020. (In Percentage)**

| Country | Year |
|---|---|
| | **2015-2016 to 2019-2020** |
| Mauritius | -7.56 % |
| Singapore | 4.93 % |
| U.S.A. | 26.95 % |
| Netherlands | 66.18 % |
| Japan | 70.21 % |
| U.K. | 99.26 % |
| Germany | 65.37 % |
| U.A.E. | 61.27% |
| Cyprus | 75.83 % |
| Cayman Islands | 50.40% |

*Source: Table 5.7.*

It is to be noted that the ranking of the FDI inflows with respect to their source country is presented according to their cumulative growth rate from 2000 to 2020. The segregation of data on the basis of the five-year period, however, has led to witnessing other patterns, with respect to the growth rate. In the case of FDI inflows, as per the destination in India, cumulative data of the top ten states can be seen in Table 5.11 as per the financial year 2000-2020. The cities (in the top ten states) that correspond to the percentage share receiving the FDI inflows are visually represented in a pie diagram in Figure 5.5. Accordingly, the Indian states in descending order, Andhra Pradesh, Gujarat, Tamil Nadu, Karnataka, Delhi and Maharashtra constituted 96.45% of the total FDI inflow of the US $ 318,263 million during the period of April 2000 to March 2020. Also, a heavy concentration of FDI inflows in these six regions due to their better infrastructure and connectivity can also be noticed. The cities corresponding to the states receiving the largest FDI inflows are also observed. These states consist of some of the most advanced cities as compared to the rest, namely, Mumbai, Delhi, Bengaluru, Chennai, Ahmedabad and Hyderabad, which hold the historic and economic significance.

**Table 5.11: Top Ten States Attracting the Total FDI Inflows in India from 2010-2011 to 2020-2020. (In US$ Million)**

| Sr. No. | States | 2010-11 April-March | 2012-13 April - March | 2012-13 April - March | 2013-14 April - March | 2014-15 April - March | 2015-16 April - March | 2016-17 April - March | 2017-18 April - March | 2018-19 April - March | 2019-20- April-March | Cumulative Inflows Apr,00-Mar,20 | %age to total Inflows |
|---|---|---|---|---|---|---|---|---|---|---|---|---|---|
| 1 | Maharash-tra | *6,097* | *9,553* | 8,716 | 3,420 | 6,361 | 9,511 | 19,654 | 13,423 | 11,383 | 21,890 | 127,089 | 30% |
| 2 | New Delhi | *2,677* | *7,983* | 3,222 | 6,242 | 6,875 | 12,743 | 5,884 | 7,656 | 10,142 | 16,170 | 84,642 | 20% |
| 3 | Karnataka | *1,332* | *1,533* | 1,023 | 1,892 | 3,444 | 4,121 | 2,132 | 8,575 | 6,721 | 7,670 | 37,670 | 9% |
| 4 | Tamil Nadu | *1,352* | *1,422* | 2,807 | 2,116 | 3,818 | 4,528 | 2,218 | 3,475 | 2,613 | 5,471 | 29,848 | 7% |
| 5 | Gujarat | *724* | *1,001* | 493 | 860 | 1,531 | 2,244 | 3,367 | 2,091 | 1,803 | 2,323 | 20,545 | 5% |
| 6 | Andhra Pradesh | *1,262* | *848* | 1,159 | 678 | 1,556 | *1,369* | 2,195 | 1,246 | 3,457 | 792 | 18,469 | 4% |
| 7 | West Bengal | *95* | *394* | 424 | 436 | 239 | 955 | 50 | 218 | 1,229 | 1,697 | 5,432 | 1% |
| 8 | Kerala | *37* | *471* | 72 | 70 | 230 | 90 | 454 | 208 | 257 | 1,155 | 2,221 | 0.5% |
| 9 | Punjab | *416* | *130* | 47 | 91 | 39 | 27 | 6 | 108 | 618 | 644 | 2,090 | 0.5% |
| 10 | Rajasthan | *51* | *33* | 132 | 38 | 541 | 50 | 165 | 117 | 363 | 422 | 1,960 | 0.5% |

*Source: Source: Compiled from various issues of the Quarterly Factsheets on FDI inflows by DIPP, Ministry of Commerce and Industries.*

*Figure 5.5: Share of Top Ten Major Cities Receiving the Largest FDI Inflows in India from April, 2000 to March 2020. (In Percentage)*

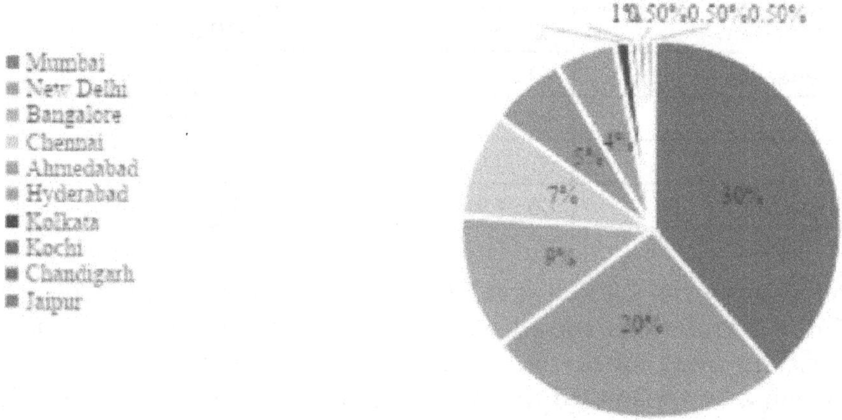


*Source: Table 5.6*

From 2000 to 2020, Maharashtra attracted 30% of the total inflows at US$ 127,089 million followed by New Delhi at 20% with US$ 84,642 million. The bottom five of the top ten, namely, Tamil Nadu, Telangana, Haryana, U.P. and Andhra Pradesh received less than 5% share. The Table 5.12 shows the CAGR for Maharashtra increasing from 0.85% in 2010-15 to 18.14% in 2015-20. The Table 5.12 also shows a decline in CAGR in percentage in the case of West Bengal, Andhra Pradesh, Gujrat, Tamil Nadu and Karnataka. In the southern state of Kerala, an increase in the CAGR was observed from 2010-15 to 2015-20. With a negative CAGR in 2010-11 to 2014-15, Punjab actually manage to improve its performance in 2015-16 to 2019-20.

**Table 5.12: The Compound Annual Growth Rate of Top Ten States Receiving FDI Inflows in 2010-2011 to 2014-2015 and from 2015-16 to 2019-20. (In Percentage)**

| **Country** | **Year** | |
|---|---|---|
| | **2010-2011 to 2014-2015** | **2015-2016 to 2019-2020** |
| Maharashtra | 0.85 % | 18.14 % |
| New Delhi | 20.76 % | 4.87 % |
| Karnataka | 20.92 % | 13.22 % |
| Tamil Nadu | 23.07 % | 3.85 % |
| Gujarat | 16.15% | 0.69 % |

| Country | Year | |
|---|---|---|
| | 2010-2011 to 2014-2015 | 2015-2016 to 2019-2020 |
| Andhra Pradesh | 4.27 % | -10.36 % |
| West Bengal | 20.26 % | 12.18 % |
| Kerala | 44.11 % | 66.59 % |
| Punjab | -37.71 % | 88.58 % |
| Rajasthan | 60.37 % | 53.20 % |

*Source: Table 5.7.*

In Rajasthan, the CAGR was at 53.20% from 2015-16 to 2019-2020. Overall, the CAGR measure has shown most rates on the top five rank holders, on the declining trend for the FDI inflows by sector, by source country and by destination as compared to the year on year growth rate, especially, for the latest five years i.e., from 2015-2016 to 2019-2020.

Although, as previously noted, India has opened its doors to international investment through much more rigorous liberalisation, privatisation, and globalisation, resulting in a significant rise in FDI inflows (quantity-wise), there is a certain lack of quality in such investments. For instance, the services sector at the top spot as the largest sector attracting FDI inflows, though contributes the largest to the national income but employs the least number of total employees, Mauritius as the major source country of FDI is a well-known tax haven and states with the four major metropolitan cities as the major states receiving the largest FDI cater mainly to the services sector snubbing the backward states that would mainly cater the agricultural and industrial sector.

## The Linkages in the Automobile Sector in India.

### *Objective 2. To Study the Industry Wise Backward Linkages and Forward Linkages in The Automobile Sector in India from 2010 to 2020.*

Before analysing the performance with respect to capital, labour, materials, power, R&D, export intensity etc. with the help of the regression-based technique of the panel data, to determine forward and backward linkages between the automobile and various other industries in the Indian economy turns relevant. The basis of linkages is that there exists a direct effect and an indirect effect upon the demand of the final product, with respect to the derived demand of the products that are used as inputs, in making the final product. The realisation of linkages based on the industry can incur in case of the automobile production. For instance, if a consumer decides to purchase a vehicle, as a result, the automobile components manufacturers adjust their production levels of the transport equipment. This is because accommodating the demand of the consumer would, in turn, require raw materials from the metal, electrical and leather industries etc. This situation would also motivate an additional production of metal, electrical and leather-based products for the initial production of automobile vehicles in accordance of the consumer's demand. The indirect effect of this consumer's demand is incurred by the metal, electrical and leather industries also.

The addition of the direct as well as the indirect effect would result in the total effect of the demand which would be captured by the relationship between various industries, primarily, with the help of input-output tables, i.e., with total output, intermediate demand and the final demand of various industries. For the second objective, this section tries to find the total backward linkages and the total forward linkages that further measures the outturn of one sector's production activity on another sector's consumption and vice-versa with the help of relevant data from the Asian Development Input-Output Database, based on World Input-Output Database. Therefore, the total (direct and indirect) effects resulting from the interdependence of the production process are quantified with the Leontief inverse for the total backward linkage. With respect to the total forward linkage Ghoshian inverse has been implemented, in line with the requirement of the input-output analysis.

In this section, Table 5.13 presents calculated values for the total backward linkages of various sectors in the Indian economy for the ten-year period of 2011-2020, taking into the total effects of final demand from all sectors on a particular sector's output.

**Table 5.13: Total Backward Linkages for various Sectors/Industries in India from the year 2011 to 2020.**

| Sectors/Industries | Years | | | | | | | | | |
|---|---|---|---|---|---|---|---|---|---|---|
| | **2011** | **2012** | **2013** | **2014** | **2015** | **2016** | **2017** | **2018** | **2019** | **2020** |
| Agriculture, hunting, forestry, and fishing | 1.41 | 1.41 | 1.41 | 1.42 | 1.44 | 1.43 | 1.43 | 1.44 | 1.44 | 1.45 |
| Mining and quarrying | 1.44 | 1.47 | 1.47 | 1.47 | 1.80 | 1.81 | 1.80 | 1.90 | 1.98 | 2.05 |
| Food, beverages, and tobacco | 2.53 | 2.49 | 2.46 | 2.47 | 2.49 | 2.48 | 2.48 | 2.46 | 2.46 | 2.45 |
| Textiles and textile products | 2.63 | 2.51 | 2.47 | 2.47 | 2.50 | 2.50 | 2.48 | 2.44 | 2.43 | 2.41 |

| Sectors/Industries | Years | | | | | | | | | |
|---|---|---|---|---|---|---|---|---|---|---|
| | **2011** | **2012** | **2013** | **2014** | **2015** | **2016** | **2017** | **2018** | **2019** | **2020** |
| Leather, leather products, and footwear | 2.68 | 2.56 | 2.51 | 2.53 | 2.55 | 2.54 | 2.53 | 2.49 | 2.47 | 2.46 |
| Wood and products of wood and cork | 2.04 | 1.96 | 1.96 | 1.96 | 1.96 | 1.96 | 1.96 | 1.93 | 1.92 | 1.91 |
| Pulp, paper, paper products, printing, and publishing | 2.71 | 2.65 | 2.61 | 2.61 | 2.62 | 2.62 | 2.60 | 2.58 | 2.57 | 2.55 |
| Coke, refined petroleum, and nuclear fuel | 2.34 | 2.21 | 2.20 | 2.22 | 2.55 | 2.62 | 2.53 | 2.63 | 2.69 | 2.76 |
| Chemicals and chemical products | 2.73 | 2.71 | 2.68 | 2.69 | 2.74 | 2.74 | 2.72 | 2.73 | 2.73 | 2.73 |
| Rubber and plastics | 2.92 | 2.88 | 2.84 | 2.85 | 2.84 | 2.83 | 2.81 | 2.79 | 2.78 | 2.76 |
| Other non-metallic minerals | 2.37 | 2.27 | 2.24 | 2.27 | 2.33 | 2.36 | 2.31 | 2.32 | 2.32 | 2.32 |
| Basic metals and fabricated metal | 2.64 | 2.54 | 2.51 | 2.53 | 2.50 | 2.49 | 2.45 | 2.43 | 2.40 | 2.38 |
| Machinery, N.E.C. | 2.76 | 2.64 | 2.59 | 2.59 | 2.54 | 2.52 | 2.49 | 2.43 | 2.40 | 2.36 |
| Electrical and optical equipment | 2.79 | 2.70 | 2.66 | 2.65 | 2.62 | 2.60 | 2.58 | 2.53 | 2.50 | 2.47 |
| Transport equipment | 2.94 | 2.83 | 2.79 | 2.78 | 2.76 | 2.73 | 2.71 | 2.66 | 2.62 | 2.59 |
| Manufacturing, N.E.C.; recycling | 2.84 | 2.64 | 2.61 | 2.62 | 2.63 | 2.65 | 2.61 | 2.56 | 2.54 | 2.52 |
| Electricity, gas, and water supply | 2.13 | 2.07 | 2.05 | 2.07 | 2.16 | 2.17 | 2.14 | 2.16 | 2.18 | 2.19 |
| Construction | 2.37 | 2.31 | 2.28 | 2.28 | 2.24 | 2.23 | 2.15 | 2.15 | 2.12 | 2.09 |
| Sale, maintenance, and repair of motor vehicles and motorcycles; retail sale of fuel | 1.31 | 1.29 | 1.28 | 1.28 | 1.27 | 1.28 | 1.27 | 1.26 | 1.26 | 1.25 |
| Wholesale trade and commission trade, except of motor vehicles and motorcycles | 1.31 | 1.29 | 1.28 | 1.28 | 1.27 | 1.28 | 1.27 | 1.26 | 1.26 | 1.25 |
| Retail trade, except of motor vehicles and motorcycles; repair of household goods | 1.31 | 1.29 | 1.28 | 1.28 | 1.27 | 1.28 | 1.27 | 1.26 | 1.26 | 1.25 |
| Hotels and restaurants | 2.30 | 2.26 | 2.24 | 2.24 | 2.26 | 2.33 | 2.24 | 2.26 | 2.26 | 2.26 |

| Sectors/Industries | Years | | | | | | | | | |
|---|---|---|---|---|---|---|---|---|---|---|
| | 2011 | 2012 | 2013 | 2014 | 2015 | 2016 | 2017 | 2018 | 2019 | 2020 |
| Inland transport | 2.18 | 2.11 | 2.09 | 2.08 | 2.09 | 2.14 | 2.06 | 2.06 | 2.05 | 2.04 |
| Water transport | 1.77 | 1.78 | 1.71 | 1.72 | 1.73 | 1.72 | 1.71 | 1.69 | 1.68 | 1.67 |
| Air transport | 2.07 | 1.43 | 1.71 | 1.72 | 1.74 | 1.74 | 1.73 | 1.68 | 1.67 | 1.66 |
| Other supporting and auxiliary transport activities; activities of travel agencies | 1.82 | 1.75 | 1.76 | 1.76 | 1.75 | 1.77 | 1.74 | 1.74 | 1.73 | 1.72 |
| Post and telecommunications | 1.55 | 1.50 | 1.35 | 1.35 | 1.35 | 1.34 | 1.34 | 1.26 | 1.23 | 1.20 |
| Financial intermediation | 1.33 | 1.31 | 1.29 | 1.29 | 1.29 | 1.29 | 1.28 | 1.27 | 1.27 | 1.26 |
| Real estate activities | 1.18 | 1.16 | 1.17 | 1.16 | 1.15 | 1.15 | 1.14 | 1.14 | 1.13 | 1.13 |
| Renting of machinery & equipment and other business activities | 1.58 | 1.55 | 1.42 | 1.42 | 1.41 | 1.41 | 1.40 | 1.34 | 1.31 | 1.28 |
| Public administration and defence; compulsory social security | 1.00 | 1.00 | 1.00 | 1.00 | 1.00 | 1.00 | 1.00 | 1.00 | 1.00 | 1.00 |
| Education | 1.20 | 1.19 | 1.19 | 1.19 | 1.18 | 1.19 | 1.18 | 1.18 | 1.18 | 1.18 |
| Health and social work | 1.86 | 1.84 | 1.82 | 1.82 | 1.83 | 1.83 | 1.82 | 1.82 | 1.81 | 1.81 |
| Other community, social, and personal services | 1.36 | 1.35 | 1.34 | 1.34 | 1.32 | 1.32 | 1.32 | 1.31 | 1.30 | 1.29 |
| Private households with employed persons | 1.00 | 1.00 | 1.00 | 1.00 | 1.00 | 1.00 | 1.00 | 1.00 | 1.00 | 1.00 |

*Source: ADB Database.*

**Table 5.14: Total Forward Linkages for various Sectors/Industries in India from the year 2011 to 2020.**

| Sectors/Industries | Years | | | | | | | | | |
|---|---|---|---|---|---|---|---|---|---|---|
| | 2011 | 2012 | 2013 | 2014 | 2015 | 2016 | 2017 | 2018 | 2019 | 2020 |
| Agriculture, hunting, forestry, and fishing | 3.58 | 3.31 | 3.23 | 3.16 | 3.33 | 3.32 | 3.23 | 3.18 | 3.14 | 3.11 |
| Mining and quarrying | 3.91 | 4.43 | 4.24 | 3.91 | 3.72 | 3.12 | 3.80 | 3.38 | 3.26 | 3.13 |
| Food, beverages, and tobacco | 2.03 | 1.83 | 1.77 | 1.78 | 1.87 | 1.95 | 1.82 | 1.83 | 1.82 | 1.81 |
| Textiles and textile products | 1.66 | 1.60 | 1.56 | 1.56 | 1.67 | 1.68 | 1.64 | 1.65 | 1.66 | 1.67 |

| Sectors/Industries | Years | | | | | | | | | |
|---|---|---|---|---|---|---|---|---|---|---|
| | 2011 | 2012 | 2013 | 2014 | 2015 | 2016 | 2017 | 2018 | 2019 | 2020 |
| Leather, leather products, and footwear | 1.45 | 1.41 | 1.38 | 1.39 | 1.44 | 1.43 | 1.42 | 1.42 | 1.42 | 1.42 |
| Wood and products of wood and cork | 1.18 | 1.30 | 1.28 | 1.29 | 1.27 | 1.29 | 1.28 | 1.30 | 1.31 | 1.32 |
| Pulp, paper, paper products, printing, and publishing | 1.80 | 1.70 | 1.68 | 1.68 | 1.71 | 1.77 | 1.71 | 1.70 | 1.70 | 1.70 |
| Coke, refined petroleum, and nuclear fuel | 3.17 | 2.35 | 2.26 | 2.29 | 2.46 | 2.77 | 2.50 | 2.41 | 2.38 | 2.34 |
| Chemicals and chemical products | 4.34 | 3.99 | 3.92 | 4.09 | 4.08 | 4.02 | 4.13 | 4.03 | 4.01 | 4.00 |
| Rubber and plastics | 1.81 | 1.73 | 1.74 | 1.74 | 1.71 | 1.79 | 1.70 | 1.71 | 1.70 | 1.69 |
| Other non-metallic minerals | 1.38 | 1.39 | 1.39 | 1.39 | 1.37 | 1.40 | 1.39 | 1.39 | 1.39 | 1.39 |
| Basic metals and fabricated metal | 4.94 | 4.37 | 4.10 | 4.04 | 3.20 | 3.20 | 3.10 | 2.60 | 2.28 | 1.97 |
| Machinery, NEC | 1.83 | 1.79 | 1.78 | 1.74 | 1.75 | 1.77 | 1.68 | 1.69 | 1.67 | 1.65 |
| Electrical and optical equipment | 2.08 | 1.98 | 1.98 | 1.99 | 2.05 | 2.02 | 1.96 | 1.98 | 1.97 | 1.96 |
| Transport equipment | 1.84 | 1.86 | 1.85 | 1.77 | 1.85 | 2.02 | 1.78 | 1.87 | 1.88 | 1.88 |
| Manufacturing, NEC; recycling | 1.96 | 2.16 | 2.09 | 2.09 | 2.09 | 2.21 | 2.09 | 2.17 | 2.18 | 2.20 |
| Electricity, gas, and water supply | 2.27 | 2.24 | 2.22 | 2.28 | 2.55 | 2.55 | 2.50 | 2.61 | 2.67 | 2.73 |
| Construction | 2.04 | 1.97 | 2.03 | 2.01 | 1.75 | 1.64 | 1.57 | 1.52 | 1.44 | 1.36 |
| Sale, maintenance, and repair of motor vehicles and motorcycles; retail sale of fuel | 1.16 | 1.15 | 1.17 | 1.17 | 1.18 | 1.19 | 1.19 | 1.20 | 1.20 | 1.21 |
| Wholesale trade and commission trade, except of motor vehicles and motorcycles | 2.27 | 2.25 | 2.35 | 2.39 | 2.45 | 2.48 | 2.48 | 2.55 | 2.59 | 2.64 |
| Retail trade, except of motor vehicles and motorcycles; repair of household goods | 2.89 | 2.83 | 2.98 | 3.08 | 3.22 | 3.28 | 3.26 | 3.40 | 3.48 | 3.56 |
| Hotels and restaurants | 1.68 | 1.61 | 1.59 | 1.61 | 1.69 | 1.62 | 1.70 | 1.67 | 1.68 | 1.68 |

| Sectors/Industries | Years | | | | | | | | | |
|---|---|---|---|---|---|---|---|---|---|---|
| | 2011 | 2012 | 2013 | 2014 | 2015 | 2016 | 2017 | 2018 | 2019 | 2020 |
| Inland transport | 3.47 | 3.30 | 3.27 | 3.35 | 3.57 | 3.56 | 3.54 | 3.58 | 3.62 | 3.66 |
| Water transport | 1.04 | 1.03 | 1.03 | 1.03 | 1.03 | 1.04 | 1.03 | 1.03 | 1.03 | 1.02 |
| Air transport | 1.06 | 1.05 | 1.04 | 1.04 | 1.04 | 1.04 | 1.04 | 1.03 | 1.03 | 1.02 |
| Other supporting and auxiliary transport activities; activities of travel agencies | 1.15 | 1.14 | 1.14 | 1.15 | 1.15 | 1.15 | 1.15 | 1.15 | 1.15 | 1.15 |
| Post and telecommunications | 1.38 | 1.33 | 1.32 | 1.33 | 1.40 | 1.40 | 1.39 | 1.40 | 1.41 | 1.42 |
| Financial intermediation | 2.71 | 2.58 | 2.54 | 2.61 | 2.75 | 2.68 | 2.64 | 2.68 | 2.68 | 2.69 |
| Real estate activities | 1.03 | 1.03 | 1.03 | 1.03 | 1.04 | 1.04 | 1.04 | 1.04 | 1.04 | 1.04 |
| Renting of Machinery & Equipment and other business activities | 1.71 | 1.71 | 1.83 | 1.92 | 2.10 | 2.22 | 2.11 | 2.30 | 2.39 | 2.48 |
| Public administration and Defence; compulsory social security | 1.02 | 1.02 | 1.02 | 1.02 | 1.01 | 1.02 | 1.01 | 1.01 | 1.01 | 1.01 |
| Education | 1.12 | 1.11 | 1.09 | 1.09 | 1.13 | 1.12 | 1.13 | 1.13 | 1.13 | 1.14 |
| Health and social work | 1.03 | 1.03 | 1.02 | 1.02 | 1.03 | 1.03 | 1.03 | 1.03 | 1.03 | 1.03 |
| Other community, social, and personal services | 1.41 | 1.38 | 1.36 | 1.38 | 1.49 | 1.52 | 1.53 | 1.55 | 1.58 | 1.61 |
| Private households with employed persons | 1.00 | 1.00 | 1.00 | 1.00 | 1.00 | 1.00 | 1.00 | 1.00 | 1.00 | 1.00 |

*Source: ADB Database.*

### Table 5.15: Normalised Backward Linkages for various Sectors/ Industries in India from the year 2011 to 2020.

| Sectors/Industries | Years | | | | | | | | | |
|---|---|---|---|---|---|---|---|---|---|---|
| | 2011 | 2012 | 2013 | 2014 | 2015 | 2016 | 2017 | 2018 | 2019 | 2020 |
| Agriculture, hunting, forestry, and fishing | 0.70 | 0.73 | 0.74 | 0.74 | 0.74 | 0.73 | 0.74 | 0.75 | 0.75 | 0.76 |
| Mining and quarrying | 0.72 | 0.76 | 0.77 | 0.76 | 0.92 | 0.93 | 0.93 | 0.99 | 1.03 | 1.08 |
| Food, beverages, and tobacco | 1.26 | 1.28 | 1.28 | 1.28 | 1.28 | 1.27 | 1.28 | 1.28 | 1.29 | 1.29 |
| Textiles and textile products | 1.31 | 1.29 | 1.29 | 1.28 | 1.28 | 1.28 | 1.28 | 1.27 | 1.27 | 1.27 |

| Sectors/Industries | Years | | | | | | | | | |
|---|---|---|---|---|---|---|---|---|---|---|
| | 2011 | 2012 | 2013 | 2014 | 2015 | 2016 | 2017 | 2018 | 2019 | 2020 |
| Leather, leather products, and footwear | 1.33 | 1.32 | 1.31 | 1.31 | 1.31 | 1.30 | 1.31 | 1.30 | 1.29 | 1.29 |
| Wood and products of wood and cork | 1.02 | 1.01 | 1.02 | 1.02 | 1.01 | 1.00 | 1.01 | 1.01 | 1.00 | 1.00 |
| Pulp, paper, paper products, printing, and publishing | 1.35 | 1.36 | 1.36 | 1.36 | 1.34 | 1.34 | 1.34 | 1.34 | 1.34 | 1.34 |
| Coke, refined petroleum, and nuclear fuel | 1.16 | 1.14 | 1.14 | 1.15 | 1.31 | 1.34 | 1.31 | 1.37 | 1.41 | 1.45 |
| Chemicals and chemical products | 1.36 | 1.40 | 1.39 | 1.40 | 1.41 | 1.40 | 1.41 | 1.42 | 1.43 | 1.44 |
| Rubber and plastics | 1.45 | 1.49 | 1.48 | 1.48 | 1.46 | 1.45 | 1.46 | 1.45 | 1.45 | 1.45 |
| Other non-metallic minerals | 1.18 | 1.17 | 1.17 | 1.18 | 1.20 | 1.21 | 1.20 | 1.21 | 1.21 | 1.22 |
| Basic metals and fabricated metal | 1.31 | 1.31 | 1.30 | 1.31 | 1.28 | 1.28 | 1.27 | 1.26 | 1.26 | 1.25 |
| Machinery, NEC | 1.37 | 1.36 | 1.35 | 1.34 | 1.30 | 1.29 | 1.29 | 1.27 | 1.25 | 1.24 |
| Electrical and optical equipment | 1.39 | 1.39 | 1.38 | 1.38 | 1.35 | 1.33 | 1.33 | 1.32 | 1.31 | 1.30 |
| Transport equipment | 1.46 | 1.46 | 1.45 | 1.44 | 1.42 | 1.40 | 1.40 | 1.38 | 1.37 | 1.36 |
| Manufacturing, NEC; recycling | 1.41 | 1.36 | 1.36 | 1.36 | 1.35 | 1.36 | 1.35 | 1.34 | 1.33 | 1.32 |
| Electricity, gas, and water supply | 1.06 | 1.07 | 1.07 | 1.07 | 1.11 | 1.11 | 1.11 | 1.13 | 1.14 | 1.15 |
| Construction | 1.18 | 1.19 | 1.19 | 1.18 | 1.15 | 1.14 | 1.12 | 1.12 | 1.11 | 1.10 |
| Sale, maintenance, and repair of motor vehicles and motorcycles; retail sale of fuel | 0.65 | 0.66 | 0.67 | 0.66 | 0.65 | 0.66 | 0.66 | 0.66 | 0.66 | 0.66 |
| Wholesale trade and commission trade, except of motor vehicles and motorcycles | 0.65 | 0.66 | 0.66 | 0.66 | 0.65 | 0.66 | 0.66 | 0.66 | 0.66 | 0.66 |
| Retail trade, except of motor vehicles and motorcycles; repair of household goods | 0.65 | 0.66 | 0.66 | 0.66 | 0.65 | 0.66 | 0.66 | 0.66 | 0.66 | 0.66 |
| Hotels and restaurants | 1.14 | 1.16 | 1.16 | 1.17 | 1.16 | 1.19 | 1.16 | 1.18 | 1.18 | 1.19 |

| Sectors/Industries | Years | | | | | | | | | |
|---|---|---|---|---|---|---|---|---|---|---|
| | 2011 | 2012 | 2013 | 2014 | 2015 | 2016 | 2017 | 2018 | 2019 | 2020 |
| Inland transport | 1.08 | 1.09 | 1.09 | 1.08 | 1.07 | 1.10 | 1.07 | 1.08 | 1.07 | 1.07 |
| Water transport | 0.88 | 0.92 | 0.89 | 0.89 | 0.89 | 0.88 | 0.89 | 0.88 | 0.88 | 0.87 |
| Air transport | 1.03 | 0.74 | 0.89 | 0.89 | 0.90 | 0.89 | 0.90 | 0.88 | 0.87 | 0.87 |
| Other supporting and auxiliary transport activities; activities of travel agencies | 0.90 | 0.90 | 0.92 | 0.91 | 0.90 | 0.90 | 0.90 | 0.90 | 0.90 | 0.90 |
| Post and telecommunications | 0.77 | 0.77 | 0.70 | 0.70 | 0.69 | 0.69 | 0.69 | 0.66 | 0.64 | 0.63 |
| Financial intermediation | 0.66 | 0.68 | 0.67 | 0.67 | 0.66 | 0.66 | 0.66 | 0.66 | 0.66 | 0.66 |
| Real estate activities | 0.59 | 0.60 | 0.61 | 0.60 | 0.59 | 0.59 | 0.59 | 0.59 | 0.59 | 0.59 |
| Renting of Machinery & Equipment and other business activities | 0.78 | 0.80 | 0.74 | 0.74 | 0.72 | 0.72 | 0.73 | 0.70 | 0.68 | 0.67 |
| Public administration and Defence; compulsory social security | 0.50 | 0.52 | 0.52 | 0.52 | 0.51 | 0.51 | 0.52 | 0.52 | 0.52 | 0.52 |
| Education | 0.60 | 0.62 | 0.62 | 0.62 | 0.61 | 0.61 | 0.61 | 0.61 | 0.62 | 0.62 |
| Health and social work | 0.92 | 0.95 | 0.95 | 0.95 | 0.94 | 0.94 | 0.94 | 0.95 | 0.95 | 0.95 |
| Other community, social, and personal services | 0.68 | 0.70 | 0.70 | 0.70 | 0.68 | 0.68 | 0.68 | 0.68 | 0.68 | 0.68 |
| Private households with employed persons | 0.50 | 0.52 | 0.52 | 0.52 | 0.51 | 0.51 | 0.52 | 0.52 | 0.52 | 0.52 |

*Source: ADB Database.*

## Table 5.16: Normalised Forward Linkages for various Sectors/ Industries in India from the year 2011 to 2020.

| Sectors/Industries | Years | | | | | | | | | |
|---|---|---|---|---|---|---|---|---|---|---|
| | 2011 | 2012 | 2013 | 2014 | 2015 | 2016 | 2017 | 2018 | 2019 | 2020 |
| Agriculture, hunting, forestry, and fishing | 1.78 | 1.71 | 1.68 | 1.64 | 1.71 | 1.70 | 1.68 | 1.66 | 1.64 | 1.63 |
| Mining and quarrying | 1.94 | 2.28 | 2.20 | 2.03 | 1.91 | 1.60 | 1.97 | 1.76 | 1.70 | 1.64 |
| Food, beverages, and tobacco | 1.01 | 0.94 | 0.92 | 0.93 | 0.96 | 1.00 | 0.94 | 0.95 | 0.95 | 0.95 |
| Textiles and textile products | 0.83 | 0.82 | 0.81 | 0.81 | 0.86 | 0.86 | 0.85 | 0.86 | 0.87 | 0.88 |

| Sectors/Industries | Years | | | | | | | | | |
|---|---|---|---|---|---|---|---|---|---|---|
| | 2011 | 2012 | 2013 | 2014 | 2015 | 2016 | 2017 | 2018 | 2019 | 2020 |
| Leather, leather products, and footwear | 0.72 | 0.73 | 0.72 | 0.72 | 0.74 | 0.73 | 0.74 | 0.74 | 0.74 | 0.75 |
| Wood and products of wood and cork | 0.59 | 0.67 | 0.67 | 0.67 | 0.65 | 0.66 | 0.66 | 0.68 | 0.69 | 0.69 |
| Pulp, paper, paper products, printing, and publishing | 0.89 | 0.88 | 0.87 | 0.87 | 0.88 | 0.91 | 0.88 | 0.89 | 0.89 | 0.89 |
| Coke, refined petroleum, and nuclear fuel | 1.58 | 1.21 | 1.18 | 1.19 | 1.27 | 1.42 | 1.30 | 1.26 | 1.24 | 1.23 |
| Chemicals and chemical products | 2.16 | 2.06 | 2.04 | 2.13 | 2.10 | 2.06 | 2.14 | 2.10 | 2.10 | 2.10 |
| Rubber and plastics | 0.90 | 0.89 | 0.90 | 0.91 | 0.88 | 0.92 | 0.88 | 0.89 | 0.89 | 0.89 |
| Other non-metallic minerals | 0.69 | 0.71 | 0.72 | 0.72 | 0.70 | 0.72 | 0.72 | 0.72 | 0.73 | 0.73 |
| Basic metals and fabricated metal | 2.46 | 2.25 | 2.13 | 2.10 | 1.64 | 1.64 | 1.61 | 1.35 | 1.19 | 1.03 |
| Machinery, N.E.C. | 0.91 | 0.92 | 0.93 | 0.91 | 0.90 | 0.90 | 0.87 | 0.88 | 0.87 | 0.87 |
| Electrical and optical equipment | 1.03 | 1.02 | 1.03 | 1.03 | 1.05 | 1.04 | 1.02 | 1.03 | 1.03 | 1.03 |
| Transport equipment | 0.91 | 0.96 | 0.96 | 0.92 | 0.95 | 1.03 | 0.92 | 0.98 | 0.98 | 0.99 |
| Manufacturing, N.E.C.; recycling | 0.98 | 1.11 | 1.09 | 1.09 | 1.07 | 1.13 | 1.08 | 1.13 | 1.14 | 1.15 |
| Electricity, gas, and water supply | 1.13 | 1.15 | 1.16 | 1.19 | 1.31 | 1.31 | 1.29 | 1.36 | 1.39 | 1.43 |
| Construction | 1.02 | 1.02 | 1.05 | 1.04 | 0.90 | 0.84 | 0.81 | 0.79 | 0.75 | 0.71 |
| Sale, maintenance, and repair of motor vehicles and motorcycles; retail sale of fuel | 0.58 | 0.59 | 0.61 | 0.61 | 0.61 | 0.61 | 0.62 | 0.62 | 0.63 | 0.64 |
| Wholesale trade and commission trade, except of motor vehicles and motorcycles | 1.13 | 1.16 | 1.22 | 1.24 | 1.26 | 1.27 | 1.28 | 1.33 | 1.36 | 1.38 |
| Retail trade, except of motor vehicles and motorcycles; repair of household goods | 1.44 | 1.46 | 1.55 | 1.60 | 1.65 | 1.68 | 1.69 | 1.77 | 1.82 | 1.87 |
| Hotels and restaurants | 0.84 | 0.83 | 0.83 | 0.83 | 0.87 | 0.83 | 0.88 | 0.87 | 0.88 | 0.88 |

| Sectors/Industries | Years | | | | | | | | | |
|---|---|---|---|---|---|---|---|---|---|---|
| | 2011 | 2012 | 2013 | 2014 | 2015 | 2016 | 2017 | 2018 | 2019 | 2020 |
| Inland transport | 1.72 | 1.70 | 1.70 | 1.74 | 1.83 | 1.82 | 1.83 | 1.87 | 1.89 | 1.92 |
| Water transport | 0.52 | 0.53 | 0.54 | 0.53 | 0.53 | 0.53 | 0.53 | 0.53 | 0.54 | 0.54 |
| Air transport | 0.53 | 0.54 | 0.54 | 0.54 | 0.53 | 0.53 | 0.54 | 0.54 | 0.54 | 0.54 |
| Other supporting and auxiliary transport activities; activities of travel agencies | 0.57 | 0.59 | 0.59 | 0.59 | 0.59 | 0.59 | 0.59 | 0.60 | 0.60 | 0.60 |
| Post and telecommunications | 0.68 | 0.69 | 0.69 | 0.69 | 0.72 | 0.72 | 0.72 | 0.73 | 0.74 | 0.75 |
| Financial intermediation | 1.35 | 1.33 | 1.32 | 1.36 | 1.41 | 1.37 | 1.37 | 1.39 | 1.40 | 1.41 |
| Real estate activities | 0.51 | 0.53 | 0.53 | 0.53 | 0.53 | 0.53 | 0.54 | 0.54 | 0.55 | 0.55 |
| Renting of Machinery & Equipment and other business activities | 0.85 | 0.88 | 0.95 | 1.00 | 1.08 | 1.14 | 1.09 | 1.20 | 1.25 | 1.30 |
| Public administration and Defence; compulsory social security | 0.51 | 0.52 | 0.53 | 0.53 | 0.52 | 0.52 | 0.53 | 0.53 | 0.53 | 0.53 |
| Education | 0.56 | 0.57 | 0.57 | 0.56 | 0.58 | 0.58 | 0.59 | 0.59 | 0.59 | 0.60 |
| Health and social work | 0.51 | 0.53 | 0.53 | 0.53 | 0.53 | 0.53 | 0.53 | 0.53 | 0.54 | 0.54 |
| Other community, social, and personal services | 0.70 | 0.71 | 0.71 | 0.71 | 0.77 | 0.78 | 0.79 | 0.81 | 0.83 | 0.84 |
| Private households with employed persons | 0.50 | 0.52 | 0.52 | 0.52 | 0.51 | 0.51 | 0.52 | 0.52 | 0.52 | 0.52 |

*Source: ADB Database.*

In other words, these values in Table 5.13 also represents the sensitivity of that sector's production, in the economy, to the demands of every other sector. With Table 5.13, in the case of a particular industry, (say transport equipment) the values of the total backward linkages for a particular year can be interpreted in the following way, since the total backward linkage of transport equipment is 2.94 in 2011 which is greater than that of (say) basic metals and the fabricated metals in the same year of 2011 at 2.64, increasing production in transport equipment industry, in comparison to basic metals and the fabricated metals industry, would have induced substantial production from sectors that are identifying, extracting or producing the raw materials, also known as upstream sector. Nonetheless, increasing production in basic metals and the fabricated metals industry would, in turn help the transport equipment sector to produce at a higher level. The same condition would apply to the sectors having value of total backward linkage lower than that of transport equipment industry. For the year 2011, all the sectors other than transport equipment would be better off, if the latter attracts the focus of attention in the matter of policy making. In this scenario, the outcome of the implementation of a policy favouring transport equipment sector could potentially be more beneficial to the other sectors and the economy as a whole. It must, however, also be noted that the value of the total backward linkage in the transport sector is substantial throughout. In the more recent year of 2020, the coke, refined petroleum, and nuclear fuel sector and the rubber and the plastic sector and with the total backward linkage value of 2.76 was greater than the rest of the sectors.

In Table 5.14, the total forward linkages for the year 2011-2020 have been computed. The interpretation of the total forward linkage in mining and quarrying, for instance, in the year of 2012, implies that, an increase in production activities of mining and quarrying sector are more beneficial or stimulating to the sectors that are closer to the end user as intermediate product or customer as the final product. Such sectors are also known as downstream sectors. Nonetheless, the fact remains that the end users of output of the downstream sector are also the producers of the final product. Therefore, the values for the total forward linkages of various sectors quantify the total (direct as well as the indirect effects) of all sectors' supply to the input of sector in India. In the given example, for the mining and quarrying sector in 2012, the value of the total forward linkage at 4.43 is greater than that of any other sector.

In the year 2020, the chemicals and chemical products with a total forward linkage value of 4.0 was greater than the rest of the sectors. To implicate the strength of the linkages, the normalised values of the same are required. In the Table 5.15, the normalised backward linkages for various sectors in India for the years of 2011-2020 are computed on the basis of Table 5.13. Similarly, Table 5.16 presents the normalised forward linkages for various sectors in India for the years of 2011-2020, with the help of Table 5.14. Both of these tables would help to draw out the relative strength of interindustry linkage among various sectors in India.

The Normalised Backward Linkages (NBL) and Normalised Forward Linkages (NFL) segregates various sectors on the extent of their reliance on the providers of inputs as a final product. This technique puts forward, the perspective of the backward linkages or users of their output as an intermediate input with respect to the perspective of forward linkages, simultaneously. With the help of the normalised values, various sectors score different values corresponding to the relatively high and low strength of the dependency among the sectors.

**Table 5.17: Normalised Backward Linkages (NBL) and Normalised Forward Linkages (NFL) for India in 2020.**

| | | Normalised Forward Linkage Coefficients | |
|---|---|---|---|
| | | **NFL<1** | **NFL>1** |
| Normalised Backward Linkage Coefficients | NBL>1 | Mining and quarrying, Coke, refined petroleum, and nuclear fuel, Chemicals and chemical products, Basic metals and fabricated metal, Electrical and optical equipment, Manufacturing, N.E.C., recycling, Electricity, gas, and water supply, Construction, Inland transport | Food, beverages, and tobacco, Textiles and textile products, Leather, leather products, and footwear, Wood and products of wood and cork, Pulp, paper, paper products, printing, and publishing, Rubber and plastics, Other non-metallic minerals, Machinery, N.E.C., Transport equipment, Hotels and restaurants |
| | NBL<1 | Agriculture, hunting, forestry, and fishing, Retail trade, except of motor vehicles and motorcycles, repair of household goods, financial intermediation, Renting of Machinery & Equipment and other business activities | Sale, maintenance, and repair of motor vehicles and motorcycles, retail sale of fuel, Wholesale trade and commission trade, except of motor vehicles and motorcycles, Water transport, Air transport, Other supporting and auxiliary transport activities, activities of travel agencies, Post and telecommunications, Real estate activities, Public administration and defence, compulsory social security, Education, Health and Social Work, Other community, social, and personal services, Private households with employed persons |

*Source: Based on Table 5.15 and 5.16.*

In Miller and Blair (2009), to show the effect of the relative strength among different sectors, the value of unity (or one) is suggested to be taken as the average value, below which a sector or an industry can display weaker linkage and above which a sector or an industry can display a stronger linkage. Following this scheme, Table 5.17 differentiates between respective sectors based on the values of the NBL and NFL. Since unity is taken as the average value, the first quadrant in Table 5.17 describes the sectors where both the normalised values of the total backward linkages and total forward linkages are greater than unity.

The first quadrant having the values of NBL and NFL greater than unity constitutes the sectors exhibiting a very large degree of interdependence on other sectors as their consumers and suppliers i.e., very strong backward and forward linkages. The second quadrant in Table 5.17 shows the sectors arranged in such a manner that their NFL is less than one but NBL is greater than one. The output in such sectors is bound to rely heavily on the producers of inputs and intermediate products whereas such output is not conditioned to be consumed further by other sectors. With the values of both NFL and NBL less than unity, the sectors with a very low degree of interdependence on each other lie in the third quadrant. With greater dependence on their buyers with NFL more than unity value, the fourth quadrant shows low dependence on suppliers of inputs, with NBL less than one.

Table 5.17 also shows the categorisation of the various sector in the case of the Indian economy for the year 2020 with respect to the normalised values of the backward linkages in Table 5.15 and the normalised values of the forward linkages in Table 5.16. Accordingly, in the Table 5.17, heavy and basic industries, construction, manufacturing, mining and quarrying, coke, refined petroleum, and nuclear fuel, chemicals and chemical products, electricity, gas, and water supply, basic metals and fabricated metal, recycling, inland transport, in the first quadrant show a strong inter-dependence among other sectors with respect to the inter-industry linkages in the upstream and downstream sectors in India. The sectors in the first quadrant can be regarded as the key industries in the Indian economy.

In the second quadrant for the year 2020, industries such as rubber and plastics, transport equipment, printing and publishing, electrical and optical equipment, leather, leather products, and footwear, food, beverages, and tobacco, wood and products of wood and cork, pulp, paper and paper products, other non-metallic minerals, machinery, hotels and restaurants, and textiles and textile products, shows a greater dependence on the upstream sectors in India. These are the industries that invigorate the production process in the other industries, in other words, supply their output to them to be used as the intermediate input. In the third quadrant the compulsory social security, sale, maintenance and repair of motor vehicles and motorcycles, wholesale trade and commission trade, activities of travel agencies, retail sale of fuel, except of motor vehicles and motorcycles, public administration and defence, water transport, air transport, other supporting and auxiliary transport activities, real estate activities, health and social work, other community, education, private households with employed persons and post and telecommunications, social, and personal services, are mentioned.

These sectors in 2020 can be seen to be exhibiting, the weakest inter-industry linkages in India. In the case of the fourth quadrant, it must be noticed that both the normalised values of the backward linkages and the normalised value of the forward linkages are less than unity in 2020. The NBL score of less than one and the NFL score of greater than one imply that the sectors in the fourth quadrant show greater inter-industry linkages corresponding to the downstream sectors. The fourth quadrant in the Table 5.17 also lists the sectors, namely, renting of machinery & equipment and other business activities, financial intermediation, except of motor vehicles and motorcycles, repair of household goods, retail trade, and agriculture, hunting, forestry, and fishing, provide for the production process of other industries in India for the year 2020. These sectors are heavily dependent on the inter-industry demand to operate well in the economy. Also, in the year 2020, the largest value (2.10) in the normalised forward linkage in Table 5.16 belongs to the chemicals and chemical products sector. Therefore, this sector acted as the top buyer or customer of the inputs from the other sectors. With respect to the largest supplier of inputs to the other sectors in India the chemicals and chemical products, nuclear fuel sector and coke & refined petroleum sector had secured the largest value of the normalised backward linkage value of 1.45.

In the ADB database, the transport equipment sector is synonymous with the automobile industry and its intricacies; and it can easily be gauged that since the value of the normalised backward linkages is greater than unity (see Table 5.15) for the entire period of 2011-2020 as compared to the normalised forward linkages which are less than unity for the same period (see Table 5.16), and therefore, the automobile industry is highly dependent on the inter-industry supply. Though the same cannot be said about this sector on the basis of its dependence on the downstream sectors. It can be deduced that changes in the automobile sector due to foreign investment, technological advancements and policy regulations etc. have the potential to bring about the positive effects on other sectors that acts as its suppliers as the inclination of this industry is on the supplier's side.

## Performance Linkages: The Impact of FDI on the Output of the Domestic Firms in the Indian Automobile Industry from 2011 to 2020

### *Objective 3. To examine the performance linkages of the selected firms in the presence of foreign-invested firms in the automobile industry from 2011 to 2020.*

This objective deals with analysing the impact of selected measures of performance linkages such as trade activities through Export Intensity (XI) and Import Intensity (MI), innovation through the Research and Development Intensity (RDI), firm-specific characteristics with the Age of the firm (Age), Size of the firm (Size) and Capital Intensity of the firm (KI) and industry-specific characteristic through Herfindahl-Hirschman Index (HHI) on the Output level, in the foreign presence measured by equity ownership (Horizontal FDI) in the domestic firms of the automobile industry. In this study, the balanced panel of one hundred thirty-nine domestic firms is investigated for the mentioned variables, mainly measuring their impact on output level at 0.05 % level of significance.

## Descriptive Statistics of the Independent Variables and the Dependent Variable

The dependent variable *Output* as an indicator corresponds to total amount of goods produced in a financial year. In this study the dependent variable of output has been constructed on the basis of sales and change in stocks variable. The sales variable acts as the main income of non-financial companies. It measures the market price of the final goods with the help of which a firm can get an idea as to how strong a company's linkages are, at generating earnings. Hence, the dependent variable (output) is displayed as the natural logarithm of sales plus change in stocks variable with respect to 139 domestic firms from 2011-2020.

The independent variables comprise mainly of Export Intensity (XI) and Import Intensity (MI) that shed a light on the export-import activities of the automobile industries, Research and Development Intensity (RDI) which tries to depict the level of innovation that would increase the domestic firms' technology grasping capacity and techniques adventitious to them, Age of the firm (Age) that acts as an indicator of experience of the firm , Size of the firm (Size) acting as measure of firm's scale of operation and Capital Intensity of the firm (KI) that acts as a measure of the operative leverage to assets of the firm; and industry-specific characteristic, Herfindahl-Hirschman Index (HHI) measures firms' size to the size of their industry i.e., market concentration of the domestic firms. While Horizontal FDI indicates the foreign presence in the automobile industry based on level of equity ownership. In the Table 5.18, the results of the descriptive statistics of the independent variables and the dependent variable (Output) with the number of observations, mean value, value of the standard deviation has been mentioned. It is also to be noticed that the minimum value and the maximum value for each of the variable has also been mentioned as follows: -

**Table 5.18: Descriptive Statistics of the Independent Variables and the Dependent Variable (Output).**

| Variables | Observations | Mean | Standard Deviation | Minimum | Maximum |
|---|---|---|---|---|---|
| Output | 1390 | 8.323093 | 1.866853 | 22.24071 | 13.44737 |
| Export Intensity (XI) | 1390 | 0.1019252 | 0.1691001 | 0 | 1 |
| Import Intensity (MI) | 1390 | 0.1261885 | 0.1977517 | 0 | 3.787234 |
| R&D Intensity (RDI) | 1390 | 0.0057825 | 0.0265656 | 0 | 0.6020326 |
| Age of the firm (Age) | 1390 | 3.335233 | 0.5925311 | 1.098612 | 4.406719 |
| Size of the Firm (Size) | 1388 | 8.170536 | 1.767426 | 3.637586 | 13.44327 |
| Capital Intensity (KI) | 1390 | 2.534641 | 1.931734 | 0.0440694 | 24.64191 |
| Herfindahl-Hirschman Index (HHI) | 1390 | 0.0534243 | 0.0042111 | 0.0480397 | 0.0639408 |
| Horizontal FDI | 1390 | 0.2559384 | 0.0146495 | 0.2301705 | 0.2773762 |

*Source: STATA 13 Output*

It can be seen that the dependent variable does not have any missing value or a zero value that would have created obstruction in the analysis of the model. The independent variable namely Size of the firm (Size) has two missing values. Nevertheless, it is not problematic from the theoretical perspective. The independent variable of export intensity, import intensity and R&D intensity has minimum values of zero. This is because not all the firms from the automobile industry are engaged in the trading activities or the expenditure on the research and development.

## Correlation between Independent Variables and Dependent Variable

In this section, the correlation analysis is performed between the independent variables and the dependent variable (output) of domestic firms in the automobile industry. The null hypothesis of correlation analysis with respect to the degree of relationship between various independent variables and the dependent variable are stated as follows: -

*Statement of Null Hypothesis in Correlation*

| |
|---|
| $H_{01}$: No significant correlation exists between the Export Intensity and the Output level. |
| $H_{02}$: No significant correlation exists between the Import Intensity and the Output level. |
| $H_{03}$: No significant correlation exists between the R&D Intensity and the Output level. |
| $H_{04}$: No significant correlation exists between the Age of the firm and the Output level. |
| $H_{05}$: No significant correlation exists between the Size of the firm and the Output level. |
| $H_{06}$: No significant correlation exists between the Capital Intensity and the Output level. |
| $H_{07}$: No significant correlation exists between the HHI and the Output level. |
| $H_{08}$: No significant relationship exists between the Horizontal FDI and the Output level. |

The results of correlation analysis in the Table 5.19, presents p-values to the corresponding coefficients, findings at two-tailed test and the remarks with respect to the independent variables and the dependent variable. With export intensity (XI), p-value for two-tailed test has turned up to be less than 0.05% level of significance. Thus, the null hypothesis $H_{01}$ of no significant correlation between the export intensity and output level gets rejected. It is also to be pointed out that due to the negative sign of coefficient, there exists an inverse relationship between the dependent variable and XI.

The Table 5.19 also depicts an insignificant and positive correlation between import intensity (MI) and output level. Hence, the null hypothesis $H_{02}$ level does not get rejected at 0.05% level of significance. Furthermore, insignificant and positive association with correlation coefficient of 0.0370 exists between R&D intensity (RDI) and output level. Hence, the null hypothesis $H_{03}$ does not get rejected.

**Table 5.19: Results of Correlation Analysis between the Independent Variables and the Dependent (Output) Variable.**

| Independent Variables | Correlation Coefficient | p-value | Findings | Remarks |
|---|---|---|---|---|
| Export Intensity (XI) | -0.1339 | (0.000) | Significant and Negative correlation exists | $H_{01}$ gets rejected |
| Import Intensity (MI) | 0.0507 | (0.0587) | Insignificant and Positive correlation exists | $H_{02}$ does not get rejected |
| R&D Intensity (RDI) | 0.0370 | (0.1684) | Insignificant and Positive correlation exists | $H_{03}$ does not get rejected |
| Age of the Firm (Age) | -0.0058 | (0.8298) | Insignificant and Negative correlation exists | $H_{04}$ does not get rejected |
| Size of the Firm (Size) | 0.9542 | (0.000) | Significant and Positive correlation exists | $H_{05}$ gets rejected |
| Capital Intensity (KI) | 0.1433 | (0.000) | Significant and Positive correlation exists | $H_{06}$ gets rejected |
| HHI | -0.1130 | (0.000) | Significant and Negative correlation exists | $H_{07}$ gets rejected |
| Horizontal FDI | 0.0065 | (0.000) | Significant and Positive correlation exists | $H_{08}$ gets rejected |

*Source: STATA 13 Output*

Similarly, the null hypothesis $H_{04}$ of significant correlation between the age of the firm and output level does not get rejected at 95% confidence with an insignificant p-value (0.8298) and a negative coefficient (-0.0058). The result, however indicates significant and positive relationship between size of a firm and output level; and capital intensity of a firm with respect to that of the output level at 0.000 p-value. With this, the null hypothesis of correlation between the size of the firm ($H_{05}$) and output level and capital intensity and output level ($H_{06}$) of the firm gets rejected, respectively.

The industry-specific variable HHI shows significant and negative correlation with the dependent variable (output level) with correlation coefficient (- 0.1130). Thus, the null hypothesis ($H_{07}$) gets rejected. The Horizontal FDI variable shows a positive and significant correlation to the output variable with its p-value (0.000). Therefore, the null hypothesis $H_{08}$ gets rejected. In order to determine how and to what extent does one (independent) variable affect the other (dependent) variable, the regression-based analysis has been undertaken.

## Pooled Regression between Independent Variables and Dependent Variable

The OLS pooled regression model to the balanced panel data of 139 domestic firms in 2011-2020 is applied in this section. The null hypothesis of the multiple pooled OLS regression analysis, where output of the domestic firms in the automobile industry is considered as the dependent variable, are stated as follows: -

*Statement of Null Hypothesis in Regression*

| $H_{01}$: No significant correlation exists between the Export Intensity and the Output level. |
|---|
| $H_{02}$: No significant correlation exists between the Import Intensity and the Output level. |
| $H_{03}$: No significant correlation exists between the R&D Intensity and the Output level. |
| $H_{04}$: No significant correlation exists between the Age of the firm and the Output level. |
| $H_{05}$: No significant correlation exists between the Size of the firm and the Output level. |
| $H_{06}$: No significant correlation exists between the Capital Intensity and the Output level. |
| $H_{07}$: No significant correlation exists between the HHI and the Output level. |
| $H_{08}$: No significant relationship exists between the Horizontal FDI and the Output level. |

The results of correlation analysis in the Table 5.19, presents p-values to the corresponding coefficients, findings at two-tailed test and the remarks with respect to the independent variables and the dependent variable. With export intensity (XI), p-value for two-tailed test has turned up to be less than 0.05% level of significance. Thus, the null hypothesis $H_{01}$ of no significant correlation between the export intensity and output level gets rejected. It is also to be pointed out that due to the negative sign of coefficient, there exists an inverse relationship between the dependent variable and XI.

The Table 5.19 also depicts an insignificant and positive correlation between import intensity (MI) and output level. Hence, the null hypothesis $H_{02}$ level does not get rejected at 0.05% level of significance. Furthermore, insignificant and positive association with correlation coefficient of 0.0370 exists between R&D intensity (RDI) and output level. Hence, the null hypothesis $H_{03}$ does not get rejected.

**Table 5.20: Results of the Pooled OLS Regression between the Independent Variables and the Dependent (Output) Variable.**

| Independent Variables | Coefficients of Multiple Regression | Standard Error | t-statistics (p-value) | Findings | Remarks |
|---|---|---|---|---|---|
| Export Intensity (XI) | -0.332 | 0.073 | -4.54 (0.000) | Significant and negative effect | $H_{01}$ gets rejected |
| Import Intensity (MI) | -0.557 | 0.063 | -8.74 (0.000) | Significant and negative effect | $H_{02}$ does not get rejected |
| R&D Intensity (RDI) | -3.155 | 0.459 | -6.87 (0.000) | Significant and negative effect | $H_{03}$ does not get rejected |
| Age of the firm (Age) | -0.153 | 0.021 | -0.72 (0.472) | Insignificant and negative effect | $H_{04}$ does not get rejected |
| Size of the Firm (Size) | 1.018 | 0.007 | 145.45 (0.000) | Significant and positive effect | $H_{05}$ gets rejected |
| Capital Intensity (KI) | 0.136 | 0.006 | 21.42 (0.000) | Significant and positive effect | $H_{06}$ gets rejected |
| HHI | -15.921 | 2.991 | -5.32 (0.000) | Significant and negative effect | $H_{07}$ gets rejected |
| Horizontal FDI | -4.165 | 0.857 | -4.86 (0.000) | Significant and negative effect | $H_{08}$ gets rejected |
| Constant | 1.747 | 0.306 | 5.70 (0.000) | Significant and positive effect | |
| Observation | 1388 | | | | |
| F-Ratio (p-value) | 2810.94 (0.000) | | | | |
| R- Square | 94.22 % | | | | |

*Source: STATA 13 Output*

The size of the firm with its positive coefficient of 1.018 is also significant at 0.05% with a p-value at 0.000. The corresponding null hypothesis $H_{05}$ , stating no significant impact of firm size on the output level of domestic firms in the automobile industry, gets rejected. The capital intensity is also significant and positive at 0.05% significance level. Consequently, the statement of "no impact" ($H_{06}$) gets rejected. The industry-specific explanatory variable shows a negative and significant relationship, therefore, the null hypothesis $H_{07}$ gets rejected.

Table 5.20 also depicts that the explanatory variable of Horizontal FDI shows a significant and a negative impact on the output level, therefore, suggesting to reject the null hypothesis, $H_{08}$. The constant or the intercept coefficient of 1.747 claims that on average a unit increase in the output level with no change in other independent variables. It must be noted that the corresponding p-values to all the independent variables (even the intercept term) to the dependent variables are highly significant except in the case of the age of the firm (at p-value = 0.472) at 95% level of confidence.

The value of the R-square that depicts the overall measure of goodness of fit tells that the independent variables explain 94.22% of the total variation, altogether, in the regression model. On the groundwork of the p-value for the F-statistic, it can also be said that the eight independent variables collectively are highly statistically significant. However, the panel data in this study consists of heterogeneous firms. Therefore, it cannot be assumed that the balanced panel used in this regression, would be free from the problem of multicollinearity among the independent variables and heteroscedasticity of the error terms. First, to know the exact level of multicollinearity among the independent variables, Table 5.21 shows the variance inflation factor (VIF) and the tolerance (TOL=1/VIF) factors, for each of the independent variables. Since, the mean VIF is less than 2, there does not exist any particular issue with the level of multicollinearity to the extent that action of dropping any variable would be necessary. Therefore, we can work with the same number of the variables as the independent variables. Also, the best remedy suggested for multicollinearity in such a case, is to do nothing and simply present the results.

**Table 5.21: Results of the Variance Inflating Factor (VIF) Test of the Multicollinearity.**

| **Independent Variables** | **VIF** | **1/VIF** |
|---|---|---|
| Export Intensity (XI) | 1.05 | 0.948 |
| Import Intensity (MI) | 1.09 | 0.915 |
| R&D Intensity (RDI) | 1.02 | 0.976 |
| Age of the firm (Age) | 1.09 | 0.921 |
| Size of the Firm (Size) | 1.05 | 0.950 |
| Capital Intensity (KI) | 1.05 | 0.095 |
| HHI | 1.08 | 0.924 |
| Horizontal FDI | 1.09 | 0.921 |
| Mean VIF | 1.07 | |

*Source: STATA 13 Output*

Now, moving to another set of challenges, in the case of the balanced panel data, i.e., heterogeneity of the error term in the regression analysis, the Breusch-Pagan/Cook-Weisberg test for heteroskedasticity has been employed to assess its presence, as the ideal case of constant variance of the error term, seldomly exists in the panel data due to ever-present cross-sectional element. At the significant p-value of chi-square (0.000), the null hypothesis of constant variance is tested. The results of the Breusch-Pagan test are presented as follows: -

**Table 5.22: Results of Breusch-Pagan/Cook-Weisberg Test for Heteroskedasticity**

| chi2(1) | p-value |
|---|---|
| 22.77 | 0.000 |

*Source: STATA 13 Output*

Therefore, with a p-value of 0.000, the situation of heterogeneity does exist in the error terms of the multiple regression. Now, since the panel data consists of elements of the cross-sectional and the time-series model, there are two different panel data models to be applied to incorporate the effect of time-based heterogeneous groups in the analysis. For this, the Hausman test is studied the proposed hypothesis stating *the preferred model is the random effects model*. The results of the test estimated from different heterogeneous units are shown below in Table 5.23.

**Table 5.23: Results of the Hausman Test between the Coefficients of the Fixed Effects Model and Random Effects Model.**

Dependent Variable: Output

| Independent Variables | Coefficients Fixed Effects | Coefficients Random Effects |
|---|---|---|
| Export Intensity (XI) | -0.236 | -0.196 |
| Import Intensity (MI) | -0.747 | -0.793 |
| R&D Intensity (RDI) | -1.173 | -1.193 |
| Age of the firm (Age) | 0.392 | 0.039 |
| Size of the Firm (Size) | 0.677 | 0.912 |
| Capital Intensity (KI) | 0.089 | 0.095 |
| HHI | -16.458 | -15.249 |

| Independent Variables | Coefficients Fixed Effects | Coefficients Random Effects |
|---|---|---|
| Horizontal FDI | -2.427 | -3.031 |
| Chi square (8) (p-value) | 133.70 (0.000) | |
| Remarks | Fixed effect model is finalized | |

*Source: STATA 13 Output*

With a p-value below 0.05% level of significance, the proposed statement that *random effects is chosen model* gets rejected. Therefore, the fixed effects model is finalised.

## Fixed Effect Regression Model between Independent Variables and Dependent Variable

In quest to examine the interpretable results from fixed effects, the null hypothesis stated intended for checking the performance linkages are as follows: -

*Statement of Null Hypothesis in Regression*

| |
|---|
| $H_{01}$: No significant impact of Export Intensity occurs on the Output level. |
| $H_{02}$: No significant impact of Import Intensity occurs on the Output level. |
| $H_{03}$: No significant impact of R&D Intensity occurs on the Output level. |
| $H_{04}$: No significant impact of Age of the firm occurs on the Output level. |
| $H_{05}$: No significant impact of Size of the firm occurs on the Output level. |
| $H_{06}$: No significant impact of Capital Intensity occurs on the Output level. |
| $H_{07}$: No significant impact of HHI occurs on the Output level. |
| $H_{08}$: No significant impact of Horizontal FDI occurs on the Output level. |

The results of the Hausman test indicated that the time-invariant effects in the panel data were significant. In addition, the results of the Hausman test also showed that the cross-sectional effects were not random. Therefore, the fixed effects model with time-invariant independent variables has been applied. The results of fixed effects are shown in Table 5.24. Table 5.24 states the regression coefficients in the model, the standard errors of the coefficients and the t-statistics and the corresponding two-tailed p-values which could be examined at 0.05% level of significance.

In the last columns, the findings of the two-tailed test corresponding to the coefficients and their respective p-values are also mentioned. Since the fixed effect model has been applied, the goodness of fit is also to be measured. The value of the reported R-square (within) is 72.06%, which means that 72.06% of the variation in the output variable within each of the firms over time is captured by the independent variables. With the help of the R-square (between) value is 91.44%. It is estimated that 91.44% of the independent variables account for the differences in the output between the firms. In simple words, 91.44% of the variation in the output variable between the firms is captured by the fixed effects model. The value of R-square (overall) states that 89.75% of the total variation in the dependent variable is explained by the independent variables in the model. In the table, the question of whether the independent variables reliably predict the output variable has to be answered by the F-statistic. The p-value of the F-statistics is 0.000. The comparison of the p-value with the 0.05% as alpha value leads to the conclusion that the independent variables reliably predict the output variable.

**Table 5.24: Results of the Fixed Effects Regression between the Independent Variables and the Dependent (Output) Variable**

| Independent Variables | Regression Coefficient | Standard Error | t-stats (p-value) | Findings |
|---|---|---|---|---|
| Export Intensity (XI) | -0.236 | 0.064 | -3.67 (0.000) | Significant and Negative effect |
| Import Intensity (MI) | -0.747 | 0.042 | -17.71 (0.000) | Significant and Negative effect |
| R&D Intensity (RDI) | -1.173 | 0.320 | -3.66 (0.000) | Significant and Negative effect |
| Age of the firm (Age) | 0.392 | 0.065 | 5.97 (0.000) | Significant and Positive effect |
| Size of the Firm (Size) | 0.677 | 0.023 | 28.45 (0.000) | Significant and Positive effect |
| Capital Intensity (KI) | 0.089 | 0.005 | 16.65 (0.000) | Significant and Positive effect |
| HHI | -16.458 | 1.837 | -8.96 (0.000) | Significant and Negative effect |
| Horizontal FDI | -2.427 | 0.524 | -4.63 (0.000) | Significant and Negative effect |
| Constant | 2.881 | 0.270 | 10.65 (0.000) | Significant and Positive effect |

| Independent Variables | Regression Coefficient | Standard Error | t-stats (p-value) | Findings |
|---|---|---|---|---|
| Observation | 1388 | | | |
| F-statistic (p value) | 28.66 (0.000) | | | |
| R-Square (within) | 72.06% | | | |
| R-Square (between) | 91.44% | | | |
| R-Square (overall) | 89.75% | | | |

*Source: STATA 13 Output*

It must be realised by now that although the fixed effects model has been finalised, it would still possess the heterogeneity of the error terms as detected in the case of the pooled estimate. In this situation, the literature has suggested a procedure of heteroscedasticity corrected (robust) standard errors. This practice does not change the value of the coefficients but adjusts the standard errors to allow for heteroscedasticity. The results pertaining to the fixed effects model with the robust standard errors must be interpreted with the help of Table 5.25. It should also be noticed that there is not much of a difference between the important estimates of the results in Table 5.24 and Table 5.25. The results of multiple regression analysis in Table 5.25, indicate regression coefficients, robust standard errors, and the p-value of the t-statistics on the basis of which certain findings are made with a two-tailed test at 0.05% level of significance.

The difference in the model with the robust errors is, however, also imbibed with the presence of an inflated value of the standard errors. Hence, the reporting of important values is done with respect to the following estimates in Table 5.25: -

**Table 5.25: Results of the Fixed Effects Regression (with Robust Standard Errors) between the Independent Variables and the Dependent (Output) Variable**

| Independent Variables | Regression Coefficient | Robust Standard Errors | t-stats (p-value) | Findings | Remark |
|---|---|---|---|---|---|
| Export Intensity (XI) | -0.236 | 0.154 | -1.52 (0.130) | Insignificant and Negative effect | $H_{01}$ does not get rejected |
| Import Intensity (MI) | -0.747 | 0.095 | -7.86 (0.000) | Significant and Negative effect | $H_{02}$ gets rejected |

| **Independent Variables** | **Regression Coefficient** | **Robust Standard Errors** | **t-stats (p-value)** | **Findings** | **Remark** |
|---|---|---|---|---|---|
| R&D Intensity (RDI) | -1.173 | 0.317 | -3.70 (0.000) | Significant and Negative effect | $H_{03}$ gets rejected |
| Age of the firm (Age) | 0.392 | 0.147 | 2.65 (0.009) | Significant and Positive effect | $H_{04}$ gets rejected |
| Size of the Firm (Size) | 0.677 | 0.060 | 11.16 (0.000) | Significant and Positive effect | $H_{05}$ gets rejected |
| Capital Intensity (KI) | 0.089 | 0.018 | 4.78 (0.000) | Significant and Positive effect | $H_{06}$ gets rejected |
| HHI | -16.458 | 2.297 | -7.16 (0.000) | Significant and Negative effect | $H_{07}$ gets rejected |
| Horizontal FDI | -2.427 | 0.766 | -3.17 (0.002) | Significant and Negative effect | $H_{08}$ gets rejected |
| Constant | 2.881 | 0.433 | 6.65 (0.000) | Significant and Positive effect | |
| Observation | 1388 | | | | |
| F (8,138) (p value) | 77.23 (0.000) | | | | |
| R-Square (within) | 72.06 % | | | | |
| R-Square (between) | 91.44% | | | | |
| R-Square (overall) | 89.75 | | | | |

*Source: STATA 13 Output*

Using the panel data, the results show that, over the period 2011-2020, the export intensity has an inconsequential and adverse influence on the output level of the Indian automobile industry, implying a unit increase in the export intensity would lead to a decline in output 0.236 units. Therefore, the null hypothesis ($H_{01}$) for the effect of the export intensity on the output level of domestic firms in the automobile industry does not get rejected. The null hypothesis ($H_{02}$) of no significant impression of import intensity on the output level of domestic corporations in the automobile business, gets rejected with a significant p-value of 0.000. As depicted by its coefficient, a unit rise in the explanatory variable would lead to a decline in the dependent variable by 0.747 units.

With an increase in the import intensity, the domestic output level seems to get affected negatively due to increase in foreign spending. There also exists a negative impact (with coefficient -1.173) of the RDI on the output level which is significant, leading to the renunciation of the statement ($H_{03}$), asserting no significant impact of R&D intensity on the output. The cause for such undesirable relations is that the domestic concerns have insufficient access to the R&D facilities. With significant p-value of 0.000, null hypothesis ($H_{04}$) of no significant impact of age of the firm on the output level of domestic firms in the automobile industry, also get rejected. As firms age, they begin to harness the advantages of becoming a brand name. The size of the firm with its positive coefficient of 0.677 is also not insignificant, with 0.000 p-value. This would be due to the fact that sizeable corporations are able to harness the scale economies due to lower average costs.

The corresponding null hypothesis ($H_{05}$) in the case of the size variable gets rejected. The capital intensity is also significant and positive at a 0.05% level of significance. This result describes that a unit increase in assets in the form of plant and machinery tends to increase the output variable by 4.78%, therefore, the null hypothesis ($H_{06}$) gets rejected. The industry-specific explanatory variable shows a negative relationship with respect to the output variable. A unit increase in the market concentration index taken as Herfindahl-Hirschman Index (HHI) decreases the output level by 16.458 units. Therefore, the null hypothesis ($H_{07}$) gets rejected. Table 5.25 also depicts that the explanatory variable of Horizontal FDI shows an adverse but substantial impact on the output level, suggesting to reject the null hypothesis ($H_{08}$). This means that the intra-industry linkages formed through the presence of foreign firms have negative effects on the level of output. The constant or the intercept coefficient of 2.881 claims that on average the output level is 2.881 units with no change in explanatory variables.

## Productivity Linkages: The Impact of FDI on the Output of the Domestic Firms in the Indian Automobile Industry from 2011 to 2020.

### *Objective 4. To examine the productivity linkages of the selected firms in the presence of foreign-invested firms in the automobile industry from 2011 to 2020.*

This objective deals with analysing the impact of selected measures of productivity linkages such as trade activities, through Export Intensity (XI) and Import Intensity (MI), innovation, through the Research and Development Intensity (RDI), firm-specific characteristics with Age of the firm (Age), Size of the firm (Size) and Capital Intensity of the firm (KI) and industry-specific characteristic, through Herfindahl-Hirschman Index (HHI) on the Total Factor Productivity level of the firms (domestic) in the presence of foreign firms calculated by the equity ownership (Horizontal FDI), in the automobile industry. In this study, the balanced panel of one hundred thirty-nine domestic firms in the automobile industry are collected for the mentioned variables, measuring their impact mainly on the TFP at 0.05 % level of significance.

## Descriptive Statistics of the Independent Variables and the Dependent Variable

The Total Factor Productivity is a statistic estimated for measuring overall productivity relative to the size of all of its primary factor inputs, in a financial year. In this study, the dependent variable of Total Factor Productivity has been constructed on the basis of primary inputs of capital, labour, material and energy variables based on the combined 170 firms (139 domestic firms and 31 foreign firms) from 2011 to 2020. However, the TFP for 139 domestic firms is taken to measure how efficiently production inputs are being employed to manufacture a given level of output and how strong a company's linkages are in the production process, in the presence of foreign firms. Hence, in order to serve this purpose, the dependent variable of *TFP* is calculated in the natural logarithm.

The independent variables comprise mainly of Export Intensity (XI) and Import Intensity (MI) to shed a light on the export-import activities of the automobile industry, Research and Development Intensity (RDI) which tries to depict the absorptive capacity that would increase the domestic firms' ability to subsume the new technology and techniques manifested by the foreign firms, Age of the firm (Age) that acts as an indicator of learning ability of the firm, Size of the firm (Size) acting by way of an indicator of scale operation of the firm and capital intensity of the firm (KI) that acts as per a measure of the operative leverage to firm's assets and industry-specific characteristic Herfindahl-Hirschman Index (HHI) describes the size of the firms with respect to the industry i.e., market concentration of the domestic firms. The Horizontal FDI indicates the presence of foreign firms based on their level of equity ownership in the automobile industry.

In Table 5.26, the results of the descriptive statistics amongst the dependent (TFP) and independent variables are presented. These results also exhibit the observations, mean values, and values of the standard deviation, in addition to the minimum and maximum value located in the variables.

**Table 5.26: Descriptive statistics of the Independent Variables and the Dependent Variable (Total Factor Productivity)**

| Variables | Mean | Standard Deviation | Minimum | Maximum |
|---|---|---|---|---|
| Total Factor Productivity | 1.123464 | 0.264179 | 0.1561607 | 2.946208 |
| Export Intensity (XI) | 0.1019252 | 0.1691001 | 0 | 1 |
| Import Intensity (MI) | 0.1261885 | 0.1977517 | 0 | 3.787234 |
| R&D Intensity (RDI) | 0.0057825 | 0.0265656 | 0 | 0.6020326 |
| Age of the firm (Age) | 3.335233 | 0.5925311 | 1.098612 | 4.406719 |
| Size of the firm (Size) | 8.170536 | 1.767426 | 3.637586 | 13.44327 |
| Capital Intensity (KI) | 2.534641 | 1.931734 | 0.0440694 | 24.64191 |
| Hirschman Herfindahl Index (HHI) | 0.0534243 | 0.0042111 | 0.0480397 | 0.0639408 |
| Horizontal FDI | 0.2559384 | 0.0146495 | 0.2301705 | 0.2773762 |

*Source: STATA 13 Output*

It can be seen that the dependent variable does not have any missing value or a zero-value that would have created obstruction in the analysis of the model. The independent variable namely the *size of the firm* has two missing values. The independent variable of *R&D intensity, import intensity* in addition to *export intensity* has a minimum value of zero. Since not all the firms from the automobile industry are engaged in the trading activities or the expenditure on the R&D.

## Correlation between Independent Variables and Dependent Variable

In this study, the correlation analysis is done between the TFP, which is taken as the dependent variable, with the measures of productivity linkages inducing spillovers as measured by XI, MI, RDI, Age, Size, KI, HHI and Horizontal FDI in domestic firms of the automobile industry. The Pearson's coefficient of correlation happens to be estimated in this study. The null hypothesis of the correlation analysis is stated as follows: -

*Statement of Null Hypothesis in Correlation*

| $H_{01}$: No significant correlation exists between the Export Intensity and the TFP level. |
|---|
| $H_{02}$: No significant correlation exists between the Import Intensity and the TFP level. |
| $H_{03}$: No significant correlation exists between the R&D Intensity and the TFP level. |
| $H_{04}$: No significant correlation exists between the Age of the firm and the TFP level. |
| $H_{05}$: No significant correlation exists between the Size of the firm and the TFP level. |
| $H_{06}$: No significant correlation exists between the Capital Intensity and the TFP level. |
| $H_{07}$: No significant correlation exists between the HHI and the TFP level. |
| $H_{08}$: No significant relationship exists between the Horizontal FDI and the TFP level. |

In the Table 5.27, correlation coefficients and the p-values between the explanatory variables and the explained variable are given as follows: -

**Table 5.27: Results of Correlation Analysis between the Independent Variables and the Dependent (Total Factor Productivity) Variable.**

| **Independent Variables** | **Correlation Coefficient** | **p-value** | **Remark** |
|---|---|---|---|
| Export Intensity (XI) | 0.1356 | (0.000) | Significant and Positive correlation exists |
| Import Intensity (MI) | -0.2273 | (0.000) | Significant and Negative correlation exists |
| R&D Intensity (RDI) | -0.1704 | (0.000) | Significant and Negative correlation exists |
| Age of the firm (Age) | -0.0296 | (0.2696) | Insignificant and Negative correlation exists |
| Size of the firm (Size) | -0.4100 | (0.000) | Significant and Negative correlation exists |
| Capital Intensity (KI) | 0.1845 | (0.000) | Significant and Positive correlation exists |
| HHI | -0.0446 | (0.0966) | Significant and Negative correlation exists |
| Horizontal FDI | -0.0214 | (0.4254) | Insignificant and Negative correlation exists |

*Source: STATA 13 Output*

IIn the case of export intensity (XI), the p-value is found to be less than the 0.05% significance level. In the view of the same, the null hypothesis ($H_{01}$) stating no significant correlation between the export intensity and TFP is rejected. It is also apparent that due to the positive sign of the coefficient, there exists a direct association between the dependent variable and export intensity. Table 5.27 also shows a significant and negative correlation between import intensity (MI) and TFP, rejecting the null hypothesis ($H_{02}$) stating no significant correlation between the import intensity and TFP. Furthermore, a significant and negative correlation with the coefficient value of -0.1704 exists between R&D intensity (RDI) and TFP, hence the null hypothesis ($H_{03}$) gets rejected.

Similarly, the null hypothesis ($H_{04}$) of a significant correlation between the age of the firm and TFP does not get rejected at 95% level of significance with an insignificant p-value (0.2696) and a negative coefficient (-0.0269). The result indicates an insignificant and negative relationship between size and TFP. With this, the statement of "no impact" in $H_{05}$ gets rejected. Capital intensity shows a significant and positive relationship in relation to the TFP. Also, the statement of "no impact" in the case of capital intensity on the TFP gets rejected in $H_{06}$.

The industry-specific HHI shows an insignificant and negative correlation with the dependent variable of the output level with a correlation coefficient (-0.0446). Thus, the statement of no impact ($H_{07}$) is not rejected at 0.05% level of significance. The Horizontal FDI variable shows an insignificant and negative correlation with respect to the output variable with its p-value (0.000). Therefore, the null hypothesis ($H_{08}$) is not rejected at a 0.05% level of significance. Nevertheless, correlation measures the degree of strength of direct or inverse association between the two variables. To determine how and to what extent does independent variable affects the dependent variable, a regression-based analysis has been undertaken.

## Pooled Regression between Independent Variables and Dependent Variable

The OLS pooled regression model to the balanced panel data of 139 domestic firms in 2011-2020 is applied in this section and the Total Factor Productivity of the domestic firms is considered as the dependent variable. The null hypothesis of the multiple pooled OLS regression analysis is stated as follows: -

*Statement of Null Hypothesis in Regression*

| |
|---|
| $H_{01}$: No significant impact of Export Intensity occurs on the TFP level. |
| $H_{02}$: No significant impact of Import Intensity occurs on the TFP level. |
| $H_{03}$: No significant impact of R&D Intensity occurs on the TFP level. |
| $H_{04}$: No significant impact of Age of the firm occurs on the TFP level. |
| $H_{05}$: No significant impact of Size of the firm occurs on the TFP level. |
| $H_{06}$: No significant impact of Capital Intensity occurs on the TFP level. |
| $H_{07}$: No significant impact of HHI occurs on the TFP level. |
| $H_{08}$: No significant impact of Horizontal FDI occurs on the TFP level. |

Table 5.28 presents the results of OLS regression analysis with coefficients, standard error, t-statistics and their corresponding p-value to test the hypothesis, as follows: -.

**Table 5.28: Results of the Pooled OLS Regression between the Independent Variables and the Dependent (Total Factor Productivity) Variable**

| **Independent Variable** | **Regression Coefficient** | **Standard Errors** | **t-statistics (p-value)** | **Findings** | **Remark** |
|---|---|---|---|---|---|
| Export Intensity (XI) | 0.203 | 0.037 | 5.46 (0.000) | Significant and positive effect | $H_{01}$ gets rejected |
| Import Intensity (MI) | -0.019 | 0.032 | -6.09 (0.000) | Significant and negative effect | $H_{02}$ gets rejected |
| R&D Intensity (RDI) | -1.072 | 0.233 | -4.60 (0.000) | Significant and negative effect | $H_{03}$gets rejected |
| Age of the firm (Age) | 0.001 | 0.010 | 0.10 (0.920) | Insignificant and positive effect | $H_{04}$ does not get rejected |
| Size of the firm (Size) | -0.055 | 0.003 | -15.58 (000) | Significant and negative effect | $H_{05}$gets rejected |
| Capital Intensity (KI) | 0.024 | 0.003 | 7.54 (0.000) | Significant and positive effect | $H_{06}$ gets rejected |
| HHI | -4.223 | 1.520 | -2.78 (0.006) | Significant and negative effect | $H_{07}$ gets rejected |

| **Independent Variable** | **Regression Coefficient** | **Standard Errors** | **t-statistics (p-value)** | **Findings** | **Remark** |
|---|---|---|---|---|---|
| Horizontal FDI | 0.013 | 0.435 | 0.03 (0.975) | Insignificant and negative effect | $H_{08}$ does not get rejected |
| Constant | 1.747 | 0.155 | 11.19 (0.000) | Significant and positive effect | |
| Observation | 1388 | | | | |
| F-Ratio (p-value) | 59.67 (0.000) | | | | |
| R- Square | 25.71 % | | | | |

*Source: STATA 13 Output*

Over the period from 2011 to 2020, export intensity shows a positive and significant impact on the TFP of the Indian automobile industry, rejecting the statement, $H_{01}$, denouncing the impact of Export Intensity on TFP level in domestic firms with 95% of confidence. Similarly, the null hypothesis ($H_{02}$) stating no significant impact of import intensity on TFP of domestic firms, gets rejected with a highly significant p-value of 0.000.

Also, there exists a negative impact of the import intensity on the TFP as depicted by its coefficient (-0.019). There also exists a significant (p-value = 0.000) and negative impact (coefficient = -1.072) of the RDI on the TFP. In this case, the null hypothesis ($H_{03}$) is also gets rejected. With a positive and insignificant p-value of 0.920, the null hypothesis ($H_{04}$) of no significant impact of age of the firm on TFP of local concerns, does not get rejected. The firm's size with its negative coefficient of -0.055 is also significant at 0.05% significance level

The corresponding null hypothesis ($H_{05}$) stating no significant impact of the size of the firm on TFP gets rejected. The capital intensity is also the significant and positive level of significance at 0.05%. Hence, the proposed null ($H_{06}$) gets rejected. The industry-specific explanatory variable HHI shows a negative and significant effect on TFP. Thus, rejecting the null hypothesis ($H_{07}$). Table 5.28 also presents that the explanatory variable of Horizontal FDI shows an insignificant and negative impact on the TFP implicating non-rejection of the null statement ($H_{08}$) of no significant impact of Horizontal FDI on the TFP at a p-value of 0.975.

The constant or the intercept coefficient of 1.747 claims that on average a TFP level is 1.747 when the explanatory variables stood at zero. The value of the R-square (within) depicts that 25.71% of the total variation incurred by the dependent variable is explained by means of all the predictors. On the basis of the p-value for the F-statistic, it can also be recognized that the eight independent variables (collectively) are highly significant at a 95% confidence level. However, the panel data in this study consists of heterogeneous firms.

The problem of multicollinearity and heteroscedasticity of the error terms has been checked. The level of multicollinearity among the independent variables is mentioned in Table 5.29. Since the mean Variance Inflating Factor (VIF) was less than 2, the best remedy suggested for multicollinearity is to do nothing. Therefore, the same number of variables as the independent variables have been worked with. Also, the best remedy suggested for multicollinearity is to do nothing and simply present the results.

**Table 5.29: Results of the Variance Inflating Factor (VIF) Test of the Multicollinearity**

| **Independent Variables** | **VIF** | **1/VIF** |
|---|---|---|
| Export Intensity (XI) | 1.05 | 0.948 |
| Import Intensity (MI) | 1.09 | 0.915 |
| R&D Intensity (RDI) | 1.02 | 0.976 |
| Age of the firm (Age) | 1.09 | 0.921 |
| Size of the firm (Size) | 1.05 | 0.950 |
| Capital Intensity (KI) | 1.05 | 0.095 |
| HHI | 1.08 | 0.924 |
| Horizontal FDI | 1.09 | 0.921 |
| Mean VIF | 1.07 | |

*Source: STATA 13 Output*

Now, moving to another set of challenges in the case of the balanced panel data, i.e., for the heterogeneity of the error term in the regression model, the Breusch-Pagan/Cook-Weisberg test for heteroskedasticity has been employed to assess its presence as the ideal case of constant variance of the error term, that usually does not exist in the panel data models due to ever-present cross-sectional element in the panel data. At the significant p-value of chi-square (0.000), the results of the heteroskedasticity test, make case for rejection of the notion of constant variance in the null hypothesis. The results for the Breusch-Pagan test for heteroskedasticity are presented in Table 5.30 as follows: -

**Table 5.30: Results of Breusch-Pagan/Cook-Weisberg Test for Heteroskedasticity**

| chi2(1) | p-value |
|---|---|
| 153.18 | 0.000 |

*Source: STATA 13 Output*

Therefore, the situation of heterogeneity does exist in the error terms of the multiple regression. At p-value (0.000) of chi-square of 153.18, the null hypothesis of constant variance gets rejected. Therefore, the situation of heterogeneity does exist in the error terms of multiple regression. Now, since panel data consists of elements of the time-series and the cross-sectional model, there are two different panel data models to be applied to incorporate the effect of time-based heterogeneous groups in the analysis. For this, the Hausman test works with the null hypothesis *that the preferred model is the random effects model*. The values of the Hausman test estimated through different heterogeneous units are shown in Table 5.31.

**Table 5.31: Results of the Hausman Test between the Coefficients of the Fixed Effects Model and Random Effects Model**

| Independent Variables | Coefficients Fixed Effects | Coefficients Random Effects |
|---|---|---|
| Export Intensity (XI) | 0.016 | 0.044 |
| Import Intensity (MI) | -0.230 | -0.225 |
| R&D Intensity (RDI) | -0.386 | -0.430 |
| Age of the firm (Age) | -0.022 | -0.007 |
| Size of the Firm (Size) | -0.068 | -0.061 |
| Capital Intensity (KI) | 0.030 | 0.030 |
| HHI | -4.998 | -4.545 |
| Horizontal FDI | -0.088 | -0.173 |
| Chi square (8) (p-value) | 16.74 (0.0329) | |
| Remarks | Fixed effect model is finalized | |

*Source: STATA 13 Output*

With p-values lower than 0.05% level of significance, the statement that the *random effects model is the preferred model* gets rejected and therefore, the fixed effects model is finalised.

## Fixed Effect Regression Model between Independent Variables and Dependent Variable

Reconsidering the results from the pooled OLS analysis to Fixed Effects model (with the Hausman test) and heteroscedasticity to check whether any major changes occur, the null hypothesis are stated as follows: -

*Statement of Null Hypothesis in Regression*

| |
|---|
| $H_{01}$: No significant impact of Export Intensity occurs on the TFP level. |
| $H_{02}$: No significant impact of Import Intensity occurs on the TFP level. |
| $H_{03}$: No significant impact of R&D Intensity occurs on the TFP level. |
| $H_{04}$: No significant impact of Age of the firm occurs on the TFP level. |
| $H_{05}$: No significant impact of Size of the firm occurs on the TFP level. |
| $H_{06}$: No significant impact of Capital Intensity occurs on the TFP level. |
| $H_{07}$: No significant impact of HHI occurs on the TFP level. |
| $H_{08}$: No significant impact of Horizontal FDI occurs on the TFP level. |

The results of the Hausman test indicated significant time-invariant effects in the panel data. Furthermore, the results of the Hausman test showed that the cross-sectional effects were not random. Therefore, the fixed effects model with time-invariant independent variables has been applied. The results of the fixed effects model are shown in the Table 5.32, as follows: -

### Table 5.32: Results of the Fixed Effects Regression between the Independent Variables and the Dependent (Total Factor Productivity) Variable

| Independent Variables | Regression Coefficient | Standard Error | t-statistics (p-value) | Findings |
|---|---|---|---|---|
| Export Intensity (XI) | 0.016 | 0.036 | 0.46 (0.647) | Insignificant and Positive effect |
| Import Intensity (MI) | -0.230 | 0.023 | -9.74 (0.000) | Significant and Negative effect |
| R&D Intensity (RDI) | -3.386 | 0.179 | -2.15 (0.000) | Significant and Negative effect |
| Age of the firm (Age) | -0.022 | 0.036 | -0.62 (0.538) | Insignificant and Negative effect |
| Size of the Firm (Size) | -0.068 | 0.013 | -5.10 (0.000) | Significant and Negative effect |

| Independent Variables | Regression Coefficient | Standard Error | t-statistics (p-value) | Findings |
|---|---|---|---|---|
| Capital Intensity (KI) | 0.030 | 0.003 | 10.26 (0.000) | Significant and Positive effect |
| HHI | -4.998 | 1.029 | -4.86 (0.006) | Significant and Negative effect |
| Horizontal FDI | -0.088 | 0.293 | -0.30 (0.763) | Insignificant and negative effect |
| Constant | 1.996 | 0.151 | 13.17 (0.000) | Significant and positive effect |
| Observation | 1388 | | | |
| F Statistic (p-value) | 21.96 (0.000) | | | |
| R- Square (within) | 19.43% | | | |
| R- Square (between) | 24.90 | | | |
| R- Square (overall) | 23.31 | | | |

*Source: STATA 13 Output*

Although, the fixed effects with time-invariant independent variables has been applied. It must be realised that the fixed effects technique would still possess the heterogeneity of the error terms, as detected in the case of the pooled OLS estimates. In this situation, the literature has recommended a way of heteroscedasticity corrected/ robust standard errors that correct standard errors to allow for the heteroscedasticity without disturbing the coefficients' values. The results of (a) Fixed Effects, as well as (b) Fixed Effects with Robust Errors, are shown in Table 5.32 and Table 5.33 respectively. Nonetheless, it should be noticed there is not much of a difference between the important estimates in the form of the coefficients. The difference in the model with the robust errors is the presence of an inflated value of the standard errors.

**Table 5.33: Results of the Fixed Effects Regression (with Robust Standard Errors) between the Independent Variables and the Dependent (Total Factor Productivity) Variable**

| Independent Variables | Regression Coefficient | Robust Standard Errors | t-statistics (p-value) | Findings | Remarks |
|---|---|---|---|---|---|
| Export Intensity (XI) | 0.016 | 0.076 | 0.22 (0.830) | Insignificant and Positive effect | $H_{01}$ does not get rejected |
| Import Intensity (MI) | -0.230 | 0.035 | -6.49 (0.000) | Significant and Negative effect | $H_{02}$ gets rejected |
| R&D Intensity (RDI) | -0.386 | 0.047 | -8.08 (0.000) | Significant and Negative effect | $H_{03}$ gets rejected |
| Age of the firm (Age) | -0.022 | 0.057 | -0.40 (0.693) | Insignificant and Negative effect | $H_{04}$ does not get rejected |
| Size of the Firm (Size) | -0.068 | 0.029 | -2.34 (0.021) | Significant and Negative effect | $H_{05}$ gets rejected |
| Capital Intensity (KI) | 0.030 | 0.015 | 2.04 (0.043) | Significant and Positive effect | $H_{06}$ gets rejected |
| HHI | -4.998 | 1.364 | -3.66 (0.000) | Significant and Negative effect | $H_{07}$ gets rejected |
| Horizontal FDI | -0.088 | 0.381 | -0.23 (0.817) | Insignificant and Negative effect | $H_{08}$ does not get rejected |
| Constant | 1.996 | 0.269 | 7.40 (0.000) | Significant and Positive effect | |
| Observation | 1388 | | | | |
| F (8,138) (p value) | 25.94 (0.000) | | | | |
| R- Square (within) | 19.43% | | | | |
| R- Square between) | 24.90% | | | | |
| R- Square (overall) | 23.31% | . | | | |

*Source: STATA 13 Output*

The p-value for the F-ratio is 0.000 in both of the tables. Also, the R-square (within) estimate, in both the tables, tells that 19.43% of within variation in the dependent variable is explained by the means of independent variables in the case of 139 heterogeneous firms. Now, reporting the important values with respect to the Fixed Effects estimates with Robust Errors in Table 5.33 is to be done. The results of multiple regression analysis in Table 5.33 indicate regression coefficients, standard errors (robust), t-statistics and their corresponding p-values to test the hypothesis.

With the panel data, the results show that, over the period 2011-2020, the export intensity has an insignificant (p-value=0.830) and encouraging impact on the TFP of the Indian automobile industry at a 0.05% significance level. Hence, the null hypothesis ($H_{01}$) of no significant impact of export intensity on the TFP of domestic concerns in the auto industry does not get rejected. The null hypothesis ($H_{02}$) stating the absence of impact of import intensity on TFP level gets rejected for the domestic establishments in the automotive manufacturing. There, furthermore, exists an adverse effect of the import intensity on the TFP. The higher foreign exchange spending on imported goods would bring a reduction in the TFP due to advanced technology put into design and process by the foreign companies. There also exists a negative impact (coefficient = -3.386) of the RDI on the output level that is substantial, prompting to repudiate the null hypothesis ($H_{03}$) of no significant impact of R&D intensity on TFP. The coefficient states that a unit increase in the research and development intensity decreases the TFP by 0.386 units. In the literature review, this phenomenon has been ascribed to the low absorptive capacity of the establishments that facilitate technology transfer to enhance the level of productivity by the inflows of direct investment.

The independent variable Age has an insignificant and negative impact on the TFP. This calls for the non-rejection of the null hypothesis ($H_{04}$). The Size variable also has a negative impact as demonstrated by its coefficient of -0.068. The null hypothesis ($H_{05}$) of no significant impact of size on TFP, however, gets rejected with its significant p-value. This is because larger firms in reality were mostly operating in the joint-ventures and mergers with the foreign-invested firms and have recently started to work independently. The larger domestic firms have spent years learning from the foreign firms.

The capital intensity tends to show a significant and positive impact on TFP, thereby, rejecting its corresponding null hypothesis ($H_{06}$). The automobile industry in India is highly capital intensive and indicates that a unit increase in physical capital per worker on average increases the TFP by 0.030 units. The industry-specific variable HHI also has a significant (p-value=0.000) and negative effect with a coefficient of -4.998. This situation favours the rejection of the null ($H_{07}$) hypothesis. It implicates a higher market concentration leading to a tougher competition within the domestic firms leading in a reduction in TFP. The variable of Horizontal FDI has an insignificant and negative influence on the dependent variable through the channel of competition effects of the FDI. The null hypothesis ($H_{08}$) does not get rejected.

# Chapter 6
# Findings Discussion and Conclusion

## Findings and Conclusion

Since the Second Five-Year Plan (1956-1961) was conceived and implemented in India, industrial sector has immensely contributed to the nation's economy. Furthermore, the manufacturing sector has been addressed as the backbone of the industrial sector with automobile sector occupying the predominant position in the Indian manufacturing sector. Most countries embarking on the road to economic development in the era of globalisation, have depended on the foreign capital due to inadequacy of the domestic capital. Such countries, therefore, have liberalised their policies to attract foreign investment to maximise its presence in their respective economies. Over the past twenty years, the colossal increase in FDI flows has been included among the apparent signs of the globalization of the world economies. Nonetheless, India faced certain challenges with respect to its economy, internally. The globalised world also witnessed the boons and the banes of the inter-linkages of various economies. This was reflected in the ups and downs in the trends of the FDI in India accompanied by policy changes by the government to attract maximum FDI.

The importance of FDI is realised in the certitude that the foreign presence classified into various categories such as Foreign Grants and Aid, Loans from International Institutions, External Commercial Borrowings and Intergovernmental Loans, FDI turned out to be the preferred source of capital and has been recognised as an indispensable tool in imparting advantages in terms of the cheaper cost of capital, access to raw material, superior management, marketing strategies, high-level technology and scale economies etc. inducing international competition to stimulate the pace of economic development, improve the efficiency of the domestic companies, augmenting their productivity and creating new opportunities for employment and production. In order to harness such benefits, the domestic firms in the host countries have to be equipped with the knowledge to imitate the new foreign technology in the form of the product or the method brought by the foreign firm to upgrade. Also, the foreign firms induce a sense of competition in the domestic firms of the host economy that bounds them to perform better in the concerned sector or the industry. This study comprised of four objectives. The major findings and conclusion corresponding to the four major objectives are stated as following: -

### *Objective 1. To study the trends and patterns of FDI in India during the selected period from 2000 to 2020.*

The first objective is to delve into trends and patterns of the FDI. A measure of CAGR was employed to check the growth of data, taking a five-year period as an interval from 2000 to 2020. The major findings and the conclusion made with respect to this objective are as follows: -

- The finding hinted at a gradual increase in FDI inflows from 2000-01 to 2019-20 mainly via automatic route. The CAGR at 16.24% was registered for the total FDI inflows from 2000-01 to 2019-2020. The CAGR from 2000 to 2005 remained at 8.47. The percentage growth of the total FDI inflows in 2006-07 was the highest at 155%, and on account of the unprecedented growth rate during 2008-2010, the CAGR of 33.04% was witnessed in the five-year period of 2005-2010. Since the foreign countries, especially the USA, went through a recession in 2008, the effects of the same were experienced in India on a magnifying level in 2012-13. The CAGR of the total FDI from 2016 to 2021 stood at 6.3% as compared to that of 2015-2020 at 6.01%. The CAGR of FIIs was 37.56% from 2016 to 2021.
- Therefore, the total FDI inflows comprising the equity, reinvested earnings and other capital witnessed a lot of fluctuations based on the macroeconomic effects. Nonetheless, the continuous efforts on the government's side in opening up various sectors for FDI inflows are reflected in the highest contribution of FIPB/RBI's automatic route component in the total FDI inflows.
- With respect to the major sectors soaking up the largest FDI inflows, it has become apparent that the services sector has managed to secure the first rank, consistently from 2005-06 to 2010-20. However, from 2005-06 to 2009-2010 the largest CAGR was observed in the housing and real estate sector. From 2010-11 to 2014-15, the trading sector presented the largest CAGR of 55.06%. In the relatively recent years of 2015-16 to 2019-20, the computer software and hardware showed

the largest CAGR. The automobile sector is an important component of the overall manufacturing sector and has also been holding ground in the top ten sectors receiving the highest FDI inflows in India from 2005 to 2020.

- The source countries granting maximum FDI inflows were majorly western, a major chunk of time being the implication of the colonial ties with India. However, Mauritius has been observed as the largest foreign investor in India, from 2005-06 to 2015-20. Mauritius has also managed to hold 30% of the cumulative total FDI inflows from 2000-01 to 2019-20. In this study, at 41.26%, Germany was calling the shots in terms of CAGR performance from 2010-11 to 2014-15. When ranked according to the order of countries attracting the FDI, Germany was placed at the eighth position, in the five-year period, from 2010-11 to 2014-15. Also, U.K. was established as the largest investor at a CAGR of 99.26% and as compared to Mauritius' CAGR of -7.56% from 2015-16 to 2019-20. In the same period, the U.K. held fifth ranking in the top ten list of major source countries of FDI inflows. As the prime tax haven in recent years, Mauritius managed to become the preferred source country in India for investments from the developed economies.
- The Indian states where the highest levels of FDI inflows incur comprise of the major metropolitan cities i.e., Maharashtra, New Delhi, Karnataka, Tamil Nadu and Gujrat. The interest of foreign direct investors in backward states, was rather, deficient. Maharashtra managed to hold 30% of the total FDI inflows from 2000-01 to 2019-20. The CAGR for Maharashtra was 0.85% from 2010-2011 to 2014-15. It improved in the next five-year period of 2015-16 to 2019-20 at 18.14%. Albeit, the highest CAGR from 2010-11 to 2014-15 was scored by Rajasthan. Rajasthan was at the tenth spot in the top ten ranking in the same time period. Whereas, from 2015-16 to 2019-20 at a CAGR of 88.58%, Punjab was able to achieve the ninth ranking in the top ten destination states for FDI inflows in India. This situation reflects the work that is left to be done in the other backward states in India to form an attractive destination for FDI.

In conclusion, direct foreign investment as an attractive source of foreign presence has benefitted the Indian economy. Nonetheless, computation of compound annual growth performance on the basis of a five-year time period has shed light on other aspects of the FDI, especially, in the case of the sectoral distribution, its source, and destination in India.

### *Objective 2. To study the industry-wise backward linkages and forward linkages in the automobile industry in India from 2010 to 2020.*

In this objective of the research, the sector-wise data for the period 2011- 20 was taken to find the strength of the backward linkages and forward linkages in 2020, with the help of input-output tables. The observations made are as follows: -

- The sectors, namely, basic metals and fabricated metal, manufacturing, coke, refined petroleum, and nuclear fuel, mining and quarrying, electricity, gas, and water supply, electrical and optical equipment, construction, recycling, chemicals and chemical products, inland transport showed both the NBL and NFL value of greater than unity for 2020. These sectors showed strong inter-industry linkages with respect to other sectors in India.
- With an NBL of greater than unity and an NFL of less than unity, sectors such as food, beverages, and tobacco, textiles and textile products, leather, leather products, and footwear, wood and products of wood and cork, pulp, paper, paper products, printing, and publishing, rubber and plastics, other non-metallic minerals, machinery, transport equipment, hotels and restaurants, are indicative of catering the upstream sector in 2020.
- In sectors such as financial intermediation, machinery & equipment and other business activities except for motor vehicles and motorcycles, repair of household goods, agriculture, retail trade, hunting, forestry, and fishing, renting, strong NFL but weak NBL were observed, in 2020, reflecting a greater dependence on the downstream sector.
- The weakest inter-industry demand and supply among various sectors were mainly seen in the retail sale of fuel, education, health and social work, post and telecommunications, public administration and defence, social security, real estate, wholesale and commission trade, air transport, water transport, activities of travel agencies, sale, maintenance, and repair of motor vehicles and motorcycles and private households with employed person sector in 2020.

In conclusion, in the year 2020 the automobile sector (reflected in the transport equipment sector of ISIC Rev 3.1) showed a strong NBL value of greater than unity but at the same period showed a weak NFL, with value of less than unity.

### *Objective 3. To examine the performance linkages of the selected firms in the presence of foreign-invested firms in the automobile industry from 2011 to 2020.*

The third objective is to measure the performance linkages of the domestic firms with respect to the output level of the automobile industry, from 2011 to 2020 with the help of fixed effects with robust errors in the presence of foreign firms. The observations made are as follows: -

- The correlation coefficient showed a significant and negative relationship of output with respect to the export intensity (XI) at a 0.05 % level of significance. With respect to the first hypothesis, the regression results showed an insignificant and negative impact of export intensity on the output level. Also, the coefficient of the fixed effects model (with robust standard errors) marked worsened performance of the domestic firms in the presence of the foreign firms due to greater emphasis on the domestic market for sales by the industry in India.
- The coefficient of correlation showed an insignificant and positive relationship between the imports intensity and the output level. However, the regression analysis demonstrated that a unit increase in import intensity resulted in a decline of 0.747 units in the dependent variable. This shows that the domestic firms' performance in the presence of foreign-invested firms gets negatively affected as increased foreign spending on imports negatively affects the revenue generated by domestic firms.
- Through fixed effect regression, it is demonstrated that the R&D expenditure to the sales ratio has a significant and negative impact on the output level. Therefore, the notion of crucial R&D efforts is supported. The regression coefficient -1.173 means that a unit increase in R&D intensity in the presence of the firms with foreign roots injured the performance of the domestic firms. The correlation coefficient, however, showed an insignificant and positive relationship between the independent and the dependent variable.
- The age of the firm showed an insignificant and negative correlation with the output level at a 0.05% level of significance. The firm's age variable has a significant and positive impact on the domestic firms' output level in the presence of foreign-invested firms with a coefficient of 0.392. It means an increment in a firm's age by a unit raised performance concerning the domestic firms by 0.392 units.

- The regression results support the idea of a significant impact of firm size on the performance of domestic firms in the overall automobile industry due to scale-based economies enjoyed by the large firms with a greater resource base in India. With a correlation coefficient of 0.9542, there existed a significant ad positive association between the size of the firm and the output. Further, the results also indicated that within a 95% confidence level, an increase in the size of the firm led to 0.677 units of enhanced performance.
- The statement of the null hypothesis was rejected at a 0.05 % level of significance implicating a significant impact of capital intensity on output level in domestic firms in the automobile industry. According to the regression analysis, increasing the independent variable of capital intensity by one-unit improved performance by 0.089 units. Also, the capital intensity showed a positive and significant correlation coefficient of 0.1433 with the level of output.
- The HHI showed a negative and significant correlation with the output level at a 0.05% level of significance. The regression with output as a dependent variable also showed a significant and negative impact of HHI at a 0.05% level of significance expressing that a unit increase in market concentration induced by the oligopolistic market structure impaired the performance level by 16.458 units.
- Finally, the results of the Horizontal FDI showed a significant and direct correlation with respect to the level of output. Nonetheless, the fixed effects regression coefficient of (-) 2.427 showed that a unit increase in the Horizontal FDI worsened the performance level by 2.427 units. The results, therefore, support the notion of the competition effects garnered by e-foreign firms in the automobile industry.

In conclusion, the automobile industry primarily focuses on the domestic sector, especially, in terms of output. This way it explains the relationship between the export and import intensity with respect to the performance level. With regard to R&D, it is essential that the domestic firms be more capable of working with foreign technology in the presence of foreign-invested firms. In contrast, the characteristics of age, size, and capital intensity of the firm hampered a high level of performance. Also, the competition effects of FDI persisted from 2011 to 2020.

### *Objective 4. To examine the productivity linkages of the selected firms in the presence of foreign-invested firms in the automobile industry from 2011 to 2020.*

The fourth objective was to evaluate the productivity linkages of the domestic firms through the TFP level of the automobile industry, from 2011 to 2020 with the help of fixed effects with robust standard errors in the presence of foreign firms. The observations made are as follows: -

- The notion that export intensity does not impact the productivity of domestic firms is supported by the analysis. The coefficient of correlation (0.1356) shows an insignificant but positive correlation between export intensity and TFP level. Nonetheless, with the regression analysis, a unit increment in the said independent variable led to an improvement in the dependent variable of TFP by 0.16 units. This shows a limited contribution on the part of the export's intensity to the TFP level of the domestic firms in the presence of foreign companies.
- The independent variable of the import intensity showed a significant and negative correlation with respect to the TFP level. But the fixed effects regression coefficient showed that a unit increase in the import intensity worsened the productivity of the domestic firms by 0.230 units. The results, therefore, support the notion that foreign spending on imports inhibits the productivity of the domestic firms in the foreign presence due to the inability to fully harness the imported technology.
- Based on the results of the regression, the productivity level of domestic firms decreased by -0.386 units for every unit increase in the R&D intensity. This is due to the inability of domestic firms to translate the R&D expenditure into productivity expanse. Nonetheless, the RDI showed a significant and negative correlation with the TFP level in the Indian automobile industry.
- The age of the firm showed a negative and insignificant correlation to TFP at a 0.05% level of significance. The fixed effects technique with TFP as a dependent variable also showed a negative and insignificant impact of the age of the firm on the productivity level of domestic companies at a 0.05% level of significance expressing that as the domestic firm's age, the increase in the output per unit increase in all inputs is insufficient to generate measurable returns.

- The notion of the significant impact of a firm's size on the output level is supported by the findings mainly because the foreign collaborations in recent years started working independently. However, the regression coefficient of -0.068 means that a unit increase in the size of the domestic manufacturers in the presence of the foreign-invested manufacturers deteriorates the former's TFP.
- In the highly capital-intensive automobile industry, the results do not support the idea of the insignificant impact of the capital intensity of the firm on the productivity level of locally owned firms. With a correlation coefficient of 0.1845, there existed a significant and direct interrelation between the capital intensity of the firm. However, the findings of the regression-based results showed that a unit increase in capital intensity led to an improvement of 0.030 units, in productivity of domestic firms with a 95% confidence level.
- A significant and negative relationship of HHI with respect to the level of productivity at a 0.05% level of significance was seen through correlation analysis. With respect to the impact of the HHI variable on the TFP level, the results showed that the independent variable has a negative and insignificant impact on the domestic firms' level of productivity, marking a higher competition between the domestic firms.
- The Horizontal FDI showed an insignificant and negative correlation with the TFP level at a 0.05 % level of significance. On a similar line, the Horizontal FDI showed an insignificant and inverse impact on the TFP level of domestic firms expressing a greater competition effect accompanying the foreign-invested firms. This marks that a unit increase in the firm's Horizontal FDI would impair the level of productivity of the domestic firms.

In conclusion, the domestic firms in the automobile industry are not benefitting from the foreign presence, at the level of productivity. The competition effects dominate the demonstration effects in the case of total factor productivity in the presence of foreign firms from 2011 to 2020. Among the findings, export intensity, firm's age, HHI, and horizontal FDI do not have a significant impact on productivity.

## Discussions and Policy Implication

This study has tried to improve the understanding of foreign presence in India, particularly in the Indian automobile industry. It is critical to emphasise that no country, especially India with steady growth rate, can expand in the absence of

FDI inflows in such globalised world. As per the findings of the study, foreign presence in the form of FDI has pushed the domestic market to look out for improving the competitiveness at the final product as well as the efficiency level. Nonetheless, international corporations invested substantially in foreign markets in order to capitalise on the significant potential of developing countries' markets. The general argument remains that the government must help boost the condition of infrastructure and the creation of social facilities and services as a strategy to garner more FDI and assist India's overall economic development, as the automobile industry has substantial linkages across all the sectors. The policies must be designed to take into the account the intricacies of the automobile industry. Moreover, investors' as well as consumer's confidence in the market remains a critical factor in boosting the industry due to the dominant domestic demand. The findings of this study show that while developing FDI policy, it is crucial to consider the function of diverse microeconomic and controllable elements while measuring the productivity of various sectors in the Indian economy. Also, certain policy implications pertinent to policymakers can be deduced based on these controllable factors that make up the majority of the determinants of this study. However, on a domestic scale, this study identifies the following characteristics as critical to promoting linkages among various sectors: -

- Encouragement of international enterprises to employ domestic inputs and providing tax breaks, developing training programmes and cooperative R&D operations for linkages to operate.
- Development of policies to boost domestic organizational upgrades (cluster-level programme) and entities that assist enterprises in acquiring high quality certification.
- Organizing trade fairs, assisting with supplier audits, and arranging trips, excursions, expositions, exhibitions, and seminars to make aware of potential trade opportunities.
- Creating supplier databases at the micro level with contact information and product specificities from possible domestic vendors to allow for smooth transactions.

However, with respect to the analysis of the domestic sales, automobile sector was already suffering a massive sluggishness from 2016-17 on the account of implementation of GST, the new safety norms, insurance regulations, axle and emission norms etc. Nonetheless, unforeseeable effects of the abrupt COVID-19 pandemic were marked by the lack of demand in the economy. In view of the same, the five steps that manufacturers should consider to hamper their effort to adapt to the new market situation are stated as follows: -

- Expand collaboration with dealer networks to expedite the adoption of digital tools meant to enable frictionless connection and meet customers where they want to conduct business, resulting in a transformative influence on the car purchase process and overall brand engagement.
- Preserve the manufacturing discipline gained during the previous upcycle, focused on creating vehicles that consumers want to buy in response to alterations in the vehicle mix driven by a growing consumer affordability concern.
- Deploy technological restructuring tools to detect and assess additional cost-cutting alternatives while safeguarding important investments that can produce significant long-term advantages in terms of output, revenue growth quality, and safety.
- Identify cash-draining areas of the organisation and make decisions necessary to repair, sunset, or dispose underperforming assets in order to reach a minimal capacity-utilization requirement.
- Increase the exploration of strategic partnerships in order to keep the focus on innovation while pooling investments and reducing risk.

By looking beyond the identification of linkages, policymakers should also concentrate on innovation, and expanding R&D efforts while improving the ability to absorb knowledge, resulting in improved productivity. In addition to attracting foreign direct investment, policy-makers must implement direct approaches to strengthening domestic firms' absorption capacities, as well as maximizing productivity gains from the international technology. In this regard, at the macroeconomic level, capacity-building operations for domestic firms, reducing the wage and skills gap of the workers with technology generation, subsidies and tax concessions on product or process innovations must be provided. In the long term, the improvements in digital infrastructure that would allow firms to operate, in line with domestic and foreign markets, would further increase FDI in India. In the long term, the improvements in digital infrastructure that would allow firms to operate, in line with domestic and foreign markets, would further increase FDI in India.

## Contribution of the Study

### Contribution to Academics

This study has tried to contribute to the existing literature by : (i) employing a rigorous and a different methodology, namely Levinsohn and Petrin (2003) approach, and (ii) it includes both the studies of the linkages i.e. the input-output tables for the backward and forward linkages, while further studying the sources of linkages affecting the performance and productivity in the process; (iii) the study peeks into the technology transfer of the FDI in the form of foreign presence on the total factor productivity and not partial measure of productivity (i.e., the labour or capital productivity) that has been the topic of interest in most of the earlier studies on finding the effects of multinational corporations on domestic firms (iv) The study employs panel data for automobile industry from 2011 to 2020, marking the recent time period. In estimation, economic activities pertaining to orientation of performance and productivity from the foreign firms in the automobile industry in the form of trade, innovation and growth with greater in-house R&D efforts has been regarded as a consequence of efforts of the domestic firms necessary to persist in the face of competition.

## Contribution to the Industry

With a focus on recent government initiatives such as National Electric Mobility Mission Plan (2020), Automotive Mission Plan (2016) and Make in India (2014), certain policy imperatives for the automobile industry are reflected in the findings of this study. As suggested by the economic theory and the literature surveyed, policy makers who focus on attracting FDI, expect FDI inflows to bring much-needed capital, management skills, marketing techniques and new technologies, resulting in a rise productivity through linkages in the form of various factors and determinants of domestic firm. The mounting Indian automobile market makes untapped opportunities apparent to the domestic firms as well as the foreign players. The recent government policies have firm determination to transform India into an auto-manufacturing hub. Also, such efforts require fresh studies on the realisation of impact on the productivity of the domestic firms from interaction with foreign players resulting from linkages, which in turn, has been essentially targeted as the prime contribution of this study. Furthermore, the COVID-19 situation has forced governments to reconsider their strategy for attracting and retaining FDI. In order to increase the links of FDI within their local enterprises, this study suggests that a large improvement in resource absorption would be required to achieve higher levels of growth.

## Limitations of the Study

This study, at various stages, faced the problem of comprehensive and homogenous availability of panel data and time-series data from different sources, especially in the case of the years preceding 2011. There was no single measure to compute the total factor productivity. The assumption that 'FDI in India resulted in the development of its automobile industry' or 'FDI has a linear relationship with productivity growth' is highly debatable, especially in the presence of the unobservable factors. No proper methods were available to separate the FDI effects due to discrepancies in the definition of FDI before 2000s. This study has taken into consideration the data belonging to the time period prior to the lockdown since March 12, 2020 in which COVID-19 had not caused disruption in the movement of FDI, labour and technology flows, causing transitions in the global supply and demand behaviour affecting consumption and production of goods. Nonetheless, the findings of this study would make certain improvements among policy makers and researchers while discussing FDI in India, which in 2021, again witnessed a fall in the economic growth rate due to COVID-19. In spite of all the limitations, reliable estimates and suggestions are provided which will be useful for planning and successful implementation of the FDI policies.

## Scope for Further Study

This study summarised the results providing useful insights into the performance and productivity level with regards to FDI and its effects in the Indian firms, since the adoption of the new base year 2011-12, while also taking into consideration the most recent year of 2020. In this regard, future research could be undertaken to examine the trends in FDI inflows into various other sectors in India. The changes in the way in which a foreign firm is defined on the basis of ownership can lead to different results and corresponding policy implications. If taken the manufacturing sector, the linkages among various sectors could also be measured. It would also be interesting to investigate and compare the extent of linkages in the manufacturing sector itself. The researchers in future can identify other factors and determinants of productivity. Since the dark days of the COVID-19 epidemic are not over and the emergency of imposing a lockdown could well be sudden, the full impact of the same will be seen in the approaching time period, adding years to the time-based estimation. There is a dire lack of studies investigating the linkages effects of FDI in the services sector, especially, amid the pandemic. Therefore, FDI linkages studies could also be undertaken in the services sector, which has been experiencing the new *Work from Home* culture.

# Chapter 7

## Pathways to a Sustainable Future: Electronic Vehicles in India

As one of the fastest-growing economies with a rapidly urbanizing population, India is facing a dual challenge ensuring sustainable urban mobility while reducing dependence on fossil fuels. With over **85% of crude oil imported** and vehicular emissions contributing significantly to urban air pollution, the shift toward electric mobility has become both an environmental necessity and a strategic imperative (Ministry of Road Transport and Highways [MoRTH], 2022; NITI Aayog & Rocky Mountain Institute [RMI], 2019).Recognizing the strategic value of electric mobility, the Indian government launched the **NEMMP 2020,** followed by the **FAME** schemes. These initiatives aim to stimulate demand, boost manufacturing, and establish a charging infrastructure network nationwide (Ministry of Heavy Industries, 2023; Invest India, 2023).

Also, India's EV sales crossed **1.5 million units in FY 2023-24**, representing more than a **50% increase from the previous year** (SIAM, 2024). Electric two-wheelers and three-wheelers account for the majority of this growth due to affordability and last-mile delivery use cases. However, electric four-wheelers and buses are also gaining traction in urban centers and public transport networks (India Energy Storage Alliance [IESA], 2023).The transition to electric mobility in India can reduce the country's oil import bill, lower urban pollution levels, create green jobs, and position India as a global manufacturing hub for affordable EVs and advanced batteries (Council on Energy, Environment and Water [CEEW], 2022). This chapter aims to examine the historical development, classification, necessity, and challenges associated with electric vehicles in India, emphasizing their potential to reduce emissions, decrease dependence on oil imports, and promote sustainable economic growth through targeted policy interventions, technological innovation, and market evolution.

### 7.1.1 Classification of Electric Vehicles

Electric vehicles in India can be classified into the following categories based on their propulsion technologies:-

*Battery Electric Vehicles (BEVs)*

BEVs are fully electric and rely exclusively on electricity stored in rechargeable batteries. They have no internal combustion engine making them zero tailpipe emission vehicles (IEA, 2023). For example, the Tata Nexon EV, MG ZS EV, and Ather 450X.

*Hybrid Electric Vehicles (HEVs)*

HEVs combine an ICE with an electric motor. The battery is charged through regenerative braking and the combustion engine, without an external plug-in feature. An example is the Toyota Camry Hybrid (Invest India, 2023).

*Plug-in Hybrid Electric Vehicles (PHEVs)*

These are similar to HEVs but include an external charging port. They operate on electricity for short distances and switch to ICE when the battery is depleted. For example, the Volvo XC90 Recharge (Bloomberg NEF, 2022).

*Fuel Cell Electric Vehicles (FCEVs) (Emerging Segment)*

FCEVs run on hydrogen fuel cells and emit only water vapor. While they hold potential for the future, India's lack of hydrogen infrastructure makes their current presence limited (IEA, 2023).

*Figure 7.1 Types of Four Wheeler EVs*

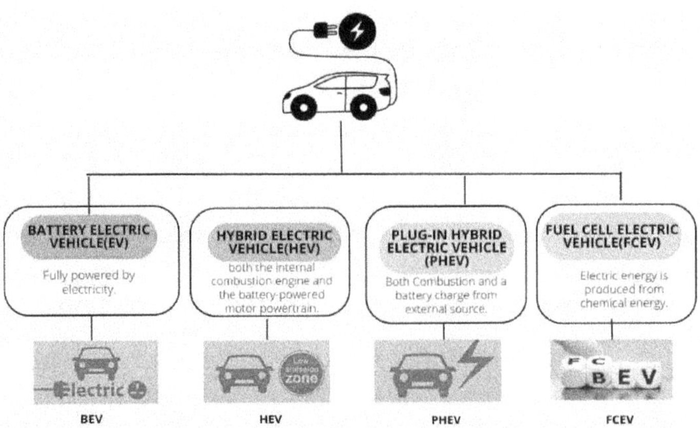

### 7.1.2 EVs by Vehicle Segment

*Two-Wheelers*

Electric two-wheelers dominate the Indian EV market, accounting for approximately 60–70% of total EV sales as of FY 2023-24 (SIAM, 2024). These vehicles are affordable and well-suited for urban commuting and deliveries. Popular electric vehicle models in India include the Tata Nexon EV, MG ZS EV, Ather 450X, and Ola S1, which reflect the growing consumer acceptance and market diversification across two-wheeler and four-wheeler segments.

*Three-Wheelers (E-Rickshaws and Cargo Autos)*

Electric three-wheelers are widely utilized in Tier II and Tier III cities, serving as a critical mode of last-mile connectivity. Their lower operating costs, combined with robust government support, have facilitated significant market penetration. Prominent manufacturers in this segment include Mahindra Treo, Piaggio Ape E-City, and YC Electric (IESA, 2023).

*Four-Wheelers (Passenger Cars)*

Electric passenger cars are increasingly being adopted by private consumers, ride-hailing services, and government fleets. This growth is driven by improvements in driving range and the availability of subsidies, with models such as the Tata Nexon EV, Tata Tiago EV, MG ZS EV, and Hyundai Kona Electric capturing a growing market share. (CEEW, 2022)

*Electric Buses*

Electric buses are witnessing growing adoption by state transport undertakings and private operators, playing a vital role in the decarbonization of public transportation systems. Key industry players contributing to this transition include Olectra Greentech, JBM Auto, Ashok Leyland, and Tata Motors (MoRTH, 2022).

### 7.1.3 Current Market Trends and Adoption

India's electric vehicle industry surpassed 1.5 million unit sales in FY 2023-24, reflecting a year-on-year growth rate of over 50% (SIAM, 2024). While two-wheelers and three-wheelers dominate the market due to cost advantages and FAME II subsidies, fleet electrification is also gaining momentum among logistics, delivery platforms, and aggregators such as Ola, Uber, and BluSmart (NITI Aayog & RMI, 2019). Furthermore, EV adoption is expanding beyond metropolitan areas, with increasing uptake in rural and semi-urban regions, particularly for e-rickshaws and low-speed electric scooters, driven by low operational costs and accessible financing options (CEEW, 2022). These achievements highlight the rapid growth of India's electric vehicle market. India's electric vehicle sector has evolved from experimental launches to a dynamic market poised for large-scale adoption. With technological innovation, supportive policy frameworks, and rising consumer demand, EV penetration is accelerating across vehicle categoriesas discussed in the next sub section.

### 7.1.4 Key Industry Players

According to the MoRTH (2022), Invest India (2023) and IESA (2023), the key industry players in India's electric vehicle sector are identified as follows:-

*Established OEMs:*

- Tata Motors: A leader in electric cars, offering models like Nexon EV, Tigor EV, and Tiago EV.
- Mahindra Electric: Among India's earliest EV players, known for e-Verito and e-Supro.
- Hero Electric: Dominates the low-speed e-scooter category

*Startups:*

- Ather Energy: Renowned for high-performance smart scooters with advanced UI/UX.
- Ola Electric: Scaled up rapidly with the Ola S1 and is building India's largest EV gigafactory.
- Bounce Infinity: Focuses on battery-swapping two-wheelers, offering flexible ownership models

*Commercial and Bus Manufacturers:*

- Ashok Leyland, Olectra Greentech, JBM Auto, and Tata Motors have introduced a wide range of electric buses for intra-city and intercity applications.

### 7.1.5 Foreign Collaborations and Investments

India's electric vehicle market has garnered increasing attention from international automobile and battery manufacturers. Firms such as MG Motor and BYD have introduced premium electric models while establishing strategic partnerships for local assembly and distribution (IEA, 2023). Additionally, Tesla has signaled its interest in entering the Indian market, subject to policy adjustments concerning import duties and incentives for domestic manufacturing (BloombergNEF, 2022). Such global collaborations are instrumental in facilitating technology transfer, enhancing production capacity, and strengthening supply chain efficiency within India's evolving EV ecosystem. The next frontier lies in strengthening the charging infrastructure, local battery manufacturing, and recycling ecosystems to ensure a resilient and sustainable EV transition.

## 7.2. Charging Infrastructure and Battery Technology

The widespread adoption of EVs in India depends not only on vehicle affordability and production capabilities but also, critically, on the development of a robust charging infrastructure and advancements in battery technology. These two foundational elements directly affect consumer convenience, economic efficiency, and the long-term sustainability of electric mobility. Although India has made considerable progress in recent years, several systemic gaps remain, particularly in public accessibility and technological self-reliance (IEA, 2023; IESA, 2023).

### 7.2.1 Types of Charging Solutions

India's EV charging ecosystem is evolving and can be categorized by charging speed and location. Alternating current (AC) or slow chargers are the most commonly used, primarily for home charging. These typically require six to eight hours for a full charge and are suited for two-wheelers and passenger vehicles that can be charged overnight. While cost-effective, their long charging time limits their utility in commercial or high-frequency use cases (Ministry of Power, 2023).

In contrast, direct current or fast chargers enable significantly quicker charging-within one to two hours-making them suitable for public charging infrastructure and fleet applications. Ultra-fast chargers, capable of charging vehicles in under 30 minutes, are gradually being introduced, although their deployment remains limited due to high energy requirements and infrastructure costs (IEA, 2023). Based on their location, chargers are classified into residential (home-based), public (in commercial zones such as malls and petrol stations), and highway or intercity stations. The Government of India's e-AMRIT initiative aims to scale up intercity charging networks to facilitate long-distance EV travel (Invest India, 2023).

### 7.2.2 Government Initiatives for Charging Infrastructure

To address infrastructure deficits, the Indian government has launched several policy measures. The FAME II scheme provides financial incentives for the establishment of charging stations across metropolitan areas, national highways, and rural clusters. Public sector entities such as Energy Efficiency Services Limited (EESL) and NTPC have been instrumental in deploying public chargers.

Additionally, regulatory provisions now permit private operators to install charging stations without a licensing requirement, thus democratizing infrastructure development (MHI, 2023).To ensure economic viability, electricity tariffs specific to EV charging are being standardized. Furthermore, the government has set ambitious targets, including the installation of at least one charging station every 3 kilometers in urban centers and every 25 kilometers along national highways

### 7.2.3 Battery Technologies in India

Battery technology is a central determinant of EV affordability, performance, and energy security. At present, lithium-ion batteries dominate the Indian EV market due to their high energy density, lower weight, and faster charging cycles. However, India's reliance on imported raw materials such as lithium, cobalt, and nickel has raised concerns about long-term sustainability and exposure to global supply chain disruptions (IESA, 2023).

To mitigate these concerns, India is investing in alternative battery chemistries and local manufacturing. Solid-state batteries, though still under research and development, promise enhanced efficiency and safety. Sodium-ion batteries, which utilize more abundant domestic materials, are also being explored as cost-effective alternatives. Furthermore, technologies such as zinc-air and flow batteries are gaining attention for their potential applications in stationary energy storage (IEA, 2023).

The government has introduced the Production-Linked Incentive (PLI) scheme for Advanced Chemistry Cell (ACC) battery storage with an outlay of ⊠18,100 crore to foster indigenous battery production. Leading domestic companies such as Ola Electric, Reliance New Energy, and Amara Raja are establishing Giga factories, signaling a major shift toward reducing import dependency and creating a localized battery supply chain (Invest India, 2023).

### 7.2.4 Battery Swapping: An Alternative Model

Battery swapping has emerged as a viable alternative to conventional charging, particularly for commercial fleets and last-mile delivery services. This model allows users to exchange depleted batteries for fully charged units at dedicated swapping stations, thereby minimizing vehicle downtime and enhancing utilization rates. Additionally, it lowers the upfront cost of EVs by decoupling battery ownership from vehicle purchase, given that batteries constitute 30–40% of the total cost (NITI Aayog & Rocky Mountain Institute [RMI], 2019).

In 2022, the Government of India proposed a draft Battery Swapping Policy aimed at standardizing battery formats, promoting interoperability, and supporting industry players like Sun Mobility and Battery Smart. Battery swapping is especially relevant for e-rickshaws and electric two-wheelers operating in dense urban environments with limited space for fixed charging setups (IESA, 2023).

### 7.2.5 Challenges in Infrastructure and Battery Ecosystem

Despite commendable progress, several challenges persist in India's EV charging and battery ecosystems. One major concern is the strain that high-capacity fast chargers can place on urban electrical grids, which are already operating near capacity. Moreover, the high cost and limited availability of land for installing public charging infrastructure in urban areas represent significant barriers.

Lack of standardization in charging connectors and battery types hampers interoperability and deters large-scale private investment. Furthermore, India's limited access to critical battery minerals makes its EV ambitions vulnerable to international market fluctuations and geopolitical tensions (IEA, 2023). While recycling programs and second-life battery initiatives offer potential solutions, they are still in nascent stages and require regulatory and technological support.

In conclusion, while India has made notable strides in expanding EV infrastructure and advancing battery technologies, substantial efforts are still needed to ensure scalability, resilience, and sustainability. Strategic investments, focused innovation, and well-defined regulatory frameworks will be critical in guiding the next phase of India's electric mobility transition, underscoring the importance of understanding the evolution of electric vehicles in the country.

## 7.3 Historical Evolution of Electric Vehicles in India

The journey of electric vehicles (EVs) in India has been characterized by cautious beginnings, incremental policy development, and a recent surge in momentum aligned with environmental and energy security goals. While the concept of electric mobility has existed for decades, its large-scale adoption in India has evolved gradually, shaped by a combination of government initiatives, technological progress, market readiness, and social awareness (NITI Aayog & RMI, 2019; IEA, 2023). Therefore, a brief account on the Historical Evolution of Electric Vehicles in India is as follows: -

### 7.3.1 Early Beginnings of EVs (1990s–2005)

India's initial experimentation with EVs began in the late 1990s and early 2000s, primarily through small-scale ventures. A notable early pioneer was the REVA Electric Car Company, which introduced the REVA a compact electric car designed for intra-city use. Despite its innovation, the REVA faced challenges such as limited battery range, high cost, and inadequate charging infrastructure, making it a niche product (Invest India, 2023).

In the two-wheeler space, companies like Hero Electric began offering low-speed electric scooters. However, these early models were often perceived as underpowered and unreliable compared to their petrol-based counterparts (CEEW, 2022). At this stage, electric vehicles were primarily viewed as experimental alternatives rather than mainstream options.

### 7.3.2 Policy Push and Recognition (2006–2015)

Government interest in promoting EVs became more visible in the mid-2000s. In 2010, the Ministry of New and Renewable Energy (MNRE) introduced a limited incentive scheme to promote EV purchases, but the absence of a national strategy and fragmented execution at the state level constrained its success (MoRTH, 2022).

A major turning point came with the launch of the (NEMMP) 2020 in 2013. The plan emphasized reducing oil dependence and greenhouse gas emissions by promoting EV adoption, while also aiming to position India as a hub for electric vehicle manufacturing. It was the first integrated national-level strategy that brought together the central government, industry, and research institutions (NITI Aayog & RMI, 2019).

### 7.3.3 Acceleration through FAME Scheme (2015–Present)

The most significant acceleration came in 2015 with the launch of the FAME. Its first phase focused on demand creation, pilot projects, and setting up basic charging infrastructure. The second phase, FAME II, launched in 2019, provided larger subsidies for electric two-wheelers, buses, and fleet vehicles, and included infrastructure development incentives (Ministry of Heavy Industries, 2023).

This period also saw a surge in participation from domestic automotive manufacturers such as Tata Motors, Mahindra Electric, and Ashok Leyland, alongside the entry of startups and global EV brands. Companies like Ather Energy, Ola Electric, and Bounce Infinity brought innovation and affordability to the urban EV market, particularly in the two-wheeler segment (IESA, 2023; SIAM, 2024).

### 7.3.4 Recent Momentum and Future Orientation (2020 Onwards)

The COVID-19 pandemic initially disrupted production and supply chains but later acted as a catalyst for consumers to shift toward personal, eco-friendly transportation (Bloomberg NEF, 2022). Simultaneously, global climate imperatives and India's commitments under the Paris Agreement increased pressure to de-carbonize the transport sector (IEA, 2023).

A growing number of Indian states, including Delhi, Karnataka, Tamil Nadu, and Maharashtra, introduced dedicated state-level EV policies offering fiscal incentives, charging infrastructure mandates, and fleet electrification targets (Invest India, 2023). At the national level, the government launched the Production-Linked Incentive (PLI) Scheme to promote domestic manufacturing of EV components and batteries (MHI, 2023).

By FY 2023–24, India had recorded over 1.5 million EV registrations, with two-wheelers and three-wheelers accounting for a substantial share of new sales (SIAM, 2024). With improving infrastructure, increasing consumer awareness, and policy alignment, India now stands at the threshold of mass-scale EV adoption.

## 7.4 Need for Electric Vehicles in India

The growing necessity for (EVs) in India is shaped by a convergence of environmental, economic, social, and strategic imperatives. As the country strives for inclusive and sustainable development, while simultaneously adhering to its global climate commitments, EVs have emerged as a promising solution. According to IEA 2023, EVs offer a path to clean mobility that not only addresses pressing domestic challenges such as air pollution and oil dependency but also aligns with India's long-term development and climate goals. In addition to this, following factors underscore the critical need for transitioning to electric vehicles:-

### 7.4.1 Environmental Concerns and Air Pollution

India ranked 22nd of the 30 most polluted cities globally in 2023, according to air quality assessments and other global monitoring agencies whereby, vehicular emissions are a significant source of urban air pollution, contributing to elevated levels of particulate matter nitrogen oxides and carbon monoxide which have direct implications for public health (MoRTH, 2022). Electric vehicles, which produce zero tailpipe emissions, offer a scalable solution to mitigate air pollution and reduce greenhouse gas emissions, particularly in densely populated urban centers.

### 7.4.2 Energy Security and Crude Oil Dependence

As per the Invest India 2023, India imports over 85% of its crude oil its energy system is highly susceptible to global oil price volatility and geopolitical tension. Furthermore, transportation accounts for a significant share of this oil demand, particularly from internal combustion engine vehicles. By shifting to electric mobility, India can reduce its oil import bill, strengthen energy independence, and promote the use of domestically produced solar and wind electricity, This transition aligns with India's goal of building a more self-reliant and resilient energy infrastructure.

### 7.4.3 Urbanization and Traffic Management

India's urban population is expected to cross 600 million by 2030, placing unprecedented pressure on public transport systems and urban infrastructure (IEA, 2023). EVs, especially electric two-wheelers, e-rickshaws, and low-speed EVs, present efficient, low-emission solutions for last-mile connectivity, a major concern in India's urban mobility network (CEEW, 2022). While incorporating EVs into integrated smart mobility platforms such as app based ride sharing and public EV bus networks-can reduce traffic congestion, lower urban emissions, and improve the overall efficiency of transport systems (IESA, 2023).

### 7.4.4 Climate Commitments and Sustainable Development Goals (SDGs)

India has committed under the Paris Climate Agreement to reduce its emissions intensity by 45% from 2005 levels by 2030 and achieve net-zero emissions by 2070 (IEA, 2023). Transitioning to electric vehicles is central to meeting these targets and addressing multiple United Nations Sustainable Development Goals (SDGs), including SDG 7: Affordable and clean energy, SDG 11: Sustainable cities and communities and SDG 13: Climate action. The widespread adoption of EVs is thus a direct enabler of India's national and international environmental commitments (Invest India, 2023).

### 7.4.5 Economic Opportunities and Innovation

The EV ecosystem is a catalyst for job creation, entrepreneurship, and technological advancement. Government initiatives such as Make in India and Atmanirbhar Bharat emphasize domestic production of EVs, batteries, and components, encouraging indigenous innovation and investment (MHI, 2023). Moreover, India's startup ecosystem considers actively contributing to the sector with ventures in battery recycling, vehicle design, charging technologies, and energy storage solutions. According to the India Energy Storage Alliance (IESA, 2023), the EV sector could create millions of green jobs across manufacturing, services, and infrastructure domains.

### 7.4.6 Health Benefits and Quality of Life

Air pollution in Indian cities constitutes a significant public health crisis, contributing to a rising incidence of respiratory disorders, cardiovascular conditions, and premature mortalityWhereas, switching to electric vehicles can greatly enhance air quality, resulting in lower healthcare expenses and improved public health and well-being. Additionally, electric vehicles are notably quieter than ICE vehicles, contributing to reduced noise pollution and improving the livability of urban environments, particularly in congested residential and commercial zones (IEA, 2023).

### 7.4.7 Technological Leapfrogging

India has historically exhibited the ability to leapfrog legacy technologies, exemplified by the rapid adoption of mobile phones in place of landline infrastructure. In a similar manner, the nation has the potential to bypass conventional fossil-fuel-based transportation systems and transition directly to clean electric mobility, thereby avoiding the limitations associated with outdated models. This transition not only ensures **long-term sustainability** but also positions India as a **global leader in affordable, scalable EV technologies**, particularly for emerging markets with similar socio-economic characteristics (Invest India, 2023).

## 7.5 Case Studies and Success Stories

India's transition toward electric mobility is characterized by a range of regional experiences that reflect the country's socio-economic and geographical diversity. These case studies illustrate how a combination of progressive policies, localized innovations, private sector engagement, and community participation can catalyze the adoption of electric vehicles.Spanning metropolitan centers to rural hinterlands, the following examples present replicable models that can inform national policy and inspire broader regional adaptation.

### 7.5.1 Delhi: A Model for Urban EV Policy and Implementation

Delhi has emerged as a frontrunner in EV adoption, owing primarily to its forward-looking and execution-oriented electric vehicle policy. Introduced in 2020, the Delhi EV Policy set an ambitious goal of ensuring that 25% of all new vehicle registrations by 2024 be electric (Delhi Government, 2021). The policy framework included a robust set of financial incentives—such as purchase subsidies, scrappage bonuses, and interest subvention on loans—with particular focus on commercial electric vehicles. It also mandated electrification across ride-hailing and logistics fleets.

Consequently, Delhi has registered over 150,000 electric vehicles, more than any other Indian metroand leads in the deployment of electric three-wheelers, supported by a conducive ecosystem and strong public awareness (NITI Aayog & RMI, 2022). Innovations such as a single-window approval mechanism for home charging installations have further enhanced user access and alleviated range-related concerns.

### 7.5.2 Uttar Pradesh and Bihar: E-Rickshaws and Grassroots Mobility Transitions

Unlike the policy-intensive model of Delhi, states such as Uttar Pradesh and Bihar have witnessed a bottom-up surge in EV adoption through the proliferation of electric rickshaws. These low-cost, accessible vehicles have revolutionized last-mile mobility in Tier II and Tier III cities, offering economical alternatives to conventional auto-rickshaws and functioning under relatively minimal regulatory constraints—including, in some cases, the absence of a driving license requirement (CEEW, 2022).

Currently, over one million e-rickshaws operate across northern India, providing sustainable employment to marginalized populations, including migrant workers and low-income youth. This transition has simultaneously advanced economic inclusion and environmental improvement by reducing dependency on fossil fuels and enhancing urban air quality.

### 7.5.3 Kerala: Advancing Public Transport Electrification through E-Buses

Kerala has made significant progress in decarbonizing public transportation by integrating electric buses into its fleet. The Kerala State Road Transport Corporation has spearheaded these efforts through both the FAME II scheme and public-private partnerships. These e-buses operate across intra-city and inter-city routes, offering enhanced commuter comfort and reduced environmental impact.

Urban centers such as Kochi and Thiruvananthapuram have reported notable reductions in diesel emissions and noise pollution. Passenger feedback indicates high levels of satisfaction concerning ride quality and hygiene. Over their lifecycle, e-buses also exhibit lower operating costs compared to diesel alternatives, reinforcing their financial viability and long-term sustainability (MHI, 2023).

### 7.5.4 Bengaluru: Innovation Ecosystem and Startup Leadership in EVs

Recognized as the technological hub of India, Bengaluru has become a key center for electric mobility innovation. The city hosts prominent EV startups such as Ather Energy, Sun Mobility, Ultraviolette Automotive, and Log9 Materials, which are at the forefront of developing high-performance electric two-wheelers, fast-charging technologies, battery-swapping solutions, and advanced energy storage systems.(IESA, 2023)

The city's vibrant startup ecosystem is supported by state-level incentives, innovation incubators, specialized EV laboratories, and prototyping facilities. Furthermore, active EV user communities enhance peer-to-peer knowledge exchange and build public confidence in electric mobility. Bengaluru thus exemplifies how public-private synergy, anchored in a robust innovation framework, can drive sectoral transformation.

### 7.5.5 Gujarat: Manufacturing Hub and Renewable Energy Integration

Gujarat's success in the EV domain stems from its dual focus on industrial development and renewable energy integration. The state's 2021 EV Policy offers substantial capital and operational subsidies to both manufacturers and end-users, attracting significant domestic and foreign investment in EV production and battery manufacturing (Invest India, 2023). Moreover, Gujarat has pioneered the integration of solar energy with EV charging stations, especially in cities like Surat and Rajkot.

This confluence of manufacturing capacity and clean energy utilization has enabled a substantial reduction in the carbon footprint of urban mobility. By leveraging solar power for EV charging, Gujarat sets a benchmark for cost-effective and environmentally sustainable infrastructure development.

### 7.5.6 Private Sector Pioneers: Ola Electric and BluSmart

In the private sector, Ola Electric has distinguished itself through rapid scaling and vertical integration. The company operates one of the world's largest electric two-wheeler manufacturing facilities in Tamil Nadu and has launched the Ola S1 Pro, one of India's top-selling electric scooters (SIAM, 2024). Ola's investments in battery cell production and extensive charging networks further position it as a comprehensive EV solutions provider.

Similarly, BluSmart has innovated within the ride-hailing space by offering India's first all-electric taxi service. Operating in Delhi-NCR and Bengaluru, BluSmart utilizes electric vehicles such as the Tata Tigor EV and offers app-based booking with fixed, surge-free pricing. Its fleet-based operational model ensures high utilization rates and underscores the environmental and economic benefits of electrified urban transport (CEEW, 2022).

These regional case studies collectively highlight the decentralized yet complementary nature of India's electric mobility ecosystem and the diversity of approaches illustrates the multifaceted path to EV adoption in India. Together, they demonstrate that with clear policy direction, inclusive incentives, and ecosystem-level collaboration, electric mobility can flourish across India's varied socio-geographic contexts.

## 7.6 Challenges to EV Adoption in India

Although India's electric vehicle (EV) sector is gaining momentum, its widespread adoption continues to be impeded by a range of structural, economic, behavioral, and infrastructural challenges. Despite policy incentives and increasing environmental consciousness, several interrelated barriers limit the potential for mass-scale deployment of EVs. Overcoming these obstacles is essential for meeting India's sustainable mobility objectives and ensuring inclusive access to clean transport technologies.

### 7.6.1 High Upfront Costs

A primary challenge in EV adoption is the relatively high upfront cost, especially for electric four-wheelers. This cost disparity stems largely from the expensive lithium-ion batteries that constitute 30% to 50% of the total vehicle cost (IESA, 2023). Since most battery components are imported, pricing remains susceptible to global supply chain volatility. While EVs promise lower operating and maintenance costs over time, the initial investment remains a critical barrier for cost-sensitive Indian consumers (CEEW, 2022). Although schemes such as FAME II and various state-level subsidies have narrowed this gap, financial support remains insufficient, particularly in the personal vehicle segment.

### 7.6.2 Inadequate Charging Infrastructure

The limited availability and accessibility of charging infrastructure remains a core impediment to EV penetration. Public charging stations are concentrated in select urban clusters, leaving rural regions, highways, and residential areas underserved (Ministry of Power, 2023). Additionally, the absence of standardized connectors and diverse charging protocols has led to fragmented networks and poor user interoperability. These limitations contribute to persistent "range anxiety," where consumers fear depleting battery levels without adequate access to recharging options (International Energy Agency [IEA], 2023).

### 7.6.3 Weak Battery Supply Chain

India's EV battery ecosystem remains heavily reliant on imported raw materials such as lithium, cobalt, and nickel, with China being a dominant supplier (Invest India, 2023). This dependency exposes the domestic industry to external supply shocks, pricing risks, and geopolitical vulnerabilities. Although the Production-Linked Incentive scheme for Advanced Chemistry Cells aims to promote indigenous manufacturing, local battery production remains in its infancy. Moreover, the lack of a formal battery recycling infrastructure raises concerns about long-term resource sustainability and environmental impacts (IESA, 2023).

### 7.6.4 Limited Consumer Awareness and Behavioral Resistance

Consumer awareness regarding EV technology, including charging logistics, battery maintenance, safety features, and performance standards, remains limited (CEEW, 2022). Persistent misconceptions regarding range reliability, battery degradation, and replacement costs create psychological barriers to adoption. Additionally, behavioral inertia shaped by longstanding reliance on internal combustion engine vehicles hampers the shift toward alternative mobility solutions, particularly in conservative or rural markets.

### 7.6.5 Restricted Model Availability

India's EV market is predominantly concentrated in two-wheeler and three-wheeler segments, with a dearth of affordable electric passenger cars in the ₹5-10 lakh price bracket (SIAM, 2024). This lack of variety limits accessibility for middle-income consumers. Furthermore, electrification in commercial vehicle categories such as trucks and intercity buses remains minimal due to the absence of technically viable and economically competitive models.

### 7.6.6 Financing and Insurance Limitations

Access to financing remains a significant barrier to EV adoption. Financial institutions and non-banking financial companies (NBFCs) have been slow to develop tailored loan products for EV buyers (NITI Aayog & RMI, 2019). Similarly, insurance firms face challenges due to insufficient historical data on

EV risk profiles, leading to higher premiums and restrictive coverage options. Additionally, ambiguity surrounding resale values further deters investment in electric mobility.

### 7.6.7 Electricity Grid and Power Supply Challenges

The integration of EVs into India's transport system imposes new demands on an already strained power grid. High-capacity chargers, particularly in urban centers, can contribute to localized overloading without appropriate infrastructure upgrades (Ministry of Power, 2023). Furthermore, unless charging networks are increasingly powered by renewable sources, the overall carbon footprint of EVs will remain significant, thereby undermining their environmental rationale (IEA, 2023).

### 7.6.8 Adoption Barriers in Rural and Tier II/III Areas

The EV ecosystem in rural and semi-urban areas is hindered by inadequate infrastructure, weak digital access, and limited repair and service facilities (Invest India, 2023). Road conditions and a lack of dependable energy supply further exacerbate these issues. Consumer hesitation in these areas is reinforced by insufficient dealership networks, making sales, servicing, and trust-building more challenging.

### 7.6.9 Policy Implementation and Coordination Gaps

While the Indian government has developed several forward-looking policies, implementation inconsistencies remain. Many state EV policies have not translated into effective deployment of charging stations or fleet electrification due to bureaucratic delays, unclear inter-agency roles, and policy fragmentation (Ministry of Heavy Industries [MHI], 2023). Variations in incentive structures and regulatory approaches across states create further confusion and limit scalability.

### 7.6.10 Environmental and Lifecycle Concerns

Although EVs reduce emissions at the point of use, concerns remain about their entire life cycle, particularly battery production and disposal. Improper handling of end-of-life batteries can lead to toxic waste accumulation and environmental degradation. In the absence of a regulated and scaled recycling framework, India risks facing an e-waste crisis in the coming decades (IESA, 2023). Establishing a sustainable end-of-life management system is thus imperative for the long-term success of electric mobility.

## 7.7 Future Prospects and Strategic Roadmap for Electric Mobility in India

India's electric vehicle (EV) transition, though still in its nascent stages, has laid the groundwork for a profound transformation in the country's mobility paradigm. The forthcoming decade will be critical, as India navigates the complex challenges of climate change mitigation, rapid urbanization, and increasing energy security concerns. To ensure that this transition is both swift and inclusive, it is imperative to adopt a comprehensive strategy that is environmentally sustainable, socially equitable, and economically robust. This section outlines key market projections, strategic priorities, and policy imperatives for the sustained advancement of electric mobility in India.

### 7.7.1 Market Forecasts and Growth Potential

Projections for India's EV sector indicate substantial growth potential. According to industry estimates, the market is expected to grow at a compound annual growth rate (CAGR) exceeding 40% over the next decade, underpinned by technological innovations, declining costs, and supportive policy frameworks (India Energy Storage Alliance [IESA], 2023). Initially, electric two-wheelers and three-wheelers are projected to dominate adoption trends, comprising nearly 80% of EV sales by 2030. Concurrently, electric passenger cars are anticipated to account for over 30% of new car registrations by the end of the decade (NITI Aayog & Rocky Mountain Institute [RMI], 2022). The integration of EVs into public transport systems and commercial logistics is also expected to play a central role in smart urban mobility strategies.

Parallel to vehicle adoption, the demand for batteries is projected to exceed 250 GWh by 2030, necessitating large-scale investment in domestic gigafactory infrastructure and the development of advanced energy storage technologies (International Energy Agency [IEA], 2023). Meeting this demand through localized production will be essential for ensuring national energy security and industrial competitiveness.

### 7.7.2 Strategic Priorities

To fully realize the potential of electric mobility, India must focus on a series of strategic priorities:

- **Infrastructure Development**: Ensuring equitable access to EV charging infrastructure across urban, peri-urban, and rural regions is essential. This includes scaling both alternating current (AC) and direct current (DC) charging stations, ensuring interoperability, and promoting open-source protocols for grid management (Ministry of Power, 2023).

- **Battery Ecosystem and Supply Chain Security**: Establishing a resilient domestic battery manufacturing ecosystem is vital. This requires not only investment in battery cell production but also strategic partnerships for critical mineral sourcing with countries such as Australia, Bolivia, and several African nations. Additionally, robust battery recycling and second-life usage frameworks must be developed to promote environmental sustainability and reduce import dependency (Invest India, 2023).
- **Affordability and Inclusivity**: Promoting EV adoption among rural populations and lower-income groups must be a core objective. This entails incentivizing the development of compact, affordable vehicle models, encouraging leasing and subscription-based ownership, and expanding access to credit for small businesses and individual consumers in underserved regions (Council on Energy, Environment and Water [CEEW], 2022).
- **Research, Development, and Skill Building**: Enhanced investment in research and development (R&D) is required to advance technologies such as solid-state batteries, AI-enabled mobility systems, and indigenous component manufacturing. Establishing specialized research hubs and supporting startup ecosystems will facilitate innovation. Simultaneously, workforce development programs must be launched to train technicians, engineers, and service professionals in EV-related domains (NITI Aayog & RMI, 2019).
- **Green Energy Integration**: The future of electric mobility must be anchored in clean energy. Integrating solar and wind power into EV charging networks will significantly reduce lifecycle emissions. The deployment of vehicle-to-grid (V2G) technologies can further enhance energy efficiency and contribute to a more decentralized and resilient power grid (IEA, 2023).

### 7.7.3 Policy and Regulatory Enhancements

The realization of these strategic objectives necessitates robust policy reform and institutional facilitation. Streamlining the regulatory procedures for land allocation, subsidy access, and charging station approvals will improve implementation efficiency. The introduction of traceability protocols and battery passports will ensure compliance with environmental and ethical standards throughout the EV value chain (MHI, 2023).

Furthermore, developing a comprehensive vehicle scrappage policy can accelerate the phase-out of older internal combustion engine vehicles and incentivize the adoption of cleaner alternatives. Active participation in global standard-setting institutions, alignment with international safety and performance benchmarks, and the exploration of carbon credit markets will further enhance India's competitiveness in the global EV ecosystem (IEA, 2023).

### 7.7.4 Role of Urban Local Bodies and City Governments

Urban local bodies and municipal administrations are poised to play a decisive role in the EV transition. Cities should prioritize the electrification of public service fleets including buses, sanitation vehicles, and official transport through mandates and procurement strategies. Additionally, local incentives such as reduced parking fees, exemption from tolls, and designated green mobility zones can encourage individual adoption. Incorporating EV infrastructure development into urban planning and Smart City initiatives will ensure integrated and future-ready mobility systems (CEEW, 2022).

### 7.7.2 Role of Youth, Academia, and Civil Society

India's youth, academic institutions, and civil society organizations constitute essential stakeholders in the broader electric mobility transition. Universities should integrate mobility innovation into their curricula, establish EV-focused clubs, and organize research challenges to foster engagement. Civil society organizations can play a critical role in public awareness, advocacy, and accountability. They are well-positioned to promote inclusivity in public incentive schemes, address gender and social equity in policy implementation, and dispel misinformation about EV technology and usage (NITI Aayog & RMI, 2022).

The transition to electric vehicles (EVs) in India represents a critical juncture in the nation's pursuit of sustainable development, energy security, and climate resilience. As this chapter has outlined, India's EV journey is shaped by a confluence of factors—rising environmental concerns, heavy dependence on imported fossil fuels, rapid urbanization, and the global push towards decarbonization. Government initiatives such as the National Electric Mobility Mission Plan (NEMMP), FAME schemes, and Production-Linked Incentives (PLI), alongside active private sector participation, have collectively established a foundation for accelerated EV adoption.

Through a detailed examination of EV classifications, market trends, technological advancements, infrastructural developments, and regional success stories, it is evident that India is progressing from a nascent to a more mature phase of electric mobility. The case studies demonstrate that both top-down policy interventions and bottom-up innovations are vital in enabling inclusive and localized transitions across urban and rural geographies.

Nonetheless, significant challenges persist, including high upfront costs, inadequate charging infrastructure, limited domestic battery supply chains, and behavioral resistance. Addressing these barriers through integrated policy frameworks, technological innovation, public awareness, and institutional coordination is imperative for achieving scale and equity in EV deployment.

Looking ahead, India's strategic roadmap must prioritize indigenous manufacturing, renewable energy integration, financial accessibility, and skill development to ensure that the EV revolution is not only environmentally effective but also economically transformative. With coordinated efforts from government, industry, academia, and civil society, India is well-positioned to emerge as a global leader in clean and affordable mobility solutions tailored for emerging economies.

# References


Agarwal, J. (1980). Determinants of Foreign Direct Investment: A Survey. *Review of World Economics. OECD (Weltwirtschaftliches Archiv), 116*(4), pp. 739–773. https://doi.org/ 10.1007/BF02696547.

Agarwal, N., & Milner, C. (2011). Connecting the Missing Link between Micro and Macro. *SSRN Electronic Journal*. https://doi.org/10.2139/ssrn.1966036.

Agarwal, P. (2003). Economic Impact of Foreign Direct Investment in South Asia. In R. M. Stern & A. Mattoo (Eds.), India and the WTO (pp. 117–140). https://openknowledge.worldbank.org/bitstream/handle/10986/15082/9780821354100.pdf?sequence=4#page=129.

Aggarwal, A. (2000) Liberalization, MNE Affiliates and Export Performance: Evidence from Indian Manufacturing, Institute of Economic Growth Discussion Papers, no 19, Delhi.

Aggarwal, A. (2002). Liberalisation, Multinational Enterprises and Export Performance: Evidence from Indian Manufacturing. *Journal of Development Studies, 38*(3), 119–137. https://doi.org/10.1080/00220380412331322371.

Aggarwal, A. (2018). The Impact of Foreign Ownership on Research and Development Intensity and Technology Acquisition in Indian Industries: Pre and Post Global Financial Crisis. *Asian Development Review, 35*(1), 1–26. https://doi.org/10.1162/adev_a_00103.

Agmon, T., & Lessard, D. R. (1977). Investor Recognition of Corporate International Diversification. *The Journal of Finance, 32*(4), p. 1049. https://doi.org/10.2307/2326511. Ibid. p. 1050.

Ahluwalia, M. S. (1986). Balance-of-Payments Adjustment in India, 1970–1971 to 1983–1984. *World Development, 14*(8), 937–962. https://doi.org/10.1016/0305-750x(86)90006-9.

Aitken, B. J., & Harrison, A. E. (1999). Do Domestic Firms Benefit from Direct Foreign Investment? Evidence from Venezuela. *American Economic Review, 89*(3), 605–618. https://doi.org/10.1257/aer.89.3.605.

Albulescu, C. T., & Tămăşilă, M. (2015). Exploring the Role of FDI in Enhancing The Entrepreneurial Activity In Europe: A Panel Data Analysis. *International Entrepreneurship and Management Journal, 12*(3), 629–657. https://doi.org/10.1007 /s11365-015-0360-9.

Alfaro, L., Chanda, A., Kalemli-Ozcan, S., & Sayek, S. (2004). FDI and Economic Growth: The Role of Local Financial Markets. *Journal of International Economics, 64*(1), 89–112. https://doi.org/10.1016/s0022-1996 (03)00081-3.

Ali, M., Roy, I., & Cantner, U. (2016). Knowledge Spillovers through FDI and Trade: The Moderating Role of Quality Adjusted Human Capital. *Journal of Evolutionary Economics, 26*(4), 837–868. https://doi.org/10.1007/s00191-016-0462-8.

Aliber, R. Z. (1970). Speculation in the Flexible Exchange Revisited. *Kyklos, 23*(2), pp. 303–314. https://doi.org/10.1111/j.1467-6435.1970.tb02560.x.

Al-Shawaf, A. M. K., & Almsafir, M. K. (2016). Economic Globalization: Role of Inward and Outward FDI with Economic Growth: Evidence from Malaysia. *Www.jbrmr.com a Journal of the Academy of Business and Retail Management, 10*. https://jbrmr.com/cdn/article_file/i-23_c-216.pdf.

Alvarez, R., & Lopez, R. A. (2005). Exporting and Performance: Evidence from Chilean Plants. *Canadian Journal of Economics/Revue Canadienne D'Economique, 38*(4), 1384–1400. https://doi.org/10.1111/j.0008-4085.2005.00329.x.

Ambrammal, S. K., & Sharma, R. (2014). R&D and Patenting by Firms in India in High- And Medium-High-Technology Industries. *Journal of Chinese Economic and Business Studies, 12*(2), 181–207. https://doi.org/10.1080/14765284.2014.900957.

Annual Report of the RBI. (1990-1991). https://rbi.org.in/Scripts/Publications.aspx?publication=Annual.

Anwar, S., & Nguyen, L. P. (2010). Foreign Direct Investment and Economic Growth in Vietnam. *Asia Pacific Business Review, 16*(1-2), 183–202. https://doi.org/10.1080/ 10438590802511031.

Anwar, S., & Sun, S. (2015). Foreign Direct Investment in R&D and Domestic Entrepreneurship in China's Manufacturing Industries. *Applied Economics, 47*(16), 1633–1651. https://doi.org/10.1080/00036846.2014.1000527.

Arslan, A., & Larimo, J. (2011). Greenfield Investments or Acquisitions: Impacts of Institutional Distance on Establishment Mode Choice of Multinational Enterprises in Emerging Economies. *Journal of Global Marketing, 24*(4), 345–356. https://doi.org/ 10.1080/08911762.2011.602323.

Athreye, S., & Kapur, S. (2001). Private Foreign Investment in India: Pain or Panacea? *The World Economy, 24*(3), pp. 399–424. https://doi.org/10.1111/1467-9701.00362.

Automobiles & Auto Components. (2020, May 30). Driving New India's Growth. https://www.investindia.gov.in/sector/automobile.

Bajrami, H., & Zeqiri, N. (2019). Theories of Foreign Direct Investment and the Significance of Human Capital. *International Journal of Business and Management, VII* (1). https://doi.org/10.20472/bm.2019.7.1.002.

Balasubramanyam, V. N., Salisu, M., & Sapsford, D. (1999). Foreign Direct Investment as an Engine of Growth. *The Journal of International Trade & Economic Development, 8*(1), 27–40. https://doi.org/doi:10.1080/09638199900000003.

Baltagi, B. H., Egger, P. H., & Kesina, M. (2014). Sources of productivity spillovers: panel data evidence from China. *Journal of Productivity Analysis, 43*(3), 389–402. https://doi.org/10.1007/s11123-014-0393-z.

Banerji, S. (2019). Data Wars. Business Today.https://www.businesstoday.in/magazine/ the-buzz/story/data-wars-235000-2019-10-30.

Banga, R. (2004). Impact of Japanese and US FDI on Productivity Growth: A Firm Level Analysis. *Economic and Political Weekly, 39*(5), 453–460. https://doi.org/10.2307/ 4414579.

Banga, R. (2005). Impact of Liberalisation on Wages and Employment in Indian Manufacturing Industries. *Econstor.eu.* https://doi.org/http://hdl.handle.net/10419/176175.

Banga, R., & Goldar, B. (2004). Contribution of Services to Output Growth and Productivity in Indian Manufacturing: Pre and Post Reforms. *Economic and Political Weekly, 42*(26), 2769–2777. https://ideas.repec.org/p/ind/icrier/139.html

Barbosa, N., & Eiriz, V. (2009). Linking Corporate Productivity to Foreign Direct Investment: An Empirical Assessment. *International Business Review, 18*(1), 1–13. https://doi.org/10.1016/j.ibusrev.2008.10.003.

Barlow, E. R., & Wender, I. T. (1955). *Foreign investment and taxation*. Halliday Lithograph Corporation.

Barrios, S., & Strobl, E. (2002). Foreign Direct Investment and Productivity Spillovers: Evidence from the Spanish Experience. *Weltwirtschaftliches Archiv, 138*(3), 459–481. https://doi.org/10.1007/bf02707949

Barry, F., Görg, H., & Strobl, E. (2005). Foreign Direct Investment and Wages in Domestic Firms in Ireland: Productivity Spillovers versus Labour-Market Crowding Out. *International Journal of the Economics of Business, 12*(1), 67–84. https://doi.org/10.1080/1357151042000323102

Basant, R., & Fikkert, B. (1993). Impact of R & D, Foreign Technology Purchase and Technology Spillovers on Indian Industrial Productivity: Some Estimates. *UNU/Initech Working Paper 18*, 1–42. https://digitallibrary.un.org/record/223528?ln=en

Behera, S. R., Dua, P., & Goldar, B. (2012a). Foreign Direct Investment and Technology Spillover: Evidence across Indian Manufacturing Industries. https://ideas.repec.org/p/cde/ cdewps/207.html

Behera, S. R., Dua, P., & Goldar, B. (2012b). Technology Spillover of Foreign Direct Investment: An Analysis of Different Clusters in India.https://ideas.repec.org/p/ pra/mprapa/43840.html.

Behera, S. R. (2014). Local Firms Productivity Spillover from Foreign Direct Investment: A Study of Indian Manufacturing Industries. *International Journal of Technological Learning, Innovation and Development, 7*(2), 167–190. https://ideas.repec.org/a/ids/ijtlid/v 7y2014i2p167-190.html.

Belloumi, M. (2014). *The Relationship between Trade, FDI and Economic Growth in Tunisia: An Application of the Autoregressive Distributed Lag Model. Economic Systems, 38(2), 269–287.* https://doi.org/doi:10.1016/j.ecosys.2013.09.002.

Bengoa, M., & Sanchez-Robles, B. (2003). Foreign Direct Investment, Economic Freedom and Growth: New Evidence from Latin America. *European Journal of Political Economy, 19*(3), 529–545. https://doi.org/10.1016/s0176-2680 (03)00011-9.

Bergman, A. (2006). *FDI and Spillover Effects in the Indian Pharmaceutical Industry* (Master's Degree (One Year). (Pp.1–78). https://lup.lub.lu.se/luur/download?func=downloadFile&recordOId=1338017&fileOId=1646193

Berrill, J., O'Hagan-Luff, M., & van Stel, A. (2018). The Moderating Role of Education In The Relationship Between FDI And Entrepreneurial Activity. *Small Business Economics, 54*(4), 1041–1059. https://doi.org/10.1007/s11187-018-0121-6

Bhattarai, K., & Negi, V. (2020). FDI and Economic Performance of Firms in India. *Studies in Microeconomics, 8*(1), 44–74. https://doi.org/10.1177/2321022220918684

Bhavani, T. A., & Tendulkar, S. D. (2001). Determinants of Firm-Level Export Performance: A Case Study of Indian Textile Garments and Apparel Industry. *The Journal of International Trade & Economic Development, 10*(1), 65–92. https://doi.org/10.1080/09638190122431

Blake, A., Deng, Z., & Falvey, R. (2009). How Does the Productivity of Foreign Direct Investment Spillover to Local Firms in Chinese Manufacturing? *Journal of Chinese Economic and Business Studies, 7*(2), 183–197. https://doi.org/10.1080/14765 280902847676

Blalock, P. G., & Gertler, P. J. (2008). Welfare gains from Foreign Direct Investment through technology transfer to local suppliers. *Journal of International Economics, 74*(2), 402–421.https://econpapers.repec.org/article/eeeinecon/v_3a74_3ay_3a2008_3ai_3a2_ 3ap_3a402-421.html.

Blomström, M. (1986). Foreign Investment and Productive Efficiency: The Case of Mexico. *The Journal of Industrial Economics, 35*(1), 97. https://doi.org/10.2307/2098609.

Blomström, M., & Kokko, A. (1998). Multinational Corporations and Spillovers. *Journal of Economic Surveys, 12*(3), 247–277. https://doi.org/10.1111/1467-6419.00056.

Blomström, M., & Persson, H. (1983). Foreign investment and spillover efficiency in an underdeveloped economy: Evidence from the Mexican manufacturing industry. *World Development, 11*(6), 493–501. https://doi.org/10.1016/0305-750x (83)90016-5.

Blomström, M., & Persson, H. (1983). Foreign Investment and Spillover Efficiency in an Underdeveloped Economy: Evidence from the Mexican Manufacturing Industry. *World Development, 11*(6), 493–501. https://doi.org/10.1016/0305-750x (83)90016-5.

Borenzstein, E., De Gregorio, J., & Lee, J.-W. (1998). How Does Foreign Direct Investment Affect Economic Growth. *IMF Working Papers, 94*(110), 115–135. https://doi.org/10.5089/9781451853278.001.

BPM6. (2009). *Balance of Payments and International Investment Position Manual (6th ed.)* (pp. 100-101). IMF. https://www.imf.org/external/pubs/ft/bop/2007/pdf/bpm6.pdf.

Brouthers, K. D., & Brouthers, L. E. (2000). Acquisition or Greenfield Start-Up? Institutional, Cultural and Transaction Cost Influences. *Strategic Management Journal, 21*(1), 89–97. https://doi.org/3.0.co;2-8">10.1002/(sici)1097-0266(200001)21:1<89:: aid-smj85>3.0.co;2-8

Brouthers, K. D., & Hennart, J.F. (2007). Boundaries of the Firm: Insights from International Entry Mode Research. *Journal of Management, 33*(3), 395–425. https://doi.org/10.1177/0149206307300817.

Buckley, P. J., Clegg, J., & Wang, C. (2007). Is the Relationship between Inward FDI and Spillover Effects Linear? An Empirical Examination of the Case of China. *Journal of International Business Studies, 38*(3), 447–459. https://doi.org/10.1016/j.ibusrev. 2006.12.006.

Burugula, P. (2019). New FPI/FDI Classification by SEBI to Hit Many Offshore Funds. https://economictimes.indiatimes.com/markets/stocks/news/new-fpi/fdi-classification-by-sebi-to-hit-many-offshore-funds/articleshow/71532706.cms?from=mdr

Busse, M., & Groizard, J. L. (2005). FDI, Regulations and Growth. SSRN Electronic Journal. https://doi.org/10.2139/ssrn.895243.

Carbonell, J.B., & Werner, R. A. (2018). Does Foreign Direct Investment Generate Economic Growth? A New Empirical Approach Applied to Spain. *Economic Geography, 94*(4), 425–456. https://doi.org/10.1080/00130095.2017.1393312.

Carkovic, M., & Levine, R. E. (2002). *Does Foreign Direct Investment Accelerate Economic Growth? SSRN Electronic Journal.* https://doi.org/. doi:10.2139/ssrn.314924.

Catik, A. N., & Karacuka, M. (2012). A Spatial Approach to Measure Productivity Spillovers of Foreign Affiliated Firms in Turkish Manufacturing Industries. *The Journal of Developing Areas, 46*(2), 65–83. https://doi.org/10.1353/jda.2012.0039.

Caves, R. E. (1974). Multinational Firms, Competition, and Productivity in Host Country Markets. *Economica, 41*(162), 176–193. https://doi.org/10.2307/2553765.

Caves, R. E., & Murphy, W. F. (1976). Franchising: Firms, markets, and intangible assets. *Southern Economic Journal*, 572-586.

Chakraborty, C., & Basu, P. (2002). Foreign Direct Investment and Growth in India: A Cointegration Approach. *Applied Economics, 34*(9), 1061–1073. https://doi.org/10.1080/00036840110074079.

Chakraborty, C., & Nunnenkamp, P. (2008). Economic Reforms, FDI, and Economic Growth in India: A Sector Level Analysis. *World Development, 36*(7), 1192–1212. https://doi.org/10.1016/j.worlddev.2007.06.014.

Chandra, B. (1981). *Nationalism and Colonialism in Modern India*. New Delhi: Orient Blackswan. Ibid. p. 15.

Chatterjee, B. (1992). *Trade, Tariffs, and Empire: Lancashire and British policy in India, 1919-1939*. New Delhi: Oxford University Press.

Chen, J. (2020). Inward Investment. Investopedia. https://www. investopedia. com/ terms/i/inward-investment.asp#:~:text=An%20inward%20 investment %20involves%20an,local%20company%20to%20foreign%20 investors.

Chen, T.J., & Ku, Y.H. (2000). The Effect of Foreign Direct Investment on Firm Growth: The Case of Taiwan's Manufacturers. *Japan and the World Economy. 12(2). (p.153-172)*. doi:10.1016/s0922-1425(99)00035-3

Chuang, Y.C., & Hsu, P.F. (2004). FDI, trade, and spillover efficiency: evidence from China's manufacturing sector. *Applied Economics, 36*(10), 1103–1115. https://doi.org/10.1080/0003684042000246812

Chuang, Y., & Lin, C. (1999). Foreign Direct Investment, R&D and Spillover Efficiency: Evidence from Taiwan's Manufacturing Firms. *Journal of Development Studies, 35*(4), 117–137. https://doi.org/10.1080/00220389908422583

Chudnovsky, D., López, A., & Rossi, G. (2008). Foreign Direct Investment Spillovers and the Absorptive Capabilities of Domestic Firms in the Argentine Manufacturing Sector (1992–2001). *The Journal of Development Studies, 44*(5), 645–677. https://doi.org/ 10.1080/00220380802009159

Coase, R. H. (1937). The Nature of the Firm. *Economica, 4*(16), 386–405. https://doi.org/10.1111/j.1468-0335.1937.tb00002.x

Consolidated FDI Policy Circular. (2020). Department for Promotion of Industry and Internal Trade. https://dipp.gov.in/sites/default/files/FDI-PolicyCircular-2020-29October 2020.pdf

Crespi, G., Criscuolo, C., Haskel, J., & Slaughter, M. (2007). Productivity Growth, Knowledge Flows, and Spillovers. *Centre of Economic Performance, Discussion Paper* (p.785). https://doi.org/10.3386/w13959

Crespo, N., & Fontoura, M. P. (2007). Determinant Factors of FDI Spillovers – What Do We Really Know? *World Development*, *35*(3), 410–425. https://doi.org/10.1016/ j.worlddev.2006.04.001

CRISIL Impact Note. (2020, March 23). The BS-IV Blow Nears. https://www.crisil.com/en/home/our-analysis/views-and-commentaries/2020/03/the-bs-iv-blow-nears.html

Das, S. (1987). Externalities, and Technology Transfer through Multinational Corporations: A Theoretical Analysis. *Journal of International Economics*, *22*(1-2), 171–182. https://doi.org/10.1016/0022-1996 (87)90028-6

Dash, R. K., & Parida, P. C. (2012). FDI, Services Trade and Economic Growth in India: Empirical Evidence on Causal Links. *Empirical Economics*, *45*(1), pp. 217–238. https://doi.org/10.1007/s00181-012-0621-1

Datt, R., & Sundaram, K. P. M. (2013). Indian Economy.69 ed. S. Chand Publications, New Delhi. pp. 20-25.

De Mello, L. (1999). Foreign Direct Investment-Led Growth: Evidence from Time-series and Panel Data. *Oxford Economic Papers*, *51*(1), 133–151. https://doi.org/10.1093/oep/ 51.1.133

Demena, B. A., & van Bergeijk, P. A. G. (2016). A Meta-Analysis of FDI and Productivity Spillovers in Developing Countries. *Journal of Economic Surveys*, *31*(2), 546–571. https://doi.org/10.1111/joes.12146

Demirbag, M., Tatoglu, E., & Glaister, K. W. (2008). Factors Affecting Perceptions of the Choice between Acquisition and Greenfield Entry: The Case of Western FDI in an Emerging Market. *Management International Review*, *48*(1), pp. 5-38.

Denisia, V. (2010). Foreign Direct Investment Theories: An Overview of the Main FDI Theories. p.55-56. *European Journal of Interdisciplinary Studies.*

Dimelis, S. P. (2005). Spillovers from Foreign Direct Investment and Firm Growth: Technological, Financial and Market Structure Effects. *International Journal of the Economics of Business*, *12*(1), 85–104. https://doi.org/10.1080/1357151042000323094

Djankov, S., & Hoekman, B. (2000). Foreign Investment and Productivity Growth in Czech Enterprises. *The World Bank Economic Review, 14*(1), 49–64. https://www.jstor.org/stable/3990034?seq=1

Domar, E. (1946). Capital Expansion, Rate of Growth, and Employment. *Econometrica, 14*(2), 137-147. doi:10.2307/1905364

Driffield, N. L., & Kambhampati, U. S. (2003). Trade Liberalization and the Efficiency of Firms in Indian Manufacturing. *Review of Development Economics, 7*(3), 419–430. https://doi.org/10.1111/1467-9361.00200

Driffield, N., Love, J. (2007). Linking FDI Motivation and Host Economy Productivity Effects: Conceptual and Empirical Analysis. *Journal of International Business Studies* .38**,** 460–473. https://doi.org/10.1057/palgrave.jibs.8400268

Du, L., Harrison, A., & Jefferson, G. (2011). Do Institutions Matter for FDI Spillovers? The Implications of China's "Special Characteristics." *Policy Research Working Papers*. https://doi.org/10.1596/1813-9450-5757

Du, L., Harrison, A., & Jefferson, G. H. (2012). Testing for Horizontal and Vertical Foreign Investment Spillovers in China, 1998–2007. *Journal of Asian Economics, 23*(3), 234–243. https://doi.org/10.1016/j.asieco.2011.01.001

Dua, P., & Rashid, A. I. (1998). Foreign Direct Investment and Economic Activity in India. *Indian Economic Review, 33*(2), 153–168. https://www.jstor.org/stable/29794166?seq=1

Dunning, J. (2008). Location and the Multinational Enterprise: John Dunning's Thoughts on Receiving the "Journal of International Business Studies" Decade Award. *Journal of International Business Studies, 40*(1), 20-34. http://www.jstor.org/stable/25483357

Dunning, J. H. (1998). Location and the Multinational Enterprise: A Neglected Factor? *Journal of International Business Studies, 29*(1), 45–66. https://doi.org/10.1057/palgrave. jibs.8490024

Dunning, J. H. (2001). The Eclectic (OLI) Paradigm of International Production: Past, Present and Future. *International Journal of the Economics of Business, 8(2), 173–190.* doi:10.1080/13571510110051441

Ekholm, K., Forslid, R., & Markusen, J. R. (2003). Export-Platform Foreign Direct Investment. SSRN Electronic Journal, (Working Paper No. 9517), (p.1). https://doi.org/10.2139/ssrn.739213

Elboishi, H. (2015). The Effect of FDI on Economic Growth and the Importance of Host Country Characteristics. *Journal of Economics and International Finance, 7*(2), 25–41. https://doi.org/10.5897/jeif2014.0602

EPWRF India Time-series. (2008). National Account Statistics. https://epwrfits.in /TypesOfNAS.aspx.

ET Auto. (2020). Indian Auto Industry Status Report 2020. https://auto. economictimes. indiatimes.com/report2020#:~:text=About%20The%20 Report Text=In% 202018%2C% 20the%20Indian%20automobile,in%20 the%20 country%20has%20doubled.

ET Auto. (2020). https://auto.economictimes.indiatimes.com/news/industry/ fdi-in-india-jumps-13-to-record-49-98-billion-in-2019-20/76082460.

FADA. (2020). FADA India. *19*(10), pp.52–55. http://www.fadaindia.org/fada-journal/january-2020-issue.html.

Ministry of Finance. (2020) https://www.fdi.finance/blog/sectors-in-which-fdi-in-india-is-allowed-under-automatic-and-approval-routes/

Foreign Investment Facilitators. (2020). Ministry of Finance. https://www.fdi. finance/ blog/explained-types-of-fdi/

Report of the Committee on Compilation of Foreign Direct Investment in India. (2002). Reserve Bank of India. https://dipp.gov.in/sites/default/files/fdi.pdf

Flores, G., Renato, J.R., Fontura, M.P. and Santos, R.G. (2000) Foreign Direct Investment Spillovers: What Can We Learn from Portuguese Data? Mimeo, ISEG, Technical University of Lisbon.

Fotopoulos, G., & Louri, H. (2004). Firm Growth and FDI: Are Multinationals Stimulating Local Industrial Development? *Journal of Industry, Competition and Trade*, *4*(3), 163–189. https://doi.org/10.1023/b:jict.0000047300.88236. f1

Franco, C., & Sasidharan, S. (2010). MNEs, Technological Efforts and Channels of Export Spillover: An Analysis of Indian Manufacturing Industries. *Economic Systems*, *34*(3), 270–288. https://doi.org/10.1016/j.ecosys.2010.02.005

G.B.N& Vashisht, P. (2008). Determinants of Competitiveness of the Indian Auto Industry. *Working paper no. 201, Indian Council for Research on International Economic Relations (ICRIER),* p.76. http://www.icrier.org/pdf/Working%20 Paper% 20201_final.pdf.

G., B. N., & Vashisht, P. (2013). Indian Auto Industry: A Global Hub in the Making? *Review of Development and Change*, *18*(2), 149–172. https://doi.org/10.1177/0972266120130205.

Gereffi, G. (1994). The Organization of Buyer-Driven Global Commodity Chains: How U.S. Retailers Shape Overseas Production. https://www.researchgate.net/publication/ 281870191_The_Organization_of_Buyer-Driven_Global_Commodity_Chains_How_US _Retailers_Shape_Overseas_Production_Networks

Ghali, S., & Rezgui, S. (2011). FDI Contribution to Technical Efficiency in the Tunisian Manufacturing Sector: Evidence from Micro-panel Data. *International Economic Journal*, *25*(2), 319–339. https://doi.org/10.1080/10168737.2010.504215

Ghosh, A. (1958). Input-Output Approach in an Allocation System. *Economica*, *25*(97), 58. https://doi.org/10.2307/2550694

Ghosh, M., & Roy, S. S. (2018). Foreign Direct Investment, Firm Heterogeneity, and Exports: An Analysis of Indian Manufacturing. *Asian Development Review*, *35*(1), 27–51. https://doi.org/10.1162/adev_a_00104

Ghosh, M, and Roy, S. S. (2013). FDI, Firm Heterogeneity and Exports an Examination of Evidence in India. Working Paper, 5 (13), Centre for Advanced Studies, Jadavpur University,

Girma, S., Görg, H., & Pisu, M. (2008). Exporting, Linkages and Productivity Spillovers from Foreign

Direct Investment. *Canadian Journal of Economics/Revue Canadienne D'économique*, *41*(1), 320–340. https://doi.org/10.1111/j.1365-2966.2008.00465.x

Glass, A. J., & Saggi, K. (2002). Multinational Firms and Technology Transfer. *Scandinavian Journal of Economics*, *104*(4), 495–513. https://doi.org/10.1111/1467-9442.00298

GOI. (1969).4th Five Year Plan (Chapter 14: Industries and Minerals), Planning Commission, Government of India. New Delhi. http://www.planningcommission. nic.in/plans/ planrel/fiveyr/4th/4planch14.html.

Goldar, B. (2004). Indian Manufacturing: Productivity Trends in Pre and Post Reform Periods. *Economic and Political Weekly*, *39*(46/47), 5033–5043. https://doi.org/10.2307/ 4415808

Goldar, B., & Banga, K. (2020). Country Origin of Foreign Direct Investment in Indian Manufacturing and Its Impact on Productivity of Domestic Firms. *FDI, Technology and Innovation*, 13–55. https://doi.org/10.1007/978-981-15-3611-3_2

Goldar, B., & Ghosh, M. (2015). Employment Growth in India's Organised Manufacturing: Trends and Determinants. *Review of Development and Change, 20*(2), 277–302. https://doi.org/10.1177/0972266120150214

Goldar, B., & Sharma, A. K. (2014). Foreign Investment in Indian Industrial Firms and Its Impact of Firm Performance. In *ninth annual Conference of the Forum for Global Knowledge Sharing, Bangalore, India*. http://www.fgks.in/images/pdf/209.pdf

Goldar, B., Renganathan, V.S. & Banga, R. (2004). Ownership and Efficiency in Engineering Firms: 1990-91 to 1999-2000. *Economic and Political Weekly, 39*(5), 441-447.http://www.jstor.org/stable/4414577

Görg, H., & Strobl, E. (2005). Spillovers from Foreign Firms through Worker Mobility: An Empirical Investigation*. *Scandinavian Journal of Economics, 107*(4), 693–709. https://doi.org/10.1111/j.1467-9442.2005.00427.x

Guerra, A.-I., & Sancho, F. (2010). Rethinking Economy-Wide Rebound Measures: An Unbiased Proposal. *Energy Policy, 38*(11), 6684–6694. https://doi.org/10.1016/j.enpol. 2010.06.038

Gujarati, D. N. (2011). *Econometrics by Example* (pp. 1–2). UK: Palgrave Macmillan.

Gunby, P., Jin, Y., & Robert Reed, W. (2017). Did FDI Really Cause Chinese Economic Growth? A Meta-Analysis. *World Development, 90*, 242–255. https://doi.org/10.1016/j. worlddev.2016.10.001

Haddad, M., & Harrison, A. (1993). Are There Positive Spillovers from Direct Foreign Investment? *Journal of Development Economics, 42*(1), 51–74. https://doi.org/10.1016/ 0304-3878(93)90072-u

Haider, F., Kunst, R., & Wirl, F. (2020). Total Factor Productivity, Its Components and Drivers. *Empirica*, 1–45. https://doi.org/10.1007/s10663-020-09476-4

Handbook of Statistics on the Indian Economy. (2008). In Gunjeet Kaur for the Reserve Bank of India, Mumbai. pp.248-251.https://www.rbi.org.in/Scripts/AnnualPublications.aspx?head=Handbook+ of+Statistics+on+Indian+Economy

Hartman, D. G. (1985). Tax policy and foreign direct investment. *Journal of Public Economics, 26*(1), pp. 107–121. https://doi.org/10.1016/0047-2727(85)90041-6

Hasan, R. (2002). The Impact of Imported and Domestic Technologies on the Productivity of Firms: Panel Data Evidence from Indian Manufacturing Firms. *Journal of Development Economics, 69*(1), pp. 23–49. https://doi.org/10.1016/s0304-3878 (02)00051-2

Hassine, H. B., Boudier, F., & Mathieu, C. (2016). The Two Ways of FDI, R&D Spillovers: Evidence from the French Manufacturing Industry. *Applied Economics, 49*(25), pp. 2395–2408. https://doi.org/10.1080/00036846.2016.1240345

Havránek, T., & Iršová, Z. (2011). Estimating Vertical Spillovers From Fdi: Why Results Vary And What The True Effect Is. *Journal of International Economics, 85*(2), pp. 234–244. https://doi.org/10.1016/j.jinteco.2011.07.004

Hayakawa, K., & Matsura, T. (2017). Impacts of Outward Foreign Direct Investment: New Firm-Level Evidence from Japan. https://voxeu.org/article/impacts-outward-foreign-direct-investment#:~:text=These%20results%20lend%20support%20to

Head, K., Mayer, T., & Ries, J. (2002). Revisiting Oligopolistic Reaction: Are Decisions on Foreign Direct Investment Strategic Complements? *Journal of Economics Management Strategy, 11*(3), pp. 453–472. https://doi.org/10.1111/j.1430-9134.2002.00453.x

Heckscher, E. F., & Ohlin, B. G. (1933). *Heckscher-Ohlin trade theory*. The MIT Press.

Hennart, J. F., & Park, Y. R. (1993). Greenfield vs. acquisition: The strategy of Japanese investors in the United States. *Management Science, 39*(9), 1054-1070.

Herzer, D. (2012). How Does Foreign Direct Investment Really Affect Developing Countries' Growth? *Review of International Economics, 20*(2), 396–414. https://doi.org/10.1111/j.1467-9396.2012.01029.x

Hicks, J. R., Mukherjee, M., & Ghosh, S. K. (1992). *The Framework of the Indian Economy: An Introduction to Economics.* Delhi: Oxford University Press. (p. 217).

Hoang, V. T. and Thanh, H. P. (2010). Productivity Spillovers from Foreign Direct Investment: The Case of Vietnam.In Hahn, C. H. and D. Narjoko (eds.). Causes and Consequences of Globalization in

East Asia: What Do the Micro Data Analyses Show? ERIA Research Project Report 2009-2. Jakarta: ERIA. Pp.228-246

Hosseini, H. (2005). An Economic Theory of FDI: A Behavioural Economics and Historical Approach. *The Journal of Socio-Economics, 34*(4), pp. 528–541. https://doi.org/10.1016/j.socec.2005.07.001

Hu, A. G. Z., & Jefferson, G. H. (2002). FDI Impact and Spillover: Evidence from China's Electronic and Textile Industries. *The World Economy, 25*(8), 1063–1076. https://doi.org/10.1111/1467-9701.00481

Hurd, J. M. (1983). Railways. In *The Cambridge Economic History of India* (pp. 737–761). https://doi.org/10.1017/chol9780521228022.016

Hymer, S. (1960). On Multinational Corporations and Foreign Direct Investment. The Theory of Transnational Corporations. London: Routledge for the United Nations.

Iamsiraroj, S., & Ulubaşoğlu, M. A. (2015). Foreign Direct Investment and Economic Growth: A Real Relationship or Wishful Thinking? *Economic Modelling, 51*, 200–213. https://doi.org/10.1016/j.econmod.2015.08.009

IBEF. (Nov,2019, updated Jan 2021). https://www.ibef.org/industry/auto components-india.aspx

Import and Export Policy of India. (1985). *Foreign Trade Review, 19*(4), 595–614. https://doi.org/10.1177/0015732515850408.

India Today. (1981). IMF Grants India Its Largest-Ever Loan of Rs 5,000 Crore, Sets Off Heated Debate https://www.indiatoday.in/magazine/cover-story/story/19811215-imf-grants-india-its-largest-ever-loan-of-rs-5000-crore-sets-off-heated-debate-773521-2013-10-28

India's Balance of Payments Concepts, Compilation, and Recent Scenario 1950-51 to 2003-04. (February, 2005). EPW Research Foundation. http://www.epwrf.res.in/upload/ BOP/BoP%20200502.pdf

India's FDI Inflows Set to Jump Massively. (2002, November 15). Indian Express. http://archive.indianexpress.com/oldStory/13038/

Indian Auto Component Industry Performance Review. (2020). ACMA. https://www.acma.in/auto-component.php

Industrial Policy Resolution. (1948). https://dipp.gov.in/sites/default/files/chap001%20%2 013.pdf

Industrial Policy Resolution. (1956). https://dipp.gov.in/sites/default/files/chap001% 20%2013.pdf

Industrial Policy Resolution. (1977). https://dipp.gov.in/sites/default/files/chap001%20 %2013.pdf

Industries Development and Regulation Act. (1951). https://thc.nic.in/Central%20 Governmental%20Acts/Industries%20(%20Development%20and%20Regulation) %20Act, %201951.pdf.

Input–Output Tables and Analysis. (2020) ADB Data Library. Asian Development Bank. https://data.adb.org/taxonomy/term/211.

Invest India. (2020). Automobiles & Auto Components Driving New India's Growth. https://static.investindia.gov.in/s3fs-public/2020-04/Auto%20%26%20Auto%20Compon ents _Non%20paginate_V7%20%281%29.pdf.

International Investment Perspectives. (2002) OECD. https://www.oecd-ilibrary.org/finance-and-investment/international-investment-perspectives-2002_iip-2002-en

IPR. (1948). https://dpiit.gov.in/sites/default/files/chap001%20%2013.pdf.

Iqbal, N., Ahmad, N., Haider, Z., & Anwar, S. (2014). Impact of Foreign Direct Investment (FDI) on GDP: A Case Study from Pakistan. *International Letters of Social and Humanistic Sciences, 16*, 73–80. https://doi.org/10.18052/www.scipress.com/ilshs.16.73

Iršová, Z., & Havránek, T. (2013). Determinants of Horizontal Spillovers from FDI: Evidence from a Large Meta-Analysis. *World Development, 42*, 1–15. https://doi.org/10.1016/j.worlddev.2012.07.001

Itagaki, T. (1981). The Theory of the Multinational Firm under Exchange Rate Uncertainty. *The Canadian Journal of Economics / Revue Canadienne D'Economique, 14*(2), 276-297. doi:10.2307/134798

Ito, B., Yashiro, N., Xu, Z., Chen, X., & Wakasugi, R. (2012). How do Chinese Industries Benefit from FDI Spillovers? *China Economic Review, 23*(2), 342–356. https://doi.org/10.1016/j.chieco.2012.02.001

Jabbour, L., & Mucchielli, J. L. (2007). Technology Transfer through Vertical Linkages: The Case of The Spanish Manufacturing Industry. *Journal of Applied Economics, 10,* 115–136. https://ideas.repec.org/a/cem/jaecon/v10y2007n1p115-136.html

Jadhav, A., & Reddy, V. (2013). Does FDI Contribute to Growth? Evidence from the Capital Goods Sector in India. *Economic and Political Weekly, 48*(12), 59-68. http://www.jstor.org/stable/23527150

Javorcik, B. S. (2004). Does Foreign Direct Investment Increase the Productivity of Domestic Firms? In Search of Spillovers through Backward Linkages. *The American Economic Review, 94*(3), pp. 605–627. https://doi.org/10.1257/0002828041464605

Javorcik, B. S., & Spatareanu, M. (2009). Tough Love: Do Czech Suppliers Learn from their Relationships with Multinationals? *The Scandinavian Journal of Economics, 111*(4), 811–833. http://www.jstor.org/stable/40587814

Javorcik, B. S., & Spatareanu, M. (2011). Does It Matter Where You Come From? Vertical Spillovers from Foreign Direct Investment and the Origin Of Investors. *Journal of Development Economics, 96*(1), 126–138. https://doi.org/10.1016/j.jdeveco.2010.05.008

Jena, P. K., & Taggar, R. (2011). Foreign Direct Investment and its Impact on the Technology Diffusion: Some Issues and Challenges Ahead. *International Journal of Research in Computer Application & Management, 1*(2 (April)), pp. 126–132. https://www.google.com/search?q=%22It%20can%20arise%20as%20a%20result%20of%20interaction%20across%20industries.%22

Jhingan, M. L. (2015). *The Economics of Development and Planning* (40th ed., pp. 1–1058). New Delhi: Vrinda Publications (P) Ltd. (Original work published 1997)

Jones, G. (1996). The Evolution of International Business. (London: Routledge). (p.6.).

Jordaan, J. A. (2008). Intra- and Inter-industry Externalities from Foreign Direct Investment in the Mexican Manufacturing Sector: New Evidence from Mexican Regions. *World Development, 36*(12), 2838–2854. https://doi.org/10.1016/j.worlddev.2008.02.006

Jordaan, J. A. (2011). Local Sourcing and Technology Spillovers to Mexican Suppliers: How Important are FDI and Supplier Characteristics? *Growth and Change, 42*(3), 287–319. https://doi.org/10.1111/j.1468-2257.2011.00554.x

Joseph, T. J., & Reddy, V. N. (2009). FDI Spillovers and Export Performance of Indian Manufacturing Firms after Liberalisation. *Economic and Political Weekly*, *44*(52), 97–105.https://www.jstor.org/stable/25663945?seq=1

Jude, C. (2012, August 31). Horizontal and Vertical Technology Spillovers from FDI in Eastern Europe.https://www.researchgate.net/publication/264850227_ Horizontal_and_ Vertical_Technology_Spillovers_from_FDI_in_Eastern_ Europe.

Kaldor, N. (1980). The Foundations of Free Trade Theory and their Implications for the Current World Recession. *Unemployment in Western Countries*, 86. https://doi.org/10.1007/978-1-349-16407-3_4

Kale, Seenaiah. (2021). The Influence of Non-R&D Channels on Innovation in a Developing Economy: an Empirical Analysis in the Context of India. *International Review of Applied Economics*. https://doi.org/10.1080/0269217 1.2021.1951682

Kathuria, A. (1966). Competing through Technology and Manufacturing: A Study of the Indian Commercial Vehicles Industry. https://www.semanticscholar. org/paper/ Competing-through-Technology-and-Manufacturing%3A-AKathuria/3f5379b36740a4eae bdb388f70956598fe666a71.

Kathuria, S. (1987). Commercial Vehicles Industry in India: A Case History, 1928-1987. *Economic and Political Weekly*, *22*(42/43), pp. 1809–1823. http://www. jstor.org/ stable/4377638.

Kathuria, S. (1996). Competing Through Technology and Manufacturing. A Study of the Indian Commercial Vehicles Industry. Oxford University Press. Delhi.

Kathuria, V. (2000). Productivity Spillovers from Technology Transfer to Indian manufacturing Firms. *Journal of International Development*, *12*(3), 343–369. https://doi.org/3.0.co;2-r">10.1002/(sici)1099-1328(200004)12:3<343::aid-jid639>3.0.co;2-r

Kathuria, V. (2001). Foreign Firms, Technology Transfer and Knowledge Spillovers to Indian Manufacturing Firms: A Stochastic Frontier Analysis. *Applied Economics*, *33*(5), 625–642. https://doi.org/10.1080/00036840121940

Kathuria, V. (2002). Liberalisation, FDI, and Productivity Spillovers: An Analysis of Indian Manufacturing Firms. *Oxford Economic Papers*, *54*(4), 688–718. https://doi.org/10.1093/oep/54.4.688

Kathuria, V. (2010). Does the Technology Gap Influence Spillovers? A Post-liberalization Analysis of Indian Manufacturing Industries. *Oxford Development Studies, 38*(2), 145–170. https://doi.org/10.1080/13600811003793079

Katrak, H. (1990). Imports of Technology of the Newly Industrialising Countries: An Inter-Industry Analysis for Mexico and Pakistan. *Journal of International Development, 2*(3), 352–372. https://doi.org/10.1002/jid.3380020304

Kaulihowa, T., & Adjasi, C. (2019). Non-Linearity of FDI and Human Capital Development in Africa. *Transnational Corporations Review, 11*(2), 133–142. https://doi.org/10.1080/ 19186444.2019.1635734

Kenton, W. (2020, November 18). Outward Direct Investment (ODI). Investopedia. https://www.investopedia.com/terms/o/outward_direct_investment.asp

Keshari, P. K. (2013). Efficiency Spillovers from FDI in the Indian Machinery Industry: A Firm-Level Study using Panel Data Models. https://ideas.repec.org/p/pra/mprapa/ 47070.html

Khachoo, Q., & Sharma, R. (2016). FDI and Innovation: An Investigation into Intra- and Inter-industry Effects. *Global Economic Review, 45*(4), 311–330. https://doi.org/10.1080/1226508x.2016.1218294

Kim, M. (2015). Productivity Spillovers from FDI and The Role of Domestic Firm's Absorptive Capacity in South Korean Manufacturing Industries. *Empirical Economics, 48*(2), 807–827. https://doi.org/10.1007/s00181-014-0804-z

Klein, M. (2017). *Technological Catch-Up and Productivity Spillovers from FDI: Evidence from Indian Manufacturing.* https://ostromworkshop.indiana.edu/pdf /seriespapers/2017spr-res/klein-paper.pdf

Knickerbocker, F. T. (1973). Oligopolistic Reaction and Multinational Enterprise. *The International Executive, 15*(2), pp. 7–9. https://doi.org/10.1002/tie.5060150205

Koizumi, T., & Kopecky, K. J. (1977). Economic Growth, Capital Movements and the International Transfer of Technical Knowledge. *Journal of International Economics, 7*(1), 45–65. https://doi.org/10.1016/0022-1996 (77)90004-6

Kojima, K. (1973). A Macroeconomic Approach to Foreign Direct Investment. *Hitotsubashi Journal of Economics, 14*(1), 1–21. https://www.jstor.org/stable/43295560? seq=1

Kojima, K. (1975). International Trade and Foreign Investment: Substitutes or Complements. *Hitotsubashi Journal of Economics, 16*(1), 1–12. https://www.jstor.org/ stable/43295590?seq=1

Kojima, K., & Ozawa, T. (1985). Toward a Theory of Industrial Restructuring and Dynamic Comparative Advantage. *Hitotsubashi Journal of Economics, 26*(2), 135–145. https://doi.org/10.15057/7891

Kokko, A. (1994). Technology, Market Characteristics, and Spillovers. *Journal of Development Economics, 43*(2), 279–293. https://doi.org/10.1016/0304-3878(94)90008-6

Konings, J. (2001). The Effects of Foreign Direct Investment on Domestic Firms Evidence from Firm-Level Panel Data in Emerging Economies. *The Economics of Transition, 9*(3), 619–633. https://doi.org/10.1111/1468-0351.0

Kumar, N. (1996). Intellectual Property Protection, Market Orientation and Location of Overseas R&D Activities by Multinational Enterprises. *World Development, 24*(4), pp. 673–688. https://doi.org/10.1016/0305-750x(95)00168-c

Kumar, N. (1998). Liberalisation and Changing Patterns of Foreign Direct Investments: Has India's Relative Attractiveness as a Host of FDI Improved? *Economic and Political Weekly, 33*(22), pp. 1321–1329. https://www.jstor.org/stable/4406834?seq=1

Kumar, N. (2003). Intellectual Property Rights, Technology and Economic Development: Experiences of Asian Countries. *Economic and Political Weekly, 38*(3), pp. 209-226. http://www.jstor.org/stable/4413100.

Kumar, N., & Siddharthan, N. S. (1993). Technology, Firm Size and Export Behaviour in Developing Countries: The Case of Indian Enterprises. *Journal of Development Studies, 31*(2), pp. 289–309. https://doi.org/10.1080/00220389408422362

Kumar, Nagesh. (1994). *Multinational Enterprises and Industrial Organization: The Case of India*, Sage Publications, New Delhi.

Kuntluru, S., Reddy, M. V., & Khan, Mohd. A. A. (2012). Foreign Direct Investment and Export Performance of Pharmaceutical Firms in India: An Empirical Approach. *International Journal of Economics and Finance, 4*(5). https://doi.org/ 10.5539/ijef.v4n5p216

L. K. Jha Committee Report. (1960). Reserve Bank of India. https://rbi.org.in/Scripts/ LKJhaLecturers.aspx.

Lall, K. B. (1978). India and the New International Economic Order. *International Studies, 17*(3-4), pp. 435–461. https://doi.org/10.1177/002088177801700305

Lall, S. (1979). The Indirect Employment Effects of Multinational Enterprises in Developing Countries. *Oxford University, Institute of Economics and Statistics*. https://doi.org/92-2-102280-3

Lall, S. (1986). Technological Development and Export Performance in LDCs: Leading engineering and chemical firms in India. *Weltwirtschaftliches Archiv, 122*(1), pp. 80–92. https://doi.org/10.1007/bf02706287

Lall, S. (1987). India's Acquisition of Technological Capability: A Synthesis. *Learning to Industrialize*, pp. 193–229. https://doi.org/10.1007/978-1-349-18798-0_8.

Lall, S., & Mohammad, S. (1983). Multinationals in Indian Big Business. *Journal of Development Economics, 13*(1-2), pp.143–157. https://doi.org/10.1016/0304-3878(83)90056-1

Larimo, J. (2003). Form of Investment by Nordic Firms in World Markets. *Journal of Business Research, 56*(10), pp. 791-803.

Le, H. Q., & Pomfret, R. (2011). Technology Spillovers from Foreign Direct Investment in Vietnam: Horizontal or Vertical Spillovers? *Journal of the Asia Pacific Economy, 16*(2), 183–201. https://doi.org/10.1080/13547860.2011.56 4746

Leontief, W. (1956). Factor Proportions and the Structure of American Trade: Further Theoretical and Empirical Analysis. *The Review of Economics and Statistics, 38*(4), 386. https://doi.org/10.2307/1926500.

Levinson, J., & Petrin, A. (2003). Estimating Production Functions Using Inputs to Control for Unobservable. *The Review of Economic Studies, 70*(2), 317–341. https://doi.org/10.1111/1467-937X.00246

Li, X., & Liu, X. (2005). Foreign Direct Investment and Economic Growth: An Increasingly Endogenous Relationship. *World Development, 33*(3), 393–407. https://doi.org/10.1016/j.worlddev.2004.11.00

Liu, X., Burridge, P., & Sinclair, P. J. N. (2002). Relationships between Economic Growth, Foreign Direct Investment and Trade: Evidence from China. *Applied Economics, 34*(11), 1433–1440. https://doi.org/10.1080/00036840110100835

Liu, X., Parker, D., Vaidya, K., & Wei, Y. (2001). The Impact of Foreign Direct Investment on Labour Productivity in the Chinese Electronics Industry. *International Business Review, 10*(4), 421–439. https://doi.org/10.1016/s0969-5931 (01)00024-5

Liu, X., Siler, P., Wang, C., & Wei, Y. (2000). Productivity Spillovers from Foreign Direct Investment: Evidence from UK Industry Level Panel Data. *Journal of International Business Studies, 31*(3), 407–425. https://www.jstor.org/stable/155649?seq=1

López, R. A. (2008). Foreign Technology Licensing, Productivity, and Spillovers. *World Development, 36*(4), 560–574. https://doi.org/10.1016/j.worlddev.2007.04.016

MacDougall, G.D.A. (1960) The Benefits and Costs of Private Investment from Abroad: A Theoretical Approach. Economic Record, 36, 13-35.https://doi.org/10.1111/j.1475-4932.1960.tb00491.x

Madsen, J. B., Saxena, S., & Ang, J. B. (2010). The Indian Growth Miracle and Endogenous Growth. *Journal of Development Economics, 93*(1), 37–48. https://doi.org/10.1016/j.jdeveco.2009.06.002

Mahambare, V., & Balasubramanyam, V. N. (2005). FDI in India. p. 6. https://www.researchgate.net/publication/23746398_FDI_in_India

Mahembe, E., & Odhiambo, N. (2014). Foreign Direct Investment and Economic Growth: A Theoretical Framework. *Journal of Governance and Regulation, 3*(2), 63–70. https://doi.org/10.22495/jgr_v3_i2_p6

Make in India. (2014). https://www.makeinindia.com/.

Malik, S. K. (2015). Conditional Technology Spillovers from Foreign Direct Investment: Evidence from Indian Manufacturing Industries. *Journal of Productivity Analysis, 43*(2), 183–198.https://www.jstor.org/stable/43550062?seq=1

Malik, S. K. (2019). Foreign Direct Investment and Employment in Indian Manufacturing Industries. *The Indian Journal of Labour Economics, 62*(4), 621–637. https://doi.org/10.1007/s41027-019-00193-6

s, S. K., & Madheswaran, S. (2012). Productivity Growth in Indian Cement Industry: A Panel Estimation of Stochastic Production Frontier. *Journal of Developing Areas, 46*(1), 287–303. https://ideas.repec.org/a/jda/journl/vol.46year2012issue1pp287-303.html

Marcin, K. (2008). How Does FDI Inflow Affect Productivity of Domestic Firms? The Role of Horizontal and Vertical Spillovers, absorptive capacity and competition. *The Journal of International Trade & Economic Development, 17*(1), 155–173. https://doi.org/10.1080/09638190701728131

Marin, A., & Bell, M. (2006). Technology Spillovers from Foreign Direct Investment (FDI): The Active Role of MNC Subsidiaries in Argentina in the 1990s. *Journal of Development Studies, 42*(4), 678–697. https://doi.org/10.1080/00220380600682298

Marin, A., & Sasidharan, S. (2010). Heterogeneous MNC Subsidiaries and Technological Spillovers: Explaining Positive and Negative Effects in India. https://ideas.repec.org/ p/mad/wpaper/2010-053.html

Markowitz, H. M. (1959). Portfolio Selection: Efficient Diversification of Investments. In *JSTOR*. https://www.jstor.org/stable/j.ctt1bh4c8h

Markusen, A. (2008). Human versus Physical Capital. *Public Policy for Regional Development. Routledge, New York*, pp.47-65.

Masron, T. A., Zulkafli, A. H., & Ibrahim, H. (2012). Spillover Effects of FDI within Manufacturing Sector in Malaysia. *Procedia - Social and Behavioral Sciences, 58*, 1204–1211. https://doi.org/10.1016/j.sbspro.2012.09.1102

Master Directions of Reserve Bank of India. (2020). https://m.rbi.org.in/Scripts/BS_View MasDirections.aspx?id=11200

McVicar, D. (2002). Spillovers and Foreign Direct Investment in UK Manufacturing. *Applied Economics Letters, 9*(5), 297–300. https://doi.org/10.1080/13504850110067487

Medda, G., & Piga, C. A. (2014). Technological Spillovers and Productivity in Italian Manufacturing Firms. *Journal of Productivity Analysis, 41*(3), 419–434. https://doi.org/10.1007/s11123-013-0351-1

Miglani, S. (2019). The Growth of the Indian Automobile Industry: Analysis of the Roles of Government Policy and Other Enabling Factors. In *Innovation, Economic Development, and Intellectual Property in India and China* (pp. 439–463). https://doi.org/10.1007/978-981-13-8102-7_19.

Mihalache-O'keef, A., & Li, Q. (2011). Modernization vs. Dependency Revisited: Effects of Foreign Direct Investment on Food Security in Less Developed Countries Vol. 55, No. 1, pp. 71-93. https://www.jstor.org/stable/23019514?read-now=1&seq=4#page_scan _tab_contents

Miller, R. E., & Blair, P. D. (2009). *Input–Output Analysis Foundations and Extensions* (2nd ed.). Washington DC: Cambridge University Press.

Mishra, B. R. (2011). Spill-Over Effects of Foreign Direct Investment: An Econometric Study of Indian Firms. https://ideas.repec.org/p/pra/mprapa/37759.html

Mishra, S. (2020, April 11). CV industry sales analysis FY19: A Turbulent Journey of a Milestone Year.https://auto.economictimes.indiatimes.com/news/commercial-vehicle/ mhcv/cv-industry-sales-analysis-fy19-a-turbulent-journey-of-a-milestone-year/68830305.

Misra, S. K. & Puri, V. K. (2013). *Indian Economy: Its Development Experience.* (32nd ed., p. 433-531.). Mumbai: Himalaya Publishing House. (Original work published 1983)

Mitra, A., Sharma, C., & Véganzonès-Varoudakis, M.-a. (2014). Trade Liberalization, Technology Transfer, and Firms' Productive Performance: The Case of Indian Manufacturing. Journal of Asian Economics, 33, 1–15. doi: 10.1016/J. Asseco.2014.04.001

Mohapatra, L. M., & Gopalaswamy, A. K. (2016). FDI, Domestic Investment and 2008 Financial Crisis: Evidence from Emerging Nations. *The Journal of Developing Areas*, *50*(6), 277–289. https://doi.org/10.1353/jda.2016.0137

Mondal, S., & Pant, M. (2014). FDI and Firm Competitiveness: Evidence from Indian Manufacturing. *Economic and Political Weekly*, *49*(38), 56–64. https://www.jstor.org/stable/24480706

Mondal, S., & Pant, M. (2018). Firm Capabilities and Productivity Spillovers from FDI: Evidence from Indian Manufacturing Firms. In N. Siddharthan & K. Narayanan (Eds.), *Globalisation of Technology. India Studies in Business and Economics.* https//doi.org//10.1007/978-981-10-5424-2_5

Monopolies Enquiry Commission. (*1965*). http://reports.mca.gov.in/Reports/44-Report%20of%20the%20monopolies%20inquiry%20commission%20 1965,%20Vo1.-I-II.pdf

Monopolies Restrictive Trade Practices Act. (1969). https://www.mca.gov.in/Ministry/ annual_reports/annualreport2006/CHAPTER4.pdf

Moosa, I. (2002). Foreign Direct Investment: Theory, Evidence and Practice. In *Palgrave.com* (1st ed.). pp.4.-42. https://www.palgrave.com/gp/book/9780333945902

Morris, Sebastian. (1994). Prospects for FDI and Multinational Activity in the 90s. *Economic and Political Weekly, 29*(19), 1141-1146. http://www.jstor.org/stable/4401170.

Morrissey, K., & O'Donoghue, C. (2013). The Role of the Marine Sector in the Irish National Economy: An Input–Output Analysis. *Marine Policy, 37*, 230–238. https://doi.org/10.1016/j.marpol.2012.05.004

Mrinalini, N., Nath, P., & Sandhya, G. D. (2014). MNCs R&D Interest in India: An Overview of Their R&D Centre Linkages with Indian Institutions. *International Journal of Technology and Globalisation, 7*(3), 217. https://doi.org/10.1504/ijtg.2014.064743

Mukunoki, H. (2017). The Welfare Effect of a Free Trade Agreement in The Presence Of Foreign Direct Investment and Rules of Origin. *Review of International Economics, 25*(4), 733–759. https://doi.org/10.1111/roie.12282

Murthy, K. V., Saran, D., & Malhotra, M. (2019). A Firm Level Study on Determinants of Spillover Effects of Foreign Direct Investment in the Manufacturing Industry in India. *Journal of International Business, 6*(1). https://doi.org/10.17492/focus.v6i1.182691

Nagraj, R. (2003). Foreign Direct Investment in India in the 1990s. *Economic and Political Weekly, 38*(17), pp.1701-1712. https://www.epw.in/journal/2003/17/special-articles/foreign-direct-investment-india-1990s.

Nair-Reichert, U., & Weinhold, D. (2001). Causality Tests for Cross-Country Panels: A New Look at FDI and Economic Growth in Developing Countries. *Oxford Bulletin of Economics and Statistics, 63*(2), 153–171. https://doi.org/10.1111/1468-0084.00214

Narayana, D. (1989). The Motor Vehicle Industry in India (Growth within a Regulatory Policy Environment). New Delhi and Trivandrum: Oxford & IBH Publishing Co. Pvt. Ltd. and Centre for Development Studies.

Narayanan, K. (1998). Technology Acquisition, De-Regulation and Competitiveness: A Study of Indian Automobile Industry. *Research Policy*, Vol. 27, pp. 215-228.

Narayanan, K. (2001). Liberalisation and the Differential Conduct and Performance of Firms: A Study of the Indian Automobile Sector. The Institute of Economic Research, Hitotsubashi University and United Nations University Institute of Advanced Studies. http://www.ier.hit-u.ac.jp/Common/publication/DP/DP414.pdf.

Narayanan, K. (2004). Technology Acquisition and Growth of Firms: Indian Automobile Sector under Changing Policy Regimes. *Economic and Political Weekly*, *39*(5), 461–470.https://www.jstor.org/stable/4414580?seq=1

Narula, R. and A. Marin (2005), Exploring the Relationship between Direct and Indirect Spillovers from FDI in Argentina. *MERIT Research Memoranda 2005-024, Maastricht Economic Research Institute on Innovation and Technology*. https://econpapers.repec.org/ paper/unmumamer/2005024.html

National Auto Policy (Draft Version 2. 2018). Department of Heavy Industry, Ministry of Heavy Industries & Public Enterprises, Government of India. http:// www.dhi.nic.in/ writereaddata/UploadFile/National%20Automotive%20 Policy%20Draft%20v2.pdf.

National Automotive Testing and R&D Infrastructure Project. https://www. NATRiP.in/.

Nayak, D., & Choudhury, R. N. (2014). A Selective Review of Foreign Direct Investment Theories (No. 143). ARTNeT Working Paper Series.

Negara, S. D., & Adam, L. (2012). Foreign Direct Investment and Firms' Productivity Level: Lesson Learned from Indonesia. *ASEAN Economic Bulletin*, *29*(2), 116–127. https://doi.org/10.2307/43184869

*National Electric Mobility Mission Plan.* https://heavyindustries.gov.in/ writereaddata/ Content/NEMMP2020.pdf

New Industrial Policy, (1991). https://dipp.gov.in/sites/default/files/ chap001%20% 2013.pdf

Nikaido, Y. (2004). Technical Efficiency of Small-Scale Industry: Application Of Stochastic Production Frontier Model. *Economic and Political Weekly*, *39*(6), 592–597.http://www.jstor.org/stable/441461

Nocke, V. and Yeaple, S. (2007). Cross-border Mergers and Acquisitions Vs. Greenfield Foreign Direct Investment: The Role of Firm Heterogeneity. Journal of International Economics, 72(2): p. 336–365.

OECD. (2008a). *OECD Benchmark Definition of Foreign Direct Investment (4th ed.)* (p. 17). http://www.oecd.org/daf/inv/investmentstatisticsandanalysis /40193734.pdfW

OECD. (2008b). *Glossary of Foreign Direct Investment Terms and Definition* (pp. 1–11). https://www.oecd.org/daf/inv/investment-policy/2487495.pdf

Okamoto, Y. (1999). Multinationals, Production Efficiency, and Spillover Effects: The Case of the U.S. Auto Parts Industry. *Weltwirtschaftliches Archiv, 135*(2), 241–260. https://doi.org/10.1007/bf02707254

Okonkwo, I. V., & Ukoh, J. E. (2020). Foreign Direct Investment and Foreign Exchange Rate Fluctuations in Nigeria: 1981-2018. *International Journal of Social Sciences and Management Review, 03*(04), 63–96. https://doi.org/10.37602/ijssmr.2020.3406

Olley, G. S., & Pakes, A. (1996). The Dynamics of Productivity in the Telecommunications Equipment Industry. *Econometrica, 64*(6), 1263–1297. https://doi.org/10.2307/2171831

Padmavathi, N. (2019). *Technical Efficiency of Unorganised Food Processing Industry in India: A Stochastic Frontier Analysis* (Working Paper, Vol. 449). http://www.isec.ac.in/WP%20449%20-%20Padmavathi%20N%20-%20Final.pdf

Page, J. M. (1984). Firm size and technical efficiency. *Journal of Development Economics, 16*(1-2), 129–152. https://doi.org/10.1016/0304-3878(84)90104-4

Pan, Y., Tse, D. (2000). The Hierarchical Model of Market Entry Modes. *J Int Bus Stud* 31, 535–554. https://doi.org/10.1057/palgrave.jibs.8490921

Pant, M., & Mondal, S. (2010). FDI, Technology Transfer and Spillover: A Case Study of India. Discussion Paper no. 10-04, Centre for International Trade and Development, School of International Studies, Jawaharlal Nehru University, New Delhi. https://jnu.ac.in/sites/default/files/DP04_2010

Pant, M., & Mondal, S. (2020). FDI Spillovers on Technical Efficiency of Indian Manufacturing Firms. *Economic and Political Weekly, 55*(7), 7–8. https://www.epw.in/journal/2020/7/special-articles/fdi-spillovers-technical-efficiency-indian.html

Parameswaran, M. (2009). International Trade, R&D Spillovers and Productivity: Evidence from Indian Manufacturing Industry. *Journal of Development Studies, 45*(8), 1249–1266. https://doi.org/10.1080/00220380902862911

Patibandla, M. (2006). *Evolution of Markets and Institutions: A Study of an Emerging Economy*. London: Routledge.

Patibandla, M., & Sanyal, A. (2005). Foreign Investment and Productivity: A Study of Post-reform Indian Industry. *Review of Applied Economics, 1*(1), 26–42. https://doi.org/10.22004/ag.econ.143483

Pattnayak, S. S., & Thangavelu, S. M. (2005). Economic Reform and Productivity Growth in Indian Manufacturing Industries: An Interaction of Technical Change and Scale Economies. *Economic Modelling*, *22*(4), 601–615. https://doi.org/10.1016/j.econmod. 2004.09.005

Paul, M., & Kumar, R. A. (2020). Import Intensity of India's Manufactured Exports: An Industry Level Analysis. *Indian Economic Review*, 1–24. https://doi.org/10.1007/s41775-020-00104-3

Pawlik.K. (2006). Foreign Ownership and Productivity in Polish Industry: The Case of Polish Manufacturing, 1993-2002. *Eastern European Economics*, *44*(5), 38-71. http://www.jstor.org/stable/4380480

Pegkas, P. (2015). The Impact of FDI on Economic Growth in Eurozone Countries. *The Journal of Economic Asymmetries*, *12*(2), 124–132. https://doi.org/10.1016/j.jeca. 2015.05.001

Petkova, N. (2013). The Real Effects of Foreign Investment: Productivity and Growth. *SSRN Electronic Journal*. https://doi.org/10.2139/ssrn.2188123

Phung, A. (2020). Why Would a Corporation Conduct Vertical FDI? Investopedia from https://www.investopedia.com/ask/answers/06/verticalfdi.asp

Piplai, T. (2001). Automobile Industry: Shifting Strategic Focus. *Economic and Political Weekly*, *36*(30), pp.2892–2897. https://doi.org/10.2307/4410922.

Porter, M. (1990). Competitive Advantage of Nations. *Competitive Intelligence Review*, *1*(1), 14–14. https://doi.org/10.1002/cir.3880010112.

Pradeep, V., Bhattacharya, M., & Chen, J.R. (2017). Spillover Effects of Research and Development, Exports and Foreign Investment on Productivity. *Journal of South Asian Development*, *12*(1), 18–41. https://doi.org/10.1177/0973174117700467

Protsenko, A. (2003). *Protsenko Alexander* (Dissertation; p. 3. https://edoc.ub.uni-muenchen.de/2105/1/Protsenko_Alexander.pdf

Quarterly Fact sheet on Foreign Direct Investment (FDI) from April, 2000 to March, 2020https://dipp.gov.in/sites/default/files/FDI_Factsheet_March20_28May_2020.pdf

Raff, H., Ryan, M., & Stähler, F. (2008). *Firm Productivity and The Foreign-Market Entry Decision* (No. 2008-02). Economics Working Paper.

Ranawat, M., & Tiwari, R. (2009). Influence of Government Policies on Industry Development: The Case of India's Automotive Industry. *SSRN Electronic Journal*.pp.22-24. https://doi.org/10.2139/ssrn.1583449.

Ranjan, P. (2018, May 27). Barring Select Sectors, Nehru Was Not Opposed to Foreign Investment. The Wire. https://thewire.in/business/barring-select-sectors-nehru-was-not-opposed-to-foreign-investment

Ranjan, V., & Agrawal, G. (2011). FDI Inflow Determinants in BRIC countries: A Panel Data Analysis. *International Business Research*, *4*(4). https://doi.org/10.5539/ibr. v4n4p255

Rath, B. N., & Bal, D. P. (2014). Do FDI and Public Investment Crowd in or Crowd out Private Domestic Investment in India. *The Journal of Developing Areas*, *48*(3), 269–284. https://doi.org/10.1353/jda.2014.0048

Rawat, P. (2017). Total Factor Productivity in Indian Manufacturing (2000-2017): A KLEM Approach (Internal Assignment: Industrial Economics MA Economics). pp. 1–14. https://www.researchgate.net/publication/321288995_Total_Factor_Productivity_in_Indian_Manufacturing_2000-2017_A_KLEM_Approach

Ray, D. (1998). *Development Economics*. Princeton University Press.

Ray, S. (2004). MNEs, Strategic Alliances and Efficiency of Firms: Emerging Trends. *Economic and Political Weekly*, *39*(5), 434–440.https://www.jstor.org/stable/4414576? seq=1

Ray, S. (2006). The Changing Role of Technological Factors in Explaining Efficiency in Indian Firms. *The Journal of Developing Areas*, *40*(1), 127–140. https://doi.org/10.1353/jda.2007.0010

RBI Vol IV. (2013). *The Reserve Bank of India: 1981-1997* (pp. 494-508). https://rbidocs.rbi.org.in/rdocs/content/PDFs/RBIvol404122018_PartA.pdf

Reganati, F., & Sica, E. (2007). Horizontal and Vertical Spillovers from FDI: Evidence from Panel Data for the Italian Manufacturing Sector. https://www.researchgate.net /publication/274964133_Horizontal_and_Vertical_Spillovers_from_FDI_Evidence_from_Panel_Data_for_the_Italian_Manufacturing_Sector

Report on the Census of India's Foreign Liabilities and Assets as on 30-th June, 1948. (1951). Reserve Bank of India. https://www.rbi.org.in/Scripts/PublicationsView.aspx? id=9479

Report of the Tariff Commission on the Automobile Industry. (1953). In *Indian Culture*. Ministry of Commerce and Industry. https://indianculture.gov.in/report-tariff-commission-automobile-industry-bombay-1953.

Ricardo, D. (1817). *On the Principles of Political Economy and Taxation: London.*

Rijesh, R. (2015). Technology Import and Manufacturing Productivity in India: Firm Level Analysis. *Journal of Industry, Competition and Trade, 15*(4), 411–434. https://doi.org/10.1007/s10842-015-0193-9

Rijesh, R. (2020). Trade Liberalisation, Technology Import, and Indian Manufacturing Exports. *Global Economic Review*, 1–27. https://doi.org/10.1080/1226508x.2020.1798267

Rodrik, D., & Subramanian, A. (2004). *From "Hindu Growth" to Productivity Surge: The Mystery of the Indian Growth Transition*. p.2. https://doi.org/10.3386/w10376.

Root, F.R. (1994). *Entry Strategies for International Markets*. Jossey-Bass, San Francisco. p.17.

Ruane, F., & Uğur , A. (2005). Foreign Direct Investment and Productivity Spillovers in Irish Manufacturing Industry: Evidence from Plant Level Panel Data. *International Journal of the Economics of Business, 12*(1), 53–66. https://doi.org/10.1080/135715104 2000323139

S.N., R. R. (2011). Technical Efficiency in the Informal Manufacturing Sector. *Journal of South Asian Development, 6*(2), 213–232. https://doi.org/10.1177/097317411100600204

Saadi, M. (2011). Essays on Foreign Direct Investment, Technology Transfer and International Trade: Ricardian Approaches and Empirical Evidence (Thesis; pp. 2–365). https://tel.archives-ouvertes.fr/tel-00592187/document

Sahoo, P., Nataraj, G., & Dash, R. K. (2013). *Foreign Direct Investment in South Asia* (p. 43). New Delhi: Springer India.

Sahoo, Pravakar. (2006). Foreign Direct Investment in South Asia: Policy, Trends, Impact, and Determinants. Asian Development Bank. http://hdl.handle.net/11540/3644.

Sahu, P. K., & Solarin, S. A. (2014). Does Higher Productivity and Efficiency Lead to Spillover? Evidence from Indian Manufacturing. *The Journal of Developing Areas, 48*(3), 175–193. https://doi.org/10.1353/jda.2014.0055

Salim, R. (2008). Differentials at firm level productive capacity realization in Bangladesh food manufacturing: an empirical analysis. *Applied Economics, 40*(24), 3111–3126. https://doi.org/10.1080/00036840600994088

Salvatore, D. (2015). *International Economics, Trade and Finance* (11th ed.). Singapore p: John Wiley and Sons. (Original work published 2011)

Sasidharan, S., & Kathuria, V. (2011). Foreign Direct Investment and R&D: Substitutes or Complements—A Case of Indian Manufacturing after 1991 Reforms. *World Development, 39*(7), 1226–1239. https://doi.org/10.1016/j.worlddev.2010.05.012

Sasidharan, S., & Ramanathan, A. (2007). Foreign Direct Investment and spillovers: evidence from Indian manufacturing. *International Journal of Trade and Global Markets, 1*(1), 5–22. https://ideas.repec.org/a/ids/ijtrgm/v1y2007i1p5-22.html

Saxena, S. (2011). Technology and Spillovers: Evidence from Indian Manufacturing Microdata. *Applied Economics, 43*(10), 1271–1287. https://doi.org/10.1080/00036840 802600301

Sengupta, P., & Puri, R. (2018). Exploration of Relationship between FDI and GDP: A Comparison between India and Its Neighbouring Countries. *Global Business Review, 21*(1), 097215091876002. https://doi.org/10.1177/0972150918760026

Sharma, C. (2012). R&D and firm performance: evidence from the Indian pharmaceutical industry. *Journal of the Asia Pacific Economy, 17*(2), 332–342. https://doi.org/10.1080/13547860.2012.668094

Sharma, C., & Mishra, R. K. (2011). Does Export and Productivity Growth Linkage Exist? Evidence from the Indian Manufacturing Industry. *International Review of Applied Economics, 25*(6), 633–652. https://doi.org/10.1080/02692171.2011.557046

Sharma, S. (2020). FDI into India may go into freefall in 2020; here's what to hit foreign investment inflows. https://www.financialexpress.com/economy/fdi-into-india-may-go-into-freefall-in-2020-heres-what-to-hit-foreign-investment-inflows/1994180/.

Shimizu, K., Hitt, M. A., Vaidyanath, D., & Pisano, V. (2004). Theoretical foundations of cross-border mergers and acquisitions: A review of current research and recommendations for the future. *Journal of international management, 10*(3), pp. 307-353.

SIAMAnnualReports.https://www.siam.in/cpage.aspx?mpgid=42&pgidtrail=89.

SIAM. (2017). Key Policy and Regulatory Initiatives in Indian Automotive Industry since 2006: Impact, Challenges and Opportunities. https://www.siam.in/cpage.aspx?mpgid =42&pgidtrail=87.

SIAM. (2020). Industry Composition. https://www.siam.in/statistics.aspx?mpgid=8& pgidtrail=12

Siddharthan, N. S. (1992). Transaction Costs, Technology Transfer, and In-House R&D. *Journal of Economic Behaviour & Organization*, *18*(2), 265–271. https://doi.org/10.1016/ 0167-2681(92)90031-6

Siddharthan, N. S., & Lal, K. (2004). Liberalisation, MNE and Productivity of Indian Enterprises. *Economic and Political Weekly*, *39*(5), 448–452.https://www.jstor.org/ stable/4414578

Siddharthan, N. S., & Nollen, S. D. (2014). MNE Affiliation, Firm Size and Exports Revisited: A Study of Information Technology Firms in India. *The Journal of Development Studies*, *3*(2), 146–168. https://doi.org/10.1080/0022038042000233849

Siggel, E., & Agrawal, P. (2009). The Impact of Economic Reforms on Indian Manufacturers: Evidence from a Small Sample Survey. *Working Paper Series No. E/300*, *37*, 1–22. http://iegindia.org/upload/pdf/wp300.pdf

Sinani, E., & Meyer, K. E. (2004). Spillovers of Technology Transfer from FDI: The Case of Estonia. *Journal of Comparative Economics*, *32*(3), 445–466. https://doi.org/10.1016/j.jce.2004.03.002

Singh, Awadhesh Pratap. (2016). R&D Spillovers & Productivity Growth: Evidence from Indian Manufacturing. *Indian Journal of Industrial Relations*, *51*(4), 563–578.https://www.jstor.org/stable/43974582?seq=1

Singh, J. (2014). India's Automobile Industry: Growth and Export Potential. *Journal of Applied Economics & Business Research*, 4(4), pp. 246–262.https://www.semanticscholar.org/paper/India%27s-automobile-industry%3A-Growth-and-export-Singh/952548286ea68e325d0e5ff278961aea16fcbdfa.

Sinha, R. (1993). Foreign Participation and Technical Efficiency in Indian Industry. *Applied Economics*, *25*(5), 583–588. https://doi.org/10.1080/00036849300000002

Sirag, A., Ahmed, S., & Ali, H. S. (2018). Financial Development, FDI and Economic Growth: Evidence from Sudan. *International Journal of Social Economics, 45*(8), 1236–1249. https://doi.org/10.1108/ijse-10-2017-0476.

Sjöholm, F. (1999). Technology Gap, Competition and Spillovers from Direct Foreign Investment: Evidence from Establishment Data. *Journal of Development Studies, 36*(1), 53–73. https://doi.org/10.1080/00220389908422611.

Slangen, A., & Hennart, J.-F. (2007). Greenfield or Acquisition Entry: A Review of the Empirical Foreign Establishment Mode Literature. *Journal of International Management, 13*(4), 403–429. https://doi.org/10.1016/j.intman.2007.08.001.

Solow, R. M. (1956). A Contribution to the Theory of Economic Growth. *The Quarterly Journal of Economics, 70*(1), 65-94.

Srivastava, S. (2003). What Is the True Level of FDI Flows to India? *Economic and Political Weekly, 38*(7), (pp. 608–610). https://www.jstor.org/stable/4413211

Staelin, C. P. (1974). The Cost and Composition of Indian Exports. *Journal of Development Economics, 1*(2), pp. 129–143. https://doi.org/10.1016/0304-3878 (74)90003-0.

Stoever, W. (1989). Foreign Collaborations Policy in India: A Review. *The Journal of Developing Areas, 23*(4), pp. 485-504. http://www.jstor.org/stable/4191788.

Sunde, T. (2017). Foreign Direct Investment, Exports and Economic Growth: ADRL and Causality Analysis for South Africa. *Research in International Business and Finance, 41*, 434–444. https://doi.org/10.1016/j.ribaf.2017.04.035

Sur, A., & Nandy, A. (2018). FDI, Technical Efficiency and Spillovers: Evidence from Indian Automobile Industry. *Cogent Economics & Finance, 6*(1). https://doi.org/10.1080/23322039.2018.1460026

Suyanto, A., & Salim, R. (2013). Foreign Direct Investment Spillovers and Technical Efficiency in the Indonesian Pharmaceutical Sector: Firm Level Evidence. *Applied Economics, 45*(3), 383–395. https://doi.org/10.1080/00036846.2011.605554

Suyanto, Salim, R., & Bloch, H. (2014). Which Firms Benefit from Foreign Direct Investment? Empirical Evidence from Indonesian Manufacturing. *Journal of Asian Economics, 33*, 16–29. https://doi.org/10.1016/j.asieco.2014.05.003

Takii, S. (2005). Productivity Spillovers and Characteristics of Foreign Multinational Plants In Indonesian Manufacturing 1990–1995. *Journal of Development Economics, 76*(2), 521–542. https://doi.org/10.1016/j.jdeveco.2004.01.006

Tambunlertchai, S. (2009a). *Foreign Direct Investment and Export Performance in Thailand* (Thesis, pp. 11–14). https://pdfs.semanticscholar.org/b5fe/228b3c7f92 54768a5fee552af1521ddd0a43.pdf

Tariff Commission. (1951). Ministry of Commerce and Industry. https://tc.nic.in/en/page /about-us.

Technical Monitoring Group on Foreign Direct Investment: First Action Taken Report. (2003). Reserve Bank of India. https://dipp.gov.in/sites/default/files/atr.pdf

Technology Policy Statement. (1983). Current Science, 65(5), 374-378.http://www.jstor.org/stable/24095781.

Tendulkar, S. D., & Bhavani, T. A. (2007). *Understanding Reforms: Post 1991 India* (p. 23). New Delhi; New York: Oxford University Press.

Teplova, T. V., & Sokolova, T. V. (2019). Building the Index of Efficiency of FDI Transformation: Economic Development and Intellectual Capital. *Emerging Markets Finance and Trade*, *55*(10), 2164–2184. https://doi.org/10.1080/1540496x.2018.1525356

Thakur, P., & Burange, L. G. (2015). Productivity Spillovers from foreign Direct Investment in the Manufacturing Sector of India. *Artha Vijnana*, *57*(1), 1–20. https://ideas.repec.org/a/gok/arviv1/v57y2015i1p1-20.html

The Competition Act. (2002). Ministry of Law and Justice. https://www.mca.gov.in/ Ministry/actsbills/pdf/The_competition_Act_2002.pdf

The Finance Act. (1965). https://www://legislative.gov.in/sites/default/files/legislative_ references/1965.pdf.

The Foreign Exchange Regulation Act. (1973). https://www.rbi.org.in/scripts/ECMUser View.aspx?CatID=12&Id=21

The Industrial Policy Statement. (1980). https://dpiit.gov.in/sites/default/files/chap001 _0_0.pdf

The Mahalanobis Committee Report. (1964). https://www.epw.in/system/files/pdf/1964_ 16/29-30-31/the_mahalanobis_committee_reportorthe_concentration_of_economists_ power.pdf.

The Patent Act. (1970). https://ipindia.gov.in/writereaddata/Portal/IPOAct/1_31_1_patent-act-1970-11march2015.pdf.

Tian, X. (2007). Accounting for Sources of FDI Technology Spillovers: Evidence from China. *Journal of International Business Studies, 38*(1), 147–159. https://doi.org/10.1057/palgrave.jibs.8400245

Tobin, J. (1958). Liquidity Preference as Behavior towards Risk. *The Review of Economic Studies, 25*(2), 65. https://doi.org/10.2307/2296205

Tomlinson, B. R. (1975). India and the British Empire, 1880-1935. *The Indian Economic & Social History Review, 12*(4), pp. 337–380. https://doi.org/10.1177/001946 467501200401

Tripathi, V., Jain, M., & Tripathi, S. (2019, February 9). Greenfield Investments: An Economic and Financial Key Driver for India's Growthhttps://www.researchgate.net/ publication/331521558_Greenfield_Investments_An_Economic_and_Financial_Key_Driver_for_India's_Growth

Tybout, J. R. (2000). Manufacturing Firms in Developing Countries: How Well Do They Do, and Why? *Journal of Economic Literature, 38*(1), 11–44. https://doi.org/10.1257/ jel.38.1.11

Ubeda, F., & Pérez-Hernández, F. (2016). Absorptive Capacity and Geographical Distance Two Mediating Factors of FDI Spillovers: A Threshold Regression Analysis for Spanish Firms. *Journal of Industry, Competition and Trade, 17*(1), 1–28. https://doi.org/10.1007/s 10842-016-0226-z

UNCTADSTAT. (2021). https://unctadstat.unctad.org/wds/TableViewer/tableView. aspx?ReportId=96740

Unel, B. (2003). Productivity Trends in India's Manufacturing Sectors in the Last Two Decades. *IMF Working Papers, 3*(22), 1–25. https://www.researchgate.net/publication/ 5124207_Productivity_Trends_in_India's_Manufacturing_Sectors_in_the_Last_Two_Decades

Velde, D. W. T. (2019). *Enhancing Spillovers from Foreign Direct Investment*.https://set.odi.org/wp-content/uploads/2019/03/Enhancing-Spillovers-from-Foreign-Direct-Investment-March-2019-1.pdf

Vernon, R. (1966). International Investment and International Trade in the Product Cycle. *The Quarterly Journal of Economics, 80*(2), 190. https://doi.org/10.2307/1880689

Virmani, A. (1997). India: Crisis, Reform and Growth. *Economic and Political Weekly, 32*(32), pp. 2064-2067.http://www.jstor.org/stable/4405736.

Virmani, A. (2003). India's External Reforms: Modest Globalisation, Significant Gains. *Economic and Political Weekly, 38*(32), pp. 3373-3390.http://www.jstor.org/ stable/4413885

Vu, T. B., Gangnes, B., & Noy, I. (2008). *Is Foreign Direct Investment Good for Growth? Evidence from Sectoral Analysis of China and Vietnam. 542-562*. https://doi.org/https://doi.org/10.1080/13547860802364976

Waldkirch, A., & Ofosu, A. (2010). Foreign Presence, Spillovers, and Productivity: Evidence from Ghana. *World Development, 38*(8), 1114–1126. https://doi.org/10.1016/ j.worlddev.2009.12.020

Wang, J.Y., & Blomström, M. (1992). Foreign Investment and Technology Transfer. *European Economic Review, 36*(1), 137–155. https://doi.org/10.1016/0014-2921 (92)90021-n

Wang, X., & Xie, Y. (2016). The Gravity of Intermediate Inputs in Productivity Spillovers: Evidence from Foreign Direct Investment in China. *SSRN Electronic Journal*. https://doi.org/10.2139/ssrn.3341965

WIR. (1999). World Investment Report 1999: Foreign Direct Investment and the Challenge of Development. In United Nations Conference on Trade and Development (UNCTAD). Geneva. United Nations. (p.465.). https://unctad.org/system/files/official-document/wir 1999_en.pdf.

WIR. (2000). World Investment Report 2000 Cross-border Mergers and Acquisitions and Development. *In United Nations Conference on Trade and Development (UNCTAD)*. Geneva. United Nations. https://unctad.org/system/files/official-document/wir2000_ en.pdf

WIR. (2007). World Investment Report 2007: Transnational Corporations, Extractive Industries and Development. In *In United Nations Conference on Trade and Development (UNCTAD). (p.245.)*.https://unctad.org/system/files/official-ocument/wir2007overview_ en.pdf

WIR. (2011). World Investment Report 2011: Non-equity Modes of International Production and Development. *In United Nations Conference on Trade and Development (UNCTAD)*.Geneva. United Nations. https://unctad.org/system/files/official-document/wir 2011overview_en.pdf.

WIR. (2017). World Investment Report 2017: Investment and the Digital Economy. *In United Nations Conference on Trade and Development (UNCTAD)*. Geneva. United Nations. p. 3. https://unctad.org/system/files/official-document/wir2017_overview_en.pdf.

WIR. (2021). World Investment Report 2021.United Nations Conference on Trade and Development.https://unctad.org/webflyer/world-investment-report-2021

Yadav, D. A. (2018). A Study of FDI Inflows in India's Service Sector: Case of German FDI (A Pragmatic Approach). https://books.google.co.in/books?id= VPZNDwAAQBAJ& printsec=frontcover&source=gbs_ge_summary_r&cad=0#v=onepage&q&f=true

Yang, J., Xu, H., Wang, C., Lai, M., & Wei, Y. (2009). Productivity Spillovers from Foreign Direct Investment in Chinese Industries. *Journal of Chinese Economic and Business Studies, 7*(4), 429–446. https://doi.org/10.1080/14765280903332314

Yi, J., Chen, Y., Wang, C., & Kafouros, M. (2015). Spillover Effects of Foreign Direct Investment: How do Region-Specific Institutions Matter? *Management International Review, 55*(4), 539–561. https://doi.org/10.1007/s11575-014-0235-2

Zheng, P. (2009). A Comparison of FDI Determinants in China and India. *Thunderbird International Business Review, 51*(3), 263–279. https://doi.org/10.1002/tie.20264

Zhou, Y. (2014). FDI and Technical Efficiency in Manufacturing Firms: A Stochastic Frontier Approach (Master's Thesis; pp. 1–27). https://repository.usfca.edu/cgi/ viewcontent.cgi? article=1102&context=thesis

BloombergNEF. (2022). *Electric vehicle outlook: 2022*. Retrieved from https://about.bnef.com/electric-vehicle-outlook/

Council on Energy, Environment and Water (CEEW). (2022). *Electric mobility in India: Leveraging fiscal instruments for sustainable development*. Retrieved from https://cef.ceew.in

Delhi Government. (2021). *Delhi electric vehicle policy 2020*. Retrieved from https://ev.delhi.gov.in

India Energy Storage Alliance (IESA). (2023). *India EV market overview report*. Retrieved from https://indiaesa.info

International Energy Agency (IEA). (2023). *Global EV outlook 2023*. Retrieved from https://www.iea.org/reports/global-ev-outlook-2023

Invest India. (2023). *Electric vehicles sector*. Government of India. Retrieved from https://www.investindia.gov.in/sector/automobile/electric-vehicles

IQAir. (2023). *World air quality report*. Retrieved from https://www.iqair.com/world-air-quality-report

Ministry of Heavy Industries (MHI). (2023). *FAME India Scheme Phase II Dashboard*. Government of India. Retrieved from https://fame2.heavyindustries.gov.in

Ministry of Power. (2023). *Charging infrastructure for electric vehicles—revised guidelines*. Government of India. Retrieved from https://powermin.gov.in

Ministry of Road Transport and Highways (MoRTH). (2022). *Annual report 2021–22*. Government of India. Retrieved from https://morth.nic.in

NITI Aayog & Rocky Mountain Institute (RMI). (2019). *India's electric mobility transformation: Progress and pathways*. Retrieved from https://rmi.org/insight/india-electric-mobility-transformation/

NITI Aayog & Rocky Mountain Institute (RMI). (2022). *State EV policies in India: An implementation update*. Retrieved from https://rmi.org/insight/state-ev-policies-in-india

Society of Indian Automobile Manufacturers (SIAM). (2024). *Vehicle statistics and trends*. Retrieved from https://www.siam.in/statistics.aspx?mpgid=8&pgidtrail=9

# Annexures

## Annexure I Information of Listed Companies from Prowess IQ Database.

| Company Name | NIC code |
|---|---|
| A S L Industries Ltd. | 2930 |
| A T S Elgi Ltd. | 29209 |
| Abilities India Pistons & Rings Ltd. | 2811 |
| Amara Raja Batteries Ltd. | 27201 |
| Anand I-Power Ltd. | 2811 |
| Apex Auto Ltd. | 29209 |
| Apollo Tyres Ltd. | 22119 |
| Ashley Alteams India Ltd. | 29209 |
| Ashok Leyland Ltd. | 29102 |
| Auto Ignition Ltd. | 29304 |
| Auto Pins (India) Ltd. | 29301 |
| Autoline Industries Ltd. | 29209 |
| Automobile Corpn. Of Goa Ltd. | 29201 |
| Automotive Axles Ltd. | 29301 |
| Automotive Stampings & Assemblies Ltd. | 29209 |
| Axles India Ltd. | 29301 |
| Bajaj Auto Ltd. | 30911 |
| Bajaj Motors Ltd. | 29209 |
| Balkrishna Industries Ltd. | 22119 |
| Banco Products (India) Ltd. | 29301 |
| Bharat Forge Ltd. | 29209 |
| Bharat Gears Ltd. | 29301 |
| Bharat Seats Ltd. | 29303 |

| Company Name | NIC code |
|---|---|
| Bimetal Bearings Ltd. | 29301 |
| Bosch Ltd. | 2811 |
| Brakes India Pvt. Ltd. | 29301 |
| C M H Tools Ltd. | 29209 |
| Canara Workshops Ltd. | 29301 |
| Ceat Ltd. | 22119 |
| Commercial Engineers & Body Builders Co. Ltd. | 29201 |
| Continental India Pvt. Ltd. | 22119 |
| Denso India Pvt. Ltd. | 29304 |
| Duncan Engineering Ltd. | 28120 |
| Dynamatic Technologies Ltd. | 28120 |
| Eastern Treads Ltd. | 22199 |
| Eicher Motors Ltd. | 30911 |
| Eimco-K C P Ltd. | 2811 |
| Enkei Wheels (India) Ltd. | 29301 |
| Exedy India Ltd. | 29301 |
| Exide Industries Ltd. | 27201 |
| Federal-Mogul Goetze (India) Ltd. | 2811 |
| Federal-Mogul T P R (India) Ltd. | 2811 |
| Fiat India Automobiles Pvt. Ltd. | 29101 |
| Fiem Industries Ltd. | 27400 |
| Force Motors Ltd. | 29102 |
| Fritzmeier Motherson Cabin Engg. Ltd. | 29201 |

| Company Name | NIC code |
|---|---|
| Frontier Springs Ltd. | 29301 |
| G K N Driveline (India) Ltd. | 29301 |
| Gabriel India Ltd. | 29301 |
| Goodyear India Ltd. | 22119 |
| H B L Power Systems Ltd. | 27202 |
| H S I Automotives Pvt. Ltd. | 22199 |
| Haldex India Pvt. Ltd. | 2930 |
| Hanon Climate Systems India Pvt. Ltd. | 29301 |
| Harita Seating Systems Ltd. | 29303 |
| Hella India Lighting Ltd. | 27400 |
| Hero Motocorp Ltd. | 30911 |
| High Energy Batteries (India) Ltd. | 27201 |
| Highway Industries Ltd. | 2930 |
| Him Teknoforge Ltd. | 29301 |
| Hindustan Composites Ltd. | 29301 |
| Hindustan Hardy Ltd. | 29301 |
| Hi-Tech Gears Ltd. | 29301 |
| Honda Cars India Ltd. | 29101 |
| Hyundai Motor India Ltd. | 29101 |
| I S T Ltd. | 2930 |
| Indag Rubber Ltd. | 22113 |
| India Nippon Electricals Ltd. | 29304 |
| Inzi Controls India Ltd. | 28120 |
| J B M Auto Ltd. | 29209 |
| J K Tyre & Inds. Ltd. | 22119 |
| J M T Auto Ltd. | 29301 |
| J T E K T Fuji Kiko Automotive India Ltd. | 2930 |
| J T E K T India Ltd. | 29301 |
| Jagan Lamps Ltd. | 27400 |
| Jamna Auto Inds. Ltd. | 29301 |
| Jay Bharat Maruti Ltd. | 29209 |
| Jay Ushin Ltd. | 29209 |

| Company Name | NIC code |
|---|---|
| K R Rubberite Pvt. Ltd. | 29209 |
| Kalyani Forge Ltd. | 29301 |
| Kalyani Maxion Wheels Pvt. Ltd. | 29301 |
| Kinetic Engineering Ltd. | 29301 |
| Krishna Ishizaki Auto Ltd. | 29302 |
| Krishna Maruti Ltd. | 29303 |
| Lakshmi Precision Tools Ltd. | 29209 |
| Lamina Suspension Products Ltd. | 29301 |
| Lucas-Tvs Ltd. | 29304 |
| Lumax Auto Technologies Ltd. | 2930 |
| Lumax Industries Ltd. | 27400 |
| M R F Ltd. | 22119 |
| Machino Plastics Ltd. | 22209 |
| Mahindra & Mahindra Ltd. | 2910 |
| Mahindra C I E Automotive Ltd. | 2930 |
| Mahindra Electric Mobility Ltd. | 29101 |
| Mahindra Vehicle Mfrs. Ltd. | 29109 |
| Mahle Anand Thermal Systems Pvt. Ltd. | 2930 |
| Maruti Suzuki India Ltd. | 29101 |
| Mehta Engineers Ltd. | 29209 |
| Menon Pistons Ltd. | 2811 |
| Minda Corporation Ltd. | 29209 |
| Minda Industries Ltd. | 29209 |
| Mitsuba Sical India Pvt. Ltd. | 2930 |
| Motherson Sumi Systems Ltd. | 29304 |
| Munjal Auto Inds. Ltd. | 29209 |
| Munjal Showa Ltd. | 29301 |
| Nelson Global Products India Pvt. Ltd. | 29301 |
| Olectra Greentech Ltd. | 29102 |
| P P A P Automotive Ltd. | 29209 |
| R A C L Geartech Ltd. | 29301 |
| Rambal Ltd. | 29301 |

| Company Name | NIC code |
|---|---|
| Rane (Madras) Ltd. | 29301 |
| Rane Automotive Ltd. | 29209 |
| Rane Brake Lining Ltd. | 2930 |
| Rane Engine Valve Ltd. | 2811 |
| Rane N S K Steering Systems Pvt. Ltd. | 29301 |
| Rane T R W Steering Systems Pvt. Ltd. | 29209 |
| Rasandik Engineering Inds. India Ltd. | 29209 |
| Remsons Industries Ltd. | 29304 |
| Rico Auto Inds. Ltd. | 2930 |
| Ring Plus Aqua Ltd. | 29301 |
| Rockman Industries Ltd. | 2930 |
| Roots Industries India Ltd. | 29304 |
| Roto Pumps Ltd. | 28120 |
| S A L Automotive Ltd. | 29209 |
| S L Lumax Ltd. | 27400 |
| S M L Isuzu Ltd. | 29102 |
| S M R Automotive Systems India Ltd. | 29302 |
| Sar Auto Products Ltd. | 29301 |
| Scooters India Ltd. | 30912 |
| Setco Automotive Ltd. | 29301 |
| Sharda Motor Inds. Ltd. | 29209 |
| Shivam Autotech Ltd. | 2930 |
| Shriram Pistons & Rings Ltd. | 2811 |
| Sibar Auto Parts Ltd. | 2811 |
| Simmonds Marshall Ltd. | 29209 |
| Sintex-B A P L Ltd. | 22209 |
| Skoda Auto Volkswagen India Pvt. Ltd. | 29101 |
| Somic Z F Components Pvt. Ltd. | 2930 |
| Sona B L W Precision Forgings Ltd. | 29301 |

| Company Name | NIC code |
|---|---|
| Special Engineering Services Ltd. | 2930 |
| Spicer India Pvt. Ltd. | 29301 |
| Sri Rama Vilas Service Ltd. | 29209 |
| Standard Radiators Pvt. Ltd. | 29301 |
| Subros Ltd. | 29209 |
| Sundaram Auto Components Ltd. | 22209 |
| Sundaram Brake Linings Ltd. | 29301 |
| Sundaram Hydraulics Ltd. | 28120 |
| Sundaram Industries Pvt. Ltd. | 29209 |
| Sundram Fasteners Ltd. | 2930 |
| Suprajit Engineering Ltd. | 29209 |
| T V S Motor Co. Ltd. | 30911 |
| T V S Srichakra Ltd. | 22119 |
| T V S Upasana Ltd. | 2930 |
| Talbros Automotive Components Ltd. | 29301 |
| Talbros Engineering Ltd. | 29301 |
| Tata Autocomp Gy Batteries Pvt. Ltd. | 27201 |
| Tata Ficosa Automotive Systems Ltd. | 29302 |
| Tata Marcopolo Motors Ltd. | 29201 |
| Tata Motors Ltd. | 29102 |
| Tata Toyo Radiator Ltd. | 29301 |
| Toyota Kirloskar Motor Pvt. Ltd. | 29109 |
| Triton Valves Ltd. | 2811 |
| Turbo Energy Pvt. Ltd. | 2930 |
| Ucal Fuel Systems Ltd. | 2930 |
| V E Commercial Vehicles Ltd. | 29102 |
| Veljan Denison Ltd. | 28120 |
| Wabco India Ltd. | 29301 |
| Wheels India Ltd. | 29301 |
| Yazaki India Pvt. Ltd. | 29304 |
| Z F Steering Gear (India) Ltd. | 29301 |

## Annexure II List of Journals, Conferences and Workshops etc.

Geet & Singh, Ombir. (2020). A Review of Determinants for the Spillover Effects of FDI in the Industrial Sector: Evidence from the Recent Studies in India. *Asiatic Society for Social Sciences and Research. (2) 2. 116-143.* e-ISSN 2582-502X.

Geet & Singh, Ombir. (2021). Revisiting the Simple Time-series Methods for Forecasting on the Domestic Sales of the Indian Automobile Industry. *International Journal of Academic Research & Development (IJAR&D).* (7) 2. 62-72. ISSN 2395-1737.

Geet & Singh, Ombir. (2021). The Indian Automobile Sector as the Flagbearer of the Sustainable. International Conference on Sustainable Development Socio-Economic, Environmental and Energy Development. St. Kabir Institute of Professional Studies, Ahmedabad, Gujrat 93-104. ISBN: 978-93-91681-51-7.

Geet & Singh, Ombir. (2022). COVID-19: Reshaping the Skills in Indian Automobile Industry National Conference on Skill Development in India Challenges and Way Forward. Department of Economics Kurukshetra University, Kurukshetra. 183-193. ISBN: 978-81-948430-7-8.

Geet & Singh, Ombir. (2020). Comparative Assessment of Intersectoral Linkages in India. 103rd Annual Conference of IEA on Reviewing the Economy towards Self-Reliant India & Role: Since 1991 to the Future. Dr. Bhimrao Ambedkar University, Agra (U.P.) India.

Geet & Singh, Ombir. (2020). A Review of Determinants In The Spillover Effects Of FDI For The Industrial Sector: Evidence from the Recent Studies. International E-Conference on Role of Technological Disruption in Management, Science and Humanities in Emerging World Order. Amity Business School, Amity University, Uttar Pradesh, Lucknow.

Geet & Singh, Ombir. (2021). Understanding the Effects of COVID-19 in the Indian Automobile Industry. International Conference on Embracing Change & Transformation - Breakthrough Innovation and Creativity. Dr. D. Y. Patil B-school, Pune, India.

Partial Least Square Structural Equation Modelling using SmartPLS-3 Workshop. December 2020.

Advanced Research Methodology and Statistical Analysis, Gautam Buddha University. October- November 2018.

# Annexure III Plagiarism Report

Annexure-

Gautam Buddha University
Plagiarism Verification

Date..6.05 2022

Title of the Thesis:....Foreign Direct Investment : An Analytical Study of the Presence of Linkages in Automobile Firms in India..........

Researcher:........Geet..........

Supervisor.........Dr. Ombir Singh..........

Department:........Department of Business Management..........

School:..........School of Management..........

Email ID (Researcher)..........geet1593@gmail.com..........

Email ID (Supervisor)..........o.dabiya@g.mail.com..........

This is to report that the above thesis was scanned for similarity detection. Process and outcome are given below:

Software used:......Turnitin.....Date:...06.05.2022.... Total Page: ..168..............

Similarity Index:......7%..........Submission ID:..1829588836 Total Word count:..71,965

The complete report is submitted for review by the Supervisor and same has been sent to researcher and supervisor by email also.

Deputy Librarian
Bodhisattva Dr. B.R. Ambedkar Library
Gautam Buddha University
Greater Noida
Deputy Librarian

The complete report of the above thesis has been reviewed by the undersigned. (Check box √)

| | |
|---|---|
| | Similarity index is below accepted norms. ✓ |
| | The similarity index is above accepted norms, because of the following reasons: ✗ |

1.............................................................

2.............................................................

3.............................................................

4.............................................................

5.............................................................

The thesis may be considered for the award of degree. (Relevant documents attached.)

Signature of Student

Signature of Supervisor

5/6/22, 10:24 AM Turnitin

Document Viewer

## Turnitin Originality Report

Processed on: 06-May-2022 10:22 AM IST
ID: 1829588836
Word Count: 71965
Submitted: 1

Foreign Direct Investment: An Analytical Stud... By Geet ...

| Similarity Index | Similarity by Source | |
|---|---|---|
| 7% | Internet Sources: | 6% |
| | Publications: | 4% |
| | Student Papers: | 2% |

include quoted include bibliography excluding matches < 10 words mode: quickview (classic) report

Change mode print refresh download

1% match (Internet from 16-Mar-2016)
https://www.iioa.org/conferences/23rd/papers/files/1964_20150312100_Vargas&Dietzenbacher-Economies_to_Die_For.pdf

<1% match (Internet from 20-Oct-2021)
https://www.adb.org/sites/default/files/publication/479656/southeastern-asia-and-pacific-input-output-tables.pdf

<1% match (Internet from 18-Feb-2022)
https://www.adb.org/sites/default/files/publication/770436/asian-economic-integration-report-2022.pdf

<1% match (Internet from 12-Sep-2018)
https://www.adb.org/sites/default/files/publication/357006/ki2017.pdf

<1% match (Internet from 08-Nov-2020)
https://dipp.gov.in/sites/default/files/FDI_Factsheet_June20_20October2020.pdf

<1% match (Internet from 26-Oct-2021)
https://zbw.eu/econis-archiv/bitstream/11159/2904/1/south-and-central-asia-input-output-tables.pdf

<1% match (Internet from 05-Feb-2022)
https://zbw.eu/econis-archiv/bitstream/11159/4342/1/1694266591.pdf

<1% match (Internet from 01-Oct-2021)
http://zbw.eu

<1% match (Internet from 08-Dec-2021)
https://Theses.ubn.ru.nl/bitstream/handle/123456789/11315/Rollfs_of_Roelofs%2c_Samme_1.pdf?sequence=1

https://www.turnitin.com/newreport_classic.asp?lang=en_us&oid=1829588836&ft=1&bypass_cv=1

turnitin

# Digital Receipt

This receipt acknowledges that Turnitin received your paper. Below you will find the receipt information regarding your submission.

The first page of your submissions is displayed below.

| | |
|---|---|
| Submission author: | Geet ... |
| Assignment title: | SOM |
| Submission title: | Foreign Direct Investment: An Analytical Study Of The Prese... |
| File name: | CHAPTER_1.docx |
| File size: | 1.02M |
| Page count: | 168 |
| Word count: | 71,965 |
| Character count: | 395,803 |
| Submission date: | 06-May-2022 10:00AM (UTC+0530) |
| Submission ID: | 1829588836 |

www.ingramcontent.com/pod-product-compliance
Lightning Source LLC
Chambersburg PA
CBHW071242230926
51849CB00001B/191
* 9 7 8 9 3 6 0 0 9 6 2 8 1 *